MW00681064

COMMERCIAL DIPLOMACY AND INTERNATIONAL BUSINESS: A CONCEPTUAL AND EMPIRICAL EXPLORATION

ADVANCED SERIES IN MANAGEMENT

COMMERCIAL DIPLOMACY AND INTERNATIONAL BUSINESS: A CONCEPTUAL AND EMPIRICAL EXPLORATION

EDITED BY

HUUB RUËL
University of Twente, The Netherlands

United Kingdom – North America – Japan
India – Malaysia – China

Emerald Group Publishing Limited
Howard House, Wagon Lane, Bingley BD16 1WA, UK

First edition 2012

Copyright © 2012 Emerald Group Publishing Limited

Reprints and permission service
Contact: permissions@emeraldinsight.com

British Library Cataloguing in Publication Data
A catalogue record for this book is available from the British Library

ISBN: 978-1-78052-674-4
ISSN: 1877-6361 (Series)

ISOQAR certified
Management Systems,
awarded to Emerald for
adherence to Quality
and Environmental
standards ISO 9001:2008
and 14001:2004,
respectively

Certificate Number 1985
ISO 9001
ISO 14001

INVESTOR IN PEOPLE

To TB

Contents

List of Contributors

Elena Bondarouk Department Business Administration, International Management, University of Twente, The Netherlands

Sander Busschers Department Business Administration, International Management, University of Twente, The Netherlands

Gorazd Justinek Department for Economic and European Diplomacy, International School for Social and Business Studies, Celje, Slovenia

Donna Lee Department of Political Science and International Studies, University of Birmingham, United Kingdom

Olivier Naray Institut de l'entreprise (IENE), Université de Neuchâtel, Switzerland

Shirin Reuvers Department Business Administration, International Management, University of Twente, The Netherlands

Huub Ruël International Management, University of Twente, The Netherlands

Annette Stadman Department Business Administration, International Management, University of Twente, The Netherlands

Jan Telgen Industrial Engineering and Business Information Systems, University of Twente, The Netherlands

Tim Vehof Department Business Administration, International Management, University of Twente, The Netherlands

Robin Visser Department Business Administration, International Management, University of Twente, The Netherlands

Lennart Zuidema Department Business Administration, International Management, University of Twente, The Netherlands

Acknowledgments

This volume would not have been possible without the contributions, help and support of a number of people. First of all, I would like to express my deepest gratitude to the great people I got the opportunity to work with on all the research projects on commercial diplomacy and international business. The outcomes of all these projects have turned into chapters in this book.

Therefore, thank you Lennart Zuidema, Tim Vehof, Robin Visser, Annette Stadman, Shirin Reuvers, Sander Busschers, and Elena Bondarouk. It was a great pleasure to work with all of you! Without you this book would have never existed, but more importantly, commercial diplomacy research would have missed great contributions. Further, I would like to express my gratitude to Donna Lee, Jan Telgen, Gorazd Justinek and Olivier Naray for their contributions. Thank you very much all of you!

I also would like to thank the Series Editors, Miquel R. Olivas-Lujan and Tanya Bondarouk, for their endless support in my endeavour to advance commercial diplomacy and international business research via their Advanced Series in Management.

I am very thankful to Annette Stadman for her managerial and editorial support!

Finally, I would like to thank my colleague and mentor Sirp de Boer, Associate Professor in International Business and co-founder of the International Management group at the University of Twente, for his support for this project and for commercial diplomacy research within the International Management group at the University of Twente. His encouragements and the discussions we had on the topic helped to generate and shape ideas. They will be of lasting value! Unfortunately, Sirp passed away on Tuesday 10 July 2012 … .

Introduction: Commercial Diplomacy and International Business: Merging International Business and International Relations

Donna Lee and Huub Ruël

International business has always been intimately linked to the politics of the global economy. Expansion and investment strategies of business play a key role in defining the architecture of the global economy. The shifting dynamic of the global economy such as the emergence of fast growing economies in, for example, India, China, South Africa and Brazil can be partly explained by the emergence of new market players such as the India transnational car manufacturer Tata, as well as the adaptation of established international businesses in the West to the new market opportunities in the South and the East. Equally, the recent (and in places ongoing) economic crises of the West owes as much to the failures of international business — notably the banking and investment industry — as it does to the failures of government policy.

At the same time the international political dimension to the global economy explains the regulatory forces which also determine the architecture of the global economy. The far reaching policy liberalization of international trade through international (namely the World Trade Organisation) and regional treaties and rule-making, and the global deregulation of the investment and financial services sector of the global economy driven by the neoliberal policies of the World Bank and the International Monetary Fund have created economic risks and opportunities for international business by opening up and creating new markets. The strategies of nation states and international business determine the architecture of the global economy and create both economic crises and dynamic growth at one and the same time in the contemporary global economy. So it is that for much of the first decade or so of the new century the West has endured an age of austerity brought on by sustained economic decline and high indebtedness. The once market dominant economies of the United States and West European economies are now struggling to reverse negative economic growth. By contrast large previously peripheral under-developed economies in Africa and Asia are enjoying remarkable and sustained growth rates and their exports and investments now fuel an overall growth in the global economy.

Expansion of Commercial Diplomacy by Nations

These structural, economic and political developments in the global economy go a long way to explaining the expansion of commercial diplomacy activities by nations. On the one hand, nations use commercial diplomacy to expand trade and investment in the context of declining economic policy sovereignty. The creation of the WTO in 1995 led to an extension of the rules and regulations of international trade and trade-related matters (including the financial services industry). This leaves national economic policy-making severely restricted. Expanding commercial diplomacy to secure new export markets and new inward investments becomes a necessary political tool for nations competing for new markets. When these new markets are in nations where the formal institutional context for doing business is underdeveloped or non-existent or where much of the economy is under state control, the need to expand and develop commercial diplomacy is all the more important.

Major nations in the South and East are now key players and the driving force behind the continuing and increasing economic integration of nations through age-old processes of international trade and foreign direct investment (FDI). Trade and FDI continue to grow, driven by state-led and business-led international entrepreneurship at regional and global levels. Growth in international trade, for example, was 25% higher in 2010 than in 2009 and driven by the increased demand within large emerging economies in the East and South for energy (oil and gas) and raw commodities such as cotton, nickel and copper. Equally, FDI investment surged as China continued to integrate into African markets. The economic decline of the West in the first decade of this century has been balanced by a remarkable growth in the economies of major states in the South and East. China, Brazil, India and South Africa have become the major engines of growth in the global economy while European economies, along with that of the United States, have declined. The mirrored experience of those nations that have grown economically in the 21st Century, like China, and those that have declined recently, like most European nations, means that international business becomes ever more significant in the global economy. Chinese investments in Africa have led to the growth of commercial diplomacy between the two to facilitate and manage their economic development. Likewise as economies decline, effective commercial diplomacy becomes ever more important to create new trade and investment opportunities or rescue and nurture existing ones. Thus, whether in the declining West or the emerging South, commercial diplomacy is vital to nations because it is a key component of international trade and FDI which are key economic processes that create capital, products, services and jobs. The ever increasing flows of capital, trade, services, people, ideas and information between states and businesses have increased the need for, and significance of, effective commercial diplomacy to help facilitate continued economic development and market integration as well as manage increased economic risks and opportunities.

Commercial Diplomacy: The International Relations of Business

Commercial diplomacy is the international relations of business that knits together political and entrepreneurial activities and agents in the global market. The dynamics in the global economy outlined above — shifting patterns of economic growth and market power from the West to the South as well as the reduced economic policy sovereignty of nations — enhance the need for effective commercial diplomacy and more integrated relations between business and diplomatic officials within the state. It is in this dynamic market and economic policy context that this book seeks to explore the practices of contemporary commercial diplomacy.

What is interesting from our perspective — that is a perspective that combines business studies and political science — is the extent to which commercial diplomacy involves the weaving together of the activities and interests of the nation state and international business, that is the public and the private in the global economy. This is because commercial diplomacy involves and creates networks of nation state (public) and business (private) actors working in domestic, regional and systemic environments in pursuit of private as well as public interests.[1] Economic integration of the sort now being seen between, for example, China and Africa is regarded to increase economic and political vulnerability and/or open up new economic opportunities for trade and investment growth between their economies as well as closer international political relations between the two nations.

Throughout the last two decades many governments have increased commercial diplomatic activities by increasing state funding for export and investment support and by formally drawing in business into foreign ministries and overseas embassies to bolster entrepreneurial skills and develop entrepreneurial networks. Responding to competitive pressures and the need to find and exploit new markets for domestic goods and services, commercial diplomacy primarily involves export and investment support and advocacy for domestic business. Commercial diplomacy focuses on building networks of diplomats and business groups based in overseas missions to promote trade and investment as well as business advocacy. For many developing countries, commercial diplomacy also includes tourism promotion as a primary activity. Diplomatic networks provide commercial intelligence, tourism marketing, business links and partner searches, as well as business assistance. Conceptually, studies of commercial diplomacy point to complex organizational networks involving ministries of commerce (often with trade promotion agencies/departments), trade and finance, in addition to the foreign ministry. Business groups are also, not surprisingly, key players in these networks and in many cases are formally placed into overseas missions and consuls through secondment programmes.[2] Business involvement is also channelled through other government departments as well as though links with national and local chambers of commerce. In this conceptualization of commercial

---

[1]See Pigman (2005) for a detailed discussion of some of the new non-state actors in economic diplomacy.
[2]See Lee (2004) for details of the UK experience of this.

diplomacy, business actors are merged with the state rather than autonomous and as such both public and private interests are included in diplomatic representation.

This book explores the international relations of business by presenting a set of studies of commercial diplomacy in the global economy. In so doing it brings new empirical evidence to the study of commercial diplomacy. It also aims to 'change the conversation' as Colquitt and George (2011) put it by creating a dialogue which incorporates concepts and understandings of commercial diplomacy from both political science/international relations and international business. The business conversation in the field of commercial diplomacy up to date has focused mostly on the role of trade shows and trade missions in export increase andFDI. Further, there is a substantial body of work on corporate political activity and the business–government interface. Primarily, this work seeks aims to understand the business–government interface at the country or state level rather than at the individual or global level. As such, ontologically, it is rendering invisible many commercial activities conducted by not only the business actors that are crucial to contemporary commercial diplomacy but also the public political and economic interests at the heart of international business and commercial diplomacy. These are important limitations of the business studies perspective of commercial diplomacy, a perspective that is overly structural since it draws almost exclusively on econometrics or economics.

This book changes the conversation by understanding the international business — government relationship at the meso (foreign post-business level) and at the micro level (individual commercial diplomat/individual international entrepreneur level) or, as political scientists would say, agency level. That is, this book highlights how and explains why individuals matter rather than focusing analysis on structural factors alone. The existing work at the macro/structural level has provided interesting and triggering insights on how government- or state-led commercial services work to increase exports and FDI by, for example, highlighting the role of overseas embassies and consulates in commercial diplomacy, but it will always be limited in its explanatory power if it fails to include analysis of the role that individuals play and the importance of micro-level networks of government and business people.

International Business Meets International Relations: An Interdisciplinary View of Commercial Diplomacy

International business is vital to nations, to their economies. It brings wealth, it creates jobs, it opens views, it changes mindsets, and it creates economic and social stability. International relations is important to nations too. It establishes relationships between nations, it exchanges political views between nations and it creates stability. International business and international relations are intertwined empirically as politicians need to boost economies through supporting entrepreneurship; international entrepreneurs need politicians and government representatives to get access to foreign markets to deal with legal issues across borders. Especially in an age where countries such as China, India, Brazil, Indonesia, South Africa and Russia have become major economies and political powers, international business and entrepreneurs need government to government contacts in many cases to get market access. International business in those cases meets international relations: business representatives and entrepreneurs meet government representatives, especially those in diplomatic service in overseas missions and consulates.

International business has been a fast growing field of academic research and international relations is a well established field of academic research. The two academic fields of study have seldom integrated despite the fact that empirically they are intertwined since they both studied cross-border economic activities. Commercial diplomacy is at the heart of the intersection between international business and international relations. Narrowly conceived, commercial diplomacy is the work of state officials in diplomatic service who carry out activities that support international business. Foreign ministries thus bring professional diplomatic skills and high-level connections to the table in support of the entrepreneur to help explore and secure new business and investment opportunities. Diplomats in overseas missions — from ambassadors to commercial officers — have expert knowledge and experience of the host nation and its economy, as well as useful networks that business can tap into. While we have some knowledge of the commercial activities of foreign ministries and their overseas missions, this is sparse. International relations scholars have largely ignored the commercial aspects of diplomacy and despite the emergence of international political economy there remain only a handful of political scientists studying commercial diplomacy. As such, commercial diplomacy as a field of international relations research has hardly been established, is not well defined, and is in need of more detailed and sustained analysis. We argue that research that integrates international business and international relations would be a very fruitful approach.

The Need of Commercial Diplomacy Research

Why is there a need for fostering commercial diplomacy as field of research? We live in a global economy, but still with national borders. Business has gone global, but national borders still exist — just ask any would be economic migrant. Of course, the creation of economic regional organizations such as the European Union, the North American Free Trade Agreement, the Southern African Development Community has made business across borders easier. But huge markets such as the Chinese and Indian which are not yet integrated institutionally through regional organizations are not easy to access for international entrepreneurs. In the absence of formal regional institutions, government to government relationship building — that is diplomacy — is needed to facilitate more open and easier business access. The commercial advantages to a nation of having an effective network of overseas consulates are well known. Rose's (2007) study of the relationship between the presence of foreign missions and a country's export demonstrated that exports to the host nation rise between 6 and 10% for each additional consulate.

The need for transparency pushes diplomacy to open up: tax payers are entitled to know what they get for their money. Embassies and consulates cost money, but what do they bring in? A study of US overseas missions by Wilkinson and Brouthers (2000a, 2000b) demonstrated the economic advantages of American commercial diplomacy and argued that federal states in particular could make far more use of overseas trade missions and trade fairs to help promote exports and FDI.

In a global economy, nations and economic regions are competing for market access, for access to natural resources and for access to procurement markets. That raises the question of how to organize commercial diplomacy effectively and efficiently. Nations have their diplomatic services organized in different ways, and international entrepreneurs are supported in different manners and with different programmes and tools. Perspectives from the field of international relations can help us analyze and understand the political and organizational aspect which business studies accounts have largely ignored.

The Aim of This Book

This book aims to advance work of this kind as well as other studies of commercial diplomacy by combining insights from two fields of study that to date have hardly spoken to each other. It will bring insights from international relations (and in particular the sub-field diplomatic studies) about the theory and practice of commercial diplomacy and it will bring insights from business studies about the theory and practice of international business. Combining the two, the book, we hope, will better define the field by being more holistic, will bring together in one place a thorough review of existing analysis of the subject from both fields, will outline the basics of a new conceptual framework, will present new empirical work and will put forward a new research agenda. This is ambitious but, we feel, worthwhile since it will help advance current understanding and encourage further analysis of commercial diplomacy as a key (and expanding) phenomenon in the global economy.

This introduction set the stage!

The further outline of the book is as follows:

Chapter 1 is on commercial diplomacy research up to date: what has been published so far on commercial diplomacy, what has been studied empirically so far, what are the results, and what is the road ahead for commercial diplomacy research.

Chapter 2 focuses on the commercial diplomat as the executor of international business support policies and practices. How do commercial diplomats actually work and which factors can help to understand the differences in the ways commercial diplomats work?

Chapter 3 is on the value of commercial diplomacy from an small and medium enterprise (SME) perspective. How do SMEs perceive commercial diplomacy services at the foreign post level? What are the factors that explain whether SME value commercial diplomacy?

Chapter 4 presents a study that aim to explain the effectiveness of commercial diplomacy through the eyes of commercial diplomats. What are the factors that influence the quality of commercial diplomacy services?

Chapter 5 continues in this line by presenting a method for measuring export support service efficiency.

Chapter 6 focuses on the interaction between international business executives and commercial diplomats. How do they perceive each other?

Chapter 7 makes a turn to the European Union and presents a comparative study on the European Union member states' commercial diplomacy policies and practices.

Chapter 8 is on the US federal procurement market as a target for foreign firms and the role of commercial diplomacy in it. It presents the results of study on the success factors and barriers for foreign firms to enter the US federal procurement market.

Chapter 9 presents a study on the lobbying tactics of commercial diplomats. How do commercial diplomats at the foreign post level lobby in order to attract international procurement contracts?

References

Colquitt, J. A., & George, G. (2011). Publishing in AMJ — part 1: topic choice. *Academy of Management Journal, 54*(3), 432–435.

Lee, D. (2004). The growing influence of business in UK Diplomacy. *International Studies Perspectives, 5*, 50–56.

Pigman, G. (2005). Making room at the negotiating table: The growth of diplomacy between nation-state governments and non- state economic entities. *Diplomacy and Statecraft, 16,* 385–401.

Rose, A. K. (2007). The foreign service and foreign trade: Embassies as export promotion. *The World Economy, 30*(1), 22–38.

Wilkinson, T. J., & Brouthers, L. E. (2000a). Trade promotion and SME export performance. *International Business Review, 15*, 233–252.

Wilkinson, T. J., & Brouthers, L. E. (2000b). Trade shows, trade missions and state governments: Increasing FDI and high-tech exports. *Journal of International Business Studies, 31*(4), 725–734.

Chapter 1

Research on Commercial Diplomacy: A Review and Implications

Shirin Reuvers and Huub Ruël

Abstract

In an ongoing process of globalization and technology improvements and due to an increase in worldwide actors in the economic sector, commercial diplomacy is an important tool for countries to support their business community during the internationalization process and afterwards. Nevertheless, commercial diplomacy literature is still in its infancy. Therefore, this chapter reviews existing research on the topic and develops a framework, which integrates the topics examined so far and provides the reader with a more complete picture of the topic at hand.

By means of a literature review, this chapter shows that the body of literature involving research of both disciplines, International Relations and International Management, is still rather limited. As a consequence, we determine a future research agenda and call for more empirical studies, especially in the field of (political) economy.

Keywords: Commercial diplomacy; literature review

Introduction

Both companies and governments face enormous challenges arising from the diminishing importance of the traditional national borders due to globalization (Friedman, 2005; Pisani, 2009; Scholte, 2000), technological change, and developments in trading systems. In a more globalized world, trade patterns and the variety of trade partners change. Trade barriers on the other hand often remain in place or

Commercial Diplomacy and International Business: A Conceptual and Empirical Exploration
Advanced Series in Management, 1–27
ISSN: 1877-6361/doi:10.1108/S1877-6361(2012)0000009005

even increase. An increasingly important means to overcome these barriers and to support businesses in the internationalization process is the use of diplomatic relations abroad. Governments have a major interest in supporting business abroad, as it often leads to domestic job creation, tax revenue increase, and a stable economy (Naray, 2010a). As a consequence, a change in the current practice of diplomacy toward more commercial activities can be observed (Kostecki & Naray, 2007). According to Lee and Hudson (2004, p. 343), "commercial activities of diplomatic services have been centralized, [...] extended, and business interests have been formally integrated within diplomatic systems." Commercial diplomacy has thereby become a foreign policy priority of many governments. Activities within the field of commercial diplomacy aim at "encouraging business development" (Naray, 2010a, p. 122), "the development of socially beneficial international business ventures" (Kostecki & Naray, 2007, p. 1), and "national economic development" (Saner & Yiu, 2003, p. 1). In this chapter, such activities will be labeled commercial diplomatic relations. While the commercial aspect seems to be increasingly important in diplomatic practice, the body of literature on the subject is still rather limited, as discussed in Kostecki and Naray (2007). The literature "fails to identify, explain and understand [...] the increased influence of private interests in diplomacy" (Lee & Hudson, 2004, p. 344) and hardly draws a complete picture of all its aspects.

The purpose of this chapter is therefore to systematically review the existing literature and identify future research opportunities that will enhance our understanding of the topic. The identified literature was grouped according to an input–throughput–output (conversion) model based on the examined topics and by the theoretical perspective, methodology, and level of analysis employed. The aim of this research is to integrate topics already elaborated on in the literature, into one central model. The literature was investigated and classified according to three different disciplinary perspectives: International Relations, Economy (Political Economy), and International Business. Next, the methodologies used in the studies were analyzed and the levels of analysis distinguished. Finally, the content and findings of the studies were examined based on our commercial diplomacy framework and a future research agenda is determined.

Review Methodology

An in-depth literature review was conducted with the aim to evaluate and critically synthesize previous research on the subject of commercial diplomacy. Our review investigated the theoretical background and perspective of the papers, their methodology, and findings. The overall aim was to distinguish "what has been done" from "what needs to be done." Relevant variables were identified and a more complete overview of the subtopics of commercial diplomacy created. Our additional objectives included identifying relationships between previous studies and understanding the nature of commercial diplomacy. A detailed explanation of our search methodology and how the identified literature was categorized, prioritized, and analytically processed, follows.

When scanning the body of literature, we included all possible publications covering commercial diplomacy. However, since the initial sample of papers was rather limited ($n = 13$), we added the terms "economic diplomacy," "government trade," and "export promotion" to the search parameters in subsequent steps to broaden its scope (see Appendix 2: Search Parameters for more details). To increase our sample of articles even further, additional key words and search terms were identified based on initial readings. The number and variety of key words consequently increased. We queried several databases with a total of 20 key words and combinations of them. In addition, we made use of back referencing, thereby identifying additional articles based on the reference lists of other articles. In total, 44 relevant studies were identified (Figure 1).

The recent publication dates (58% of all articles are published after 2004; 88% of all articles are published after 1999) support our initial statement that commercial diplomacy is a topic for which there is increasing academic interest (Table 1).

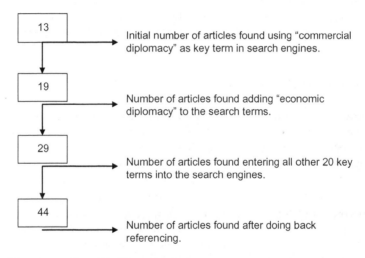

Figure 1: Numbers of articles identified.

Table 1: Number of publications per year.

Year of publication	Number of publications
1992–1999	5
2000–2003	10
2004–2007	15
2008–2011	14

Article, Publication date	Definition	Level of analysis	Methodology	Disciplinary perspective	Conclusion
Coolsaet, R. (2004)					
Czinkota, M. (2002)					

Figure 2: Concept matrix for database.

After reading all 44 articles, a framework for commercial diplomacy was produced on the basis of which the findings and topics discussed in the articles were structured. In order to work accurately and clearly, a database was created (Figure 2).

Review

Having described the method we used to produce the database, we shall proceed by defining the topic on the basis of the articles found and present and explain the framework we created to structure the subtopics of commercial diplomacy.

Definition of Commercial Diplomacy

In the literature the concepts of economic and commercial diplomacy are often used interchangeably. Definitions of both concepts vary, and consequently the relationship between them is also described in different ways. Some authors argue that commercial diplomacy is a part of economic diplomacy (Okano-Heijmans & Ruël, 2011). It is certain, however, that both kinds of diplomacy are "irrevocably intertwined" (Potter, 2004, p. 55) and thus "distinct [but] obviously closely related to [each other]" (Berridge, 2001, p. 128). Since the definitions of commercial and economic diplomacy used in the identified literature vary significantly and since in practice there is not much of a differentiation between the two, we will solely use "commercial diplomacy" as an umbrella term for both — economic and commercial diplomacy — in this chapter. We shall first discuss both definitions briefly and then present a conclusive definition, which will be used in the remainder of this chapter.

In a rather broad sense, economic diplomacy is defined as diplomacy where diplomatic means are used to achieve economic, foreign policy goals (Haan, 2010; Okano-Heijmans, 2008). In addition, economic diplomacy "seeks to secure the nation's interests [and] to serve economic interests through diplomatic means" (Muller, 2002, p. 1). "The use of international political tools to obtain economic objectives and [economic diplomacy] as such has actually existed ever since ancient civilizations have engaged themselves in commerce and trade" (Coolsaet, 2004, p. 61). As a consequence, economic diplomacy is "the process through which countries tackle the outside world, to maximize their national gain in all the fields of activity, including trade, investment and other forms of economically beneficial exchanges, where they enjoy comparative advantage, it has bilateral, regional and multilateral dimensions, each of which is important" (Rana, 2007, p. 1).

Commercial diplomacy, on the other hand, emphasizes the government's role, being defined as "government service to the business community [and the state], which aims at the development of socially beneficial international business ventures" (Naray, 2010a). It is "the work of diplomatic missions in support of the home country's business and finance sectors" and "includes the promotion of inward and outward investment, as well as trade" (Ozdem, 2009, p. 8). Commercial diplomacy consequently includes "all aspects of business support and promotion (trade, investment, tourism, science, and technology, protection of intellectual property)" (Naray, 2010b, p. 8). Lee (2004, p. 51) additionally mentions the role of the private sector by defining commercial diplomacy as "the work of a network of public and private actors who manage commercial relations using diplomatic channels and processes."

The definition we will use in this chapter includes economic and commercial diplomatic aspects and is phrased as follows: Commercial diplomacy is the use of diplomatic means to support commercial activities, such as export and foreign direct investment (FDI) promotion. It is pursued with resources available to the home country, aiming at outputs such as economic stability, home country welfare, and a national competitive advantage. Countries thereby target one or several foreign countries on a bilateral or multilateral basis. Commercial diplomacy functions as an umbrella term, including nation branding and participation in multilateral meetings, such as those of the WTO, and rewarding and sanctioning other countries in order to achieve foreign policy objectives.

Framework

Matching the above-mentioned definition and based on insights from previous conceptual work, we created a general framework in order to structure the relevant topics. A straightforward input–throughput–output (conversion) model was chosen and applied to the topic. Our choice for a conversion model is reasoned in the fact that we define commercial diplomacy as an activity pursued by the government (input) via several channels (throughput) aiming at benefits for the business community and the state (output) in a certain environment (context). The model enables us to identify the shapers, drivers, actions, context, and benefits of commercial diplomacy. In addition, we differentiate between three levels: the national policy level, the organizational level, and the individual level. The four constructs and their indicators on each level will be discussed below (Figure 3).

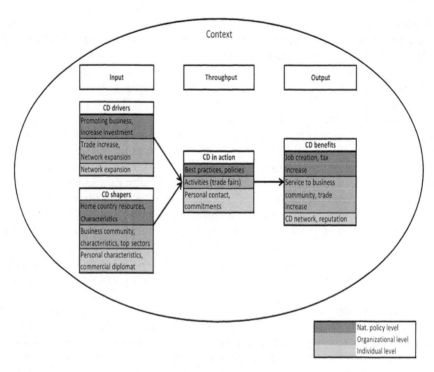

Figure 3: Literature framework input–throughput–output model (commercial diplomacy).

Commercial Diplomacy Input — Drivers and Shapers

As input to commercial diplomacy we define drivers, i.e., the objectives and rationales behind investments in commercial diplomacy, and shapers, i.e., the resources of the home country and the organization devoted to commercial diplomatic activities and the personal characteristics of the commercial diplomat.

Drivers to pursue commercial diplomacy, as discussed in the literature, include the prospect of increasing trade, arranging a level playing field for companies (or even a national competitive advantage), increasing employment and internal revenue in the country, increasing business intelligence and network possibilities, and strategic and political concerns at the national policy level and the organizational level. In addition, arguments about why commercial diplomacy should be conducted by the state and not by private entities are presented in the literature (Heemskerk, 2010; Henrikson, 2006; Hibbert, 1998; Kostecki & Naray, 2007; Naray, 2010a; Ozdem, 2009; Rose, 2005; Wilkinson & Brouthers, 2000b). At the individual level on the other hand personal network expansion and reputation building are the most important driving forces.

The identified literature also provides several shapers of commercial diplomacy, including home country resources and characteristics at the national policy level, business community characteristics and the identified top sectors at the organizational level, and the personal characteristics of the diplomat at the individual level. The latter covers the background, education, and skills of the diplomatic actor in charge. While research on home country resources and on commercial diplomatic actors is rather well established (Coolsaet, 2004; Henrikson, 2005; Kelly, 2000; Lee & Hudson, 2004; Mercier, 2007; Morrow, Siverson, & Tabares, 1998; Muller, 2002; Ozdem, 2009; Potter, 2004; Rana, 2007; Sherman & Eliasson, 2006, 2007; Sridharan, 2002; Van Dooremalen & Quaedvlieg, 2010; Yang, Shin, Lee, & Wrigley, 2008), studies on the personal characteristics of the state representative in diplomatic function are rather scarce (Hocking, 2004; Naray, 2010b; Saner & Sondergaard, 2000) and only recently addressed by Naray (2010b). In addition, there are certain home and host country characteristics that shape the context for commercial diplomacy. Home country characteristics include the national government structures and the influence of public and private actors on commercial diplomacy within the country (Coolsaet, 2004; Henrikson, 2005; Kelly, 2000; Lee & Hudson, 2004; Mercier, 2007; Morrow et al., 1998; Muller, 2002; Ozdem, 2009; Potter, 2004; Rana, 2007; Sherman & Eliasson, 2006, 2007; Sridharan, 2002; Van Dooremalen & Quaedvlieg, 2010; Yang et al., 2008). Host country characteristics include the level of economic and political development and the diplomatic ties between the home and the host country (Morrow et al., 1998; Okano-Heijmans, 2008; Okano-Heijmans & Ruël, 2011; Van Bergeijk, Veenstra, & Yakop, 2010; Van Bergeijk, 1992; Yakop & Van Bergeijk, 2009).

Commercial Diplomacy Throughput

Throughput indicators refer to the transformation process of inputs into outputs, that is to say commercial diplomacy in action. This includes activities and practices, such as trade fairs and other export promotion activities, and interactions between the home and the host countries, such as state visits, information markets, and meetings. Many authors discuss those activities at the organizational level, some include a list of possible activities, and others evaluate specific activities separately (Czinkota, 2002; Haan, 2010; Herbst, 1996; Kotabe & Czinkota, 1992; Lee & Hudson, 2004; Mercier, 2007; Naray, 2010a; Nitsch, 2005; Sridharan, 2002; Van Dooremalen & Quaedvlieg, 2010; Wilkinson & Brouthers, 2000b). Table 2 shows a list of the possible activities discussed in the literature.

Along with these activities, best practices and policies are part of the commercial diplomacy throughput at the national policy level, as are the personal contacts and commitment of the commercial diplomat at the individual level. However, so far no research concerning those indicators has been published.

Commercial Diplomacy Output

The output of commercial diplomacy, i.e., the results and benefits at the national policy level, can be differentiated into three kinds: economic benefits (Czinkota, 2002; Nitsch, 2005; Rose, 2005; Yakop & Van Bergeijk, 2009), political benefits (Haan,

Table 2: Possible activities within commercial diplomacy.

Network activities	Intelligence	Image campaigns	Support business
Developing business and government contacts	Gathering/ disseminating commercial information	Promoting goods and services	In negotiations; contract implementation and problem-solving
State visits/ delegation	Market research	Participating in trade fairs, introducing potential exporters	Gathering export marketing data
Buyer-seller meetings	Reporting to home country	Sensitizing potential foreign investors	Supervision of violations of IPRs and contracts
Match-making	Consultant to both countries	Gathering export marketing data	Advocacy activities
Search for partners/ distributors/ investors/ lawyers	Image studies, joint scientific research	Tourism promotion activities	Coordination of legal actions
Personal network of commercial diplomat		Awareness campaigns	

2010; Neumayer, 2007; Okano-Heijmans & Ruël, 2011), and nation branding (Potter, 2004; Yang et al., 2008). Economic benefits include wealth and knowledge creation and an increase in international trade. Political benefits include developmental aid (Haan, 2010; Okano-Heijmans, 2008), economic means to pursue political goals, and the global pattern of diplomatic representation. Nation branding has a positive effect on both economics and politics (Potter, 2004). In their study, Yang et al. (2008) demonstrate a measurement for country reputation and examine its effect by means of a single-country study. Commercial diplomacy creates benefits for the business community (organizational level) and the commercial diplomat himself/herself by increasing his/her network and positive reputation (individual level).

Commercial Diplomacy Context

Commercial diplomacy is highly influenced by external forces or what we call its context. Many articles describe phenomena, such as globalization, that influence commercial diplomacy externally. In this chapter, they will be referred to as factors in the commercial diplomacy context. These factors may facilitate or constrain commercial diplomacy. The relevant influences of the diplomatic environment, such as increasing use and improvements in technology and a growing influence of developing countries, are mostly discussed in more recent studies (Haan, 2010; Henrikson, 2005; Kostecki & Naray, 2007; Lee, 2004; Lee & Hudson, 2004; Muller, 2002;

Potter, 2004; Saner & Yiu, 2003; Sherman & Eliasson, 2007; Van Dooremalen & Quaedvlieg, 2010).

Findings

Disciplinary Perspectives

Within the research on commercial diplomacy, a variation in the chosen disciplinary approaches is found. Naray (2010a) identifies three different approaches: international relations and diplomacy; the political economy of commercial diplomacy; and the international trade promotion/international marketing approach. Lee and Hudson (2004) only differentiate between international relations/diplomacy-related studies and ones with a background in political economy. In this study, we use both disciplines mentioned by Lee and Hudson, adding international business as a third, which includes the research topics discussed and findings on the promotion of trade and investment from the point of view of businesses.

International Relations

The discipline of international relations is the most visible discipline in the literature. However, literature with this disciplinary approach is still limited (Lee & Hudson, 2004). Many authors, such as Coolsaet (2004), Van Dooremalen and Quadvlieg (2010), Heemskerk (2010), Herbst (1996), Lee (2004), Mercier (2007), Morrow et al. (1998), Muller (2002), Neumayer (2007), Nitsch (2005), Rana (2007), Sherman and Elliasson (2006), Stringer (2007), Van Bergeijk et al. (2010), and even Naray (2008, 2010a), use the international relations' perspective to look at all commercial aspects within the broader sense of diplomacy between governments. According to Lee and Hudson's meta-analysis (2004, p. 360), literature based on an international relation perspective uses a "predominantly rationalist approach to diplomacy, an approach that is based largely on a statist reading of international relations." While many authors argue that this view is of great importance because commercial diplomacy is often integrated in the foreign service and vital for the national interest, Lee and Hudson (2004, p. 360) criticize that "much of the diplomatic studies literature is unable to perceive, let alone analyze, the commercial elements of diplomacy."

The Political Economy

According to Lee and Hudson (2004, p. 359), the "political economy approach to diplomacy has a double advantage — it adds to the theoretical and empirical utility of diplomatic studies as well as international political economy." Literature with a political economy approach discusses the funding of commercial diplomatic activities

(Hocking, 2004; Lee & Hudson, 2004; Ozdem, 2009; Sherman & Eliasson, 2006; Wilkinson & Brouthers, 2000a, 2000b; Wright, 2000; Yakop & Van Bergeijk, 2009), presenting a number of fundamental arguments in favor of and against funding by the government, thereby discussing the involvement of private actors. Publications in the field of (political) economy especially stress the influence of economics on diplomacy, thereby focusing on effectiveness and efficiency aspects (Naray, 2010a). Lee and Hudson (2004, p. 360), for example "adopt a political economy approach that integrates market relations with political relations and thus conceptualizes diplomacy as a continuous political-economic dialogue."

International Business

Articles within the international business perspective discuss the promotion of trade and investment "from the point of view of international business firms and countries' promotional efforts" (Naray, 2010a, p. 128). Commercial diplomatic activities, such as FDI, export and trade promotion, are most often researched from an international business perspective and are quite common in the literature (Czinkota, 2002; Haan, 2010; Hibbert, 1998; Kelly, 2000; Kotabe & Czinkota, 1992; Nitsch, 2005; Potter, 2004; Rose, 2005; Saner & Yiu, 2003; Yakop & Van Bergeijk, 2009; Yang et al., 2008; Yannopoulos, 2010). Naray (2008, p. 128) stresses the importance of those studies "with regard to trade representation, possible business models, institutional arrangements and country comparisons, even though quantifying the influence of commercial diplomacy remains very difficult."

Methodological Approaches

Of all identified articles, 59% are empirical studies and 41% make use of a conceptual approach. Of the empirical studies, 11 articles are case studies (42%), 5 articles make use of a survey/questionnaire (19%), and 5 articles employ established data and a gravity model to analyze trade flows (19%). The rest of the studies can be considered meta-analyses (20%). However, the identified studies do not always state their methodologies clearly. Mixed research methods occur rather incidentally without a clear description and/or justification.

Level of Analysis

The studies identified refer obviously to one or more level(s) of analysis. However, level issues are often not specified, and mixed-level studies seem to occur rather coincidentally or at least with no clear announcement of explicit multilevel research. In a nutshell, the current research in commercial diplomacy generally demonstrates a low degree of clarity of level. Though there are studies that refer to several levels, multilevel studies are rather scarce. The levels identified are presented in Table 3.

Table 3: Levels of analysis.

Levels of analysis found	Number of times	Percentage
Countries	13	29.5
Individual actors	11	25
Concept diplomacy	8	18.1
Activities	6	13.6
Companies	5	11.3
Literature	1	0.22

The Commercial Diplomacy Framework — Topics and Findings

In order to systemize the rather scattered picture of the topics covered and the related findings, the following review draws on the proposed framework (Figure 3) and provides an overview of the current state of the literature on commercial diplomacy.

Studies that aim to provide a complete picture of commercial diplomacy and incorporate the drivers, shapers, context, and benefits of both forms of diplomacy are rather rare. Most studies focus on subtopics of the framework that are often rather specific, thereby isolating the topic from other aspects of the commercial diplomacy model discussed above.

The model differentiates between three different levels: the national policy level, the organizational level, and the individual level. We consequently include indicators for the input, throughput, and output of commercial diplomacy for all three levels based on what can be found in the literature. Overall, we can conclude that most research is done at the national policy level and only a few at the organizational and individual levels. In fact, only Naray (2010a, 2010b) and Kostecki and Naray (2007) focus on the individual level of the commercial diplomat.

Commercial Diplomacy Input

As mentioned before, commercial diplomacy input can be divided into drivers and shapers. While drivers cover the rationales for countries to invest in commercial diplomacy, shapers include home country resources and the personal characteristics of the commercial diplomat.

Drivers. More straightforward objectives for governments at the national policy level to promote business include creating jobs and increasing tax revenue and FDI and economic growth (Kotabe & Czinkota, 1992; Van Bergeijk et al., 2010; Wilkinson & Brouthers, 2000b), thereby maintaining country competitiveness (Lee & Hudson, 2004). In addition, Kostecki and Naray (2007) mention that commercial diplomacy may be used as an instrument of government policy. Strategic concerns and nation branding (improving or shaping the country's image) may play a role as well (Potter, 2004; Yang et al., 2008).

At the organizational level, objectives for enterprises include reducing the risk of entering a foreign market, improving economies of scale, growth, support in conflict situations, and access to decision makers through the support of government delegations (Kostecki & Naray, 2007; Nitsch, 2005; Saner & Sondergaard, 2000; Wilkinson & Brouthers, 2000a; Yannopoulos, 2010). Commercial diplomacy drivers at the individual level are not discussed in depth in the literature. They include personal network expansion and reputation building.

In addition to the above-mentioned objectives at the national policy level, the literature also discusses other rationales for governments to invest in commercial diplomacy, i.e., why business interests abroad should be promoted by the public administration instead of privately or vice versa. One of the arguments is that embassies can gather intelligence rather easily through their broad networks and influential role in the host country community (Kostecki & Naray, 2007). Diplomats also have immunity, which encourages risk-taking intelligence activities. Kostecki and Naray (2007) argue that diplomats attract more attention due to their visibility in the mass media. As a consequence, stage promotion events can be organized at a relatively low cost (*ibid.*). Diplomatic actors' positions additionally function as access gates to important decision makers in the host country and come with a high level of credibility (*ibid.*). Another rationale is the fact that economies of scale and scope can be achieved by centralizing support and diminishing the costs of the promotion effort.

Shapers. The amount of resources assigned to commercial diplomatic activities varies based on national policies and priorities. According to Naray (2010b, p. 8), governments "invest considerable amounts financed by public contributions" with the aim of supporting home country companies. This also includes investing time, e.g., by the commercial diplomat or the ambassador himself. Rana (2007) concludes in his research that 60% of the work of the French and German ambassadors concerns economic promotional efforts. Kostecki and Naray (2007, p. 12) conducted a study on the "allocation of commercial diplomat time between various business-support activities," differentiating between activities in the field of trade fairs, promotion of FDIs, government relations, business intelligence and partner search, support in business negotiations and disputes, and tourism, which all belong to commercial diplomacy. The authors also studied the number of commercial diplomats working abroad and the local professional staff assisting them for 12 developed countries (Kostecki & Naray, 2007, p. 6). In addition to the government, the private sector and semi-public entities are also involved in commercial diplomatic activities, according to Mercier (2007). Not only time investments, but also factors such as "offering attractive working conditions [...] material conditions [and the] length of employment contract" play a role (Naray, 2010a, p. 146). Neumayer (2007) adds the costs of setting up and maintaining diplomatic representations, and the fact that opening up a representation in one country may imply losing representation in another. In his study, he concludes that the "global pattern of diplomatic representation is significantly determined by geographical distance between countries, the power of both sending and recipient countries and by the degree of their ideological affinity" (Neumayer, 2007, p. 228), calling for these aspects to be considered in the academic discussion. Another important factor of the inputs of a country is the degree of participation in multilateral meetings, through which countries may increase their worldwide influence significantly (Muller, 2002).

Concerning the home country, Mercier (2007) identifies three different structural aspects of its governmental system on commercial diplomacy: (1) whether the structure is mainly public, private, or a mixture; (2) the level of government; and (3) the number of departments and ministries involved. Naray (2010a) elaborates on the differences between national commercial diplomacy systems in terms of their organizational and institutional arrangements. Based on those differences and earlier research (Hibbert, 1998), he distinguishes six types of arrangements[1] according to criteria such as the Trade Promotion Organization's (TPO's) relative independence from ministries, its position in the trade promotion structure, and the responsible ministry. Ozdem (2009) conducted a case study on the issue (in three developed countries), thereby identifying two different structures: the unified ministries approach and the two separate ministries approach. Lee and Hudson (2004) concluded in their study that governments are currently making the effort to reorganize their diplomatic systems so that commercial activities are more centralized and extended. Mercier (2007) and Rana (2007) also speak of a "public-private partnership tendency." In this context, Sherman and Eliasson (2006) analyze the US and EU petition process for private-public partnerships and what they call the "privatization of commercial diplomacy."

Regarding the government level, Stringer (2007) argues for more honorary consuls as commercial diplomatic actors due to the increasing importance of local areas and regions. Also, Saner and Yiu (2003, p. 5) state that the "decentralization of power to provincial government [also means] that these regional levels take [...] a more active role in pursuing commercial diplomacy."

Along with the home country resources, such as time and financial investments, and the policies employed, the actors engaged in commercial diplomacy also shape its outcomes. In the literature, a wide spectrum of actors has been identified, including at the high-policy level, i.e., the head of state, prime ministers, ambassadors, ministers, and members of the parliament; the lower level of diplomatic envoy, such as trade representatives, commercial attachés, and commercial diplomats; and actors of government-sponsored organizations, including trade promotion organizations and investment promotion agencies (Kostecki & Naray, 2007). Ozdem (2009) identifies the following commercial diplomatic actors: the Foreign Ministry, the Ministry of Foreign Trade, the Ministry of Finance, the Treasury, and specialist export and investment promotion agencies. Rana, on the basis of his worldwide study of the structures of foreign affairs and external economic management, adds business

---

[1]The Corporatist type (independent trade promotion structures); the Pragmatist type (coordination mechanisms); the Northern Europe type; the Commonwealth type (combination of foreign affairs and trade); the Classical type (trade promotion as part of trade policy and Ministry of Trade); and the Developing Country type (trade promotion in the Ministry of Foreign Affairs).

schools, academics, think tanks, the tourism industry, media, and a host of domestic actors "that are both stakeholders and prime movers" (Rana, 2007, p. 3) to the list.

While the above-mentioned studies focus on the different actors in commercial diplomacy, Kostecki and Naray (2007) and Naray (2010a, 2010b) investigate the individual level, that is to say the personal characteristics of the state representative in diplomatic function. Recently, Naray (2010b) published an empirical study on the successfulness of certain working styles of a commercial diplomat. In his research, he differentiates between the business promoter, civil servant, and generalist styles (Kostecki & Naray, 2007; Naray, 2010a). He argues that "ideally a new [commercial diplomat] recruit's profile ought to combine strengths in international experience and business, preferably in senior marketing, and a solid understanding of involved institutions" (Naray, 2010b, p. 9). Suggestions about a return of the commercial diplomat to the private sector after a few years in diplomatic service are also mentioned, based on the idea of having a "natural access to international business and marketing issues while understanding the broader context of bilateral relationships" (*ibid.*) Lee (2004) and Mercier (2007) refer to this idea as "cross-fertilization" (between the public and private sector). In this context, the personal network and commitment of the commercial diplomat is also of great importance. Naray (2010a) argues that two more basic elements seem to be crucial for the future commercial diplomat's recruitment: business knowledge and experience.

Overall, there is a limited body of literature on home country resources. Furthermore, whereas the actors involved in commercial diplomacy are discussed more explicitly, Kostecki and Naray (2007) are almost the only scholars conducting research on the personal characteristics of the commercial diplomat. The biggest gap in the existing literature, however, concerns research on policy-making on commercial diplomacy at the national level.

Commercial Diplomacy Throughput: Commercial Diplomacy in Action

This section describes the current state of research on commercial diplomacy in action, thereby investigating commercial diplomacy activities and practices as well as interactions between home and host countries.

The literature on practices and activities is rather extensive, in comparison to all other subtopics. According to Kostecki and Naray (2007), two types of activities are distinguished: primary ones (relating to trade and FDIs, research and technology, tourism and business advocacy) and supporting ones (relating to the inputs needed for the primary activities: intelligence, networking, involvement in the "made-in" image campaign, and support for business negotiations, contract implementation, and problem-solving). Lee (2004) categorizes activities slightly differently by allocating commercial diplomacy-related activities to three categories: gathering and disseminating commercial information and market research; developing business and government contacts; and promoting goods and new products in the host market. In his current research, Naray (2010a) included a matrix with all the activities of a commercial diplomat, thereby differentiating between the following five activity areas: promotion of trade in goods and services; protection of intellectual property rights (IPR); cooperation in science and technology; promotion of "made-in" and corporate images; and promotion of FDI. Ozdem (2009), Mercier (2007), and Coolsaet (2004) also collected a very detailed list of commercial diplomatic activities. Mercier (2007) thereby stressed the point that export promotion activities and inward investment promotion activities should be considered together. However, Rana (2001, p. 5f) distinguishes between activities for export promotion, such as "market studies, visits by business delegations, participation in international trade fairs, and buyer-seller meetings" and activities mobilizing FDI, which he calls "salesmanship" activities, such as "sensitizing potential foreign investors on the opportunities in the home country, [...and] targeting promotion." Kostecki and Naray (2007, p. 10) add "match-making" to the activities of commercial diplomats, stating that a few countries in particular devote significant resources to the process.

Many other studies focus solely on one of the above-mentioned categories, or more specifically on one of the activities conducted by a commercial diplomat, as for example on the individual level. Herbst (1996) thereby mentions that a large part of a commercial diplomat's work consists of reporting from the host country to the home country. Potter (2004) reinforces this by stating that the trade commissioner functions as the home country's eyes and ears in the foreign market. Saner and Yiu (2003), on the other hand, studied the function of a commercial diplomat as a consultant to both domestic and foreign companies. At the organizational level, Yakop and Van Bergeijk (2009) follow up on this by presenting a list with relevant topics for which firms mainly need commercial diplomatic support. A number of other studies, including Czinkota (2002) and Yannopoulus (2010), focus solely on the promotion of exports as an activity of commercial diplomat and evaluate their performance (Herbst, 1996; Hibbert, 1998; Nitsch, 2005; Wilkinson & Brouthers, 2000a, 2000b; Yannopoulos, 2010). In this context, Van Veenstra, Yakop, and Van Bergeijk (2010) conclude that export promotion agencies are mostly ineffective in their work, whereas Yannopoulos (2010) nuances this statement by arguing that export assistance programs cannot be viewed as "equally useful" (Yannopoulos, 2010, p. 36) to all exporters.

An additional topic at the national policy level is policy-making itself. So far, only a few studies on commercial diplomacy policies have been published. This is mainly due to the fact that commercial diplomacy remains an unspoken part of diplomatic activities, or as Lee (2004, p. 344) puts it: commercial diplomacy is "present-but-invisible." A few authors have approached the subject, including Muller (2002), who focus on the policy shift of the South African government toward a universal model, which excluded hardly anyone from the commercial diplomacy efforts of the country. Van Bergeijk and Melissen (2010) also provide arguments in favor of more economic diplomacy policy, mainly based on the current changes in the global environment. Many other authors refer to a policy shift when studying the increased number and frequency of commercial diplomatic activities (Coolsaet, 2004; Lee, 2004; Muller, 2002; Potter, 2004; Rana, 2007; Saner & Sondergaard, 2000; Sridharan, 2002;

Stringer, 2007). Some, such as Heemskerk (2010) and van Dooremalen and Quaedvlieg (2010), also elaborate on countries' policy choice to focus on certain sectors to bundle their commercial diplomatic efforts.

All countries use a number of commercial diplomatic instruments to pursue their national economic and foreign policy goals. Depending on the situation of the country and their economic or political partners, those instruments vary in strength and assertiveness. They include free trade agreements and preferential trade agreements (bilateral and regional basis), agreements that tackle nontariff obstacles, transportation agreements, and investment protection and facilitation accords (Okano-Heijmans, 2008; Rana, 2007; Sherman & Eliasson, 2007; Van Bergeijk, 1992). Recent trends show that governments make use of "comprehensive economic cooperation accords" (Rana, 2007, p. 6) with their network of embassies and consulates.

In general, the literature on commercial diplomacy in action, i.e., its activities or practices, is rather well established in the body of literature investigated. However, the number of evaluation studies still needs to be increased, making use of different levels of analysis, in order to provide applicable results.

Commercial Diplomacy Output: Commercial Diplomacy Benefits

The aim of commercial diplomacy is to benefit business enterprises as well as the government and society. In any case, it should be a value-creating activity since it is dealing with both managerial and governmental concerns (Kostecki & Naray, 2007; Potter, 2004).

Political benefits.   According to a study by Kotabe and Czinkota (1992), commercial diplomacy creates jobs, increases tax revenue, and stimulates economic growth. Another potential benefit, studied by Yang et al. (2008), is augmenting the positive reputation of a country, which means the "relative attractiveness of a country in the minds of foreign publics" (Yang et al., 2008, p. 422), which may stimulate trade patterns. Heemskerk (2010) also stresses the influence of commercial diplomacy on protectionism and free trade.

Economic benefits.   Along with government benefits, Naray (2010b) also includes business beneficiaries. According to him, the purpose of commercial diplomat activities varies according to the size of the business firms. As a consequence, SMEs are usually supported in taking their first steps in a new foreign market, whereas larger firms use diplomatic channels to "gain advocacy support in international tenders [and] influence relevant policy-making and regulations in the host country" (Naray, 2010b, p. 8). Economic benefits in the form of an increase in exports were studied by Czinkota, who stated that exports shape the "public perception of the competitiveness of a nation and determine [...] the level of imports that a country can afford" (2002, p. 315). Yakop and Van Bergeijk (2009) and Veenstra et al. (2010) conclude in their studies that commercial diplomacy is only effective when the home country is a high-income country and the host country a low- or middle-income country and that diplomatic representation via embassies or consulates "is not a relevant trade enhancing factor for trade within the OECD" (Yakop & Van Bergeijk, 2009, p. 4).

In their research, Kostecki and Naray (2007) present the value chain of commercial diplomacy, thereby stating that commercial diplomacy is a value-creating activity. Empirical evidence is provided by a number of authors (Nitsch, 2005; Rose, 2005; Saner & Yiu, 2003; Stringer, 2007; Yakop & Van Bergeijk, 2009) who argue for more input (diplomatic missions, etc.) in order to receive better and greater output (higher trade volume, etc.). Rose (2005, p. 13), for example, states that "bilateral exports rise by approximately 6–10% for each additional consulate abroad." This is in line with the study of Veenstra et al. (2010), which concludes that a 10% increase in consulates and embassies can lead to a 0.5–0.9% larger trade flow. Heemskerk (2010) adds that according to estimates, economic diplomacy accounts for a growth in welfare of between 100 and 200 million euros a year. And Nitsch (2005) expresses the added value of commercial diplomacy by stating that international trade missions explain 6–10% of the trade volume worldwide.

Taken as a whole, there is a limited body of conceptual papers on the outcome of commercial diplomacy. There is a significant need for empirical studies, especially from a political economy perspective, researching the effectiveness of commercial diplomacy and its benefits for society.

Commercial Diplomacy Context

Several phenomena are discussed in the literature on commercial diplomacy, such as globalization. In addition, government characteristics, such as market size, bilateral history, and current relation between the two countries, are aspects of the commercial diplomacy context.

Host country characteristics include the bilateral relations and its economic, cultural, legal, and political situation. According to Rose (2005) and Kostecki and Naray (2007), the host country's market size and potential are the most significant determinants for investments in commercial diplomatic relations. Another factor of influence may be "the gravity center" (Kostecki & Naray, 2007, p. 13) or top sectors, implying that some regions/countries are very important markets for certain products. Other authors add decisive variables to the discussion, such as the legal environment of a country and its reliability, the possibility to obtain satisfaction in court, and the level of corruption. The efficiency of commercial diplomatic efforts therefore depends on the host country's business regime, cultural differences, and efficiency of governance (Kostecki & Naray, 2007; Yakop & Van Bergeijk, 2009). Foreign pressure based on ideological differences may prevent the establishment of diplomatic representation in the first place (Kostecki & Naray, 2007; Neumayer, 2007). In this respect, history, especially colonial ties (Yakop & Van Bergeijk, 2009), may influence diplomatic relations between countries and therefore also commercial diplomacy significantly. Okano-Heijmans (2008) conducted an in-depth study on the economic and diplomatic relations between Japan and China. Other factors of importance are military alliances, the importance of possible aid programs, economic importance, etc. (Kostecki & Naray, 2007). Neumayer (2007, p. 229) studied why "some nation-states host many more foreign representations at home than others." He concluded that three factors exert a strong influence on the representation pattern: distance, power, and ideology. Based on his argumentation, Kostecki and Naray (2007) studied the number of commercial diplomats by country of origin. Yakop and Van Bergeijk (2009) supplemented the literature by doing research between different country groups according to different income and development levels, concluding that especially for less developed countries outside the OECD, economic relations are of great importance.

Along with the home and host country characteristics, worldwide phenomena are also commonly discussed in the literature. They include trends such as increasing internationalization and globalization (Kostecki & Naray, 2007; Muller, 2002; Potter, 2004; Saner & Yiu, 2003; Van Dooremalen & Quaedvlieg, 2010), encouraging more interdependencies between states, but especially between the political and economic sphere. Increasing use and improvement of technologies (Henrikson, 2005; Kostecki & Naray, 2007), but also phenomena such as the blurring of barriers, common threats such as terrorism (Potter, 2004), and an ever stronger commercial influence play important roles (Van Dooremalen & Quaedvlieg, 2010). An often discussed topic is also the increased influence of developing countries (Haan, 2010; Saner & Yiu, 2003; Van Dooremalen & Quaedvlieg, 2010) and of private actors (Henrikson, 2005; Saner & Yiu, 2003; Sherman & Eliasson, 2007; Van Dooremalen & Quaedvlieg, 2010).

In general, research on the context of commercial diplomacy is of great importance since commercial diplomacy is conducted in an ever-changing environment. As a consequence, there is an urgent call for new studies on the influence of modern technology development and other globalization phenomena.

Conclusion

As stated before, most studies focus on rather specific subtopics of this framework, thereby isolating the elaborated topic from other aspects of the commercial diplomacy model. Studies that aim at the complete picture of commercial diplomacy are rather rare, even though authors such as Kostecki and Naray (2007) and Rana (2007) try to capture a broader picture of commercial diplomacy, thereby including aspects of the input, throughput, and output of the model constructed in this chapter. By employing a general and plain outline, the framework is supposed to present at least the basic issues of commercial diplomacy and should be refined for future work. Commercial diplomacy is a new and evolving field of research at the interface of the fields of International Relations (IR) and International Management (IM). Reviewing the initial body of literature and discussing a future research agenda, this chapter would like to stimulate further debate and research on the topic of commercial diplomacy (Figure 4).

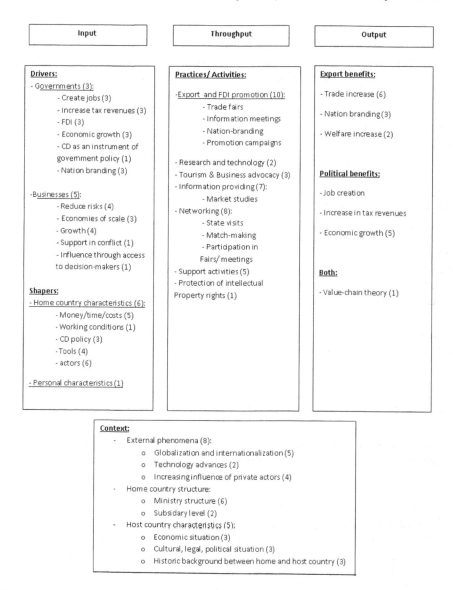

Figure 4: Framework of input–throughput–output model (commercial diplomacy) including context and number of publications.

Practical Implications

As this critical literature review demonstrates, the relative importance of commercial diplomacy and its input, throughput, and output is a topic of inquiry in the fields of international relations as much as in international management. Arguments for and against commercial diplomacy often depend on the perspective chosen. Presenting an overview of the current body of literature emphasizes the patchiness of the work and the need for a more complete picture of the topic to enable well-informed advice to be given to governments and involved organizations. Since commercial diplomacy forms an important part of governmental policy, recommendations should be based on a complete analysis of commercial diplomacy, including effectiveness and efficiency studies. The presented model informs the reader about the current state of research and encourages scientists to continue researching it.

Limitations to This Study

There are a number of limitations to this chapter. The review is restricted to studies published in international peer-reviewed journals. In addition, language restrictions limited the search to articles published in English, Dutch, and German. As a consequence, further research published in books, unpublished papers, or other languages may be available and could be added. The framework, designed to systematize the current body of literature on commercial diplomacy, is normative since it is not based on proper theoretical foundations. However, an appropriate theory for framing commercial diplomacy is lacking at present.

Commercial Diplomacy Research Agenda

This chapter's proposed framework and conceptualizations give a useful overview of the current state of the literature on the topic of commercial diplomacy. In this section, we would like to describe a future research agenda. First of all, empirical research should be conducted on the key research topics to support the theoretical perspectives. It is of great importance to collect meaningful data and translate the findings of these studies into useful recommendations for practitioners, especially since the empirical literature on commercial diplomacy is still in its infancy. So far, we have produced some valuable insights into the nature of commercial diplomacy. The theoretical development of the literature needs to continue, however. Future research on the output, a number of factors, and possible changes in the context of commercial diplomacy is needed, thereby making use of different disciplinary perspectives and methodological approaches. The following section elaborates on these demands by discussing some initial implications concerning theoretical perspectives, methodological approaches, and levels of analysis. So far, research has mainly focused on commercial diplomacy in action. In this chapter, however, we see there needs to be a shift of attention to other parts of the model, but especially toward obtaining a broader view on commercial diplomacy. This includes business studies and a more managerial approach. There is a constant need to update empirical findings and apply different approaches and perspectives.

Disciplinary Perspectives

Due to a predominantly international relations approach to diplomacy, commercial elements of diplomacy are often either neglected or not entirely comprehended by the literature. This is what Lee and Hudson (2004, p. 360) refer to when they speak of the "present-but-invisible" status of commercial diplomacy. Recently, some scholars have picked up the topic, but there is a need to increase the use of the international business and economic-political perspectives to gather more information on the effectiveness and efficiency of commercial diplomacy. Adopting these approaches enables the integration of market relations with political relations and consequently conceptualizes diplomacy as a "political-economic dialogue" (Lee & Hudson, 2004, p. 360). In addition, due to recent changes in the political environment, governments and nation-states should be investigated from a business rather than an international relations approach. Efficiency and cost-benefit analyses are vital tools for practical appliance in this case. A dialogue on public-private relationships within state structures, as currently employed by many International Political Economic (IPE) studies, is also of great use in the commercial diplomatic debate.

Methodological Approaches

Because commercial diplomacy is a developing field with diverse topics, methodological pluralism should be present. All of the empirical studies presented in this chapter are cross-sectional, and only the conceptual case studies take historical relations between the home and the host country into account. Since commercial diplomacy is subject to change, longitudinal studies would help identify the direction of the transformation and may support strategic choices. A drawback of the studies identified is that most of them rely on single source respondents, nearly all being the commercial diplomats themselves. To increase the level of awareness, multiple respondents should be included. Most important is the necessity to increase the number of empirical studies, thereby taking into account additional ways of data collection. Recent studies often lack description, explanation, and justification of the choice of methodology. Future studies should improve on this drawback by explicitly stating and justifying their methodological choices.

Level of Analysis

Due to the fact that issues of level create particular problems when "the levels of topic, theory, data collection and/or analysis are incongruent" (Strohmeier, 2007, p. 30), future work should explicitly address them. Commercial diplomacy includes the micro as well as the macro level and there is consequently a necessity for more multilevel approaches, as applied by Kostecki and Naray (2007). So far, most articles have employed case studies, i.e., they mostly used countries and individuals as their level of analysis, which is common for studies with international relations as a theoretical background. We call for more research on business firms as the level of analysis. In order to investigate the entirety of commercial diplomacy, multilevel research is needed, incorporating supranational institutions (EU, WTO, IMF, and more), the government level, public and private actors, and business firms. This chapter contributes to the current state of research by focusing on the existing literature as the level of analysis.

Topics

Analyzing the existing literature as summarized in Figure 2, it becomes apparent that current studies mainly refer to specific subtopics of commercial diplomacy. One of their central limitations is their lack of an overview. In fact, we possess scientific knowledge of several parts of the above-presented framework, while there is only a hint of the complete picture. What we consequently need in order to advance the current state of the literature are three different kinds of studies: First, specific studies that address a new subset of the framework: its concepts and the relationship between them are needed to gain more in-depth information. Second, specific studies that address already examined subtopics of the framework in order to support prior findings by replication are vital. Third, there is a need for general studies that embrace several aspects concurrently.

First of all, a better understanding of the output of commercial diplomatic activities should be created. There is a need to replicate and extend empirical studies, such as the ones by Rose (2005), Nitsch (2005), and Veenstra et al. (2010), making use of different methodological approaches. The central question is whether the benefits of commercial diplomacy justify the burdens for the public, as Rose already points out. Mercier (2007) adds thoughts to this discussion about the possibility of recovering costs through charging fees and raises the critical question about the nature of companies that should be supported: those with headquarters in the home country or those that deliver the most added value to the home country. Studies focusing on the value of commercial diplomacy for the government (job creation, internal tax revenues, etc.) and for businesses (economies of scale and scope, economic growth, etc.) are needed to support the value-chain theory of commercial diplomacy as presented by Kostecki and Naray (2007) and answer those questions. Additional research should thus include the extent to which government and business objectives are met and their satisfaction achieved, thereby measuring the commercial diplomat's effectiveness. Follow-up studies lend robustness to prior findings and alleviate possible contradictions. In addition, they may justify prior findings and the methodologies used and take reliability and validity measurements into account.

Along with a gap in the literature concerning the efficiency and effectiveness of commercial diplomacy, in-depth research is lacking on its context, i.e., on the external influences. An ever-changing environment demands new studies, which take into account the role of technological advances, the blurring of barriers, the development of e-government (Kostecki & Naray, 2007), and the increasing number of actors involved in commercial diplomacy. While a number of authors include some thoughts on these issues in their studies, empirical research will support their argumentation, as also claimed by Saner (2000).

Another topic yet to be investigated is how the tendency to centralize commercial diplomacy may be affected by the autonomy given to local and regional governments, and subsequently, how countries should deal with regional rivalries over FDI (Mercier, 2007; Rana, 2007). More research on how to overcome a lack of impetus, cultural differences, and ineffective governance will be needed (Yakop & Van Bergeijk, 2009), and aspects such as country reputation, relational and historical dimensions, and affinities between countries should be taken into account (Yang et al., 2008). The question of whether a best practice approach could be developed should be discussed in the literature, and factors that influence the success of commercial diplomacy should be pointed out (Mercier, 2007). Evaluation studies, such as the ones by Wilkinson and Brouthers, could be of great use here.

All in all, we conclude that firstly concerning the disciplinary perspectives, more studies with an international business and/or political-economic approach need to be conducted in order to receive a complete picture of commercial diplomacy, including the priorities of receivers of the diplomatic effort (businesses), and efficiency and effectiveness issues. Second, concerning the empirical methods, combining different ones enables the literature to present in-depth, reliable, and generalizable findings. Third, issues of level should be solved by conducting more multilevel research, including studies focusing on companies and supranational institutions as levels of analysis. Fourth, considering the patchiness of the current body of literature, future studies should focus more on the systematic framework presented in this study. And fifth, studies focusing on the individual level of commercial diplomacy, that is to say on the actors involved, should be conducted in order to increase the commitment of commercial diplomats. All this will allow governments to adapt and reorganize existing commercial diplomatic structures and increase efficiency and effectiveness on the basis of theoretical conclusions. A joint debate taking advantage of different methodological and theoretical approaches should yield insights for future research which will help to advance our understanding of commercial diplomacy.

Acknowledgment

The authors would like to thank Michel L. Ehrenhard for his insightful comments to earlier versions of this chapter.

References

Babbie, E. R. (2009). *The basics of social research.* Belmont, CA: Thomson Wadsworth.
Berridge (2001). *A dictionary of diplomacy.* Basingstoke, UK: Palgrave Macmillan.
Coolsaet, R. (2004). Trade and diplomacy: The Belgian case. *International Studies Perspectives,* 5(1), 61–652.

Czinkota, M. (2002). Export promotion: Framework for finding opportunity in change. *Thunderbird International Business Review*, *44*(3), 315–324.

Friedman, J. (2005). Globalization and the emerging culture of planning. *Progress in Planning*, *64*, 183–234.

Haan, A. (2010). Omvat economische diplomatie ook ontwikkelingssamenwerking? *Internationale Spectator*, *64*(2), 70–72.

Heemskerk, F. (2010). Toenemend belang van economische diplomatie voor Nederland. *Internationale Spectator*, *64*(2), 85–87.

Henrikson, A. (2005). Diplomacy's possible futures. *The Hague: Journal of Diplomacy*, *1*(1), 3–27.

Henrikson, A. (2006). *What can public diplomacy achieve?* Clingendael Discussion Papers in Diplomacy 104. Netherlands Institute of International Relations "Clingendael", The Hague.

Herbst, A. (1996). The commercial counsellor's field of activity. *Intereconomics*, *4*(10), 323–325.

Hibbert, E. (1998). Evaluating government export promotion: Some conceptual and empirical approaches. *The International Trade Journal*, *XII*(4).

Hocking, B. (2004). Privatizing diplomacy. *International Studies Association Perspectives*, *5*, 147–152.

Kelly, D. (2000). *The International Chamber of Commerce as a diplomatic actor* (July, 21 pp.). Leicester: Centre for the Study of Diplomacy, University of Leicester.

Kostecki, M., & Naray, O. (2007). *Commercial diplomacy and international business* (April, 41 pp.). Den Haag: Nederlands Instituut voor Internationale Betrekkingen "Clingendael".

Kotabe, M., & Czinkota, M. R. (1992). State government promotion of manufacturing exports: A gap analysis. *Journal of International Business Studies*, *23*(4), 637–658.

Lee, D. (2004). The growing influence of business in U.K. diplomacy. *International Studies Perspectives*, *5*, 50–54.

Lee, D., & Hudson, L. (2004). The old and the new significance of political economy in diplomacy. *Review of International Studies*, *30*, 343–360.

Mercier, A. (2007). *Commercial diplomacy in advanced industrial states: Canada, the UK and the US*. Clingendael Discussion Papers in Diplomacy 108. Netherlands Institute of International Relations "Clingendael", The Hague.

Morrow, J. D., Siverson, R. M., & Tabares, T. E. (1998). The political determinants of international trade: The major powers, 1907–90. *American Political Review*, *92*(3), 649–661.

Muller, M. (2002). South Africa's economic diplomacy: Constructing a better world for all? *Diplomacy and Statecraft*, *13*(1), 1–30.

Naray, O. (2008). Commercial diplomacy: A conceptual overview. Paper presented at the 7th World Conference of TPOs, The Hague, The Netherlands.

Naray, O. (2010a). Commercial diplomats in the context of international business. *The Hague Journal of Diplomacy*, *6*, 121–148.

Naray, O. (2010b). What a good commercial diplomat has to know and be capable of. *Exchange: The Magazine for International Business and Diplomacy*, *2*(December), 8–9.

Neumayer, E. (2007). Distance, power and ideology: Diplomatic representation in a world of nation-states. *Area*, *40*(2), 228–236.

Nitsch, V. (2005). *State visits and international trade*. CESifo Working Paper 1582. CESifo Group, Munich.

Okano-Heijmans, M. (2008). Economie en diplomatie in de relatie Japan-China: Voorwaarts ondanks het verleden. *Internationale Spectator*, *62*(3), 155–159.

Okano-Heijmans, M., & Ruël, H. J. M. (2011). Commerciële diplomatie en internationaal ondernemen. *Internationale Spectator*, *65*(9).

Ozdem, M. I. (2009). *Government agencies in commercial diplomacy: Seeking the optimal agency structure for foreign trade policy.* Raleigh NC, USA: North Carolina State University.

Pisani, N. (2009). International management research: Investigating its recent diffusion in top management journals. *Journal of Management, 35*(2), 199–218.

Potter, E. H. (2004). Branding Canada: The renaissance of Canada's commercial diplomacy. *International Studies Perspectives, 5*, 55–60.

Rana, K. S. (2001). Serving the private sector: India's experience in context. In N. Bayne & S. Woolcock (Eds.), *The new economic diplomacy: Decision-making and negotiation in international economic relations* (1st ed.). Farnham, UK: Ashgate Publishing Limited.

Rana, K. S. (2007). Economic diplomacy: The experience of developing countries. In N. Bayne & S. Woolcock (Eds.), *The new economic diplomacy: Decision-making and negotiation in international economic relations* (pp. 201–220) Aldershot: Ashgate.

Rose, A. K. (2005). The foreign service and foreign trade: Embassies as export promotion. *World Economy, 30*(1), 22–38.

Saner, R. (2000). *The expert negotiator.* The Hague, The Netherlands: Kluwer Law Publisher.

Saner, R., & Yiu, L. (2003). *International economic diplomacy: Mutations in post-modern times* (January, 37 pp.). The Hague: Netherlands Institute of International Relations "Clingendael".

Saner, R. Y. L., & Sondergaard, M. (2000). Business diplomacy management: A core competency for global companies. *Academy of Management Executive, 14*(1).

Scholte, J. A. (2000). *Globalization a critical introduction.* Basingstoke, UK: Macmillan.

Sherman, R., & Eliasson, J. (2006). Trade disputes and non-state actors: New institutional arrangements and the privatisation of commercial diplomacy. *World Economy, 29*, 473–489.

Sherman, R., & Eliasson, J. (2007). Privatizing commercial diplomacy: Institutional innovation at the domestic-international frontier. *Current Politics and Economics of Europe, 18*(3/4), 351–355.

Sridharan, K. (2002). Commercial diplomacy and statecraft in the context of economic reform: The Indian experience. *Diplomacy and Statecraft, 13*(2), 57–82.

Strohmeier, S. (2007). Research in e-HRM: Review and implications. *Human Resource Management Review, 17*(1), 19–37.

Van Bergeijk, P. A. G. (1992). Diplomatic barriers to trade. *The Economist, 140*(1), 45–64.

Van Bergeijk, P. A. G., & Melissen, J. (2010). Diplomatie economen. *Internationale Spectator, 64*(2), 98–99.

Van Veenstra, M.-L. E. H., Yakop, M., & Van Bergeijk, P. A. G. (2010). *Economic diplomacy, the level of development and trade* Clingendael Discussion Papers in Diplomacy 119. Netherlands Institute of International Relations "Clingendael", The Hague.

Stringer, K. (2007). *Think global act local: Honorary consuls in a transforming diplomatic world.* Discussion Papers in Diplomacy, No. 109. The Hague: Netherlands Institute of International Relations "Clingendael".

Van Bergeijk, P., Veenstra, M., & Yakop, M. (2010). *Economic diplomacy, the level of development and trade.* Discussion Papers in Diplomacy, No. 119. The Hague: Netherlands Institute of International Relations "Clingendael".

Van Dooremalen, S., & Quaedvlieg, W. (2010). Nederlandse economische diplomatie heeft overkoepelende visie nodig. *International Spectator, 64*(2), 77–80.

Wilkinson, T. J., & Brouthers, L. E. (2000a). Trade promotion and SME export performance. *International Business Review, 15*, 233–252.

Wilkinson, T. J., & Brouthers, L. E. (2000b). Trade shows, trade missions and state governments: Increasing FDI and high-tech exports. *Journal of International Business Studies, 31*(4), 725–734.

Wright, J. (2000). Economic education, executive education, and the training of commercial diplomats for the global economy. Crossroads of the New Millennium, United Arab Emirates, TEND 2000.

Yakop, M., & Van Bergeijk, P. A. G. (2009). *The weight of economic and commercial diplomacy.* International Institute of Social Studies Working Paper No. 478, International Institute of Social Studies, The Hague.

Yang, S., Shin, H., Lee, J., & Wrigley, B. (2008). Country reputation in multidimensions: Predictors, effects, and communication channels. *Journal of Public Relations Research, 20*(4), 421–440.

Yannopoulos, P. (2010). Export assistance programs: Insights from Canadian SMEs. *International Review of Business Research Papers, 6*(5), 36–51.

Appendix

Appendix 1: Search Criteria

Babbie (2009) identifies the following search criteria: selection, relevance, validity, and completeness. While the selection criteria are explained in detail in the main text, the other three are discussed in this section. To progress to the next step in the evaluation phase and limit the resources needed for evaluation, only academic papers published later than 2000 were considered. The academic source requirement, also a criterion for validity, ensures that only papers with a certain level of quality were considered, i.e., that tools and techniques were applied correctly and in a scientific sense. In order to check the completeness of the body of literature, an intensive reference check was performed. In addition, the cross-search test employed increased the probability of completeness.

Appendix 2: Search Parameters

In order to plan the literature search strategy, a number of parameters for the search were defined:

Parameters	Narrow	Broad
Language of publication	English	English, German and Dutch
Subject area	Commercial diplomacy	Economic diplomacy
Geographical area	Worldwide	Worldwide
Publication period	1995–2011	1950–2011
Literature type	Secondary	Primary, secondary, and tertiary sources

Chapter 2

Commercial Diplomats as Corporate Entrepreneurs: An Institutional Perspective

Robin Visser and Huub Ruël

Abstract

This chapter presents a study on the work of commercial diplomats as international business promoters at foreign posts. Research has largely overlooked the actual roles and activities of commercial diplomats in explaining the effectiveness of commercial diplomacy and international business support. In this study, it is assumed that commercial diplomats' behavior is influenced by informal institutions. Face-to-face semi-structured interviews with 23 commercial diplomats at foreign posts from different countries were conducted and analyzed. The results show three different types of role behavior and differences in proactivity per type. Informal institutions such as background, skills, and experience, cultural differences, and the working environment suggest to explain the differences in levels of proactive international business support behavior of commercial diplomats. Further research is needed to assert these findings.

Keywords: Commercial diplomacy; corporate entrepreneurship; role behavior; informal institutionalism; proactivity

Introduction

Commercial diplomacy is of growing concern to governments and features two types of activities: policy-making and business support. Embassies, being active within networks of organizations that deal with business support and promotion (Kostecki & Naray, 2007), especially for SMEs (Kostecki & Naray, 2007; Naray,

Commercial Diplomacy and International Business: A Conceptual and Empirical Exploration
Advanced Series in Management, 29–70
ISSN: 1877-6361/doi:10.1108/S1877-6361(2012)0000009006

2011), are at the front-end of this spectrum. Commercial diplomacy research is relatively young and hence also quite unexplored field (Kostecki & Naray, 2007; Naray, 2011; Potter, 2004). Due to the increasing importance of commercial diplomacy in a globalizing world, there is a demand for more research on commercial diplomacy. A particular topic that hardly has been studied is the work and activities of the executors of commercial diplomacy policies and practices, the commercial diplomats at the foreign posts. Increasing our understanding of how commercial diplomats work will not only help to advance theory that can explain commercial diplomacy's contribution to a country's economy, its effectiveness, its relevance, and usefulness but also lead to more systematic insights that can help commercial diplomats to improve commercial diplomat policies and practices. Therefore, the objective of this research is to expand the current body of knowledge on this subject.

The environment in which commercial diplomats perform their activities, the business–government interface, can be better understood "by incorporating the institutional settings through which business and government must interact" (Hillman & Keim, 1995, p. 212). Kostecki and Naray (2007) point out several elements of such institutional settings, indicating that commercial diplomats with different styles have different backgrounds and professional experience in business. Naray (2008, p. 9) suggests that a commercial diplomat's style "can evolve quickly due to foreign influence, (…) background and personality." Furthermore, the role of a commercial diplomat strongly depends on host country characteristics such as proximity, culture, and local business regime (Kostecki & Naray, 2007). The effects of informal institutions can be seen through a lens of corporate entrepreneurship, which deals with the way entrepreneurial behavior manifests in the individual (Burgelman, 1983; Kuratko, 2007).

Theoretical Framework

Diplomacy is "the conduct of relations between sovereign states through the medium of officials based at home or abroad" (Berridge & James, 2003). The implications of this definition for embassies are both political-economic and commercial (Yakop & Bergeijk, 2009).

A comparison of economic diplomacy and trade and export promotion shows that commercial diplomacy, as opposed to economic diplomacy, focuses on business support and promotion and that it is a more entailing concept than trade and export promotion (Kostecki & Naray, 2007; Mercier, 2007; Naray, 2011; Potter, 2004; Rose, 2005; Saner & Yiu, 2003; Spence & Crick, 2004; Wilkinson & Brouthers, 2000a, 2000b, 2006; Yakop & Bergeijk, 2009).

A definition of commercial diplomacy that considers the terms and the definitions mentioned above, can be found in the academic literature, such as in Potter (2004), Berridge and James (2003, p. 42), who define commercial diplomacy as "the work of diplomatic missions in support of the home country's business and finance sectors." Distinct from although obviously closely related to economic diplomacy, it is now common for commercial diplomacy to include the promotion of inward and outward investment, as well as trade" and Naray (2008, p. 2), who says that commercial diplomacy "is an activity conducted by state representatives with diplomatic status in view of business promotion between a home and a host country. It aims at encouraging business development through a series of business promotion and facilitation activities." An integration of these considerations and definitions leads to the following definition of commercial diplomacy that will be adopted in this study:

> *"Commercial diplomacy is an activity conducted by state representatives which is aimed at generating commercial gain in the form of trade and inward and outward investment for the home country by means of business and entrepreneurship promotion and facilitation activities in the host country based on supplying information about export and investment opportunities, keeping contact with key actors and maintaining networks in relevant areas."*

The activities and areas in business and entrepreneurship promotion and facilitation have been comprehensively identified by Naray (2011), who identifies five areas in which commercial diplomats operate (promotion of trade in goods and services, protection of intellectual property rights, cooperation in science and technology, promotion of made-in and corporate image, and promotion of FDI) and six types of activities they perform (intelligence, communication, referral, advocacy, co-ordination, and logistics).

Commercial diplomats, the performers of these activities, can be said to be actors that operate in a host country as members of either the diplomatic envoy or of a trade promotion agency (Kostecki & Naray, 2007; Naray, 2011; Saner & Yiu, 2003). Such

Table 1: Three styles of commercial diplomats based on Kostecki and Naray (2007) and Naray (2011).

	Business promoter	**Civil servant**	**Generalist**
Approach	Commercial issues are understood mainly as business issues	Commercial issues are seen as an integral part of international relations	Commercial issues are perceived in a broader diplomatic and political perspective
Leading concern	Focus on client satisfaction	Focus on satisfaction of the ministry of trade	Focus on satisfaction of the ministry of foreign affairs
Level of activity	Proactive due to know-how and entrepreneurial approach	Reactive due to focus on policy implementation and government instructions	Ad hoc basis due to additionality to diplomatic duties
Strength	Having know-how and hands-on vision of support activities	Providing a link between business and ministry	Having high-level contacts and seeing commercial issues in broad diplomatic

commercial diplomats are categorized by Kostecki and Naray (2007) and Naray (2011) into three broad styles of which Table 1 provides an overview.

A caveat regarding these styles is that this table "only shows broad and so far typical tendencies" (Naray, 2008, p. 10) of empirical observations. However, due to the emergent status of the field, no other classification has yet been made of commercial diplomats. Sridharan (2002) gives a number of attributes that he sees as important for the development of the Indian commercial diplomatic apparatus, but a closer look at his suggestions reveals that they relate to economic diplomats rather than commercial diplomats.

On the subject of these roles, Kostecki and Naray (2007) observe that commercial diplomats with different styles usually have different backgrounds and professional experience in business. Naray (2008, p. 9) suggests that a commercial diplomat's style "can evolve quickly due to foreign influence, (...) background and personality." Furthermore, the role of a commercial diplomat strongly depends on host country characteristics such as proximity, culture, and local business regime (Kostecki & Naray, 2007).

Institutionalism

The commercial diplomat in the business–government interface.   The environment in which commercial diplomats perform their activities is the business–government interface, an interface that can be better understood "by incorporating the institutional settings through which business and government must interact" (Hillman & Keim, 1995, p. 212). This importance of institutions in the business–government interface is reflected in Harris and Carr (2007, p. 103) who assert that "different institutional arrangements are a clear reason why management behavior varies between countries," in Nasra and Dacin (2009), and in Li and Samsell (2009), who point to the largely ignored effects of informal institutions in this interface and call more attention to it by contrasting rule-based and relation-based governance systems for international trade.

Institutional arrangements are "the rules of the game in a society (...) that shape human exchange, whether political, social or economic" (North, 1990, p. 3). These rules "reduce uncertainty by establishing a stable (but not necessarily efficient) structure to human interaction" (North, 1990, p. 6) and are of both formal and informal nature. Formal institutions include rules and structures, and informal institutions, referred to as the informal constraints of society by Hillman and Keim (1995), include cultures, values, and norms (North, 1990). The informal institutions "are important aspects of the institutional setting through which business and government interact in different countries" (Hillman & Keim, 1995, p. 200) and are symbolic frameworks that provide guidelines for behavior, and lend stability, regularity, and meaning to social life (Orr & Scott, 2008).

According to Hillman and Keim (1995, p. 195), a "discussion of informal constraints will lead to consideration of the individual actors who are the members of government and business organizations. Informal rules, customs and practices are enacted and observed by these individuals." As the commercial diplomat is the individual actor to whom Hillman and Keim's (1995) reference pertains to, it becomes evident that the informal element of new institutional theory provides the key to understanding what influences the commercial diplomat.

New institutional theory and the commercial diplomat. As said before, institutions can be formal and informal. While formal institutions usually exist in some tangible form, informal institutions are harder to identify. Helmke and Levitsky (2004, p. 727) define informal institutions as "socially shared rules, usually unwritten, that are created, communicated, and enforced outside of officially sanctioned channels." The resultant informal rules are "not consciously designed or specified in writing — they are the routines, customs, traditions and conventions that are part of habitual action" (Lowndes, 1996, p. 193).

Informal institutions fall into two pillars: the normative and the cultural/cognitive (Bruton, Ahlstrom, & Li, 2010; Ingram & Clay, 2000; Ingram & Silverman, 2002). The normative pillar constitutes "organizational and individual behavior based on obligatory dimensions of social, professional, and organizational interaction, (...) typically composed of values (what is preferred or considered proper) and norms (how things are to be done, consistent with those values) that further establish consciously followed ground rules to which people conform" (Bruton et al., 2010, pp. 422–423) and includes "the informal norms, values, standards, roles, conventions, practices, taboos, customs, traditions, and codes of conduct that guide behavior and decisions" (Orr & Scott, 2008, p. 565).

The cultural/cognitive pillar describes "individual behavior based on subjectively and (often gradually) constructed rules and meanings that limit appropriate beliefs and actions" (Bruton et al., 2010, p. 423) and includes elements such as "shared beliefs, categories, identities, schemas, scripts, heuristics, logics of action and mental models" (Orr & Scott, 2008, p. 565).

Another way of approaching and clarifying the distinction between formal and informal institutions is by identifying whether an institution is centralized or decentralized, and whether it is public or private. Public-centralized and private-centralized institutions are formal and include (respectively) laws and rules. Public-decentralized and private-decentralized institutions are informal and include (respectively) culture and the norms derived from culture (Ingram & Clay, 2000; Ingram & Silverman, 2002). This view differs from the three-pillar system in its more extensive coverage of the regulative pillar.

Commercial diplomats, the actors in this research, as individuals occupy the normative (private-decentralized) pillar and theory predicts this pillar will "exert the most immediate control on individuals" (Ingram & Clay, 2000, p. 537). This is pointed out by Naray (2008, p. 9) who suggests that a commercial diplomat's style "can evolve quickly due to foreign influence, (...) background and personality."

When looking at how commercial diplomats shape their role, the focus of attention will be on elements such as working habits, the immediate environment, and personal experience, as such indicators are most likely to directly influence the way a commercial diplomat operates, as can be derived from specific elements found by

Searing (1991) and Zenger, Lazzarini, and Poppo (2002). Seeing the observable behavior by individual actors as a "proximate" cause, with the informal institutional context functioning on a higher level as a "remote" cause is actor-centered institutionalism, a form of new institutionalism (Van Lieshout, 2008).

The business–government interface, the environment in which commercial diplomats operate, can be better understood by looking at formal and informal institutions through an actor-centered new institutional lens. This research focuses on informal institutions on the normative (personal) level as the formal institutions that drive role adoption by commercial diplomats have already been identified by Kostecki and Naray (2007) and Naray (2008).

Corporate Entrepreneurship

Commercial diplomats as agents of opportunity identification.   Considering Naray's (2008) area-activity matrix (see Table 1), it is clear that commercial diplomats adopt both a reactive and a proactive role in their activities. For example, identifying potential partner firms on a business request is a reactive action, while organizing briefings for potential investors is a proactive element.

This contrast is addressed in Spence and Crick (2004), who also question the effectiveness of proactive activities by stating "that the multitude of export information including that from government sources is often confusing and its relevance to the needs of managers is sometimes questionable" (Spence & Crick, 2004, p. 283). They identify motivational (risks are perceived to be too high), informational (the lack thereof), and operational (lack of resources) barriers for international business and entrepreneurship. Wilkinson and Brouthers (2006), approaching the issue from a resource-based perspective, share this view.

The potential that lies here for the commercial diplomat is underlined by Spencer, Murtha, and Lenway (2005), who categorize ways in which governments shape institutional structures for new industry creation, by Bruton, Ahlstrom, and Obloj (2008), and by Nasra and Dacin (2009, p. 584), who suggest that "the state can actively engage in entrepreneurial behavior, identifying and discovering opportunities that emerge within their environments," adopting an informal institutional standpoint in their analysis. The challenge for the commercial diplomat, then, is in adopting a proactive approach in situations where this could be beneficial and relevant to home country businesses or entrepreneurs.

Proactive behavior as described by Bruton et al. (2008) and Nasra and Dacin (2009) pertains to elements in the area-activity matrix (see Table 1) that are aimed at increasing the success of home country businesses by active opportunity identification in the host country. Reactive behavior pertains to elements that are aimed at helping businesses and entrepreneurs that are already present in the host country.

The perception of commercial diplomats about proactive as opposed to reactive behavior and the way they act accordingly is the final aspect of the research question, as the academic literature suggests this may constitute an important part of the way they shape their roles.

Corporate entrepreneurship as the key to understanding proactive behavior. A succinct rationale for using corporate entrepreneurship to address the proactive versus reactive issue is provided by Kuratko (2007, p. 151) in stating that proactive behavior is "the type of behavior that is called for by corporate entrepreneurship." The academic literature is dedicated to business manager behavior, and consequently, corporate entrepreneurship is virtually always seen in the light of business continuity and competitiveness. While elements such as continuity and competitiveness are of considerably less concern to a commercial diplomat, the principles and processes of corporate entrepreneurship concern individual actors, and are as such transferable to others actors such as commercial diplomats.

The theory's transferable character is reflected in the academic literature, in which Sharma and Chrisman's (1999, p. 18) view that corporate entrepreneurship is "the process whereby an individual or group of individuals, in association with an existing organization, create a new organization or instigate renewal or innovation within that organization" finds widespread agreement and recurrence (Dess et al., 2003; Ireland, Covin, & Kuratko, 2009; Keupp & Gassmann, 2009; Peredo & Chrisman, 2004). The parallel with commercial diplomats becomes even starker when adopting the strategic entrepreneurship focus of corporate entrepreneurship, which involves "simultaneous opportunity-seeking and advantage-seeking behaviors (...) by emphasizing an opportunity-driven mindset" (Kuratko, 2007, p. 159) and the concept of autonomous strategic behavior, which states that entrepreneurial behavior surfaces in a bottom-up and informal manner (Burgelman, 1983; Kuratko, 2007).

On the individual actor level, several factors eliciting entrepreneurial behavior have been identified. These factors are top management support for corporate entrepreneurship, reward and resource availability, organizational structure and boundaries, risk-taking, and time availability (Hornsby, Kuratko, & Zahra, 2002; Kuratko, 2007; Kuratko, Montagno, & Hornsby, 1990). Like the concept of corporate entrepreneurship, these factors are transferable to commercial diplomats. However, due to the inductive nature of this research, these factors cannot be taken as a starting point; what the factors are for commercial diplomats is the topic of this research.

Corporate entrepreneurship, albeit a field of theory that is usually of concern in business sciences, is used in this research to address the contrast between reactive and proactive behavior of commercial diplomats. Reactive and proactive elements of commercial diplomacy will be tied to the three roles that commercial diplomats adopt, as the degree to which a commercial diplomat is proactive most likely depends on the role that is taken up.

Interlinkages between the theories. The theory of commercial diplomacy is the overarching theme of this theoretical framework to which new institutionalism and corporate entrepreneurship are tied. As the research question concerns the commercial diplomat as an individual actor within the definition of commercial diplomacy given in the section theoretical framework, and the areas and activities of commercial diplomacy as can be seen in Table 1, actor-centered new institutionalism, its normative viewpoint in particular, is a useful tool to investigate what elements influence the commercial diplomat within his/her role. In this case, normative institutional elements are the independent variables that influence the way that the commercial diplomat shapes being either a business promoter, a civil servant, or a generalist, as the behavior that can be observed in either one of these roles is influenced by normative institutions.

Corporate entrepreneurship provides a means to distinguish between reactive and proactive behavior, an element that is a direct consequence of what role a commercial diplomat has.

Research model.   The framework in Figure 1 is a synthesis of the theoretical review and hence covers all elements of the literature review. It represents a conceptual model of the research question.

The informal institutions that govern the behavior of commercial diplomats are given on the left. No particular elements are indicated as "preordained theoretical perspectives or propositions may bias and limit the findings" (Eisenhardt, 1989, p. 536).

This influence on the commercial diplomat, situated here within the confines of the activities of commercial diplomacy to indicate the boundaries of his/her endeavors, is represented by a line (indicating possible but uncertain causality) between informal institutionalism and the commercial diplomat. Kostecki and Naray's (2007) and Naray's (2008) three styles of commercial diplomats are elements of the term "Commercial Diplomat" and therefore overlap it. Proactive and reactive elements are set to the background of these styles, as they are expected to be important elements in the way commercial diplomats perform activities within their roles.

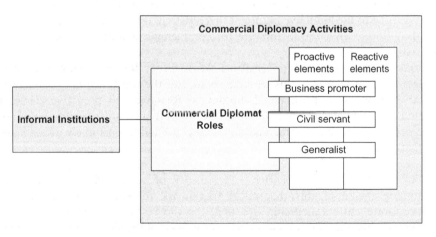

Figure 1: The research model based on the literature review.

Operationalization

A multimethod qualitative and cross-sectional case study was chosen as the focus lies on mapping the behavior of commercial diplomats to enrich the understanding of a number of similar units and the processes being enacted within single settings (Eisenhardt, 1989; Gerring, 2007), resulting in testable emergent theory based on empirically valid findings (Eisenhardt, 1989; Eisenhardt & Graebner, 2007; Pawson, 1996).

Face-to-face semi-structured interviews were conducted, as this allowed for an interview-dependent variation of complex and open questions in relation to an exploratory study in which it is necessary to understand the reasons for the decisions, attitudes, and opinions of interviewees (Darlington & Scott, 2002; Esterberg, 2002).

Systematic observation and recording of the actions of a commercial diplomat in the form of a "participant as observer," which focuses on discovering meanings behind actions (Saunders, Lewis, & Thornhill, 2009), mainly by means of primary and experiential data kept track of in a logbook was chosen to complement the interviews as it provided a background for them (Esterberg, 2002) and "heightens the researcher's awareness of significant social processes" (Saunders et al., 2009, p. 299).

Sample selection of most-similar cases occurred on the basis of self-selection seeing as this method was most useful where qualitative, exploratory research is needed (Darlington & Scott, 2002; Gerring, 2007; Saunders et al., 2009). The choice of participants was based on the difference in institutional backgrounds between them and their expected expertise so as to increase the likelihood that the emergent theory of commercial diplomacy was enhanced (Darlington & Scott, 2002; Eisenhardt, 1989; Eisenhardt & Graebner, 2007; Esterberg, 2002). A total of 33 possible participants were contacted, of whom 23 responded positively. The balance between participants from European and non-European countries is 14 to 9, which upholds the need for a wide variety of institutional backgrounds. All interviewees were stationed in Helsinki, and Table 2 provides an overview of them, including the number of years they had been stationed at Helsinki at the time of the interview and, for those appointed rotationally, the length of their careers.

Results

Interviewee Styles

The transcripts, notes, and responses via e-mail are reviewed for each individual interview and descriptive text segments and meanings are written down in list form in the terms as used by the interviewees. Such categorization of the interviews in terms of the theoretical concepts by means of open coding, the first step in the analysis process (Esterberg, 2002), allows for an assessment of the roles that the interviewees have adopted in terms of Kostecki and Naray's (2007) and Naray's (2008) three styles of commercial diplomats (see Table 1).

Table 2: Overview of the interviewees.

Code	Country	Function	Appointed	Interview type	Years in Helsinki and years in career	Nationality (if different from country)
G01	Argentina	Chargé D'Affaires	Rotationally	Face to face	3 and 25+	
G02	Belgium	Investment and Trade Commissioner	Rotationally	Face to face	2 and 9	
G03	Anonymous	Senior Trade Commissioner	Rotationally	Face to face	2 and 8	
G04	Chile	Third Secretary and Consul	Rotationally	Face to face	3 and 10	
G05	Czech Republic	First Secretary	Rotationally	E-mail	2 and 12	
G06	Denmark	Commercial Adviser	Locally	Face to face	6	Finnish
G07	Estonia	Second Secretary for Economic Affairs	Rotationally	Face to face and e-mail	4 and 8	
G08	Germany	Counselor	Rotationally	Face to face	3 and 15	
G09	Hungary	Counselor-Trade, Science and Technology	Rotationally	Face to face	7 and 20+	
G10	Italy	Commercial Attaché	Rotationally	Face to face	2 and 12	
G11	Japan	First Secretary	Rotationally	Face to face and e-mail	1 and 1	

G12	Korea	Third Secretary and Vice-consul	Rotationally	Face to face	3 and 3
G13	Mexico	Trade Commissioner	Rotationally	E-mail	3 and 13
G14	Spain	Economic and Commercial Counselor	Rotationally	Face to face	6 and 13	Finnish
G15	Sweden	Second Secretary	Rotationally	Face to face	2 and 2
G16	Switzerland	Deputy Head of Mission	Rotationally	Face to face	3 and 25+
G17	Turkey	Commercial Counselor	Rotationally	Face to face	1 and 1
G18	UK	Director of UKTI	Locally	Face to face	9
G19	USA	Regional Senior Commercial Officer	Rotationally	Face to face	2 and 16
P01	Austria	Commercial Counselor	Rotationally	Face to face	3 and 15
P02	Germany	Assistant Managing Director	Locally	Face to face	25
P03	Korea	Senior Consultant	Locally	Face to face	7	Finnish
P04	Norway	Manager	Locally	Face to face	4	Finnish

As Kostecki and Naray (2007) and Naray (2011) only provide general terms with which to determine where a particular commercial diplomat stands, initial categorization of the interview results suffices to result in Table 3.

Seventeen of the 23 interviewees have styles that are consistent with Kostecki and Naray's (2007) and Naray's (2008) typology (see Table 1), meaning that their approach toward commercial issues, leading concern, and level of activity is fully in line with the style they have adopted.

However, not all of the interviewees are fully in line with Kostecki and Naray's (2007) and Naray's (2008) typology: G04, G05, G07, G10, G13, and G14 all have an approach toward commercial issues, a leading concern or a level of activity that deviates from their style. An explanation as to why these interviewees are considered to belong to a certain style even though they deviate from their style's characteristics follows.

Whereas a civil servant's usual leading concern is satisfaction of the ministry of trade, G04, G07, and G10 all answer to their ministries of foreign affairs. The type of info and feedback they give to the ministry of foreign affairs does not differ from the deliverables of other civil servants to their ministries of trade. For this reason, this deviance is not a significant one.

Another ministerial setup is seen in G05, who answers to both the ministry of trade and the ministry of foreign affairs. This is "a relic of the past system" (G05) and as with G04, G07, and G10, the deliverables do not differ from other civil servants.

Different from other business promoters, G13's leading concern is not client satisfaction but satisfaction of the ministry of trade. The reason this interviewee is a business promoter and not a civil servant like other interviewees whose leading concern lies with the ministry of trade is the distinct approach toward commercial services and the proactive level of activity. These two factors, both indications of a business promoter, outweigh the interviewee's leading concern.

Where other civil servants maintain a reactive level of activity, G14 adopts a proactive approach. The reason this interviewee is not a business promoter is his strong emphasis on and identification with his responsible ministry, as well as the emphasis he places on formal contacts with governmental bodies in Finland.

By determining the styles that the interviewees adopt, Table 3 constitutes the "commercial diplomat" part of the conceptual framework of Figure 1. Of the interviewees, nine are business promoters (P01, G02, G06, P02, P03, G13, P04, G18, and G19), nine are civil servants (G03, G04, G05, G07, G09, G10, G11, G14, and G17), and five are generalists (G01, G08, G12, G15, and G16). The next step is to ascertain the proactive and reactive elements for each of these styles and the informal institutions that play a role herein.

Cross-Case Analysis

As can be seen, the theory of corporate entrepreneurship functions as a means to distinguish between proactive and reactive behavior. As individual within-case analysis has provided a distinction between business promoters, civil servants, and

Table 3: The interviewees' styles.

	G01	G02	G03	G04	G05	G06	G07	G08	G09	G10	G11	G12	G13	G14	G15	G16	G17	G18	G19	P01	P02	P03	P04
Approach toward commercial issues																							
Understood mainly as business issues		x				x							x					x	x	x	x	x	x
Integral part of international relations			x	x	x		x		x	x	x			x			x						
Perceived in a broader political perspective	x							x				x			x	x							
Leading concern																							
Client satisfaction		x				x							x					x	x	x	x	x	x
Satisfaction of the ministry of trade			x		x				x		x			x		x	x						
Satisfaction of the ministry of foreign affairs	x			x			x	x		x		x			x								
Level of activity																							
Proactive		x				x							x	x	x			x	x	x	x	x	x
Reactive			x	x	x		x		x	x	x												
Ad hoc	x							x				x				x	x						
CD style																							
Business promoter		x				x							x					x	x	x	x	x	x
Civil servant			x	x	x		x		x	x	x			x			x						
Generalist	x							x				x			x	x							

generalists, cross-case analysis will now be applied to assess elements of corporate entrepreneurship and informal institutions for each of the three styles.

Corporate entrepreneurship.   The elements pertaining to corporate entrepreneurship that arise through an inductive analysis of the data concern the reactive part of the interviewees' daily activities, their views on the importance of the proactive part, and the manner in which they perform proactive activities. For each of the three styles, an assessment in terms of these elements will now follow.

The business promoter
The business promoter's reactive activities.   Business promoters are *"very actively involved with the 'actual work'"* (G19), as exemplified by G02[1] (who, commenting on what his trade office does, stipulates *"trade and investments. Not the politics. Nor political economy, or economic policy"*) and P01, who says that *"our main work is what the companies are doing. It's not so much what the others have to do, report to the ministry, more political reports (…). This we do only reacting when somebody's asking for it."*

The major part of the "actual work" requires them to respond to requests they receive from businesses as *"they are our paying customers"* (G06). For the most part, the business promoters provide a wide array of services[2] that covers the majority of the area-activity matrix, yet some of these services are much more popular than others. *"Some years ago, we used to make a market analysis and things like that and (…) there's not really a demand for that anymore. (…) a very big portion of our assistance is building the contact service. (…) And that's basically what we mostly do. (…) Its rich possibilities that we can offer what's on the website, but there is a very small demand for most of the services"* (G06). The most commonly provided services are summarized by G19 "the *most commonly provided services include matching programs (…) and partner search.*" It is not uncommon for business promoters to stay involved during the entire process, as is the case with P01 and P04.

> **P01.** *"This reactive can be everything from the simple list of potential Finnish partners to some sort of market survey or then next step and they have some legal questions or and the last when they have problems with the Finnish partners. Like when they do not pay or other things. We can be (…) involved in the whole chain of the normal business like that."*

Being as involved with commercial issues as the business promoters are, the approach they adopt toward their reactive activities and services is generally a highly involved and personal one. As G19 says, the *"job is hard to do without keeping close*

---

[1]As the interview with G02 was conducted in Dutch, the quotes here are translated versions of the originals.
[2]See, for example, the websites of G06 (http://www.ambhelsingfors.um.dk/da/menu/Eksportraadgivning), P03 (http://www.kotra.fi/index.jsp), P04 (http://www.innovasjonnorge.no), and G18 (http://www.ukti.gov.uk/export/countries/europe/northerneurope/finland.html) for an extensive overview of the services these organizations provide.

personal contact with businesses." As for the differences in approach between members of private and governmental organizations, neither can be said to be more involved than the other. A comparison between G02 and G13, both members of a governmental organization, and P01 and P03, both members of a private organization, of the depth of their involvement with businesses from the home country shows that affiliation is of no influence on the level of involvement. For example, while G02 makes appointments for home country business, saying that "*the only thing they[3] have to do is score of course,*" G13's involvement is much more superficial. The same is true for P03, who says that he operates as though he were "*kind of an extension of their export sales department here*" and P01, who offers "*almost everything but only on the first level support. (…) We can give hints in almost every aspect (…). That's why I said behind the whole thing, but I would not say really accompanying to 100%.*"

The importance of proactivity. While reactive activities form the predominant part of the business promoter's daily activities, the importance of proactive behavior is recognized and underlined by most of them (most notably by G02, G06, G18, P01, and P03) and most business promoters find a healthy balance between the two. In the words of G02, "*there are actually two main functions, namely exporting Flemish businesses (…) and investment by Finnish businesses in Flanders. Those are the main activities. Including for example trade missions.*" P03 summarizes the main sentiment expressed by the interviewees: "*I understand this proactive part, I would like to do more that perhaps, but then of course these days paying customers first*" (P03), thereby acknowledging the importance of proactive efforts over reactive ones for reasons stipulated by G06 and P01.

G06. "*I think it's very important (…) for us to increase the knowledge and market, or (…) sales potential in Finland (…) because (…) we have our sales target to meet (…) so it's extremely important for us to attract assignments given to us.*"

P01. "*It is indeed the lesser part but I think the more important part. Because this is where we can promote new exports.*"

Proactive efforts. Business promoters pursue proactive efforts on levels ranging from the company level to the higher institutional level. What it boils down to is that business promoters "*need to explore the market and actually identify for the business, these are the possibilities, take a look at that, this is in development. So we kind of need to be the eyes and ears*" (G02). In other words, "*to actively look for opportunities in the Finnish market and communicating those*" (G19) to home country businesses by means of organizing and attending events and deploying activities in the host country.

The most prominent example of a business promoter who combines company-level efforts with institution-level efforts is P01, who attends and co-organizes events in addition to his activities on the B2B level. "*We are trying to look for interesting fields*

---

[3]In this context, "they" refers to Flemish businesses.

and we are organizing events. (…) Co-organizing could be with Finnish ministry or with Finpro or also perhaps a seminar about Austrian wines with Alko together. (…) And of our own, it is different types, one which is more really with B2B (…) and others what we call Marktzundieringsreise[4] (P01).

G02 provides an example of active opportunity seeking through keeping close contact with businesses, i.e., the company level. "*I went to Kuopio in August (…) and that resulted in two leads for investments. (…) Those are investment leads and then there are of course opportunities that translate into propositions for trade (…). You make sure to bring something back from that trip. And those are things you do not know beforehand, so that is why you absolutely have to visit other cities, other regions*" (G02).

Representation at fairs is another very common method of getting an idea of where the opportunities lie and is the preferred weapon of choice of G18, P02, and P03.

That not every opportunity is one to be chased after is stipulated by P01, who focuses on markets "*where the others are not already running to.*" His reasoning is that "*if for example everybody would be running here to the wood industry because they say it's the new market, I would not. I would promote it in Austria but I would think very long about really proactively doing an event for this sector. Because there are already too many others here.*" While the business promoters are in general agreement as to the level at which proactive efforts are effective, which is in most cases a combination of the institutional level and the company level, there is no consensus when it comes to the approach needed at the latter level.

For example, while G13 operates "*mostly by cold-calling and writing email to companies we believe might be interested in importing from Mexico,*" P03 moves away from cold-calling by saying that "*whenever there is some kind of inquiry or request from Korea, I think first, do I already know somebody who might be the right person to contact about this matter. The same goes for buyer search. I start with the usual suspects, but if it's not enough I'll try to find new ones.*"

G02 provides the most extreme example of P03's approach. His view is that one has to "*make sure that people know you, because that's how you get more and more propositions. Business is always done between people and that's why we need to make sure that you are known, or that you know the people*" (G02).

A third and completely different opinion on this matter is presented by G06, who does not deem it "*worthwhile visiting the companies. Because the electronic way to describe the assignment giver for the potential partners its good enough. It would be a waste of time to visit the companies I would say.*"

The business promoter's corporate entrepreneurship in a nutshell.   Commercial issues are the business promoter's only concern that shows in the extensive reactive agenda they have on the business level, though partner search is the most commonly asked for service. Most business promoters underline the importance of proactive efforts

---

[4]"Marktzundierungsreise" is the German word for trade missions.

and actively make room to pursue efforts to identify opportunities for home country businesses on the institution and business levels.

The civil servant

The civil servants' reactive activities. Most civil servants are responsible for a dedicated trade/export promotion section. One interviewee, G09, has a focus that is different from the others; his is a more technology- and science-oriented one with trade being "*the cream on the cake*" (G09). Due to being part of an (often small) embassy, some civil servants (e.g., G03, G05, and G09) have other functions as well.

All civil servants are very occupied with their reactive tasks on a higher level, meaning they maintain a distant relationship with home country businesses. G07 provides an overview of the variety of issues that civil servants cover and the challenges that lie therein:

> **G07.** "*We must put some red line we can't step over because we simply can't. We have our heavy work load and also some other diplomatic regions, so what we can do (…) for our businessmen, we can help them when there are some problems here (…). Then we can help in creating contacts here in Finland, give them advice, explain what business environment here, habit, and how to behave in one or another situation for example. (…) We can also find suitable people who can take over and continue this advisory services. (…) Then we organize different events here, seminars and business mission here at the embassy or at Enterprise Estonia (…). And we offer also our premises for the firms if necessary for the Estonian counties or Estonian different trade associations if they ask. But (…) there are also some aspects below the red line. (…) We are not (…) trying to do some market investigations, we have not time and resources for that and this is not our job actually.*"

Resource and time constraints render civil servants to not be deeply involved with home country businesses. Exemplary of this is G07's take, which is that "*we can make some general (…) presentations concerning Estonian economy (…) but we never do something concerning only one firm*" (G07); a remark that resonates in almost every other case. As a result, the approach that most civil servants (apart from G03 and G04) take in providing their services is a distant one. Those who employ more involved approaches (such as G03, G04, and G14) are the final link in a chain of organizations that reaches from the home to the host country, in addition to being part of a dedicated trade office. The immediate advantage these two factors bring becomes apparent when considering G14's approach, which indicates a much more involved approach than most civil servants' approaches:

> **G14.** "*The normal process is, first of all, trying to understand as much as possible why the Spanish company needs, which is something, I won't say difficult but of course this is something that we need to invest time on, (…) and then, once we get a good clarification of the matter on interest, on how they get projected its position here and the like, then we are ready to start an integrated strategy.*"

The importance of proactivity.   While six of the nine civil servants indicate that they have neither time nor resources for the proactive side of their job, mostly due to having a strict mandate to maintain which makes it *"very hard for the embassy to turn down requests"* (G03), they do see its importance. G14 is the only one to explicitly stipulate this, by saying that *"this is a kind of word which is not always very much emphasized but which is I think a key part of our work, being proactive, and having things ready before they even start."* The usual way in which proactive efforts are approached is from a reactive point of view, as G03 points out.

> **G03.** *"In essence the section initiates a lot of ideas and projects but is also very adept at leveraging expressions of interest from others such as encouraging business missions visiting the region to visit Finland or spend more time in country."*

Proactive efforts.   Three main approaches toward proactive efforts, unrelated to the organizational setup, can be discerned. There are those who focus on the institutional level (G07, G09, and G14), those who focus on a business level (G04, G05, and G17), and one who adopts an approach that is a mixture of the institutional and business levels (G03).

In the group with an institutional focus, one (G07) is the head of a commercial section that is integrated with the embassy, one (G09) is the head of a section that mainly deals with science and technology, and one (G14) is the head of a commercial section that exists separately from the embassy. They share the same approach when it comes to proactive efforts, which comes down to maintaining relationships on an institutional level with local unions (G07), chambers of commerce (G09), and ministries (G14). In their capacity as diplomats, they make use of these institutions to identify opportunities, communicating these to their home countries.

> **G14.** *"So it is a matter of (…) integrate information we have as a ministry and as an agency about Spain, and see what is happening here and then try to find good matches. And then be able to manage the office time and our resources in a way that really allows us to try to find analytical responses to certain topics which are not hot topics that exact day, you know, so that you have to always a background activity going on as well, which is proactive."*

The group that focuses on the business level is as diverse as the previous group in their organizational setup. In their efforts to identify opportunities for entrepreneurs and businesses from their home countries, they adopt a different approach that involves utilizing their personal contact with businesses.

> **G05.** *"My key role is making people meet and keeping good memory. Why? You never ever know if an inquiry sent long ago cannot match with a recent offer."*

A special case in this group is presented by G04, who says that export quota and an export capacity that is still lacking inhibit proactive efforts to increase Chilean exports, and, by extension, his opportunity-seeking behavior. Instead of trying to attract new opportunities, he deals with Finnish businesses with the objective to make the most out of possible (future) cooperation.

G04. *"First, phone conversation (...). I tell him we have from Chile a delegation and if (...) we could meet. Then I request a personal meeting to bring them the (...) information on paper. What companies, what is it about, what are the products they are offering, what is their international experience (...). We believe a lot in personal contact. (...) Contact person, you can't beat that. Then you get the card from this guy (...) and usually I use them then a year later, three years later."*

The rationale of G03's mixed approach is that institutional relations are kept to stay informed on a number of topics (akin to the way G14 operates) while individual businesses are contacted to identify highly specific opportunities.

G03. *"While keeping in touch with organizations that enable business is very important, our primary focus is on companies and key organizations like VTT, Tekes and regional development agencies. The latter are critical to learning of technology transfer and partnership opportunities that can be communicated to home country companies and similar organizations. This is part of the innovation side of our integrated commercial approach. The same is true of individual companies. We set specific outcall targets to meet companies in a variety of sectors, focusing on our priority sector areas. Through meeting companies we learn of opportunities for home country suppliers (our export promotion function), investment and expansion interests and technology and innovation opportunities. Our experience in Finland suggests that meeting companies is key however most companies are also linked or involved with key RandD and other organizations so emphasizing both private and public entities completes the circle."*

The civil servants' corporate entrepreneurship in a nutshell. Civil servants deal with commercial issues on a broad level, usually taking an institutional viewpoint in performing reactive and proactive activities. Because of a high-level viewpoint and the heavy workload they experience in the reactive sense, they find it difficult to leverage proactive efforts. They usually maintain institutional-level contacts rather than business-level ones to proactively identify opportunities for home country businesses.

The generalist
The generalist's reactive activities. The generalists are generally not very involved in commercial issues. They are career diplomats (e.g., G16 is in his 10th posting) in high-level functions dealing with a variety of issues. They are essentially *"professional nomads,"* as G08 puts it.

When it comes to providing services and facilities to business and entrepreneurs, they never deal with business issues specifically. Instead, their main role in this respect is to accompany trade missions and to attend trade fairs every now and again. This is due to both the small number of inquiries generalists get from the home country, and an integration of the commercial side with the economic and/or cultural side, either intended or necessitated because of the small size of the organization as a whole.

When generalists do tend to business issues, it usually entails standardized responses such as a standard list of buyers in Finland. G01 presents a prime example of this when he says that he acquires most inquiries *"per computer. They'd like to know for example continuously importers of meat, importers of wine, importers of fruit and I will have a list and we reply with the list"* (G01). On why the number of inquiries is as low as it is, G08 says:

> **G08.** *"in my opinion it's a trend in the EU, because everything is so much coordinated, starting this or last year you have a single contact point for young entrepreneurs who want to open business in other EU countries, so there's no need really for an embassy to give advice. A company that wants to come to Finland, well, comes to Finland."*

The second reactive activity is a referral to a different agency (e.g., G15 and G16). In G16's case, whenever the service asked for can be provided by a private institution, the commercial office is obliged by its mandate to refer to a private institution.

Proactive efforts.   When it comes to proactive behavior, none of these interviewees adopt a very involved approach. This is simply due to lack of time (as with G01, who, when asked if there are any awareness-increasing activities, replied with *"No. The time, I haven't time"*), a focus on different elements (such as G08 and G15), and lack of resources (G01 and G16). In three cases (G08, G15, and G16), an integration with the cultural aspects leads to a focus on what can be identified as nation branding[5]; essentially a proactive effort to a small extent.

> **G15.** *"my job is more on a higher level actually to promote the Swedish image together with the cultural attaché here and his assistant. So they're doing, dealing with more, like, promoting Swedish, theater, literature, and, so we cooperate a lot and I have a business view. For example, Clean Tech is the area that the Swedish want to export or renewable energies and then we have a seminar, we get some Swedish speakers."*

> **G16.** *"There is a huge potential for Swiss businesses in Finland, but there are no sufficient means (money- and personnel-wise) to better promote the Finnish market. The cultural side of the office helps in a small amount by increasing general awareness in Finland of and Switzerland, as a country with a wide variety of cultural competences, but also with a strong economy and a competitive financial sector."*

Most generalists employ virtually no proactive efforts, mainly due to their type of appointment. G12, for example, is appointed specifically for larger economic issues

---

[5]Nation branding "concerns applying branding and marketing communications techniques to promote a nation's image" (Fan, 2006, p. 6).

such as trade barriers and legal issues regarding economic regulations rather than commercial issues because *"the embassy's role in this commercial area has been decreasing. (...) There isn't much from our side to help them out."* Rather than an integration with other, e.g., cultural, departments, the commercial department is outsourced and the embassy's focus lies with economic issues.

The generalist's corporate entrepreneurship in a nutshell. Due to the nature of their appointment, the low amount of requests they receive, and a lack of resources, generalists hardly ever deal with reactive issues and when they do, they adopt a distant approach in providing them. Nation branding is the only type of proactive behavior a generalist performs, though this, too, is a rare occurrence.

Informal Institutions

The elements pertaining to corporate entrepreneurship that arise through an inductive analysis concern the influence of culture on the way the interviewees deal with businesses as well as on the personal level, their background, the role of the skills and experiences obtained from their background, and the influence of the work environment. For each of the three styles, an assessment in terms of these elements will now follow.

The business promoter
The influence of culture
Being focused solely on business issues, and the proactive part of their work being recognized as a highly important element, business promoters generally accredit high value to cultural differences between the home and host countries, small though these differences may be. This is most likely due to all business promoters (except for G13) being from Western countries, a point that is touched upon by P02 and exemplified by G02 when he pinpoints the small scale of these differences in a comparison between his current and former postings: *"the bridge between Flanders and France is much bigger and longer than that between Flanders and Finland. They are two countries that like to get to-the-point, where the Finns are even more to-the-point than we are, so in that sense there might be a difference."* His view is supported by most business promoters (most notably G06, P01, and P04), and none of them point to any major obstacles that national cultural differences pose for home country businesses except for P04, who points to language issues rather than cultural ones.

Rather than national cultural differences, P03 and G19 point out differences between business cultures, yet here, too, the differences are small. As G19 says, *"the only thing that is noticeable is the importance of relationships in business: US business are happy to employ an 'arms-length' approach, while that is not a common practice in Finland."* In contrast to what most Western-based business promoters experience, P03, who deals with Korean business coming to Finland, has a much more extensive agenda when it comes to business culture differences seeing as Korean businesses have *"very much of an ad hoc way of doing things,"* which, *"from a Finnish viewpoint (...)*

looks very disorganized and even unprofessional" (P03), the basis of which lies in the general cultures of both countries. "*I think it's more about the culture. As you know, in Finland people are not accustomed to working so much when it comes to working hours and things like that, and they are not so keen on taking risks in business*" (P03).

Even though the culture differences may be small, several business promoters (G02, P01, P02, and P03) point out that they do communicate these to businesses in order to prepare them as much as possible. "*The approach that we continuously have to point out (…) is that mailing doesn't work. It's much too easy. (…) So those are very concrete things*" (G02) is a remark that resonates around the field in different forms.

Though such recommendations may seem trivial and easy to comply with, the necessity of a trade office, in the cultural sense, shows in the way business promoters speak of how such issues influence the personal style of working. The most important element here is forming the bridge between the home and host countries. "*You have to adapt and make sure to be some sort of chameleon that is accepted by the local party*" (G02).

In their efforts to form the bridge between the home and host country, G02 and P03 point to the cultural differences as taking up a lot of time in dealing with home country businesses, thereby reasserting the necessity of the trade office as a bridge between the home and host countries.

G02. "*I was posted in Rijsel, that is 15 kilometers off the border. And people wondered of course if it was necessary to have a post there. Absolutely, because if a Flemish company does business in France, (…) the culture is totally different. So they think it's close, it'll work out quickly, but that is not true. And then they contact us.*"

G02 notes that despite the differences between host countries (France and Finland in his case), the general outline of his work remains the same to some extent. "*It works in Finland, to a lesser degree, but it always works (…). I can say yes, but I have seen this person (…) and it will work that way*" (G02). What it comes down to, in the end, is that "*you have to be admitted. (…) You have to ensure that you integrate well enough for them to let you in*" (G02). P01 adds to this by saying that "*many questions normally are quite the same we get all over the world. It is the answers that differ and that's what makes it interesting, that you have to learn to get the right answer*" (P01).

Background
Much like the way most interviewees are in agreement on the role that culture plays, their backgrounds show striking similarities. Most business promoters, such as P02, P03, and P04, have an educational background in economics, though others (e.g., G02 and P01) have decidedly different educational backgrounds. As for what drives the business promoter to take up a specific study, pure personal interest is the main determinant in this area rather than an intended career in commercial diplomacy, even to those who chose functionality over interest: "*Law you need everywhere. (…) Law, (…) in my view, is only another view on the things. (…) You get another view on the things that you had before and that might help*" (P01).

Most business promoters have a strong background in the practical side of their work, gained from both their backgrounds in business and their previous postings. For example, G02 *"started this job when I had been in international trade for 15 years"* and has been posted in France and Lithuania before, adding to a total of 10 years in this job. Stories much akin to G02's are told by G06, G13, G18, and G19. Furthermore, in their capacities as commercial diplomats, P01 has *"worked in Venezuela, China, Spain and Latvia"* and G19 has *"been posted to 4 or 5 embassies all over the world,"* indicative of the rich experience in business and the international field that business promoters possess of.

As may be evident from their educational and professional backgrounds, commercial diplomacy is not something that business promoters choose for early on in their career or during their studies but evolved in some form from what they were doing previously. The cases of G02, G06, P02, P03, and G19 are the most evident examples of this, with P03 saying that *"it was not exactly the kind of career I had been thinking about a long time, but then an opportunity comes and I take it"* and G06 relating being a commercial diplomat to his former job by pointing out that *"this job is being quite much as being an export manager but you are (…) local."*

The role of skills and experience
Much like their backgrounds, the business promoters' opinions on the role of skills and experience are quite parallel. As a starting point, *"on the paper it's always the same thing we have to do, in reality it is not"* (P01), necessitating quick adaptability and both practical and theoretical skills. When it comes to actual theoretical skills, the business promoters accredit importance to psychologically oriented skills (G02 and P01) such as *"the skill to study the people"* (P01), philological skills as *"knowing the language is 50% of business done"* (G02), and the ability to learn, meaning *"finding information from various sources and analyzing it"* (P03).

However, the prevalence with which most business promoters mention skills gained through practice rather than formal education is telling, with G06 taking up the most extreme viewpoint on the matter, saying that *"studies concerning economics and especially marketing and sales, it's all true, but theoretical. (…) it's a huge gap between the university and real life, I think. And of course you learn systematic ways of doing your ways and work independently. But you can learn that anywhere (…). So in a way I think you have to have that (…) certificate that you are not totally dumb or lazy. But I don't give so much worth on my education, (…) I have almost highest education you can have in my field but in a way I think it was a waste of time"* (G06). Most business promoters though take up a more mellow opinion, such as G02's. *"Books and reality differ a lot you know, you shouldn't get too much from economic books because it doesn't always work. (…) With us they hire people with an economic background in that sense, international experience, so most people have lived abroad."*

Experience is gained by doing (P03), hence P01's and P03's takes on learning are based mainly on their current posts, saying that commercial diplomats *"need more or less two years till we are really in the country with enough contacts we need"* (P01). P03 adds to this by pointing out that *"in this kind of work, the longer experience you have, the easier your work becomes because when you get some random (…) company coming here, then because of your experience you can pretty much say in about five seconds whether it is something you can approve, meaning you can try to find them customers, or whether you can just reject the request. And then, once we have accepted it for this buyer search project, then in most cases you can already remember, yeah I did something like this one or two years ago, let's see the old report.*"

Turning from the importance of experience in the contemporary environment of the business promoter to a more precisely defined set of practical skills, flexibility, knowledge of the market, and the approach toward contacting host country businesses are the ones G02 mentions, added to by G13 with communication skills and an understanding of the home country business' product.

Two business promoters (G13 and P04) regard a balance of theoretical and practical skills as the most beneficial one in their line of work. In the theoretical department, they place their focus on economic skills such as finance, economics, sales, and marketing and practical skills such as networking, understanding of the technical product, and multitasking (G13 and P04).

Skills gained because of either the predecessor or because of trainings followed at the commercial office or ministry are rare to find with business promoters and seem to have not as prevalent a role as the other skills mentioned before.

When it comes to speaking the language of the host country, G06, P02, P03, and P04 do so fluently, stemming from either having a long history in the host country (P02) or having been born there (G06, P03, and P04). Knowing a host country's language is highly advantageous according to these three interviewees, seeing as "*when it comes to looking for certain kind of people it still helps to know Finnish*" (P03). Only one of the business promoters that is employed on a rotational basis is making an effort to study Finnish, saying that "*you have to integrate. (…) because we are here for a period of four years minimum (…), usually up until seven years*" (G02). Remarkably, while G06, P02, and P03 see the advantage in knowing the language from their jobs' perspectives, G02 learns Finnish to know "*what people are saying. I don't like it when people say something and I can't understand it.*"

The work environment

None of the business promoters is a lone ranger, all having a team that consists of two or more local employees, the exception to which being G02, whose team consists of one local employee. Furthermore, G06, P02, P04, and G18 either have (P02) or are (G06, P04, and G18) locally employed heads of their respective offices. The business promoters of the latter group work in a team that solely consists of locally employed personnel, an arrangement that is highly valued by P04 and G18 over one in which a diplomat that is subject to rotational appointment heads the team.

G18. "*There used to be a diplomat running the UKTI department in Helsinki who had no business background and changing every four year. (…) Connections with Finnish government and businesses are now much better because of the local* *employees connections and continuity in their positions. The level of activity is much higher these days.*"

The prevalence of locally employed personnel provides a stable work environment, one which is usually "*already firmly established beforehand*" (G19). The benefit of a fully locally employed team becomes clear when considering G18's experience, whose "*working environment hasn't changed much at all. For the most part, the same people still work here that did two years ago*" (G19).

However, there are cases when the working environment isn't as stable as in others. Great benefit can lie in such situations, most obviously in shaping things the way that the business promoter likes to see them, such as G04, G13, and P04 experienced.

P03. "*When I came here this office was very disorganized but while I worked here I started gathering this kind of information bit to bit. (...) Basically at the time when I started here a lot of staff (...) had changed almost entirely within a relatively short period of time. At the time we had three locally hired as now and each of us was relatively new to this work. So basically we all had to just figure out ourselves what is the best way of doing this.*"

The business promoter in a nutshell
The business promoter has a background in business and is in the possession of a substantial amount of experience therein, never having had the express intent to become a commercial diplomat. Their business-oriented background renders them to place heavy emphasis on the use of practical skills rather than ones gained from education and considers a team of locally employed personnel to be crucial. Business promoters see cultural differences, as small as they may be, as an important element in dealing with businesses.

The civil servant
The influence of culture
The civil servants are in agreement as to the sizeable impact that cultural differences have, G05 being the only exception ("*Do we really need to know whether and how we are different? Does it really matter?*"). Nonetheless, most of the civil servants have adopted ways to deal with cultural differences between the home country and Finland in a business perspective.

The benefits that a similar culture may hold are pointed out by G09 and underlined by G03, who states that "*common interests and experiences makes it easier to initiative and pursue projects (...). As a result I can use these as references of common values we share with Finns. This helps break down barriers more quickly and leads to trust — I can empathize/understood Finnish perspectives.*" In most cases though, cultural differences are very small to begin with, as G04 indicates: "*there are some differences in that sense. But I think we share with Finns some things, like Chileans are a bit shy, like Finns are. (...) And for Latin-American standards, we are considered very organized, very tedious people. (...) In general, businessmen are a very organized, serious, attached to compromises and schedules. (...) Probably because we're a sort of mixture."*

These small differences are not often communicated to home country businesses by the civil servants. G03 presents the most in-depth approach in this regard: *"in the case of business development, to ensure cultural awareness and sensitivity to specific issues, I always meet or correspond with a home-country business person before they meet with Finnish contacts"* (G03).

Organizing meetings with Finnish businesses *"is quite complicated, many times from a cultural standpoint but also from a business standpoint"* (G14). G04 is a striking example of how being a cultural "curiosity" can benefit a personal approach toward contacting Finnish businesses. Showing knowledge of the Finnish business culture in saying that *"when I tell them, you know, I want to come there to your office, I know makes them a bit uncomfortable, first because they are not used to it, second, probably because they have no time to waste"* his is a personal approach, even though *"here you can almost manage everything by phone or via email."* In the end, G04's meeting with any Finnish businesses *"usually lasts more than 15 minutes because they're not used to this thing so they wait for me with their coffee and cookie (...) and then they talk, I mean they're curious about a guy from Chile. Probably the first time they see somebody from Chile, so they start making queries. (...) Then, lasts for one hour. Always, but from their side."*

Background

The educational background of the civil servants is more diverse than their opinion on cultural differences, implying that they are not as focused on business issues as business promoters are. Two have completed studies in politics (G03 and G17), four have completed economic studies (G05, G09, G10, and G14), and two have completed more practice-oriented studies (G04 and G07), with one of them (G07) having completed studies in agriculture engineering, linguistics, and information technology.

Much like the diversity in backgrounds, the reasons as to why a certain study was chosen are manifold. Two (G04 and G10) chose with a career in diplomacy in mind. *"I studied journalism to then have my university degree because you need a university degree to get into the Chilean diplomatic academy. Even before I started journalism, I wanted to go to diplomatic academy to do what I do"* (G04). Another civil servant that wanted to enter the public rather than private field, but not diplomacy in particular, is G17. *"After I graduated from the faculty of political science in Ankara (...) I thought I was confident to work in private sector but personally, I found really risky for me."*

Other civil servants have chosen certain studies to fulfill their own interests (G07), for job performance (G09 and G14), or to gain skills needed for a future career (G03):

> **G03.** *"It combined practical learning in areas such as law, management and financial accounting with theoretical studies such as macro and micro economics and policy development. This program was more encompassing than pure economics or political science."*

Furthermore, two of the civil servants (G09 and G14) have studied at the University of Helsinki to study the national economy of Finland for one semester (G09) in order to *"understand much better the different aspects in the economic development"* and to study an MBA (G14). Especially G14 indicates to benefit from this experience, where he *"had the occasion to interact with a lot of Finnish people at the company level, and see how they tick. (...) And this is really something which is quite useful, because (...) if you know how a person reasons (...) you are already halfway through the entire rationalization process. (...) Also, I happen to know something more about their business culture."*

The role of skills and experience
Turning from educational background to skills gained from education as G14 has already done, it becomes clear that some civil servants argue that it does not matter what type of education one receives in economic diplomacy (G04 and G10) and that practice is much more valuable than theory (G05 and G07). Nevertheless, the position that G03 takes up toward education is exemplary for most civil servants when he says that *"the skill set acquired in university 'streamed' me to the commercial side of the department and (...) the skills are applicable to the type of initiatives we undertake but also provide a basis for more non-commercial activities. (...) The combination of skills and experience acquired is portable (...) and more widely applicable than narrower fields of study. For example, understanding key managerial accounting concepts such as just in time production and inventories allows me to more fully engage with Finnish producers and this can lead to identifying opportunities for home country suppliers or technologies."*

Where G03 mainly mentions skills that stem from education, some (G07, G14, and G17) lean more toward practical experience. *"Finnish language skills, experience in preparing business contacts, salesmanship in larger sense, ability to manage a business and evaluate financial positions/economic conditions, knowledge concerning some industry fields which are most developed in Finland"* are the ones that G07 mentions, added to by G17, who sees that *"in general it needs quite a lot of government experience but also the private sector experience to reply all these demands."* What G14 sees as the most important skill, in which he finds support from G04, is that *"you have good and sound working knowledge about what is happening, in Finnish society as well as in the Finnish economy.(...) And the same goes for the business environment."*

Speaking of practical skills, G07 and G09 speak Finnish, both indicating that they feel they have an advantage over other diplomats in the same position because of this: *"sometimes I have more background information than those who don't speak Finnish"* (G09). In these specific cases, learning Finnish is made easy by the linguistic backgrounds of the civil servants. Especially G09 benefited from learning Finnish. *"I started to learn Finnish with my children at the time. And it was very good because after that in 1997 and a post for the scientific and cultural center was open for a bid in Hungary the only requirement was Finnish language"* (G09). All other civil servants (with the exception of G10) indicate that knowing the language provides an advantage in either business or cultural terms, but they point out that English works equally well, *"as these relationships are largely based on how well people get along"* (G03).

When it comes to skills gained from predecessors, the civil servants form two camps. Those that have virtually nothing to do with their predecessor (G04, G05, G07, and G10) have, in general terms, not had any overlap, and show no direct continuation in working style or approach (save G07). G04 presents the usual practice in this case in saying that *"when I arrived, he was leaving. (...) So he left, and he left me a bunch of business cards, people he met, and bye."* To G05 this lack of contact carries no importance, as *"what has to be carried on is the brand name."*

The second group consists of those civil servants that relate their approach to that of their predecessor (G03, G11, and G17). In G17's case, he and his predecessor *"could find time to meet and talk and meet other businessmen and we started a new kind of approach this year, and this is true for all other Turkish trade counselors from now on."* While G03 has been in touch with his predecessor, one element that he purposely points out is that *"the least amount of disruption is probably (...) the best"* (G03).

The work environment

Whereas the predecessor is not often seen as a crucial source of information, the civil servants that lead a team accredit high value to it, as G14 and G03 indicate. *"The less specialized part of our home staff (...) do not provide the kind of expertise that you expect from a market analyst, so (...) we hire market analysts from the country of course"* (G14). *"The local team at any posting must be recognized as a critical resource given their experience and local knowledge. (...) That type of knowledge is very useful when it comes to developing business programs, opening doors to home country companies, delivering key messages to host country decision makers and keeping in touch with contact persons"* (G03). Balancing an own style of working and the established working style of a team of locally employed personnel takes time, as G03 found out. *"Despite my preference and expectations were for a highly proactive work environment (i.e. provide what was asked as well as possible problems and solutions and areas to expand upon) (...) it was clear that this was not an inherent area of focus or experience for the team. (...) The subject adjusted their expectations for the short term and began to build up an awareness of this requirement in the team"* (G03). The main obstacle in this process is recognized by G03 to be the host country culture. *"The government has placed a much stronger emphasis on flexibility and adapting to change. This does not seem to come easily in Finnish culture and therefore it was important to make clear that adopting new working approaches was expected and part of the job while explaining how and why this was to occur and be measured as well as listening to the arguments or concerns raised"* (G03).

When it comes to living in Finland, the civil servants' international experience is such that they have little difficulty adapting to Finland, even though there is a slight contradiction in expectation and reality, as G14 calls it. *"The idea you had about Finland before coming here for good, was that Finland was a very open country. (...) But then you come here and you (...) find out (...) they certainly project something which is a little bit different from what it feels. So in that sense, perhaps there is, (…) a minor contradiction perhaps"* (G14). Only one of the interviewees (G11) has difficulties in Finland due to his lack of international experience as well as him doing *"as I did in Japan"* (G11). The exact opposite of this is G03, who says that *"the previous stay in Sydney (which was also quite laid-back) helped ease that transition. In general, I try to go with the flow of the host country as this is the most effective way to ensure productivity and maintain the work/life balance. I try to incorporate the way things work in the host country to my own way of working"* (G03).

Some of the civil servants (G03, G04, G09, and G14) regard adapting to the host country as essential to their work. *"You've got to be on their side, (…) I try to do things that Finnish people do. Really, I feel from my business counterparts, that it makes a difference"* (G04). G04 is backed by G03, who says that *"common interests and experiences makes it easier to initiative and pursue projects (…). As a result I can use these as references of common values we share with Finns. This helps break down barriers more quickly and leads to trust."* In G09's case, adapting to the host country was important for personal reasons: *"it was my aim.[6] I prepared the road to that, but the most, more important was that I had that time two small children they went to Finnish school."*

The civil servant in a nutshell
The civil servant has an educational background in economics and substantial work experience in business and usually enters the diplomatic field in a later stage in his/her career. Practical skills are more important than skills gained from education, and teams of locally employed personnel are highly valued. The civil servant has a keen sense for cultural differences, indicating that these have a larger impact on the personal style of working than on contact with businesses.

The generalist
The influence of culture
As the generalists are uninvolved in commercial affairs, none of them deal with cultural differences between the home and host countries in the business sense. Only two of the interviewees, G15 and G16, do stipulate that their home countries differ only slightly in this regard and that the host country should therefore constitute a more appealing market for home country businesses than the amount of inquiries would suggest. According to G16, the main agent of stagnation here is his home country culture, thereby explaining the generalist's approach toward proactive behavior as relying on nation branding:

G16. *"it is a tenet of Swiss culture, and therefore also the business culture, to solve a problem or handle a situation yourself first. Only when there is no other possible solution do businesses turn to the Embassy for help."*

---

[6]To return to Finland.

For generalists, cultural differences do not significantly impact the way they perform their jobs but tend to dictate the type of job they do. In the one case where cultural differences between the home and host country are quite large (G12) the commercial section is outsourced.

Background
When it comes to being posted, "*any civil servant[7] has to be multifunctional*" (G16). This is emphasized by G01, who indicates that "*there are colleagues who choose always legal sectors, juridical, economics (…). I prefer political sector (…)*" and G12: "*When I first joined the Ministry they always emphasized the fact that I have to be an all-round player. So if you're a soccer player you have to be able to strike, defend, goalkeeper sometime, wing, centre back, everything. You have to do everything. I can be in charge of economic affairs at the moment, but if I move to another embassy they might already have a person in economy there, so I can be in charge of consul matters, I can be anything. I think we have to be prepared.*"

Both in addition to and as a consequence of this multifunctionalism, all generalists are assigned to a different post every three or four years. Only G12 sees a downside in this, saying that "*sometimes we lack the expertise, (…) let's say I was in charge of economic affairs for like three years for the Finnish, like, Northern part, or South America. Those are different things, that can be a possibility so we have to be prepared for everything. That's the limitation.*" All other generalists herald the rotation system as a good thing, with four out of five generalists indicating that career diplomacy is what they purposely chose for. Given this inclination to enter the field early on, it is not surprising that the backgrounds of the interviewees show great similarities: three of the five generalists are in the midst of a long diplomatic career that was taken up after graduating in either law or international politics and two more are in their first posting, one coming from a different ministry (G15), and the other (G16) coming from a multinational.

The role of skills and experience
The generalists opt for a career in diplomacy with a set of general skills derived from previous studies and, in one case, derived from work experience at a multinational corporation. The most prominent skill the generalists possess is their adaptability, a result of their international orientation. This is even true for generalists of non-Western origin such as G01 and G12, who refer to their past to point out that adapting is a nonissue. "*If you were nine years in Germany, Europe, North Europe it's not very difficult*" (G01).

The general nature of their work translates to their views on the usefulness of the Finnish language. Four of the five generalists do not speak Finnish and have not made an effort in doing so as it is viewed as "*impossible*" (G01) or not useful because it is not a recurring language in any other posting (G12). The fifth generalist speaks

---

[7]In this case, the term "civil servant" is used by the interviewee as an interchangeable term with "career diplomat." Its meaning therefore differs from the way it is used throughout this research.

Finnish because it is her second language, but she does not indicate having any advantages over other diplomats in the same position.

The generalist in a nutshell
Having fulfilled the ambition to become a career diplomat, the generalist is a multifunctional person who is well-versed in the international environment without having the skills or experience to make a deep impact in the commercial sense. They are used to change in the cultural sense but do not provide a link to businesses in this area.

The Observations as a Background for the Interviews

In order to see whether or not the data presented above upholds in a noninterview method for one of the three styles of commercial diplomats, observations have been made over a four-month period at the Embassy of the Kingdom of the Netherlands in Helsinki (Finland). These observations comprise entries from a logbook that was kept during the four-month period spent at the embassy.

Over the course of four months, the head of the commercial department has not been deeply devoted to commercial affairs, leaving most of the contact to the locally employed commercial officer. This is mostly due to the embassy being a small organization causing the diplomat in charge of commercial affairs to be involved in a broad spectrum of affairs, including (but not limited to) political, cultural, and consular ones. In taking up issues across the diplomatic spectrum, his focus lies with the ministry of foreign affairs. As the commercial issues are mainly dealt with by the trade officer (given the low occurrence of the subject's involvement in the commercial section's daily activities) and the diplomat oftentimes seeing commercial issues in the broader sense (e.g., the national economic system, or innovation on the country level), then the subject can be said to be a generalist.

Given the classification of generalist, the findings presented in this section provide an indication of how the subject opines on the matter of activity and proactivity, and what role informal institutions play herein.

As far as reactive activity goes, requests by home country businesses and entrepreneurs are almost exclusively dealt with by the trade officer rather than the commercial diplomat. Proactive efforts are equally rare and only arise once from an experience in the personal environment. This is in line with most generalists' activities in commercial diplomacy in the sense that they hardly deal with home country businesses, let alone opportunity-seeking behavior, yet whether this is due to the low amount of data gathered from observations or due to the low amount of inquiries received from home country businesses as well as the EVD placing high emphasis on other markets rather than Finland in the first place remains uncertain.

When it comes to informal institutions, the observations do not show much in this direction other than the fact that the subject is a career diplomat who entered the diplomatic service at an early stage in his career, having a background in law. The one thing that is noticeable is the high amount of appreciation he directs toward the activities of the trade officer, yet this in itself is not an indication of his views on the work environment. The nonoccurrence of remarks on informal institutions regarding culture and the working environment are most likely due to the commercial diplomat being hardly involved in the commercial section's daily activities. Comparing this to the results section, it becomes clear that this is in line with what is to be expected as the interviewees hardly speak of cultural issues while the work environment is not commented on at all due to the small scale of the organizations that generalists usually operate in.

Conclusion

The Business Promoter

Business promoters play very active roles in commercial issues and provide a multitude of services that pervades Naray's (2008) area-activity matrix, their main reactive function being partner search. This activity is usually undertaken on a very personal level, keeping close contact with both home and host country businesses.

Business promoters see proactivity as the more important element of their job even though it is, quantitatively speaking, the smaller part. Not surprisingly, the methods business promoters employ showing "opportunity-seeking and advantage-seeking behaviors" (Kuratko, 2007, p. 159) are extensive. Representation at fairs and events to achieve name-recognition, collaboration and contact with host country institutions such as trade unions and ministries as well as close contact with host country businesses to stay aware of opportunities for home country businesses are used evenly by business promoters and it is not uncommon that many leads for proactive behavior are gathered through their reactive activities.

The business promoter has an educational background in business or economics, usually chosen out of personal interest and without the intention to enter the diplomatic field. Having a lot of (international) experience in business, the business promoter places heavy emphasis on practical business skills rather than theoretical ones and sees the psychological component, knowing the people, as the most crucial one. Language skills are seen to add to the business promoter's success, yet Finnish is hardly attempted as it is seen as virtually impossible to learn. Equally important is experience at the current post, which enables the business promoter to more quickly resolve issues and respond to requests, as well as being beneficial to proactive behavior, explaining why business promoters prefer longer lengths of stay than what is usual for diplomats. Moreover, many business promoters are locally appointed or acknowledge the benefit hereof. More often than not, the working atmosphere is firmly established and the absence of change is seen to be very beneficial for the functioning of the team by those that are locally employed. The business promoter regards (business) cultural differences as crucial, even though they are quite small in most cases, and relates them to the importance of the existence of trade offices, their communication of these differences to home country businesses, and the way they deal with host country businesses. The degree to which these three elements are seen as important depends greatly on the difference in home and host country cultures.

The Civil Servant

Civil servants are involved in commercial issues on a higher level than business promoters and in many cases, have other functions beside the commercial one. As a result, the reactive activities they perform are manifold yet the approach toward providing their services and activities is a more distant one in which they rarely maintain personal contact with businesses.

The importance of proactive behavior is recognized, yet a busy agenda in the reactive sense impedes on taking according action. Opportunity-seeking behavior is most commonly displayed on the institutional level, i.e., with ministries, trade unions, and the like rather than the business level.

The civil servants have educational backgrounds that vary from politics to business to more practice-oriented studies, chosen out of personal interest in some cases though more often in consideration of a future career or for job performance. This reflects in how they opine on the role of skills and experience as the civil servant is keen to mention language[8] and business skills as well as cultural awareness over skills gained during education, though does not negate the importance of the latter. Having a practical mindset, the team of locally employed personnel is seen as a critical resource and leveraging the personal work style with that of the team can be hindered by cultural differences between the host and home countries, though international experience helps dealing with such situations. The civil servant sees cultural differences as being of utmost importance to his/her own adaptation to and functioning in the host country, small though these differences are in most cases. In dealing with local businesses, they leverage what is expected of them with their own method of working.

The Generalist

Generalists rarely deal with commercial issues, mostly due to the nature of their appointment and the low amount of requests they receive. When they do receive inquiries, they respond in a distant and usually somewhat standardized manner. Where the occurrence of reactive activities is low, proactive efforts are even more uncommon and can be identified to pertain to nation branding.

The generalist's noninvolvement with commercial issues can be related to background, which features an intention to enter the field of career diplomacy at

---

[8]Even though the Finnish language is generally seen as virtually impossible to learn.

an early age, usually after having completed studies in politics. The generalist's multifunctionalism and a career that warrants rich international experience result in an absence of skills and experience pertaining to business.

Discussion

The findings of this research will be compared with the theoretical framework and with the theoretical background to this framework. The findings and concepts will be discussed to assess their implications for and possible contribution to the current body of knowledge on commercial diplomacy as one of the final two steps of the inductive analysis as performed in this research is a *"comparison of the emergent concepts (…) with the extant literature"* (Eisenhardt, 1989).

Additionally, the limitations of this research will be pointed out to assess the strength of the findings.

Theoretical Implications

The conceptual framework revisited.   In Figure 1 the commercial diplomat is depicted as being influenced by a number of informal institutions whilst performing both reactive and proactive activities as a business promoter, a civil servant, or a generalist. The answer to the research question provides a means to fill this model for each of the three styles in order to add to the current literature.

The informal institutions that were found to influence the commercial diplomat are culture, the commercial diplomat's background, the skills and experiences that arise from this background, and the work environment. The influence that these elements have increases for higher levels of activity in the commercial sense in a specific order.

Background is the most influential one as this affects the commercial diplomat's affiliation with business issues and has a direct relationship with the role of skills and experience, both determinant of the commercial diplomat's view on proactive issues and his/her according actions as an educational and practical background in business warrants a deeper understanding of such issues.

Of lesser impact is the difference between host and home country cultures. The more involved a commercial diplomat is with commercial issues, the more importance he/she will recognize cultural differences to have and the more they are seen to influence the personal work style, though this is also strongly dictated by the size of the cultural gap between the home and host countries. The influence of the working environment, partially falling under the influence of cultural differences, is marginal yet increases as the expectations between the commercial diplomat and the locally employed team differ.

Given the direct influence that the aforementioned informal institutions have on how the commercial diplomat acts, the commercial diplomat's relationship with proactivity can be described along the lines of the influence that these informal institutions exert and coincides with the increased proactive behavior that has been shown to exist in the three styles (with the generalist displaying the lowest amount of proactive behavior and the business promoter the highest amount).

In general, the "proactivity" element in Figure 1 pertains to commercial diplomats undertaking proactive efforts on the institutional level and the business level to increasing levels of involvement, both in a quantitative sense (meaning the actual time they spend pursuing said activities) and a qualitative sense (meaning their view on its importance and their commitment to the cause).

Generalists hardly ever exhibit proactive behavior and ascribe little importance to it. When they do engage in such activities, it is a superficial effort pertaining to nation branding, and is usually performed in collaboration with other departments of the same governmental organization.

Civil servants undertake proactive efforts on both the institutional and business levels, having a preference for the former and maintaining close contact with host country institutions to achieve the highest amount of success whilst leveraging their reactive duties. In some cases, a combination of the institutional and business levels is employed, though here, too, the emphasis lies with the institutional level.

Business promoters display the highest amount of proactive behavior and actively budget and pursue proactive efforts on both the institutional and business levels, favoring direct contact with businesses through (e.g.) promotional events and visits though oftentimes employing all possible means to identify opportunities for home country businesses.

The results' fit with informal institutionalism and corporate entrepreneurship. This research's main value was aimed to be its contribution to the existent literature on commercial diplomacy, or more specifically, the role of the commercial diplomat herein by taking a closer look at Kostecki and Naray's (2007) and Naray's (2008) division of the commercial diplomat in three styles (being business promoter, civil servant, and generalist) as one of the theory's constituents. The results have shown that this contribution has been accomplished, as both the theory of institutionalism and the theory of corporate entrepreneurship have been linked to these three styles. An assertion of the strength of these contributions now follows.

Corporate entrepreneurship has resulted in a means to identify how the commercial diplomat approaches "opportunity-seeking and advantage-seeking behaviors" (Kuratko, 2007, p. 159). Several factors eliciting entrepreneurial behavior were found in literature (e.g., resource availability and organizational structure), and this research mainly yields methods of "identifying and discovering opportunities that emerge within their environments" (Nasra & Dacin, 2009, p. 584) rather than underlying causes for proactivity, though the factors found by Kuratko et al. (1990), Hornsby et al. (2002), and Kuratko (2007) have been touched upon during this research and can be seen to have some effect on the commercial diplomat's proactive behavior, alongside informal institutions. All in all, the results suggest that Nasra and Dacin's (2009, p. 584) assertion that "the state can actively engage in entrepreneurial behavior" is justified. However, whether or not businesses benefit greatly from the info they receive remains unclear, hence Spence and Crick's (2004) and Wilkinson and Brouthers' (2006) pessimistic view on this subject cannot be turned into optimism yet.

An assessment of the informal institutions that affect the commercial diplomat has resulted in a list of elements that are the source of the commercial diplomat's approach toward proactive behavior, specifying Kostecki and Naray's (2007) observations that commercial diplomats with different styles usually have different backgrounds and professional experience in business by inductively connecting them to the commercial diplomat's daily activities.

Elements such as cultural differences and background have been identified to influence the commercial diplomat in his approach toward proactive efforts. However, while the results indicate that a commercial diplomat's background and the resulting skills and experience "exert the most immediate control on individuals," as Ingram and Clay (2000, p. 537) put it, it is still uncertain whether these elements do indeed constitute the "informal rules, customs and practices" that "are enacted and observed by these individuals" (Hillman & Keim, 1995, p. 195). The same is true for the elements of culture and work environment. They do have a less pronounced effect on proactive behavior, as the cultural/cognitive pillar has according to literature (Bruton et al., 2010; Orr & Scott, 2008), but whether they describe "individual behavior based on subjectively and (often gradually) constructed rules and meanings that limit appropriate beliefs and actions" (Bruton et al., 2010, p. 423) is not clear.

Another issue that the data analysis is subject to is whether the elements found are spoken of by the interviewees within the three different styles at the same level, implying that the meaning that these elements have may differ per interviewee. This pertains more to the cultural element than to the other three elements, as the interviewees do not describe elements of culture as uniformly as they do with (e.g.) background and skills.

The indication that culture has a different meaning to different interviewees shows in the amount they speak of it, which is an indication of the importance they accredit to it. Some of the interviewees, most notably G02 with the business promoters and G03 with the civil servants, place much more emphasis on cultural issues than others (e.g., G06 and G10 with the business promoters and the civil servants, respectively). However, the possibility that overreliance on remarks by interviewees who accredit more importance to cultural issues renders the results to go askew is counteracted by the support that these interviewees receive for their remarks from other interviewees.

The level at which the interviewees speak about cultural issues is approached from national, societal, business, and personal levels, all of which have been described separately in the data analysis. However, the possibility exists that remarks from interviewees cover multiple levels and that the analysis therefore does not sufficiently distinguish between these levels.

While we stipulate that the difference in institutional backgrounds is needed to increase the likelihood that the emergent field of commercial diplomacy is added to, this brings forth the question whether and to what degree the cultural differences between the interviewees themselves have an impact on their views on cultural issues. A comparison of interviewees from dissimilar environments, e.g., G02 and G04, and G03 and G14, shows that generally, interviewees accredit high value to cultural differences in a manner that does not depend on the institutional background, but on the style that is adopted. This is mainly caused by background seeing as virtually all interviewees are highly experienced in the international environment, rendering the cultural differences between the interviewees themselves to be of low impact on their differing views on cultural matters.

The consequences for commercial diplomacy. Now that the contributions of corporate entrepreneurship and institutionalism to the field of commercial diplomacy have been assessed, a review of the results' impact on the three-style framework developed by Kostecki and Naray (2007) and Naray (2008) is in order.

Table 4 is based on the general terms provided by Kostecki and Naray (2007) and Naray (2008), which are very loosely defined and lack substantial evidence as their three styles only show "broad and so far typical tendencies" (Naray, 2008, p. 10) of empirical observations.

Comparing their findings to this research's results shows that broadly speaking, the division into three styles holds for all elements in Table 4. The results have particularly deepened the understanding of what they refer to as "level of activity" by adding the exact approach that each of the three styles adopts toward proactive efforts, thereby relieving this element of the table of its largely undefined status. Furthermore, the results suggest that "approach," "leading concern," and "level of activity" are interdependent elements that can be described along the lines of the proactive approaches as determined in this research.

Therefore, instead of looking at the individual elements as described by Kostecki and Naray (2007) and Naray (2008), this research suggests that the approach toward

Table 4: A new typology based on proactivity.

	Proactor	Reactor	Non-actor
Importance of proactivity	Seen as the most important element of the job	Recognized but marginal due to lack of time and resources and reactive duties	Not important
Level of proactivity	Institutional and business levels	Institutional level	Institutional level, if at all
Intensity of proactive efforts	Highly intensive, including representation at fairs and events, as well as contact with host country institutions and businesses	Moderately intensive with a focus on host country institutions	Sporadic efforts pertaining to nation branding

proactivity is the main determinant of the commercial diplomat's role as it encompasses the aforementioned authors' elements and provides deeper insight into a commercial diplomat's role. The benefit of such a division would be that it is relatively more measurable than the three styles as determined by Kostecki and Naray (2007) and Naray (2008), seeing as how a commercial diplomat approaches proactive behavior (in terms of the importance accredited to it, the level at which it is pursued, and the intensity with which it is pursued) can now be more narrowly defined than general outlines regarding "approach," "level of activity," and "leading concern." Table 4 shows the typology that arises from this research in terms of proactivity.

Limitations

In general, findings from case study research are too small to generalize to an entire population. However, seeing as the findings of this research relate to existing theory and result in testable theoretical propositions (Eisenhardt, 1989; Saunders et al., 2009) in addition to the sample selection representing an accurate cross section of the population of commercial diplomats in Helsinki and hence, by extension, Western nations, the results are considered to be generalizable to Western nations.

This research is based on emergent theory that has not seen rigorous empirical testing yet and does not add to resolving this issue due to its inductive nature. As for possible heaps in the collection of said data, issues of interviewee bias were resolved by means of the nonsensitive nature of the info that was asked for using open-ended questions and the interviewees having been offered anonymity, as well as them being in charge of the recording device and acting as the final editors of their own interview transcripts.

Researcher bias in the analysis of the data persists as Eisenhardt's (1989) and Darlington and Scott's (2002) recommendation that multiple researchers perform the data analysis has not been followed while "the convergence of observations from multiple investigators enhances confidence in the findings" (Eisenhardt, 1989, p. 536). This limitation is counteracted by the fact that Eisenhardt's (1989) method was followed as closely as possible.

The observation method was chosen to mitigate the impact of validity issues yet the results are too thin to provide a substantial background for triangulation. Furthermore, the amount of data gathered from interviews with the five generalists is significantly lower than that gathered from the business promoters and civil servants. Given the great similarities in their stories, it is believed that what has been found in this research represents an exhaustive overview of the generalists' actions.

The causal relationship between informal institutionalism has not been found, which weakens the link as proposed in the research model and affects construct validity as it is unclear whether the elements found to influence the commercial diplomat can be tied to institutionalism.

Recommendations for Further Research

An addition to literature, as has been enacted in this research, implies that concrete suggestions for further research can be made. While this research has connected commercial diplomacy to institutionalism and corporate entrepreneurship, generally speaking, commercial diplomacy holds many opportunities for expansion in (e.g.) HR or development studies.

First of all, to alleviate the generalization problem that arises due to the fact that this research took place in Finland, a Western nation, the same research is recommended to be carried out in other Western nations in order to see whether or not this research's conclusions will hold in similar institutional environments. Moreover, it is recommended that this type of research be repeated in far different institutional environments such as South America, Africa, the Middle East, and South-East Asia. If the principles of what has been found in this research hold for dissimilar institutional environments as well, this would add strength to the findings and conclusions.

Second, to increase the reliability of the results, it is recommended that the interviews be reanalyzed by different and multiple researchers to alleviate researcher bias problems that may have affected data analysis.

Third, deductive research is needed to ascertain the link between informal institutions and commercial diplomacy, as well as for the order in which the elements discovered seem to influence the commercial diplomat in adopting a proactive approach; further research as to what "weight" these elements have and why this particular order is present would give more insight into how and why they influence the commercial diplomat.

Fourth, certain types of proactive efforts have been found to become increasingly heavily used by the commercial diplomat when it comes to the progression from generalist to business promoter. Deductive research is recommended to empirically test the results of this inductive research. In addition, the use of the commercial diplomat's proactive efforts for businesses remains unclear and therefore requires that further research be undertaken to assess the success gained by businesses from such efforts.

Acknowledgment

The authors would like to thank Martin Stienstra for his comments to an earlier version of this chapter.

References

Berridge, G. R., & James, A. (2003). *A dictionary of diplomacy*. Basingstoke: Palgrave Macmillan.

Bruton, G. D., Ahlstrom, D., & Li, H.-L. (2010). Institutional theory and entrepreneurship: Where are we now and where do we need to move in the future?. *Entrepreneurship Theory and Practice*, *34*(3), 421–440.

Bruton, G. D., Ahlstrom, D., & Obloj, K. (2008). Entrepreneurship in emerging economies: Where we are today and where should the research go in the future. *Entrepreneurship Theory and Practice*, *32*(1), 1–14.

Burgelman, R. A. (1983). Corporate entrepreneurship and strategic management: Insights from a process study. *Management Science*, *29*(12), 1349–1364.

Darlington, Y., & Scott, D. (2002). *Qualitative research methods in practice: Stories from the field*. Crows Nest, Australia: Allen & Unwin.

Dess, G. G., Ireland, R. D., Zahra, S. A., Floyd, S. W., Janney, J. J., & Lane, P. J. (2003). Emerging issues in corporate entrepreneurship. *Journal of Management*, *29*(3), 351–378.

Eisenhardt, K. M. (1989). Building theories from case study research. *Academy of Management Review*, *14*(4), 532–550.

Eisenhardt, K. M., & Graebner, M. E. (2007). Theory building from cases: Opportunities and challenges. *Academy of Management Journal*, *50*(1), 25–32.

Esterberg, K. G. (2002). *Qualitative methods in social research*. Boston, MA: McGraw-Hill.

Fan, Y. (2006). Branding the nation: What is being branded?. *Journal of Vacation Marketing*, *12*(1), 5–14.

Gerring, J. (2007). *Case study research*. New York, NY: Cambridge University Press.

Harris, S., & Carr, C. (2007). National cultural values and the purpose of business. *International Business Review*, *17*(1), 103–117.

Helmke, G., & Levitsky, S. (2004). Informal institutions and comparative politics: A research agenda. *Perspectives on Politics*, *2*(4), 725–740.

Hillman, A., & Keim, G. (1995). International variation in the business-government interface: Institutional and organizational considerations. *The Academy of Management Review*, *20*(1), 193–214.

Hornsby, J. S., Kuratko, D. F., & Zahra, S. A. (2002). Middle managers' perception of the internal environment for corporate entrepreneurship: Assessing a measurement scale. *Journal of Business Venturing*, *17*(3), 253–273.

Ingram, P., & Clay, K. (2000). The choice-within-constraints: New institutionalism and implications for sociology. *Annual Review of Sociology*, *26*, 525–546.

Ingram, P., & Silverman, B. S. (2002). Introduction: The new institutionalism in strategic management. In P. Ingram & B. Silverman (Eds.), *The new institutionalism in strategic management* (pp. 1–30). Oxford, UK: Elsevier Science Ltd.

Ireland, R. D., Covin, J. G., & Kuratko, D. F. (2009). Conceptualizing corporate entrepreneurship strategy. *Entrepreneurship Theory and Practice*, *33*(1), 19–46.

Keupp, M. M., & Gassmann, O. (2009). The past and the future of international entrepreneurship: A review and suggestions for developing the field. *Journal of Management*, *35*(3), 600–633.

Kostecki, M., & Naray, O. (2007). Discussion papers in diplomacy. *Clingendael Discussion Paper in Diplomacy*, The Hague, Clingendael Institute. Retrieved from http://www.clingendael.nl/publications/2007/20070400_cdsp_diplomacy_kostecki_naray.pdf

Kuratko, D. F. (2007). Corporate entrepreneurship. *Foundations and Trends in Entrepreneurship*, *3*(2), 151–203.

Kuratko, D. F., Montagno, R. V., & Hornsby, J. S. (1990). Developing an entrepreneurial assessment instrument for an effective corporate entrepreneurial environment. *Strategic Management Journal*, *11*, 49–58.

Li, S., & Samsell, D. P. (2009). Why some countries trade more than others: The effect of the governance environment on trade flows. *Corporate Governance: An International Review*, *17*(1), 47–61.

Lowndes, V. (1996). Varieties of institutionalism: A critical appraisal. *Public Administration, 74*(2), 181–197.

Mercier, A. (2007). Commercial diplomacy in advanced industrial states: Canada, the UK and the US. *Clingendael Discussion Paper in Diplomacy*, The Hague, Clingendael Institute. Retrieved from http://www.clingendael.nl/publications/2007/20070900_cdsp_diplomacy_mercier.pdf

Naray, O. (2008). Commercial diplomacy: A conceptual overview. Paper presented at the 7th World Conference of TPOs, The Hague, The Netherlands.

Naray, O. (2011). Commercial diplomats in the context of international business. *The Hague Journal of Diplomacy, 6*, 121–148.

Nasra, R., & Dacin, M. T. (2009). Institutional arrangements and international entrepreneurship: The state as institutional entrepreneur. *Entrepreneurship Theory and Practice, 34*(3), 583–609.

North, D. C. (1990). *Institutions, institutional change and economic performance*. Cambridge: Cambridge University Press.

Orr, R. J., & Scott, W. R. (2008). Institutional exceptions on global projects: A process model. *Journal of International Business Studies, 39*(4), 562–588.

Pawson, R. (1996). Theorizing the interview. *British Journal of Sociology, 47*(2), 295–313.

Peredo, A. M., & Chrisman, J. J. (2004). Toward a theory of community-based enterprise. *Academy of Management Review, 31*(2), 309–328.

Potter, E. H. (2004). Branding Canada: The renaissance of Canada's commercial diplomacy. *International Studies Perspectives, 5*, 55–60.

Rose, A. K. (2005). *The foreign service and foreign trade: Embassies as export promotion.* Working Paper 11111. National Bureau of Economic Research, Cambridge, MA.

Saner, R., & Yiu, L. (2003). International economic diplomacy: Mutations in post-modern times. *Clingendael Discussion Papers in Diplomacy*, The Hague, Clingendael Institute. Retrieved from http://www.clingendael.nl/publications/2003/20030100_cli_paper_dip_issue84.pdf

Saunders, M., Lewis, P., & Thornhill, A. (2009). *Research methods for business students.* Essex, England: Pearson Education Limited.

Searing, D. D. (1991). Roles, rules and rationality in the new institutionalism. *The American Political Science Review, 85*(4), 1239–1260.

Sharma, P., & Chrisman, P. P. (1999). Toward a reconciliation of the definitional issues in the field of corporate entrepreneurship. *Entrepreneurship Theory and Practice, 23*(3), 11–28.

Spence, M., & Crick, D. (2004). Acquiring relevant knowledge for foreign market entry: The role of overseas trade missions. *Strategic Change, 13*(5), 283–292.

Spencer, J. W., Murtha, T. P., & Lenway, S. A. (2005). How governments matter to new industry creation. *The Academy of Management Review, 30*(2), 321–337.

Sridharan, K. (2002). Commercial diplomacy and statecraft in the context of economic reform: The Indian experience. *Diplomacy and Statecraft, 13*(2), 57–82.

Van Lieshout, H. A. M. (2008). *Different hands: Markets for intermediate skills in Germany, the U.S. and the Netherlands.* Doctoral dissertation, University of Groningen. Retrieved from gitur-archive.library.uu.nl/dissertations/2008-0402-200621/lieshout.pdf. Accessed on March 22, 2011.

Wilkinson, T. J., & Brouthers, L. E. (2000a). An evaluation of state sponsored promotion programs. *Journal of Business Research, 47*(3), 229–246.

Wilkinson, T. J., & Brouthers, L. E. (2000b). Trade shows, trade missions and state governments: Increasing FDI and high-tech exports. *Journal of International Business Studies, 31*(4), 725–734.

Wilkinson, T. J., & Brouthers, L. E. (2006). Trade promotion and SME export performance. *International Business Review, 15*, 233–252.

Yakop, M., & Bergeijk, P.A.G. van (2009). *The weight of economic and commercial diplomacy.* Working Paper 478. International Institute of Social Studies. Retrieved from http://papers.ssrn.com/sol3/papers.cfm?abstract_id=1469137

Zenger, T. R., Lazzarini, S. G., & Poppo, L. (2002). Informal and formal organization in new institutional economics. In P. Ingram & B. Silverman (Eds.), *The new institutionalism in strategic management* (pp. 277–305). Oxford, UK: Elsevier Science Ltd.

Chapter 3

The Value of Commercial Diplomacy from an International Entrepreneurs Perspective

Sander Busschers and Huub Ruël

Abstract

One powerful public support instrument to support the economic interests abroad is via commercial diplomacy (CD). CD is practice gaining more importance in today's economy, but is poorly addressed in research. The available existing research, however, lack detail on the beneficiary perspective and the value-added function of CD, let alone specific enterprises to small and medium enterprises (SMEs). This study contributes to the field of CD by identifying the determinants of the value of CD from an SME (beneficiary) perspective. Out of a random sample of 450 SMEs contacted, 115 of them agreed to fill out a scale-based questionnaire and answer to open questions in the questionnaire. The results demonstrate that the perceived service quality by SMEs of CD influences the overall value SMEs attach to CD. No evidence was found in support of the hypothesis that institutional environment of a host country is negatively related to the value SMEs attach to CD. But we found a negative relationship between the international experience of an SME and the overall value SMEs attach to CD, and a positive relationship between the extent of having foreign public customers and the overall value attached to CD by SMEs. Opposite to what existing literature suggests, smaller SMEs do not attach more value to CD services. Also, for the business network we did not find evidence that SMEs with an established business network attach less value to CD. We did, however, find evidence that SMEs with an established business network attach less value to partner search services. Suggestions for further research are provided.

Keywords: Commercial diplomacy; SMEs; service quality; institutional profile; value of commercial diplomacy

Commercial Diplomacy and International Business: A Conceptual and Empirical Exploration
Advanced Series in Management, 71–103
ISSN: 1877-6361/doi:10.1108/S1877-6361(2012)0000009007

Introduction

While largely responsible for the economic growth of many countries, small and medium enterprises (SMEs) experience a higher exposure to barriers compared to the larger organizations in their internationalization endeavor, due to information and financial limitations (Spence, 2003). Similarly a research from EIM Business and Policy Research (2010) identifies the lack of capital and adequate information as an important trade barrier but also recognizes a lack of adequate public support as one of the most important trade barriers. For businesses with international expansion plans, the experience and knowledge of firms operating in foreign markets are important for the internationalization of other SMEs due to the transmission of knowledge to other firms (Hessels, 2008). This so-called "knowledge spillover" is, however, limited due to the self-interest and the rationale of gaining competitive advantage as a private firm over others. As Lederman, Olarreaga, and Payton (2009) mentioned, private firms alone will not provide, e.g., foreign market information. Therefore, to address information asymmetries and other market failures, governments have the important task to support companies to internationalize, thereby creating a stronger and more competitive economy.

One powerful public support instrument to support the economic interests abroad is via commercial diplomacy (CD). CD is defined as "the activities conducted by state representatives with diplomatic status in view of business promotion between a home and a host country" (Naray, 2008). CD is practice gaining more importance in today's economy, but is poorly addressed in research. Bergeijk and Melissen (2010) identified three main factors increasing the importance of CD. First, new players in the world economy ask for more economic diplomacy. The "big four" or BRIC countries (Brazil, Russia, India, and China) require more governmental involvement due to cultural and institutional factors. BRIC countries hold many state-owned companies and private parties are not taken seriously, requiring more commercial diplomatic involvement to support businesses. Second, the European integration plays an important role in the extent of economic diplomacy. While trade diplomacy (trade policy-making) is no longer a national matter and rather lies at the responsibility of the European Commission, CD (business support activities) remains a national matter. As an English proverb goes "Charity begins at home," or in other words, one's own country comes before any other responsibility. This shows how CD will retain its importance disregarding a further integration of the EU. Third, the Dutch unique selling points (USPs) play an important role in the importance of economic diplomacy. USPs as energy, water, and road construction happen to be governmental customers that make bilateral governmental relationships imperative.

Although increasing in importance, CD has had an invisible status within diplomatic studies (Lee & Hudson, 2004). Only recent research has started to explore the field of CD (Kostecki & Naray, 2007). One important focus within the existing literature in the field of CD is the effectiveness of CD and the environment in which, and the instrument with which, CD is effective in terms of export increase (e.g., Rose, 2007; Lederman et al., 2009; Yakop & Bergeijk, 2009). These studies measured the effectiveness of CD on a macroeconomic level and recognize that CD has a positive effect on international trade. Although these results are very essential, the results lack detail on the beneficiary perspective and the value-added function of CD, let alone specific enterprises such as SME's. Neither did existing literature nuance the determinants of CD value. This study contributes to the field of CD by identifying to what extent, where, to whom and under which quality conditions CD is perceived as valuable from an SME (beneficiary) perspective.

Literature Review

Commercial Diplomacy

Ruel and Zuidema (2012) define commercial diplomacy as activities conducted by state representatives with diplomatic status, or acting on behalf of them, aimed at business promotion between a home and a host country. This definition is based on Naray (2011), who focuses on public actors who perform business promotion and facilitation activities. Kostecki and Naray (2007) nuance this in earlier work by stating that the services of CD are commonly employed by members of diplomatic missions, the staff, and related agencies. Related agencies such as business support agencies National Business Support Offices (NBSO) and foreign investment agencies do not have a diplomatic status but are, however, public services to promote trade and are thus seen as part of the CD construct. We therefore adjust the definition of Naray (2008) and use the nuance made by Kostecki and Naray (2007) in earlier work and see CD as an activity conducted by state representatives abroad (with diplomatic status) in view of business promotion between a home and a host country.

Economic Diplomacy — Commercial Diplomacy

As Mercier (2007) notes, CD is often confused with economic diplomacy. This necessitates an elaboration on the concept of economic diplomacy in relation to CD. Okano-Heijmans (2010) explicated on the concept of economic diplomacy, which gives a clear perspective on the strands of economic diplomacy and provides more clarity into the concept. Okano-Heijmans identifies CD as a strand of economic diplomacy. Economic diplomacy is defined as "the political means as leverage in international negotiations with the aim of enhancing national economic prosperity, and the use of economic leverage to increase the political stability of the nation" (Okano-Heijmans, 2010). The concept of economic diplomacy is based on the countries desire to have economic security, which has two dimensions: the business end (prosperity) and the power-play end (stability). By excluding military actions, many economic diplomacy strands fall between the prosperity and stability end. The strands identified by Okano-Heijmans are CD, trade diplomacy, financial diplomacy, inducements, and negative sanctions. CD is positioned at the business end and is defined in this research as an activity conducted by state representatives abroad (with diplomatic status) in view of business promotion between a home and a host country. The actors involved in CD range from high policy level to lower level specialized diplomatic envoys. It is important to understand that the other strands of economic activities and commercial activities are not to be seen as separate activities. As Potter (2004) argued, economic diplomacy and CD are irrevocably intertwined since CD aims at exploiting the opportunities that are more or less created via the other strands of economic diplomacy.

Rationale and Justification of Commercial Diplomacy

There are a variety of reasons why governments consistently use CD. Naray (2008) posed six rationales for CD that provides a comprehensive picture. First, the need of firms to have access to reliable and neutral business information is important. Naray (2008) also mentioned that CD is important for the support for newcomers with regards to their credibility and image in foreign markets. Additionally, partners search, conflict handling, support of home country delegations, and strategic concerns such as the improved access to energy supplies are important rationales for governments to use CD.

Since CD is publicly funded, the justification needs to be based on an assessment of the social costs and benefits associated with the CD services. Lederman et al. (2009) pose that the social benefits would be bigger if large positive externalities are associated with higher national exports within an exporting country. The assessment of the CD on economic welfare grounds is, however, difficult, if not impossible. Existing research has therefore focused on assessing whether CD increases export and found that CD increases national exports, which leads to the main objectives of the government to increase tax revenue and the creation of jobs (Lederman et al., 2009; Rose, 2007). The justification of CD as a trade-off between social benefits and social costs is not the only debate. A divergent yet interrelated topic concerns the perspective of a capitalistic economy system where classical liberals hold the ideal of no governmental interference, i.e., laissez-faire. However, realists pose that governmental intervention such as CD is a "necessary evil" for the economic system. The justification of this necessary evil is based on the theory of asymmetric information and other market failures. As Lederman et al. (2009) mentioned, private firms alone will not provide, e.g., foreign market information. The rationale for a private firm to gain competitive advantage over others limits knowledge spillovers and thus the ability for other firms to collect the knowledge to internationalize. These market failures lead to the task of the government to provide support services to address information asymmetry, imperfect networks and informal institutions, such as culture and language barriers. The extent to which the government is involved in the market can best be described as a facilitating role where CD opens doors but the actual business is conducted by the companies.

The Rationale and Justification of Commercial Diplomacy for SMEs

Governmental business support services, such as CD, are generally focused on SMEs (Kostecki & Naray, 2007; Mercier, 2007; Seringhaus & Rosson, 1989). The topic and focus of the internationalization support for SMEs are of considerable relevance for two reasons. First, the observed growth effects of internationalized SMEs and the capacity of SMEs to drive the economic development of a nation make SMEs give weight to this group of firms (OECD, 2009). The capacity of SMEs to drive economic development is also shown in the case of the Netherlands, where a recent study shows that SMEs stand for almost 30–40% of the export of the Netherlands, including indirect exports — a stunning 60% of the total export in the Netherlands comes from SMEs (EIM Business and Policy Research, 2010).

Second, although of considerable relevance for the economic development of a nation, SMEs have a higher exposure to trade barriers, compared to the larger organizations, in their internationalization endeavor. The main barriers are, as Spence (2003) denotes, the information and financial limitations. More specifically, a research of the OECD (2009) demonstrates the top-ranked internationalization barriers of SMEs are (1) the shortage of working capital to finance exports, (2) limited information to locate/analyze markets, (3) the inability to contact potential overseas customers, and (4) the lack of managerial time, skills, and knowledge. The barriers addressed by the OECD (2009) are largely internal and are mainly a reflection of the resources and capabilities of an SME. The EIM Business and Policy Research (2010), however, also depicted the external barriers and demonstrates that the lack of public support is one of the most important external barriers in the internationalization of SMEs.

Moreover, the aforementioned rationale for public internationalization support is simultaneously the main rationale for taking an SME perspective in this research, i.e. the high impact of SMEs on the development of the national economy, more prone to trade barriers, and the perceived lack of public support in their internationalization endeavor.

Services of CD

The concept of CD can best be described by its observable business promotion services. CD is, to a large extent, based on the export promotion services. Kotabe and Czinkota (1992) separated export promotion services into the categories of export service programs and market development programs. The former program is more focused on export counseling and export advice questions (making companies export ready), whereas the latter is more focused on identifying opportunities within the host market and preparing market analysis in the host country. The CD services of foreign posts are more focused on market development programs. This is also acknowledged by Potter (2004) who makes the distinction in "boarder in" and "boarder out" services. Potter (2004) states that the responsibility in making companies "export ready" is a "boarder in' task constituting domestic agencies and "boarder out" is focused on market development. The activities of foreign posts are therefore more focused on promoting export by delivering valuable host country market/country information, establishing contacts and by organizations or support in organization trade fairs, seminars and trade missions. This research will thus focus on the "boarder out' activities.

Lee (2004a, 2004b) gives an overview of the "boarder out' activities by separating them into three main categories. The first one is gathering and dissemination of host country market information. A second category concerns the development and introduction of host country business and governmental relations to the home country. The third and final category is the promotion of home country services into the host market by means of trade fairs, lobbying and the organization of seminars.

Another perspective comes from Kostecki and Naray (2007). They position CD as a value-creating activity and define value by Potter (2004) definition as the "combination of benefits delivered to the beneficiaries minus the cost of those benefits to business and government". In broad terms, the areas of CD can be defined according to the area-activity matrix of Naray (2008), comprising promotion of trade in goods and services, protection of intellectual property rights, cooperations in science and technology, promotion of made-in corporate image, and the promotion of foreign direct investment. These activities are identified as the primary activities of CD in the value chain posed by Kostecki and Naray (2007). Activities in these areas can come in forms such as export advice, legal assistance, and backstopping, if needed. Such kinds of support include helping national firms to enter new markets or old markets with new products and to help foreign companies interested in investing in the home country (Saner & Yiu, 2003). The inputs to support the primary activities are identified as the support activities, constituting intelligence, networking, contract negotiator implementation, and problem solving. The supply of information and dealing with inquiries from home and host country, referred to by Kostecki and Naray (2007) as the support activity "intelligence," is identified as the main support activity of CD. Following the aforementioned synopsis of CD activities, we propose our own exhaustive groups of service. A systematic overview was made with the most important conceptual clusters of CD services proposed by other authors. After a thorough analysis, we proposed our own comprehensive and nonoverlapping cluster of CD services based on the synopsis of previous literature, i.e., (1) intelligence, (2) problem solving, (3) partner search, (4) assistance at fairs and trade missions, and (5) presence of diplomat at fairs, contract signing/ceremonies. Intelligence is subdivided into the areas such as cultural information, regulatory information, information on markets, and public tenders.

Customer Value in the Field of CD

By means of the CD services, governments intend to promote and facilitate SMEs to internationalize. The government is ultimately looking for economic stability and security in the home country. CD comprises a range of services that intend to contribute to this objective by boosting import, export, and economic growth. Where the previous sections have discussed the definition, the rationale, the specific services, and the objective of CD, the prevailing section will assess whether the objective of CD is accomplished by assessing the existing literature on the value adding role of CD.

The value of CD is researched from the perspective of the beneficiary. We are therefore interested in the "customer value" of CD. A diversity of definitions have been given to customer value, such as "the customer's overall assessment of the given utility of a product based on perception of what is received and what is given" (Zeithaml, 1988) or "a trade-off between perceived quality and perceived psychological and monetary sacrifice" (Dodds & Monroe, 1984). However, in this research, customer value will not be defined as a trade-off between what is given and the monetary costs. Rather this research defines customer value as "the worth in usefulness to the organization." This definition leaves out a trade-off between monetary costs and what is received, which seems more applicable since no costs are charged for CD services in the Netherland at this stage.

Several publications have attempted to capture the value of export promotion programs, and more specifically, the value of CD on international trade in terms of increase in export. Gençtürk and Kotabe (2001) tested the US organizational perspective by linking export programs to sales and profitability figures of the beneficiary and argues that the usage of export promotion programs increased profitability but not sales. This questions the necessity of export promotion since it implies that the likelihood of export success for a company is just as likely with or without foreign posts' support where companies use CD services merely to save costs in export endeavors. Nevertheless, Gençtürk and Kotabe's (2001) study does acknowledge the importance of export promotion for SMEs. Similarly, Spence (2003) noted that SMEs would arguably need these services due to financial and information limitations. Furthermore, Rose (2007) and Yakop and Bergeijk (2009) focused their research specifically on CD and both found quantitative evidence of an export increase rather than mere profit in the field of CD. Both articles used a gravity model to demonstrate the effectiveness of CD. In these gravity models, export figures of a large number of export and import countries are analyzed. Rose identified a significant effect of consulates and embassies on export promotion. Yakop and Bergeijk (2009) replicated the study of Rose but used a more heterogeneous sample constituting a larger sample of low- and medium-income countries. Yakop and Bergeijk (2009) conclude that the impact of CD in developed countries is not significant and is therefore not a relevant factor for trade, rather it is suggested that the significant impact of CD on exports is driven by developing countries. This finding is also acknowledged by Lederman et al. (2009).

The aforementioned literature is highly focused, or in some cases solely focused, on an increase in export that would justify the existence of foreign posts in the context of business internationalization. However, this type of research has little focus on the perspective of the beneficiary, other than a general, nevertheless important notion whether it has a significant effect on export figures. Kostecki and Naray (2007) started to address this gap in literature by providing more insight into the perspective of the beneficiary with a useful client-provider gap of CD services, identifying the discrepancy between the offered services and the actual needs of the beneficiary.

Similar to Gençtürk and Kotabe (2001), Kostecki and Naray (2007) made a distinction in the importance of CD between SMEs and multinational enterprises (MNEs). Where Gençtürk and Kotabe (2001) acknowledge the importance of CD for SMEs, Kostecki and Naray (2007) nuanced this perspective by citing an Anglo-Saxon diplomat who stated that the focus of CD is both on SMEs and MNEs, but the interest in specific CD activities differ. SMEs would arguably be more technical and less relationship-based, and MNEs would have more interest in public relationships involving the host country government. This statement, however, lacks generalizability and is based on merely one quote.

As can be concluded from the aforementioned discussion, the importance of CD for SMEs is recognized in existing literature. Nevertheless, the extent to which it is valued by SMEs has not been measured, neither has any research tried to capture the factors determining the value of CD activities or attempted to capture the value adding improvement points posed by SMEs. Second, the client provider gap posed by Kostecki and Naray (2007) gave a better overview of the needs of the beneficiary, yet lacks nuances specified to SMEs. Additionally, in existing literature, indications are given that the interest in specific CD services differs between SMEs and MNEs. These statements, however, lack generalizability and merely portrays an indication of a difference in value between SMEs and MNEs (cross-case analysis) but do not display heterogeneity in the perceived value within the case of SMEs (within-case analysis).

It is this gap that we try to fill in literature by measuring the value of CD within the case of SMEs. Having conceptualized the value of CD and identified the gaps in current literature in relation to the customer value of CD, the following section will elucidate the potential determinants of the value of CD in the field of service quality, institutional theory and the resource-based theory.

Determinants of Customer Value

In the existing literature, Kostecki and Naray (2007) pose 16 propositions that might impact the activity profile, the business orientation and the performance of CD services. Performance is recognized to be an important factor of the perceived value (Zeithaml, 1988; Bolton & Drew, 1991; Oh, 1999). The outset of this framework therefore functions as a meaningful starting point for our framework to determine the factors influencing the customer value. The 16 propositions posed by Kostecki and Naray (2007) are grouped into five categories, i.e., client characteristics, home country features, host country features, the global business environment, and the commercial diplomatic arrangements.

Besides the influence of performance on the customer value of CD, Lederman, Olarreaga, and Payton (2007) show the importance of the client firm, which is also acknowledged by Zeithaml (1988) who argues that a customer's assessment of value is dependent on the customer's frame of reference that implies the client firm characteristics.

Additionally, the customer assessment of value is, as Woodruff (1997) described, dependent on the use situation. Woodruff poses that if the use situation changes the actual value changes as well. The use situation of CD is inherently dependent upon the host country characteristics. Yakop and Bergeijk (2009) demonstrated this in terms of effectiveness by making a distinction between developed and developing countries, arguing that the different institutions and cultural backgrounds have impact on the effectiveness of CD.

From a home country market perspective, Kostecki and Naray (2007) argue that every country has its government-business relationships that, logically speaking, also concerns the perception of organizations toward commercial diplomatic activities. They argue that in France, the culture exists to automatically go to the embassy once being abroad. Since this research solely focuses on foreign posts of the Netherlands, it will not be viable to determine the intra-country differences. It is, however, interesting to take this determinant in account as an underlying reason for not going to an embassy, which might be due to managerial expectations, perception of the role of the state, or cultural considerations (Kostecki & Naray, 2007).

As can be concluded from the aforementioned, there are numerous potential determinants that can affect the customer value of CD. According to the aforementioned literature and feasibility considerations, the most important potential determinants of CD value seem to be the service quality of the foreign posts, the institutions within the host country, and the client firm characteristics.

Service Quality.   Service quality is recognized to be an important factor of the customer value (Zeithaml, 1988; Bolton & Drew, 1991; Oh, 1999). Kostecki and Naray (2007) acknowledge this but recognize that the performance of CD is hard to evaluate. They do, however, propose that one way of evaluating the CD service performance is by organizational feedback. One way of measuring the performance of a foreign post is in terms of service quality. Service quality can be defined as "the discrepancy between the customer's perceptions of services offered by a particular firm and their expectations about the firms offerings of such service" (Parasuraman, Zeithaml & Berry, 1988). The service quality in the field of CD is yet another poorly researched area and there are no generally accepted explanations on how service quality factors affect the value of CD. The research of Kostecki and Naray (2007) does, however, provide rich qualitative data in the field of CD service quality. Potential shortcomings of the service quality of CD have been addressed by Kostecki and Naray (2007) and are mainly due to the generalist and civil servant type of diplomats active at foreign posts. Critics include "exporters do not use the same language as diplomats," "diplomats do not understand business concerns," "diplomats are overloaded with issues other than trade and investment," and "commercial attaches are bureaucratic and ineffective." Kostecki and Naray (2007) give a good indication of critics and possible determinant of service quality in relation to the style of the diplomat. We try to expand the current quality factors by quantifying the service quality of CD by means of an extensive service quality model developed by Parasuraman et al. (1988), measuring the service quality along five performance dimensions: (1) reliability, (2) responsiveness, (3) assurance, (4) empathy, and (5) tangibles. We are interested in how the knowledge and courtesy of employees, the willingness to help and provide prompt service, the ability to perform the promised services dependably and accurately, the physical representation of the service, and finally the caring individualized attention provided to

SMEs influence the customer value of CD. Previous research in the field of CD has not measured the perceived service quality of CD with an extensive list of performance indicators, nor has it attempted to identify the relative impact service quality had on the customer value of CD. Therefore, the aforementioned five dimensions are used to measure the service quality of CD.

Institutional Country Profile

A basic principle in the international management literature is that firms are entrenched in a country-specific institutional environment that reflects the relatively stable rules, social norms and cognitive structures (Scott, 2008). Scott (2008) defines the institutional environment as relatively stable rules, social norms, and cognitive structures, whereas North (1990) defines institutions as the humanly devised constraints that shape human interactions. Many authors have difficulty in finding a universal definition and there is little consensus in the conceptualization of the institutional environment. Institutions are classified informally and formally (North, 1990) as tangible and intangible institutions and Scott (2008) introduces the interrelated regulatory, cognitive, and normative dimensions. Inspired by Scott's (2008) three interrelated institutional pillars, the regulatory, cognitive, and normative dimension, Kostova (1999) introduced a three-dimensional country institutional profile constituting the governmental policies (regulatory), the widely shared social knowledge (cognitive), and the value systems (normative) that affect domestic business activities. The country institutional profile was set up by Kostova (1999) as a way for conceptualizing and measuring relational and regulatory home country–level features affecting organizational development. We, however, are interested in host country–level features, affecting the international development of an SME. We suggest that the value SMEs attach to CD, at least partly, relies on the institutional country profiles (regulatory, cognitive, and normative pillars) that constrain and shape the organizational behavior.

Client Firm Characteristics. The value attached to CD is dependent on the customer's frame of reference (Zeithaml, 1988). A resource-based view can give a useful insight into the client firm's characteristics that potentially determine the value attached to CD. The firm's resources can be defined as "all assets, capabilities, organizational processes, firm attributes, information, knowledge, etc. controlled by a firm that enable the firm to conceive of and implement strategies that improve its efficiency and effectiveness" (Barney, 1991). However, a distinction is to be made in resources and capabilities, which in the definition of Barney (1991) are seen as one. This chapter adopts the view that resources are tradable and non-specific. Capabilities are, however, firm specific and used to engage the resources within the firm (Makadok, 2001). Capabilities can therefore be seen as the capacity to deploy resources. As capabilities are used to deploy resources in order to improve efficiency and effectiveness, a lack of either could inhibit a firm's ability to achieve its goals. Translating this to the perceived value of companies toward CD activities of foreign posts, one can argue that the extent of available resources and capabilities affect a firm's ability to internationalize.

The extent of available resources and capabilities of the organization are determined by, but not limited to, specific host country context. This section, however, focuses on the internal resources and capabilities available and the effect it has on the perceived value of CD services. Wilkinson and Brouthers (2006) and Gençtürk and Kotabe (2001) argue that the foreign posts can complement the internal resources of a firm, thereby making them more successful in the host country. Specific determinants (resources) of the perceived value of CD services are related to SME. Kostecki and Naray (2007) state that most CD services focus on SMEs rather than on MNEs, since the larger companies have no need for commercial diplomatic activities. SMEs would arguably need these services, as Spence (2003) noted, due to financial and information limitations. The information limitations that are caused by but not limited to financial limitation could therefore affect the necessity of using public services. Information limitations are also potentially caused by an underdeveloped network in the host country that can possibly affect the attached value to CD services. A network has the benefit of resource sharing, allowing firms to combine knowledge, skills and physical assets. Second, a network can provide access to knowledge spillovers and serve as information conduits (Ahuja, 2000). Additionally, one main activity of CD services is to "open doors" by offering partner searches to firms, an activity that can be considered as a network building activity. The available network of a firm therefore has a potential indirect effect on CD value (network information limitations value of CD) and a potential direct effect on the value of specific partner search activities (network partner search). In addition to the extent of available resources, Ionascu, Meyer, and Estrin (2004) have stressed that organizations may mediate the impact of distance through the accrual of experience that represents the capabilities of a firm. Subsequently, the mitigation of distance might also mitigate the need for CD services as SMEs are more experienced in exporting abroad, thus indicating that companies with more international experience would attach less value to CD services. Additionally, Czinkota and Johnson (1983) and Cavusgil (1980) demonstrated that experienced exporters are able to rely more on in-house export experience.

Another client firm arrangement that has potential impact on whether CD activities are perceived as important is brought up by Bergeijk and Melissen (2010). They argue that Dutch USPs play an important role in the activities of economic diplomacy. The USPs being energy, water, and road construction happen to be governmental customers that make bilateral governmental relationships imperative. Subsequently, CD activities might not be immune to foreign governmental customers and partners. It is therefore argued that CD services are potentially perceived as more valuable by firms that to a large extent rely on foreign public customers and partners. The aforementioned review on client firm characteristics uncovered resources and capabilities and client firm arrangements that potentially influence the degree of value. The most important client firm characteristics taken into account in this research are therefore the number of employees, the available business network in the host country, the international experience, and the extent of having public customers/partners abroad.

Research Model

The determinants are categorized into three groups: the service quality the institutional country profile, and the client firm characteristics that potentially influence the value attached to CD. The hypotheses are formulated after an extensive literature review using a resource-based view, institutional theory, and service quality theory.

First, we assert that the service quality delivered by foreign posts is positively associated with overall value of CD. We included five dimensions, each measuring a different aspect of the service quality of CD.

Second, we propose that a favorable institutional country profile based on regulative, cognitive and normative pillars are negatively associated with the value of CD. Asserting that a reliable legal system, high information availability, and an economic system–based market relations decrease the necessity (value) for public support, i.e., commercial diplomacy.

The third and final group depicts the client firm characteristics that are believed to influence the value of CD. From a resource-based view we included the number of employees, the available network, and the international business experience the firm has. We assert that the more resources and capabilities an organization possesses, the less value a firm attaches to CD. An additional client firm characteristic that potentially influences the value of CD is the extent to which the firm has foreign public customers/partners and we propose that firms with high public customer/ partner involvement attaches more value to CD.

This research will measure the determinants on the overall CD value. After testing the relationships on the overall value, this research will also explicate on the value of specific CD services in association with the client firm characteristics and institutional profile.

The relationships are displayed in Figure 1 and the proposed hypotheses are formulated in Table 1.

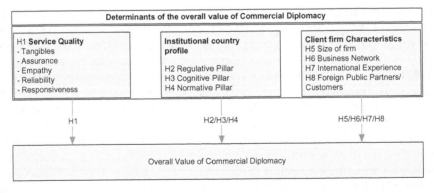

Figure 1: Research model.

Table 1: Hypotheses.

Area	No.	Hypothesis
Service quality	1	Higher perceived service quality is associated with higher value of CD
Institutional country profile	2	Higher security of transactions and contracts is negatively associated with the perceived value of CD
	3	Higher information availability in the host country is negatively associated with the perceived value of CD
	4	Higher reliance on market relations in the host country is negatively associated with the value of CD
Client firm characteristics	5	Larger SMEs attach less value to CD
	6	An increase in international experience is associated with a decrease in the value of CD
	7	An increase in the available business network in the host country decreases the value of CD
	8	An increase in foreign public customers/partners increases the value SMEs attach to CD

Method

A mixed method research is adopted using both quantitative and qualitative data in which the quantitative and qualitative data is analyzed at the same time (parallel). A mixed method research is used because both quantitative and qualitative research have their strengths and weaknesses. One drawback of quantitative data is the limited in-depth descriptive power, whereas qualitative data has low statistical power. We therefore choose to adopt a combination of quantitative and qualitative methods, which allows us to obtain statistically reliable information from numerical measurements, which is, thereafter, complemented with enriched explanations. In addition to aiding interpretation, the mixed method research design allows triangulation in which two or more independent data sources can uphold research findings.

The quantitative data is used to test the hypothesized relationships of CD in numbers and frequencies, allowing us to statistically analyze the central research question. This analysis is backed up by qualitative data obtained from open questions in the online questionnaire, a telephone questionnaire and a semi-structured interview. The multi-method data collection technique consists of a (1) telephone questionnaire, (2) an online questionnaire, and a (3) semi-structured interview. This section will elaborate on the justification and operationalization of the three data collection methods used.

Telephone Questionnaire

The rationale for choosing the telephone requests is threefold. Initially it served the purpose of profiling the right respondents for the online questionnaire, in this case the owner, the export manager, or the international sales manager who has a general overview of the international business activities within the firm. A large obstacle to overcome in this research was the ability to get contact details from the appropriate respondents within the company. A second challenge was the ability to get a large enough sample size. Approaching respondents via telephone gives the researcher the ability to build report and commitment, increasing your likely response rate (Saunders, Lewis, & Thornhill, 2009).

The telephone questionnaires were conducted in a call center. A big drawback of telephone questionnaires in case of a large sample is the time taken to complete the data collection, but the benefits of a larger and reliable sample size outweighed the costs. A telephone script/questionnaire was created in which the purpose of this research was explained. After the approval of sending an online questionnaire to their personal email, the possibility arose to obtain more qualitative data. This was operationalized by asking the respondents (1) if they used CD services, (2) what the rationale was for using or (not) using CD services, and (3) and how they experienced the services.

Online Questionnaire

Within a time span of 4 hours after contacting the response via telephone, a structured questionnaire was dispersed per email to the panel of respondents who gave their consent in us sending an online questionnaire. The use of a survey strategy with a questionnaire gives us the ability to collect quantitative data that can be analyzed quantitatively using both descriptive and inferential statistics.

The tool used to electronically disperse the questionnaires was NETQ. This questionnaire application helped to address several challenges to optimize the response and reliability of this research. First, NETQ allowed us to use condition-based questioning instead of a static questionnaire where the same questions are posed to all respondents. The set of respondents can be divided into the respondents who used CD services and the respondents who did not. Since respondents who have used CD services are able to answer a divergent set of questions (e.g. service quality) and respondents who did not use CD are, e.g., asked to explain the rationale for not using CD, condition-based routing is imperative to guarantee a questionnaire that is user-friendly and poses only relevant questions to the respondents. Second, the system gave the ability to use condition-based questioning, track response ratings, send request to respondents in a personalized manner, and send reminders efficiently, thus allowing us to obtain and manage a large amount of information in a relatively highly economical way.

Although the support system to manage the data collection is imperative, the task to produce a questionnaire that collects the data that you require to answer the research question and achieve the objectives is an even bigger challenge. As Oppenheim (2000) argue, it is far harder to produce a good questionnaire than you might think. Additionally, Saunders et al. (2009) pose that it is important to precisely define the questions prior to the data collection.

At last the questionnaire used also contains an open-ended question in which the respondents are asked to give their vision on possible improvement points or expansion of the CD services that would increase the value of CD for their organization. This question contributes to the fourth objective to get a better insight into improvement suggestions to increase the value of CD from an SME perspective. These qualitative suggestions, together with the quantitative findings, are reflected upon in a semi-structured interview, discussed in the following section.

Sample Techniques and Response

This study focuses on exporting SMEs. The sample used in this research was purposively drawn from an export company list from "company-info" in the Netherlands. The purposive sample was selected on the number of employees between 1 and 300. A total of 450 export and international managers/owners were contacted by telephone, of which 48% (214 out of 450) agreed to fill out a questionnaire or was willing to send it to the designated person.

Apart from getting the approval of sending an online questionnaire to the potential respondents, this telephone conversation was also held to obtain more qualitative data from the respondents. From the 214 contacts, 48 respondents provided meaningful qualitative information on the rationale for using or not using CD services via telephone questionnaire. The rather low response rate on the telephone questionnaire (48 out of 214) was due to the fact that the majority of international managers/export managers/owners were not available since they were either on a business trip or had time constraints at that time. The gatekeeper, in many cases the receptionist, was, however, able to give his or her personal email and name that allowed us to proceed and sent the online questionnaire with a personalized email explaining the purpose of this research. A reminder was sent after 1 week and subsequently resend 2 weeks later in case the online questionnaire was not started or completed.

From the respondents/gatekeepers who gave their approval of us sending the online questionnaire, 57% (121 out of 214) started the questionnaire, of which 85% (103 out of 121) completed the questionnaire. The non-completion rate is for a large extent due to the length of the questionnaire. There is a noticeable pattern where respondents terminate the questionnaire, which is at the start of a rather lengthy question matrix. Nevertheless, respondents not completing the questionnaire but having filled out a minimum of five questions are included into this questionnaire. A question completion rate of five questions has been installed to filter out the respondents who did not terminate the questionnaire due to its length. A total of 5% (6 out of 121) did not meet this threshold and were omitted from the questionnaire. The total sample response was therefore $N = 115$. The four objectives of this research have, however, different sample requirements that have an effect on the valid N. In order to measure the use and the extent of value attached to CD services (objectives 1 and 2) and in order to get a better vision on possible improvement points to increase the value of CD services (objective 4), a sample of both users and nonusers of CD services is necessary to get a representative picture of all exporting SMEs in the Netherlands.

The third objective "measuring the determinants of the value of CD" can, however, only be measured from a user perspective, since the proposed independent variables of the value CD, such as the service quality and the host country characteristics, necessitate the respondents to have actually used CD services. The sample response of respondents who used CD services in the last 2 years has an N of 38, which is no more than 33% of the total sample. Therefore, Table 2 gives a

Table 2: Sample: 'total count and user-only count'.

Variable	Scale	Total count	Table N (%)	User-only count	Table N (%)
Number of	1–9	19	16	4	11
employees	10–50	47	41	13	34
	51–250	40	35	15	39
	>250	9	8	6	16
	Total	115	100	38	100
Years of	0	1	1	0	0
international/	<1–10	15	13	4	11
export experience	11–20	28	24	9	24
	21–30	28	24	4	11
	31–40	18	16	10	26
	>40	25	22	11	29
	Total	115	100	38	100
Number of foreign	Never	60	54	14	38
public customers/	Seldom	19	17	7	19
partners abroad	Occasionally	15	13	6	16
	Very frequently	15	13	9	24
	Almost always	2	3	1	3
	Total	111	100	37	100

distribution of the number of employees, years of international experience, and number of foreign public customers/partners from both the total sample and from a subsample, excluding the respondents who have not used CD services. This list has not been included here due to its length. The sample visualized in Table 2 has a fair number of respondents in each group, only respondents with no international export or export experience is rather low or nonexistent. This is due to the fact that the company list consisted of existing exporting SMEs.

Findings

Service Quality and its Effect on the Value of CD

We hypothesize that the service quality of foreign posts leads to an increase in the overall value of CD. We therefore computed a Pearson's correlation coefficient to examine the relationship between the service quality and the perceived value per country (Table 3). The overall service quality ($r = .477$) positively correlates with the value of CD per country and is significant. These results support hypothesis 1 that there is a positive relation between the service quality and the value attached to CD. Replicating the analysis on the individual performance dimensions, assurance ($r = .613$) and empathy ($r = .530$) are highly significantly correlated with the value of CD. Tangibles ($r = .466$), responsiveness ($r = .289$), and reliability ($r = .329$) are moderately significant. The observed data therefore suggests that all five performance dimensions are positively associated with higher customer value. Moreover, the knowledge and courtesy of commercial diplomats (assurance) and their ability to understand the needs of firms and provide individualized attention (empathy) show the highest and most significant association with the value attached to CD.

Table 3: Pearson's correlation coefficients — service quality on overall CD value.

Variable	Correlation coefficient	*p*-Value	N
Service quality, overall	.477**	.012	22
Tangibles	.466*	.054	12
Assurance	.613***	.001	22
Responsiveness	.298*	.084	23
Reliability	.329*	.067	22
Empathy	.530***	.006	22

*Correlation is significant at the 0.1 level (one-tailed).
**Correlation is significant at the 0.05 level (one-tailed).
***Correlation is significant at the 0.01 level (one-tailed).

Institutional Country Profile and Value of CD

In this section, the relation between the institutional country profile and the overall value of CD is examined. We hypothesized a negative relationship between the host countries' regulative, cognitive, and normative pillars and value of CD. The institutional country profile was also measured as an aggregate of the regulative, cognitive, and normative pillars. We hypothesized a negative relation between the overall institutional country profile and the customer value of CD.

We examined the relationships by calculating a Pearson's correlation coefficient (Table 4). The overall institutional country profile ($r = -.128$), the regulative pillar ($r = .084$), the cognitive pillar ($r = -.150$), and the normative pillar ($r = -.221$) do not significantly correlate with the overall value of CD. Therefore, the quantitative data in this study indicates that the institutional environment does not relate to the overall value SMEs attach to CD.

Additionally, we examined whether the overall institutional country profile, the regulative, cognitive, and normative pillars, is related to the value of specific CD services. The value of two types of services is significant and relate to the institutions. The partner search activities are negatively correlated and moderately significant with the cognitive pillar ($r = -.319$, $p < .10$) and the normative pillar ($r = -.373$, $p < .10$). This suggests that more value is attached to partner search activities in host countries with poor information availability and high governmental involvement. Moreover, a negative association was found between the normative pillar and the value attached to the intelligence services ($r = -.482$, $p < .05$), which suggests that intelligence services are more valued in host countries with high governmental involvement.

We also examined whether CD is more valued in developing countries. A striking 86% (32 out of 37) of the foreign posts addressed for CD services were located in non-European countries, and 70% (26 out of the 37) in a developing country. To see whether the potential increase in the use of CD could be due to a less favorable institutional country profile, we first performed a *t*-test and verified whether developing countries were indeed categorized by a less favorable institutional environment. The *t*-test showed a significant difference between the institutional country profile $t(17) = 4.156$, $p < .001$ in developed countries ($M = 5.23$) and in developing countries ($M = 3.32$), indicating that the institutional country profile in developing countries is less favorable than the one in developed countries. We

Table 4: Pearson's correlation coefficients — institutional country profile on the overall CD value.

Variable	Correlation coefficient	*p*-Value	*N*
Overall institutional profile	−.128	.319	16
Regulative pillar	.084	.374	17
Cognitive pillar	−.150	.277	18
Normative pillar	−.221	.214	15

therefore argue that CD services in developing countries are more valued by the respondents than those in developed countries. We examined this by performing a *t*-test to analyze whether the overall value attached to CD and the value of specific CD services differed between developed and developing countries. No significant differences were observed. This indicates that the smaller group of SMEs using CD in developed countries does not value CD (services) less than the larger group of SMEs using CD (services) in developing countries. Moreover, qualitative data aided the interpretation about why CD was valued in developed countries even though the institutional country profile appeared to be more favorable in these countries.

> I can imagine that markets like Germany and France can really be valuable for starting exporters. A lack of experience in the host country is the most important determinants for using CD service. (exporter in the agricultural sector)

> Although Europe is a familiar market with similar regulations, we can really use assistance because we are just starting to export and we do not have the financial resources to hire a consultant. (anonymous)

There were also SMEs that claimed that although the institutions in developed neighboring countries were more favorable, CD still added value with reasons related to institutions.

> We are currently exploring new markets in both European and more distant countries. I find the value of CD in distant countries higher. Nevertheless, CD services in the EU are still interesting. EU regulations might have eased international business within the EU, the interpretation of rules and regulations are very different in each country. (export manager, fruit and vegetable wholesaler)

Another exporter who contacted the consulate in Germany noted: "The Dutch consulate in Germany does good work, and I experience a positive influence on the trade between Germany and the Netherlands. Although it is a familiar market, we experience that the German chamber of commerce is a somewhat bureaucratic organization, and the Dutch consulate addresses this problem" (anonymous).

The statements demonstrate that the reasons for using CD in developed countries are related to a lack of experience and financial limitations. Additionally, some SMEs believe that foreign posts still add value with arguments related to the institutional country profile.

Although CD services in developed countries are not less valued by SMEs, most SMEs used CD (services) in developing countries with less favorable institutional profiles. The qualitative data obtained from the telephone questionnaire aids the interpretation of why a larger group of SMEs values CD services within developing countries instead of developed countries. Respondents were asked in which scenario they would use foreign posts. Respondents argued that CD services would become more valuable when their company starts operating in non-European countries or, more specifically, in developing countries, for reasons relating to the institutional country profile.

> We know our European market very well, and we do not need governmental involvement in these markets. In case of expansion it might be interesting, especially in developing countries where the export infrastructure is limited. (anonymous)

> We are not operational in developing countries, but if this would be the case then an embassy would certainly be more valuable since there are simply more trade barriers. (export manager, water sport equipment exporter)

> We only import and export in Western European countries, and we do not need foreign posts in this process. Foreign posts could become more useful when we would operate in Sudan or other countries with an underdeveloped legal system. (international manager, exporter of building equipment)

The aforementioned statements give evidence that existing exporters that are not using CD services see CD as more valuable if they were to start operations in non-European/developing countries because of a lack of experience, but more importantly for this section, a poor export infrastructure, a poor legal system, and an increase in trade barriers, reasons that are heavily intertwined with the institutional country profile. It therefore appears that the rationale for using CD services is indeed influenced by the institutional country profile. Thus, SMEs involved in exporting appear to use CD more frequently in developing countries with a less favorable institutional environment. Nevertheless, the smaller group of SMEs using CD in developed countries does not value CD less than the larger group of SMEs using CD within developing countries. Similarly, this study indicates that the regulative, cognitive, and normative pillars and overall institutional country profile do not relate to the overall value SMEs attach to CD, regardless of whether or not it is a developing/developed country. The quantitative data of this study does support the view that more favorable cognitive and normative pillars in the host country have a negative effect on the value attached to partner search activities, and a more favorable normative pillar is associated with less value being placed on the intelligence services of foreign posts.

Client Firm Characteristics

In this section, the hypothesized relationships between the client firm characteristics and the overall value of CD are examined. Moreover, this section also assesses the value of the specific CD services in relation to the client firm characteristics. The relationships are assessed by means of a Pearson's correlation test. Table 5 depicts the correlation coefficients and the significance levels of the hypothesized relationships between the client firm and the *overall* CD value. Two client characteristics are significantly correlated with the perceived value of CD. First, the international experience in number of years is negatively correlated with the CD value ($r = -.330$, $p < .10$) and is moderately significant. The negative association conforms with our hypothesis.

Referring to the frequency of use, we previously demonstrated that SMEs with more international experience are more likely to use CD services, which was partly

Table 5: Pearson's correlation coefficients — client firm characteristics on the overall CD value.

Variable	Correlation coefficient	p-Value	N
Number of employees	.228	.136	25
International experience	−.330[*]	.053	25
Public customers/partners	.445[**]	.013	25
Business network	.191	.180	25

[*]Correlation is significant at the 0.1 level (one-tailed).
[**]Correlation is significant at the 0.05 level (one-tailed).

explained by the variance in awareness. Interestingly, however, within the group of users of CD, international experience is negatively associated with the value attached to CD. This indicates that SMEs with less international experience use CD less frequently compared to SMEs with more international experience, but when they do use it, SMEs with less international experience value CD more.

The second client firm characteristic significantly related to the CD value is the extent to which SMEs have foreign public customers/partners ($r = .445$, $p < .05$). The observed positive relation supports hypothesis 7. The number of employees ($r = .228$) and the available business network ($r = .191$) within the host country did not appear to be significantly correlated with the CD value. From this we can conclude that SMEs with more international experience appear to attach less value to CD and SMEs with many foreign public customers/partners seem to attach more value to CD.

The *overall* CD value gave us a good indication of which client firm characteristics are associated with greater CD value. These results do not tell us, however, which specific CD services are valued more or less in association with which client firm characteristics. The following section elaborates on the value of specific CD services in relation to the client firm characteristics: (1) number of employees, (2) international experience, (3) foreign public customers/partners, and (4) the available business network.

Of these four client firm characteristics, three variables are significantly associated with the value attached to specific CD services: (1) international experience, (2) foreign public customers/partners, and (3) the business network.

International experience. To analyze whether international experience is related to specific CD services, we performed an independent *t*-test on the eight predefined CD services. The six-point measurement scale of international experiences was employed by two groupings of SMEs. The groups were formed because the sample size was not sufficient to compare the means for all six scales. The first group consisted of SMEs with 0–20 years of international experience and the second group consisted of SMEs with 21–40+ years of international experience. Interestingly, the only service with a mean score significantly different between both groups was the assistance with trade disputes $t(21) = 2.64$, $p < 0.01$, with SMEs with 0–20 years of international experience attaching a high average value ($M = 5.71$) and SMEs with 21–40+ years of international experience attaching a moderate value ($M = 4.44$), which indicates that SMEs with more international experience attach less value to the assistance with trade disputes.

Foreign public customers/partners.   To examine which CD services are more or less valued, an independent sample *t*-test was conducted to compare the perceived value between SMEs with no or very few foreign public customers/partners and SMEs with several or many foreign public customers/partners. CD services were valued significantly different between the two groups. Our results suggest that SMEs with more foreign public customers/partners attach more value to six specific CD services:

1. (Trade) cultural information, $t(25) = 1.457$, $p < .10$
2. Information about public tenders, $t(19) = 2.829$, $p < 0.01$
3. Partner search, $t(24) = 2.432$, $p < 0.05$
4. Assistance with trade disputes, $t(21) = 3.221$, $p < 0.01$
5. Assistance at fairs and missions, $t(21) = 3.350$, $p < 0.01$
6. Presence of a diplomat at ceremonies, $t(24) = 3.488$, $p < 0.01$

Interestingly, four out of six CD services that are valued more by SMEs with several/many foreign public customers/partners are relationship-based CD services (i.e., services that involve the commercial diplomat using his or her network in the host country). This data supports our line of thought that relationship-based services in particular are perceived as valuable in a government-to-government (G2G) context. The increased value of relationship-based services for SMEs with several/ many foreign public customers/partners was also seen in the frequency of use for the service "presence of a diplomat at meetings/negotiations," as this service was only used by them.

In addition, a statement from a sales manager of a manufacturer of high-quality blast cleaning abrasives clarifies the interpretation of the positive association between the value of relationship-based services and SMEs with several/many public customers.

> Our goods were blocked at customs in Romania although all our paperwork was correct. We contacted the embassy, and it did not take long before we were able to export the goods to the country. Embassies are particularly helpful in trade disputes where governments are involved. In the B2B market they are of less use since we then use our lawyer more often instead of embassies. (international manager, transport industry)

The observed data presents a good indication of the importance of G2G relations where especially SMEs who deal with several/many public customers and partners attach a higher value to the relationship-based services than SMEs who have no or very few public customers/partners abroad.

Note that for the total sample, we concluded that all CD services are equally valued. Interestingly, when we control for the number of foreign public customers/ partners an SME has abroad, we have to nuance our conclusion. Within the subsample of SMEs with few or no foreign public customers/partners, relationship-based services ($M = 4.03$) are significantly less valued, $t(11) = -3.01$, $p<0.01$, than the intelligence services ($M = 4.92$). The diminished value for relationship-based services is not observed within the subsample of SMEs with several/many foreign public customers/partners. On the contrary, the value score of relationship-based services was higher ($M = 5.63$), although not significantly higher than that for the intelligence services, ($M = 5.49$).

Business network.   We also conducted an independent sample t-test to examine whether SMEs with an undeveloped network attach more value to specific CD services than those with a developed business network. The results showed a significant difference, $t(24) = -1.607$, $p<0.10$, in the mean value of partner-search activities between SMEs with no or underdeveloped network within the host country and those with one. More specifically, respondents with a developed business network ($M = 4.09$) attached less value to partner-search services than those with no or undeveloped business network ($M = 4.93$).

Testing the Research Model

The aforementioned sections examined the hypothesized relationships separately. Testing the bivariate relationships is interesting, yet does not investigate whether the relationships hold when included with other potential determinants. We are therefore interested in decomposing the unique contribution of each variable as a predictor of the overall value of CD. This section aims to combine the determinants into one regression model. This regression model is based on a stepwise regression method in order to find the most parsimonious set of variables to explain the model. Pairwise deletion of cases is used due to the limited number of respondents. Table 6 presents the regression model. The model examines the impact of the client firm characteristics, the service quality and the institutional country profile. It is subdivided into two regression models to clarify the relative impact of the two independent variables found to be significant in the multiple regression analyses.

Model 1.   The first model examines the impact of the service quality. Due to multicollinearity reasons, the five performance indicators could not be included in this regression model. Instead, we measured the overall service quality as an aggregate of the five dimensions. The service quality is positively related to the CD value with a standardized coefficient of .477, $t(20) = 2.429$, $p<0.05$. The model is statistically significant ($f(20) = 5.898$, $p<0.05$) and has an explained variance of 22.8% ($R^2 = .228$).

Model 2.   The second model includes model 1 in concert with the impact of the client firm characteristics (number of employees, international experience, business network, public foreign customers/partners) on the CD value. After controlling for the included client firm characteristic and the service quality, the "foreign public

Table 6: Multiple regression model for the overall CD value.

Dependent variable	CD value (1)			CD value (2)		
	B^a	SE	*t*-value	B^b	SE	*t*-value
Constant	1.890	1.182	1.599	1.258	1.100	1.143
Service quality	.477	.195	2.429*	.453	.195	2.552**
Foreign public partners/ customers				.419	.171	2.358*
N	21			21		
R^2	.228			.403		
S	1.02063			.92103		
F	5.89*			6.401**		
R^2 change				.175		

*Coefficient is significant at the 0.05 level (one-tailed).
**Coefficient is significant at the 0.01 level (one-tailed).
aWe used the standardized regression coefficient.

customers/partners" and "service quality" variables appear to be the most parsimonious set of variables explaining the CD value. The service quality is significant in model 2 with a standardized coefficient of .453, $t(19) = 2.552$, $p < 0.01$. The foreign public customers/partners variable is added to this model and helps explain the observed variance in CD value ($B = .419$, $t(19) = 2.358$, $p < 0.05$). By including the "foreign public customers/partners" variable, the model seems to improve the explained variance with $R^2 = .175$. In addition, model 2 is statistically significant ($f(19) = 6.401$, $p < 0.01$) and has an explained variance of 40.3% ($R^2 = .403$). In the previous bivariate analysis, "international experience" was negatively associated with the CD value. However, in this regression model, "international experience" does not add anything to CD value after allowing for the other independent variables. This does not mean that the initial relationship does not exist, however. In a third attempt to improve the model, we included the regulative, normative, and cognitive pillars of the institutional host country profile. Including these variables did not increase the explained variance in this model and were therefore excluded in the stepwise regression method.

The final results of this model indicate that the service quality and the extent of having foreign public partners/customers are important determinants of the CD value. Other variables (number of employees, business network, institutional pillars) did not appear to be significant in this model, nor did they appear to be significant in the bivariate correlation testing (apart from international experience). Thus, service quality and the extent of having foreign public partners/customer partially explain the variability in the CD value. Additionally, international experience is related to the CD value in a one-to-one relation but does not add additional information to the explained variance of CD value after allowing for the other independent variables.

Discussion and Implications

Service Quality

In this research, we demonstrated that the service quality influences the overall value SMEs attach to CD, which is in line with previous work (Zeithaml, 1988; Bolton & Drew, 1991; Oh, 1999). Our research expands existing research and signaled that the quality dimensions representing the knowledge and courtesy of commercial diplomats (assurance) in addition to the ability of the commercial diplomat to understand the needs of the firms and deliver individualized attention (empathy) are the most important value adding dimensions.

The (increasing) importance of a commercial diplomat to understand the needs of firms and provide individualized attention is also recognized by Naray (2008), who claims that due to the development of the Internet, a shift is occurring to more value-added and tailor-made services based on personal contact. Furthermore, existing literature displayed that the type of commercial diplomats who demonstrate the best ability to understand the needs of firms and provide individualized attention (empathize) are the business promoters (Ruel & Zuidema, 2012). Our results, therefore, also offer indirect support that business promoters are the most suitable commercial diplomats to increase the value of CD. This is also conform in the existing literature where business promoters are claimed to be the most suitable commercial diplomat for CD and are characterized by their proactive behavior, their focus on the client and their practical business skills (Kostecki & Naray, 2007; Visser, 2011).

The aforementioned also has managerial implications. We pose that practitioners who are increasing the value of CD by optimizing the service quality of CD services should focus on the business knowledge and courtesy of commercial diplomats in addition to the ability of the commercial diplomat to understand the needs of the firms and deliver individualized attention. Moreover, the business experience of a commercial diplomat, the available business network, and available employees within a foreign post are believed to be important aspects in achieving higher service quality.

Institutional Country Profile

This research does not provide significant evidence in support of a negative relation between the institutional country profile and the value SMEs attach to CD. Similarly, this research dichotomized the countries into developed and developing countries and provided evidence that the institutional country profile is less favorable in developing countries. This finding also conform earlier empirical studies (Djankov, Glaeser, La Porta, Lopez-de-Silanes, & Shleifer, 2003; Lederman et al., 2007). Nevertheless, there is no difference in the value attached to CD, between SMEs doing business in developing countries and those doing business in developed countries.

However, our research does demonstrates that the justification of governmental intervention in developed countries has a less definite reference to market failures since our research demonstrated that the trade institutions are more favorable in developed countries. Existing research even questions the effectiveness of CD in developed countries (Lederman et al., 2007; Yakop & Bergeijk, 2009) with reasons related to more developed institutions that make governmental involvement obsolete. Yakop and Bergeijk (2009) imply that the effect of export facilitation in developed countries is zero and argues that this is due to more developed institutions that are less prone to market failures in comparison to developing countries.

Nevertheless, our research demonstrated that CD services in developed countries are valuable for two reasons. First, although institutions are developed, qualitative data indicated that foreign posts still have a positive effect on the institutions in developed countries as these can be bureaucratic and less effective than the information provision of foreign posts. Second, CD provision is claimed to be important in neighboring (developed) countries. SMEs who are starting to internationalize, and most often do so in developed neighboring countries, lack experience and need support in their first international endeavor, but do not have the financial resources to address a private business support supplier. This last justification is also acknowledged by the European Commission (EIM Business and Policy Research, 2010). Although we cannot debunk the zero effect of export facilitation in developed countries demonstrated by Lederman et al. (2007) and Yakop and Bergeijk (2009), our research does demonstrate that most SMEs valued and experience a positive effect of CD in developed countries.

The aforementioned tells us something about the individual value SMEs attach to the use of CD in a specific host country context. However, this does not tell us anything about the scope of SMEs valuing CD services in a specific institutional environment. The frequency of use between developed and developing countries filled this gap and demonstrated that the group of SMEs using CD services in developing countries is far greater than the group who used CD services within developed countries. SMEs also suggest that this is (apart from a lack of experience) due to a poor export infrastructure, a poor legal system, and an increase in trade barriers, reasons that are heavily intertwined with the institutional country profile. Indeed, we suggest that a larger group of SMEs use CD services within developing countries due to the institutional country profile. Our findings also conform with earlier empirical studies, claiming that CD is more frequently needed in developing countries (Kostecki & Naray, 2007; Yakop & Bergeijk, 2009). The study of Yakop and Bergeijk (2009) suggested that market failures hamper international exchange and are more apparent in developing countries. Moreover, Yakop and Bergeijk (2009) implied that embassies and consulates succeed in reducing or solving some of these market failures. Similarly, our research demonstrated that markets in developing countries have a less favorable institutions and is used more frequently by SMEs with motives related to unfavorable trade institutions, implying that market failures might be more of a problem in developing countries, thus increasing the rationale for SMEs to use CD in these countries.

The aforementioned also has managerial implications. We demonstrated that a larger group of SMEs use and value CD services within developing countries. Nevertheless, a smaller group of SMEs use, but equally value CD, within developed countries. We believe that it is the task of the government to balance the demand for CD services with the proportionate supply of CD services. Ergo, emphasizing CD within developing countries, serves the interests of the largest share of SMEs. Nevertheless, the demand for CD in specific developed countries (e.g., developed neighboring countries) should not be ignored. This research suggest that the use of CD in developed countries is important for a smaller group of SMEs, who lack the expertise to, e.g., identify business opportunities and lack the financial resources to address a private business support provider. The allocation of CD resources to developed countries, in relation to developing countries, can therefore be less profound, but should not disappear.

The Client Firm Characteristics

The findings with respect to the client firm characteristics are in line with Zeithaml (1988), claiming that the perceived value is dependent on the customer's frame of reference. We found that the international experience of an SME is associated with the overall value SMEs attach to CD, and the extent of having foreign public customers explains a part of the variability in the overall value attached to CD.

The observed negative association between the international experience of SMEs and the perceived value is in line with existing literature. Wilkinson and Brouthers (2006) and Gençtürk and Kotabe (2001) argue that the foreign posts can complement the internal resources and capabilities of a firm, thereby making them more successful in the host country. Additionally, Czinkota and Johnson (1983) and Cavusgil (1980) demonstrated that experienced exporters are able to rely more on in-house export experience. Similarly, Ionascu et al. (2004) stressed that international experience may mediate the impact of "distance." In line with this argument, our research indicates that CD is more important for those SMEs with little international experience. We argue that many SMEs who have a lack of international experience, lack the expertise/capabilities to identify, e.g., business opportunities abroad, market requirements, or potential partners. Subsequently, it is within this group of SMEs that we believe CD can add most value.

Furthermore, our results have demonstrated that the extent of having foreign public partners/customers influences the value of CD. This finding conforms earlier research of Bergeijk en Melissen (2010), who argue that Dutch USPs play an important role in the activities of economic diplomacy. The USPs being energy, water, and road construction happen to be governmental customers that make bilateral governmental relationships imperative. Our findings support this thought and demonstrate that CD is particularly perceived valuable in a G2G context.

Additionally, we found evidence that SMEs with several/many foreign public customers/partners attach more value to relationship-based CD than SMEs with no or few foreign public customers/partners. More specifically, SMEs with several/many foreign public customers/partners abroad perceive the relation-based services as a "high value" service, whereas SMEs with no or few foreign public customers/partners abroad are neutral about the value. This findings contradicts a citation of an Anglo-

Saxon diplomat within the research of Kostecki and Naray (2007) who claims that
SMEs are less interested in relationship-based services involving public relationships
with the government.

This finding also has managerial implications on the effective and efficient
provision of CD services. As we have previously discussed, understanding the needs
of SMEs is imperative. We therefore stress that commercial diplomats should be
aware that many SMEs who deal with public customers/partners appreciate
relationship-based services, such as their presence in meetings and negotiations.
Conversely, SMEs who deal with private parties attach less value to the relationship-
based services and are more interested in intelligence services. These findings
demonstrate that there is no "one size fits all" strategy on the provision of CD service.
We therefore recommend foreign posts that are very frequently addressed by SMEs
who deal with foreign public customers/partners should, in addition to offering the
intelligence services, also put emphasis on delivering relationship-based services.
Conversely, foreign posts that are frequently addressed by SMEs who only deal with
private parties should put more emphasis on the intelligence service of CD.

In addition to the international experience and the extent of having foreign public
customers/partners, we also examined whether the number of employees and the
available business network within the host country affected the value of CD. We did
not find evidence that SMEs with less employees attach more value to CD services.
This does not conform existing literature in which it is suggested that the size of the
client firm matters (Hogan, Keesing, & Singer, 1991).

Also, for the business network we did not find evidence that SMEs with an
established business network attach less value to CD. We did, however, find evidence
that SMEs with a established business network attach less value to partner search
services. This finding is also partly conform the findings of Ruel, De Boer, and Ten
Haaf (2012) who claims that companies with an established network are able to
manage business by themselves. We, however, argue that this only holds for partner
search activities. It seems that a developed network only has a negative effect on the
value of partner search activities, i.e., the development of a network. Nevertheless a
developed network does not seem to provide the access to knowledge spillovers and
serve as information conduits as Ahuja (2000) describes, which would make, e.g.,
market intelligence or information about trade and culture less valuable for SMEs.

Limitations

This study has several limitations that future research should overcome. The most
important limitations are discussed in the following section.

First, the low statistical power of this research calls for caution in making any
inferences. In addition, an insufficiently powered research lowers the ability to reject
the null hypothesis when it is false. The institutional country profile and two client
firm characteristics that we hypothesized to be associated were not statistically
significant. These outcomes should be interpreted with caution as the chance of type 2
errors are more profound. Additionally, the five performance indicators were

multicollinear on the value of CD. Multicollinearity can be reduced by increasing the sample size, thereby allowing to understand the unique contribution of the five performance indicators on the value of CD. This study should therefore be replicated with a larger sample size.

Second, our research is based on a single country analysis, "the Netherlands." The extent to which CD services are valued are also subject to the home country characteristics because every country has its own government-business relationships (Kostecki & Naray, 2007). The extent to which CD is valued by SMEs is therefore hard to generalize over other countries. Future research should address this limitation and preferably conduct a cross-country analysis, thereby indentifying the home country characteristics influencing the value of CD.

Third, this research used several existing instruments (i.e., customer value, SERVPERF, institutional country profile) and adapted the instruments according to the domain of CD. As Straub (1989) points out, the more the original instrument is changed, the greater the chance that the instrument will lack the qualities of the original instrument, thereby affecting the reliability and validity of the instruments.

Fourth, we assessed the internal consistency by calculating the Cronbach's alpha. The Cronbach's alpha of the performance indicators, assurance, and tangibles were below the threshold of .7. The poor internal consistency necessitates caution in the interpretation of these constructs. The poor reliability is likely induced by the small sample size and by the translation and adaption of original models (Lumpkin & Dess, 2001).

At last, our sample was consistent of users and nonusers of CD. There is a possibility that this research overestimated the "users" of CD, as they seemed more prone in collaborating with this research. This would affect the overall value ratings of SMEs and inflate the percentage of SMEs using CD services. Moreover, our unit of analysis was the export manager/international manager of an SME, yet our unit of observation was the SME itself. This might have induced a single 'informant bias." As a result, we could not check the reliability among other respondents within the firm.

Future Research

This research attempted, and partly succeeded, in answering the central research question. Yet, every answer poses new questions and every unanswered question remains to be solved. This section will therefore elucidate on both and suggest future research topics.

First, we urge future research to include a number of variables that have not been included within this research due to time constraints. We propose to include the following potential determinants of CD value: the home country characteristics, the industry in which an SME is operational, the host country experience of an SME, the number of countries exported to, and the financial resources. Additionally, we suggest future research to include the export manager/international manager as a unit of observation by researching its business experience, country experience, and experience within the firm.

Existing research indicates that the home country characteristics might affect the value of CD. This study focused on the case of "the Netherlands"; therefore, it was not viable to determine the intra-country differences. Kostecki and Naray (2007) argue that the managerial expectations, perception of the role of the state, and other cultural considerations might influence the government-business relationship in the home country. Therefore, we suggest future research to replicate this study in other countries or conduct a cross-country analysis to identify possible home country characteristics. Additionally, a transparent industry was a reason for not using CD and might, therefore, also affect the value of CD and its specific services. In addition to comparing the value of CD between industries, future research should focus on within-case analysis for specific industries to get an in-depth view on the business support needs of SMEs in specific industries. Moreover, our research did not find an association between the size of an SME and the value attached to CD that does not stroke with the thought and existing research that a lack of internal resources would increase the value of CD (Hogan et al., 1991). This research measured the size of an SME by measuring the number of employees. We urge future research in adding, e.g., level of sales turnover to improve the determination of the size of an SME. Furthermore, this research measured the international experience of firms according to their number of years of export experience. However, our qualitative data gave strong indications that the experience within the specific host country is an important factor for not using CD. Therefore, future research should (in addition to the overall export experience) include the experience within the host country as a potential determinant of the value of CD. Additionally, we pose that the number of countries in which the SME has experience might influence the value of CD.

Second, our research provided answers on the central research question, which brought up new domains of future research. This research identified unawareness as a major concern for the effectiveness of CD. Additionally, we posed that awareness campaigns are pivotal, and SMEs submitted suggestions about which medium to use since the current external communications systems lacks effectiveness. Nevertheless, this was not the main focus of this study. We identified the problem and it is now key to conduct thorough research in effective communication tools and messages to reach SMEs.

Third, our research provided evidence that the value of specific CD services differ within the group of SMEs. Future research is, however, necessary in the differing needs of services for different types of SMEs in different host country contexts. Our research demonstrates that the international experience, the extent of having foreign public customers, and the available business network of an SME are associated with the value SMEs attach to specific CD services. This outcome is satisfactory for this research but should be seen as a starting point for the segmentation of SME target groups. In addition, existing literature addressed other forms of target group segmentation, in which services coordinate across programs to address the firm's different requirements, depending on their export process (Seringhaus & Botschen, 1991; Mercier, 2007). This target group segmentation is based on the different stages of internationalization development such as "start ups" and "established and growing firms" (European Commission, 2008). We, however, pose that it is important to look not only at the development stage, but also at the specific client firm characteristics, industry, and host country context in determining the most appropriate services across different programs. The identification of such determinants is, however, limited and should be expanded in future research.

At last, our research demonstrates that the justification of governmental intervention in developed countries has a less definite reference to market failures since our research demonstrated that the trade institutions are more favorable in developed countries, which also conforms existing literature (Lederman et al., 2007; Yakop & Bergeijk, 2009). The role of CD in developed countries is therefore questioned. Nevertheless, our research quantitatively demonstrates that SMEs equally value CD in developed countries. Yet, our study does not take a potential dead-weight loss in account. Future research should therefore examine whether CD results in more international activities or if it merely facilitates operations without necessarily resulting in more international activity.

Acknowledgment

The authors would like to thank Harry van der Kaap for his support and help in the statistical analyses presented in this chapter.

References

Ahuja, G. (2000). Collaboration networks, structural holes, and innovation: A longitudinal study. *Administrative Science Quarterly, 45*(3), 425–455.

Barney, J. (1991). Firm resources and sustained competitive advantage. *Journal of Management, 17*(1), 99–120.

Bergeijk, P., & Melissen, J. (2010). Diplomatie economen. *Internationale Spectator, 64*(2), 98–99.

Bolton, R. N., & Drew, J. H. (1991). A multistage model of customers' assessments of service quality and value. *Journal of Consumer Research, 17*(4), 375–384.

Cavusgil, S. T. (1980). On the internationalization process of firms. *European Research, 8,* 273–279.

Czinkota, M. R., & Johnson, W. J. (1983). Exporting: Does sales volume make a difference? *Journal of International Business Studies, 14*(1), 147–153.

Djankov, S., Glaeser, E., La Porta, R., Lopez-de-Silanes, F., & Shleifer, A. (2003). The new comparative economics. *Journal of Comparative Economics, 31*(4), 595–619.

Dodds, W. B., & Monroe, K. B. (1984). The effect of brand and price information on subjective product evaluations. *Advances in Consumer Research, 12,* 85–90.

EIM Business and Policy Research. (2010). *Internationalisation of European SMEs.* Brussels: DG Enterprise and Industry, European Commission.

European Commission. (2008). *Supporting the internationalisation of SMEs: Good practice selection.* Brussels: DG Enterprise and Industry, European Commission.

Gençtürk, E. F., & Kotabe, M. (2001). The effect of export assistance program usage on export performance: A contingency explanation. *Journal of International Marketing, 9*(2), 21.

Hessels, J. (2008). *International entrepreneurship: Value creation across national borders*. ERIM PhD Series in Research in Management, 144. Erasmus Research Institute of Management (ERIM), Rotterdam.

Hogan, P., Keesing, D. B., & Singer, A. (1991). *The role of support services in expanding manufactured exports in developing countries* (Vol. 53). Washington, DC: Economic Development Institute, World Bank.

Ionascu, D., Meyer, K. E., & Estrin, S. (2004). *Institutional distance and international business strategies in emerging economies*. The William Davidson Institute, University of Michigan, MI, USA.

Kostecki, M., & Naray, O. (2007). *Commercial diplomacy and international business*. Discussion Papers in Diplomacy No. 107. Netherlands Institute of International Relations 'Clingendael', The Hague, the Netherlands.

Kostova, T. (1999). Transnational transfer of strategic organizational practices: A contextual perspective. *Academy of Management Review, 24*(1), 308–324.

Kotabe, M., & Czinkota, M. R. (1992). State government promotion of manufacturing exports: A gap analysis. *Journal of International Business Studies, 23*(4), 21.

Lederman, D., Olarreaga, M., & Payton, L. (2007). Export promotion agencies: What works and what doesn't. Policy Research Working Paper No. 4044 (Vol.1). The World Bank, The World Region.

Lederman, D., Olarreaga, M., & Payton, L. (2009). *Export promotion agencies revisited*. Policy Research Working Paper No. 5125. The World bank, Washington, DC.

Lee, D. (2004a). *The embedded business-diplomat: How institutional reform upholds the role of business in UK diplomatic practice*. Paper presented at the Diplomacy and Business: Beyond the Hegemony of the State, Montreal, Canada.

Lee, D. (2004b). The growing influence of business in U.K. diplomacy. *International Studies Perspective, 5*(1), 50–54.

Lee, D., & Hudson, D. (2004). The old and new significance of political economy in diplomacy. *Review of International Studies, 30*(1), 343–360.

Lumpkin, G., & Dess, G. (2001). Linking two dimensions of entrepreneurial orientation to firm performance: The moderating role of industry and life cycle. *Journal of Business Venturing, 16*(5), 429–451.

Makadok, R. (2001). Toward a synthesis of the resource-based and dynamic-capability views of rent creation. *Strategic Management Journal, 22*(5), 387–401.

Mercier, A. (2007). *Commercial diplomacy in advanced industrial states*. Discussion Papers in Diplomacy No. 108. Netherlands Institute of International Relations 'Clingendael', The Hague, the Netherlands.

Naray, O. (2008). *Commercial diplomacy: A conceptual overview*. Paper presented at the 7th World Conference of TPOs, The Hague, the Netherlands.

Naray, O. (2011). Commercial diplomats in the context of international business. *The Hague Journal of Diplomacy, 6*, 121–148.

North, D. C. (1990). *Institutions, institutional change, and economic performance*. Cambridge, NYY: Cambridge University Press.

OECD. (2009). *Top barriers and drivers to SME internationalization*. Report by the OECD Working Party on SMEs and Entrepreneurship, OECD. Retrieved from http://www.oecd.org/dataoecd/16/26/43357832.pdf

Oh, H. (1999). Service quality, customer satisfaction, and customer value: A holistic perspective. *Hospitality Management, 18*, 67–82.

Okano-Heijmans, M. (2010). Hantering van het begrip economische diplomatie. *Internationale Spectator, 62*, 73–76.

Oppenheim, A. N. (2000). *Questionnaire design, interviewing and attitude measurement.* New York, NY: Continuum.

Parasuraman, A., Zeithaml, V. A., & Berry, L. L. (1988). SERVQUAL: A multiple-item scale for measuring customer perceptions of service quality. *Journal of Retailing, 64*(1), 12–40.

Potter, E. H. (2004). Branding Canada: The renaissance of Canada's commercial diplomacy. *International Studies Perspective, 5,* 5.

Rose, A. K. (2007). The foreign service and the foreign trade: Embassies as export promotion. *The World Economy, 30*(1), 16.

Ruel, H. J. M., De Boer, S., Ten Haaf, W. (2012). Commercial diplomacy in practice: Experiences of international business executives and representatives. *Proceedings of the 1st REDETE Conference on Economic Development and Entrepreneurship in Transition Economies* (pp. 537–546). Banja Luka, Bosnia-Herzegovina, October 27–29, 2011.

Ruel, H. J. M., & Zuidema, L. (2012). *The effectiveness of commercial diplomacy. A survey among Dutch embassies and consulates.* Discussion Papers in Diplomacy No. 123. Netherlands Institute of International Relations 'Clingendael', The Hague, the Netherlands.

Saner, R., & Yiu, L. (2003). *International economic diplomacy: Mutations in post-modern times.* Discussion Papers in Diplomacy No. 84. Netherlands Institute of International Relations 'Clingendael', The Hague, the Netherlands.

Saunders, M., Lewis, P., & Thornhill, A. (2009). *Research methods for business students.* Essex, UK: Pearson Education Limited.

Scott, W. R. (2008). *Institutions and organizations: Ideas and interests.* Thousand Oaks, CA: Sage.

Seringhaus, F. H. R., & Botschen, G. (1991). Cross-national comparison of export promotion services: The views of Canadian and Austrian companies. *Journal of International Business Studies, 22*(1), 115–133.

Seringhaus, F. H. R., & Rosson, P. J. (1989). *Government export promotion: A global perspective.* London: Routledge.

Spence, M. M. (2003). Evaluating export promotion programmes: U.K. overseas trade missions and export performance. *Small Business Economics, 20*(7), 83–103.

Straub, D. (1989). Validating instruments in MIS research. *MIS Quarterly, 13*(2), 147–169.

Visser, R. (2011). *How commercial diplomats work.* Master's thesis, University of Twente, Enschede.

Wilkinson, T., & Brouthers, L. E. (2006). Trade promotion and SME export performance. *International Business Review, 15*(1), 233–252.

Woodruff, R. B. (1997). Customer value: The next source for competitive advantage. *Journal of the Academy of Marketing Science, 25*(2), 139–153.

Yakop, M., & Bergeijk, P. A. G. (2009). The weight of economic and commercial diplomacy. Working Paper No. 478. International Institute of Social Studies, The Hague, the Netherlands.

Zeithaml, V. A. (1988). Consumer perceptions of price, quality and value: A means-end model and synthesis of evidence. *Journal of Marketing, 52*(3), 2–22.

Chapter 4

The Effectiveness of Commercial Diplomacy: A Survey Among Embassies and Consulates

Lennart Zuidema and Huub Ruël

Abstract

The global economic power shift towards the East has caused the governments of developed economies to support national businesses which are involved in the process of internationalizing and expanding across borders. Commercial diplomacy provides a means for governments to increase their international trade and to stimulate their national economies. Foreign posts play a crucial role in offering effective diplomatic support for international business. But what are the factors that can explain commercial diplomacy effectiveness at the foreign post level? This chapter presents the results of a survey that was conducted among commercial diplomats stationed at foreign posts. It appears that the amount of experience that commercial diplomats acquired at these foreign posts, combined with their established business network, form two of the most important factors which have a positive impact on the quality of commercial diplomacy. This extends further to include the importance of the client (business) preparedness in terms of knowledge and skills as well. Furthermore, the results indicate that the less favourable a cognitive institutional environment in a host country is, for instance in terms of information availability, the more relevance commercial diplomacy will have. The results of this study promote the understanding of how commercial diplomacy works and show how the debate on the future of commercial diplomacy can be taken a step further. This study should also be seen as a starting point for a holistic framework of commercial diplomacy effectiveness.

Keywords: Commercial diplomacy; effectiveness; quality

Commercial Diplomacy and International Business: A Conceptual and Empirical Exploration
Advanced Series in Management, 105–140
Copyright © 2012 Emerald Group Publishing Limited
All rights of reproduction in any form reserved
ISSN: 1877-6361/doi:10.1108/S1877-6361(2012)0000009008

Introduction

Commercial diplomacy is important in today's global economy (Kostecki & Naray, 2007). The global economic power has shifted from developed economies to emerging economies. This in turn has caused governments of developed economies to support national business which is involved in the process of internationalizing and expanding across borders. Commercial diplomacy is a means for governments to increase international trade and support their national economies. As emerging economies will most likely remain a fact, and as they will function as the economic growth engines in the coming decades, governments of developed economies need to strengthen the instruments they use such as commercial diplomacy, while at the same time they will have to deal with budget cuts at home. For instance, the United Kingdom and the Netherlands have rethought their strategies and prioritized commercial diplomacy (*The Economist*, 2011).

Although commercial diplomacy as such is not new, research on commercial diplomacy is a relatively recent phenomenon (Kostecki & Naray, 2007). Examples of studies that have investigated commercial diplomacy are those from Rose (2007) and Yakop and van Bergeijk (2009). They specifically studied the relationship between diplomatic representations abroad on trade volumes. However, explanatory studies on commercial diplomacy at the foreign post level are simply non-existent. This chapter fills this void. It focuses on the characteristics that make commercial diplomacy successful. It aims to identify those characteristics of commercial diplomacy that can enhance commercial diplomacy effectiveness. The research presented in this chapter stems from the following central research question: To what extent do characteristics within the field of commercial diplomacy determine the effectiveness of commercial diplomacy?

The remainder of this paper is structured as follows: In the first section, commercial diplomacy is defined. In the second section, the main objectives of commercial diplomacy are described in order to clarify commercial diplomacy effectiveness. The third section elaborates on the determinants of commercial diplomacy. This section is concluded with a theoretical framework. The fourth section presents and analyses empirical data to test the framework. The empirical data has been collected through questionnaires and semi-structured interviews. Finally, in the last section, the research is concluded and theoretical and practical implications are discussed.

Commercial Diplomacy Defined

Commercial diplomacy is often confused with economic diplomacy (Mercier, 2007) and other types of diplomacy such as trade diplomacy and financial diplomacy (Okano-Heijmans, 2010; Okano-Heijmans & Ruël, 2011). Economic diplomacy is concerned with general economic policy issues and trade agreements (Yiu & Saner, 2003). Even though both have an overarching economic objective (Potter, 2004), commercial diplomacy is much more specific. Mercier (2007) and Kostecki and Naray (2007) both recognize that the term commercial diplomacy is often used to cover two different types of activities: policy-making and business support. While many agree that the core of commercial diplomacy focuses on the specific business support (Berridge & James, 2001; Kostecki & Naray, 2007; Mercier, 2007; Naray, 2008; Potter, 2004; Yiu & Saner, 2003), many of the proposed definitions by various authors differ. Potter, for instance, defines it as:

> the application of tools of diplomacy to help bring out specific commercial gains through promoting exports, attracting inward investment, and preserving outward investment opportunities, and encouraging the benefits of technological transfer. (Potter, 2004, p. 3)

Lee (2004) defines it as 'the work of a network of public and private actors who manage commercial relations using diplomatic channels and processes' (2004, p. 21). This definition suggests that both private and public actors conduct commercial diplomacy. Yiu and Saner (2003) have noted that when commercial diplomacy is conducted by private actors, it is called corporate or business diplomacy. Consequently, private actors should preferably be excluded from the definition of commercial diplomacy. Finally, Naray defines it as:

> *An activity conducted by public actors with diplomatic status in view of business promotion between a home and a host country. It aims at encouraging business development through a series of business promotion and facilitation activities.* (Naray, 2008, p. 2)

These activities are performed by members of foreign diplomatic missions, their staff and other related agencies (Kostecki & Naray, 2007). This notion slightly contradicts the definition offered by Naray (2008), as it only focuses on those public actors who possess diplomatic status, whereas in our view the regular staff can also conduct commercial diplomacy. Having taken this consideration into account (i.e. those actors without diplomatic status), the definition of Naray (2008) will be used in this chapter.

Commercial diplomacy centres around a series of activities in order to promote and facilitate international business. These activities have been identified and classified by numerous researchers. Naray (2008) distinguishes six types of activities: intelligence, referral, communication, advocacy, coordination and logistics. He relates these activities to specific areas such as markets and goods or intellectual property rights. Country image building, export support services, marketing, and market research and publications are other activities that belong to commercial diplomacy, according to Lederman, Olarreaga, and Payton (2007). In contrast to the former activities identified by Naray (2008), the ones identified by Lederman et al. (2007) are focused on a more general country level. Kostecki and Naray (2007) distinguish between support activities of commercial diplomacy and primary activities of commercial diplomacy. The support activities, which include intelligence, networking and public relations, contract negotiations, and problem solving, provide the input for primary activities: trade promotion, promotion of FDI, science and technology cooperation, promotion of tourism, and national business community advocacy.

Interestingly, Kotabe and Czinkota (1992) only distinguish between export service programmes and market development programmes. The former focuses on export counselling and advice. The latter identifies market opportunities. Potter (2004) adds the distinction of broader-in and broader-out activities. Broader-in activities are carried out by domestic actors and aim at preparing firms to do business across borders. Broader-out activities are carried out by actors at foreign posts and focus on market development. It appears that broader-out activities deliver the most value since they are carried out in a host country. Preparing firms to do business in a foreign country can be achieved more easily by domestic actors. Lee (2004) divides the broader-out activities into three main categories. She distinguishes gathering and dissemination of market information, development and introduction of government relations, and promotion of home country products and services by means of trade fairs, lobbying and organizing seminars.

As the aforementioned classifications differ, systematic clustering can lead to the following most important activities of commercial diplomacy: (1) intelligence, and (2) assistance with fairs, trade missions and networking, (3) problem solving and assistance with trade disputes and (4) partner search and negotiation. The first activity comprises information search and dealing with business inquiries, the second activity includes organizing business and export promotion events, the third activity is about advising in cases where businesses face problems with creditors, contract disputes or market access issues, and the fourth activity deals with bringing together business partners from home and target countries.

Objectives and Effectiveness

Commercial diplomacy aims at encouraging business development (Naray, 2008). Naray (2008) specifically indicates that firms which enter foreign markets need to have access to reliable and neutral information, they need to enhance their credibility and image, they must search for potential partners, and/or they need to be able to handle conflicts effectively. It appears that public actors can support these firms by means of commercial diplomacy, thus leading to increased international trade and economic growth. Ultimately, commercial diplomacy aims to create a prosperity-enhancing effect in the home country (Okano-Heijmans, 2010).

Interestingly, researchers have measured the extent to which some of the objectives are achieved. Rose (2007) for example used a gravity model to estimate the effect of commercial diplomacy on international trade. Rose (2007) found that the presence of embassies and consulates had a significant effect (i.e. commercial diplomacy) on international trade. Yakop and van Bergeijk (2009) replicated that study and supported the findings of Rose (2007). It was also found that firms which use state export promotion programmes enjoyed greater export success (Wilkinson & Brouthers, 2006). Another study revealed that the profitability of firms increases when they made use of commercial diplomacy increased. However, these firms failed to increase sales (Gençtürk & Kotabe, 2001).

The above suggests that commercial diplomacy can be effective in multiple ways (Figure 1). The objective that is most frequently referred to is increasing import, export and international trade (e.g. Rose, 2007; Yakop & van Bergeijk, 2009).

Figure 1: Objectives of commercial diplomacy.

Economic growth and prosperity are indirect and ultimate objectives. The direct objective seems to provide added value for those firms which make use of commercial diplomacy. But added value is not easy to monetize because it is hard to directly relate commercial diplomacy to monetary beneficiaries for firms.

Kostecki and Naray (2007) composed an initial framework for value-added commercial diplomacy that could be used as a starting point. In their framework, they situate activity profile and performance as value-added commercial diplomacy. Kostecki and Naray (2007) further indicate that a good activity profile should include those activities that are relevant for a firm which does business in a specific country. The importance of relevance and performance, or quality, is also acknowledged by a commercial diplomat cited in a paper by Hogan, Keesing, and Singer (1991). Essentially, these concepts reflect the relevance of the activities and the quality of the activities of commercial diplomacy. Both the relevance and the quality should be important to firms which wish to succeed in a foreign market and which ultimately achieve the more indirect objectives of commercial diplomacy, such as increasing international trade and economic growth.

In conclusion, relevance of commercial diplomacy is defined as the importance and applicability of business promotion support tools and means offered by public actors with a diplomatic status to home country firms which wish to succeed in a host country market. The quality of commercial diplomacy activities can be defined by using the definition of service quality: 'The degree of discrepancy between customers' normative expectations for the service and their perceptions of the service performance' (Parasuraman, Zeithaml, & Berry, 1988, p. 13).

Determinants of Commercial Diplomacy Effectiveness

The previous section has suggested that commercial diplomacy should add value for client firms, by offering activities (or services) that are relevant and of high quality, but it is not clear how this value is added. The framework used by Kostecki and Naray (2007) introduces several determinants. They included the characteristics of the home and host country, the foreign post, the commercial diplomat, the client firm and the global business environment. Other researchers, such as Lederman et al. (2007), Keesing and Singer (1991), Yakop and van Bergeijk (2009) and Hogan et al. (1991), also acknowledge the importance of the foreign post, commercial diplomat, client firm and the host country.

Resource-Based View and Foreign Post Resources

Most of the aforementioned studies do not provide a generally accepted explanation for how characteristics of both the foreign post and the commercial diplomat influence commercial diplomacy effectiveness. The resource-based view of the firm can provide useful insights. The resource-based view fundamentally relates resources as important antecedents to products and services, and ultimately a firm's performance and hence, effectiveness (Priem & Butler, 2001).

A basic assumption of the resource-based view is that if a firm's resources are both rare and valuable (they contribute to firm efficiency or effectiveness), they can produce a competitive advantage (Barney, 1991). Caves (1980) defined resources as 'those assets which are tied semi-permanently to the firm' (Caves, 1980, p. 32). Barney (1991) includes 'all assets, capabilities, organizational processes, firm attributes, information, knowledge, etc. controlled by a firm that enable the firm to conceive of and implement strategies that improve its efficiency and effectiveness' (Barney, 1991, p. 101). However, commercial diplomacy does not necessarily aim at obtaining a sustained competitive advantage. It is of key importance for public organizations to identify and build strategic capacities so as to produce the greatest public value for stakeholders (Bryson, Ackermann, & Eden, 2007). A foreign post aims to satisfy the stakeholders of commercial diplomacy. From this perspective, the resource-based view can provide a useful explanation in support of resources and their influence on commercial diplomacy. For instance, because a foreign post is embedded in the host country and has a local political and business network, it should have rare and valuable resources. A firm can make use of these rare and valuable resources which enable it to operate successfully during a foreign venture and to create a sustained competitive advantage. A foreign post's rare and valuable resources create value for the firm. In support of this application of the resource-based view, Wilkinson and Brouthers (2006) and Gençtürk and Kotabe (2001) argue that commercial diplomacy services of foreign posts can complement the internal resources of firms, thereby enabling firms to become effective in the host country.

Specific Foreign Post Resources

Although resources are arguably one of the main determinants of commercial diplomacy effectiveness, it still remains an unknown mystery in regard to which specific resources are important. The role of organizational arrangements has been discussed by several researchers (Lee & Hudson, 2004; Potter, 2004). Naray (2008) summarizes and notes that criteria such as the independence of agencies, decentralization, the position in the structure, and the responsible ministry are the most important organizational arrangements. Hogan et al. (1991) propose specific key success factors such as autonomy, sufficient finance, and the experience and training of commercial diplomats. Commercial diplomats are even considered as being 'the most important success factor for effective commercial diplomacy' (Hogan et al., 1991, p. 51). They also elaborate on this by arguing that a combination of academic and practical training, and overseas experience should be the standard. It appears that having a thorough knowledge of subjects such as marketing, the local market, and commercial and financial techniques stands a commercial diplomat in a good stead (Carron De La Carriere, 1998).

Commercial diplomats appear to have different styles (Kostecki & Naray, 2007). Based on their approaches to commercial issues and their leading concerns, three types of commercial diplomats can be distinguished: business promoters, civil servants or generalists (Kostecki & Naray, 2007). Business promoters understand commercial issues mainly as business issues and their leading concern is client (firm) satisfaction. Civil servants understand how commercial issues play an integral role in international relations and their main concern is how they can please the Ministry of Trade. The generalist perceives commercial issues in a broader diplomatic and political sense and their main concern is how they can please the Ministry of Foreign Affairs (Naray, 2008). Hogan et al. (1991) note that in the past, commercial diplomats used to act as civil servants but they were not successful since they brought practices of government bureaucracy to foreign posts. This was not an effective way of dealing with business needs and inquiries. Business promoters tend to have solid technical know-how and they have an entrepreneurial approach. They are often considered as the most successful commercial diplomats (Naray, 2008; Visser, 2011). Naray (2008) concludes that both business knowledge in international marketing and business experience appear to be the two most critical aspects which can make a commercial diplomat effective. Many of the commercial diplomats today have some background in economics, but they possess very little first-hand business experience as they seem to be learning on the spot (Naray, 2008). In conclusion, the resources that are assumed to be the most important determinants of commercial diplomacy effectiveness comprise the characteristics of the commercial diplomat (style and background) and characteristics of the foreign post (budget, business network and communication facilities).

Client Firm Preparedness

The firm which makes use of commercial diplomacy, or the client firm, may also be an important determinant of commercial diplomacy effectiveness. Indeed, the 'clients of service organizations have important roles to perform in creating services' (Mills & Morris, 1986, p. 728). Clients have to acquire knowledge and skills to participate effectively in the service creation process. Bitner, Faranda, Hubbert, and Zeithaml (1997) note that the required level of participation changes per type of service. For commercial diplomacy, a moderate level of participation is needed. At times co-creation is also required since a client firm needs to participate during trade missions. According to Bitner et al. (1997), the service outcome is negatively influenced when a client participates less than what is required.

Based on this line of reasoning, it can be argued that the client firm can influence the outcomes of commercial diplomacy. It is often the case that client firms do not positively participate in the service process, but instead they tend to be unprepared and their requests may be unspecific or unrealistic. Therefore, this research focuses on the extent to which client firms are prepared (have the knowledge and skills) to go abroad, in which preparedness is defined as 'a state of readiness' (Simpson, Weiner, & Press, 1989).

Host Country's Institutional Environment

Finally, the environment in which commercial diplomacy is conducted is the host country. Through its institutional environment, the outcomes of commercial diplomacy can be better understood. Institutions are 'the humanly devised constraints that shape human interaction' (North, 1990). One of the basic principles of the institutional perspective is that organizations within the same institutional environment employ similar practices. Institutions can be classified as formal versus informal institutions (Hodgson, 2006; North, 1990), or intangible versus tangible. However, Scott (2008) introduced three interrelated pillars that reflect the regulatory, cognitive and normative environment. The regulatory dimension reflects 'the existing laws and rules in a particular national environment that promote certain types of behaviours and restrict others' (Kostova, 1991, p. 310). The cognitive dimension reflects 'knowledge and skills possessed by the people in a country' (Busenitz, Gómez, & Spencer, 2000, p. 995). The normative dimension reflects 'the values, beliefs, norms, and assumptions about human nature and human behaviour held by the individuals in a given country' (Kostova & Rott, 2002, p. 217). These dimensions reflect different parts of a country's institutional environment. This institutional profile might exert pressure on a firm in order to adapt to the environment. Kostova (1991), however, recognizes that foreign firms are buffered from the host country's institutional pressures and are not necessarily expected to become completely isomorphic.

In keeping with this argument, it can be suggested that cross-country differences in commercial diplomacy effectiveness rely partly on the set of institutions that guide and constrain foreign firms in the host country and that a country's institutional profile can serve as 'a viable alternative for exploring broad country differences' (Busenitz et al., 2000, p. 1000). Consequently, foreign firms that are exposed to unfavourable institutional environments may find it more difficult to adapt and to operate successfully in the host country than foreign firms which enter countries that have more favourable institutional environments. Firms that operate in unfavourable institutional environment may therefore have an increased need for commercial diplomacy. Considering the aforementioned, the following framework can be constructed. The determinants are classified into four groups: foreign post [resources], commercial diplomat [characteristics], client firm [preparedness] and the host country [institutional context]. It is assumed that these determinants determine the quality or relevance of commercial diplomacy. These relationships are based on the aforementioned literature review and are reflected in the following hypotheses:

H1. An increase in years of business, country and post experience of the commercial diplomat increases the quality of commercial diplomacy.

H2a. An increase in the level of tertiary education of the commercial diplomat increases the quality of commercial diplomacy.

H2b. Commercial diplomats with business education background demonstrate a greater quality of commercial diplomacy than commercial diplomats with other subjects of education.

H3. Commercial diplomats that act as business promoters demonstrate a greater quality of commercial diplomacy than commercial diplomats that act as civil servants and/or generalists.

H4. An increase in the foreign post's resources (i.e. number of employees, budget, business network and communication facilities) increases the quality of commercial diplomacy.

H5. An increase in preparedness of client firms increases the quality of commercial diplomacy.

H6. A less favourable host country's regulatory, cognitive and normative environment for foreign firms increases the relevance of commercial diplomacy (Figure 2).

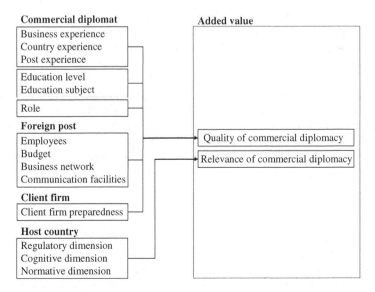

Figure 2: Research model.

Methodology

Most of the literature on commercial diplomacy employs qualitative research techniques. Almost none of the current literature focuses on validating the findings quantitatively. This research builds on previous research and tests the hypotheses formulated. By means of a questionnaire, quantitative data was collected in a survey. The unit of observation was those persons who work for Dutch foreign posts (e.g. embassies or consulates) and who carry out the activities of commercial diplomacy. The respondents all worked for economic and trade departments of Dutch foreign posts and performed the activities of commercial diplomacy. Invitations to fill out a questionnaire were sent to personal e-mail addresses. Not all personal e-mail addresses were publicly available. Therefore, snowball sampling techniques were employed. Respondents were asked to forward the invitation to other commercial diplomats. Additionally, the invitation was sent to general e-mail addresses of the economic and trade departments of foreign posts. A total of 140 respondents commenced filling out the questionnaire, whereas 110 respondents fully completed the questionnaire. Over 65 Dutch foreign posts are represented in the sample, which further include 62 male and 77 female commercial diplomats and have a mean age of 40 years. Almost 53% of the commercial diplomats in the sample have the Dutch nationality. The Indian and Chinese nationalities are also significantly represented in the sample. The response rate (with a total of 270 invitations without the figures of the snowball samples techniques) was almost 41%, which is rather high. This allows the results at least to be generalized to all Dutch commercial diplomats at the foreign post level, but it also allows the results to be indicative for foreign post commercial diplomats of European countries, and perhaps even all developed economies.

In order to verify the results of the survey and to interpret the results, semi-structured face-to-face interviews were carried out. The interviewees selected worked at more strategic levels and were assumed to provide different perspectives on commercial diplomacy. Five semi-structured interviews were conducted with interviewees from an embassy, the Ministry of Foreign Affairs, the Ministry of Economy, Innovation, and Agriculture, the Network of International Entrepreneurship and the Netherlands Institute of International Relations 'Clingendael'. The interviews allowed for a more in-depth discussion on the quantitative findings. The interviews included questions that are deduced from the research model and hypotheses. There was room to deviate from the questions if other interesting, but relevant subjects came to the table. Detailed interview transcripts were generated and interviewees were invited to verify the transcripts to enhance reliability.

Measurement

Earlier in this chapter it was explained that both the relevance and the quality of commercial diplomacy are the underlying concepts of value-added commercial diplomacy. The measuring of the quality of commercial diplomacy is based on the SERVPERF tool. The SERVPERF scale is a tool designed for measuring service quality; that is, the measurement of a specific long-term attitude at a single point in time (Cronin & Taylor, 1994). The construct of the quality of commercial diplomacy thus consists of five dimensions: responsiveness, assurance, tangibles, empathy and reliability. Consistent with other applications of SERVPERF (Cronin & Taylor, 1994), a 7-point Likert scale is used to measure the commercial diplomat's perception of the dimensions. The reliability, assurance, tangibles, empathy and responsiveness subscales consist of 5 ($\alpha = 0.84$), 4 ($\alpha = 0.77$), 5 ($\alpha = 0.71$), 4 ($\alpha = 0.81$) and 3 ($\alpha = 0.84$) items, respectively. The scale reliability of the overall quality construct is rather high (21 items; $\alpha = 0.91$). The relevance of commercial diplomacy is composed of four items to enhance reliability (Van Aken, Berends, & van der Bij, 2009). Consistent with the quality construct, the relevance construct is measured on a 7-point Likert scale. The construct is found to be highly reliable (4 items; $\alpha = 0.85$). For a full operationalization of the independent construct, the table in Appendix 1 can be consulted.

Analysis and Results

Table 1 gives an overview of descriptive statistics for all variables that are included in this research. On average commercial diplomats perceived the quality of commercial diplomacy $M = 5.96$ on a scale of 1 to 7. The lowest score is 4.01. On average commercial diplomats rated the relevance of commercial diplomacy $M = 5.88$.

Quality of Commercial Diplomacy

For testing the hypotheses, regression analyses were conducted. A regression analysis presents whether, and to what extent, an independent variable (characteristics of the commercial diplomat, characteristics of the foreign post and client firm preparedness) explains the variance in a dependent variable (commercial diplomacy quality). Table 2 displays three regression models on the relationship between the independent variables and the quality of commercial diplomacy. The first model examines the impact of the characteristics of the commercial diplomats, such as business experience or level of education (H1–H3). The second model includes the characteristics of the commercial diplomat and adds the characteristics of the foreign post, such as business network or budget (H4). The third model includes both types of characteristics and adds the extent to which the client firm is prepared (H5). Only significant results are included in Table 2 from all models.

The first model (Table 2) shows that only post experience, with an unstandardized coefficient of 0.02 ($t(105) = 3.18$, $p < 0.01$), is positively related to the quality of commercial diplomacy. This model is statistically significant at $p < 0.01$ ($F(105) = 10.127$) and has an explained variance of $R^2 = 0.08$. Country experience, business experience, educational level and field of study, and role are not significantly determining the quality of commercial diplomacy. Hence, from the characteristics of the commercial diplomat included in this study, only post experience of the

Table 1: Descriptive statistics.

Variable	N	Mean	SD	Min	Max	Scale reliability	No. of items
Dependent variables							
Reliability	113	5.85	0.72	3.40	7	0.838	5
Assurance	113	6.12	0.62	4.25	7	0.772	4
Tangibles	113	5.54	0.92	2.67	7	0.708	5
Empathy	112	6.13	0.64	4.00	7	0.811	4
Responsiveness	112	6.17	0.69	3.33	7	0.844	3
Quality of CD	112	5.96	0.56	4.01	7	0.915	21
Relevance of CD	112	5.88	0.78	3.25	7	0.854	4
Relevance intelligence	108	6.01	1.02	2	7		
Relevance fairs/ missions	111	6.05	0.90	2	7		
Relevance problem solving	108	5.94	1.03	3	7		
Relevance partner search	112	6.26	0.84	2	7		
Independent variables							
Experience business	133	4.72	6.36	0	33		
Experience country	133	19.02	17.25	0	56		
Experience post	133	7.80	7.86	0	38		
Education level	134	3	1	1	5		
Field of study	132	2[a]					
Role	134	1[a]					
Employees	125	4.72	1.68	1	7		
Budget	120	4.02	1.65	1	7		
Business network	123	5.10	1.370	1	7		
Communication	125	5.06	1.526	1	7		
Resources	125	4.7333	1.1697	2	6.75	0.751	4
Client firm preparedness	110	4.64	0.91	1.25	6.50	0.792	4
Regulatory	110	4.5756	1.2458	1.62	6.88	0.898	8
Cognitive	110	4.1395	1.2771	1.00	6.40	0.901	5
Normative	110	3.7356	0.9988	1.00	7.00	0.480	4
Institutional profile	110	4.1502	0.9789	1.25	6.69	0.813	17

[a]Instead of means, modes are used (mode is a measure for the most frequently reported response).

Table 2: Quality of commercial diplomacy regression models.

Dependent variable	Service quality (1)			Service quality (2)			Service quality (3)		
	B	SE	t-Value	B	SE	t-Value	B	SE	t-Value
Constant	5.798	0.071	81.601*	5.242	0.194	27.070*	4.598	0.269	17.095*
Post experience	0.020	0.006	3.182*	0.018	0.006	2.988*	0.018	0.006	2.975*
Business network				0.131	0.036	3.688*	0.097	0.037	2.640*
Client firm preparedness							0.155	0.055	2.819*
N	113			113			113		
R^2	0.084			0.187			0.245		
F	10.127*			12.303*			11.153*		
R^2 change				0.103			0.058		
F change				13.221*			7.947*		

*Coefficient is significant at the 0.01 level (1-tailed).

commercial diplomat is a significant determinant of the quality of commercial diplomacy. This implies that the more post experience a commercial diplomat has, the higher the quality of commercial diplomacy is.

The second regression model adds the characteristics of the foreign post. The hypothesis (H4) asserted positive relationships between the types of resources and the quality of commercial diplomacy. Results show that one resource has a significant impact: business network has a positive impact on the quality of commercial diplomacy, with an unstandardized coefficient of 0.13 ($t(104) = 3.688$, $p<0.01$). This implies that the larger the business network of the foreign post, the higher the quality of commercial diplomacy. This model explains a significant proportion of variance in service quality ($R^2 = 0.19$, $F(104) = 12.303$, $p<0.01$.). The change in R^2 is significant 0.103 ($p<0.01$). It implies that adding the business network variable improves the model and accounts for the quality of commercial diplomacy. H4 is thus partly supported. Other resources (i.e. employees, budget and communication facilities) do not significantly determine the quality of commercial diplomacy.

Finally, it was hypothesized that client firm preparedness is positively related to the quality of commercial diplomacy (H5). Results reveal that client firm preparedness indeed significantly determines the quality of commercial diplomacy, $B = 0.16$, $t(103) = 11.153$, $p<0.01$. Client firm preparedness accounts for a relatively high proportion of variance in the quality of commercial diplomacy, $R^2 = 0.11$, $F(103) = 11.153$, $p<0.01$. The R^2 change is significant (R^2 change $= 0.06$, $p<0.01$). This indicates that client firm preparedness improves the regression model used for explaining the quality of commercial diplomacy. Therefore, H5, which asserted that client firm preparedness is positively related to the quality of commercial diplomacy, can be supported. The better client firms are prepared to start doing business with the host country, the higher the quality of commercial diplomacy will be.

Relevance of Commercial Diplomacy

Table 3 displays the stepwise regression models for the relevance of commercial diplomacy. The model examines the impact of the institutional aspects of the host country, such as the regulatory or cognitive environment on the relevance of commercial diplomacy. The sample is split into developed and developing countries since there is a considerable difference between their institutional environments. The cognitive environment is negatively related to the relevance of commercial diplomacy ($B = 0.29$, $p<0.01$) for the subsample of developed countries. The regulatory and normative dimensions are not significant in this model. This model, which only includes the cognitive dimension, explains a significant proportion of variance in the relevance of commercial diplomacy ($R^2 = 0.22$) in developed countries. The regulatory, cognitive and normative dimensions are not significant for the subsample of developing countries. Therefore, we can partly support Hypothesis 6, which asserted a negative relationship between the regulatory, cognitive and normative dimensions of the host country and the relevance of commercial diplomacy. The result implies that it is only in developed countries that the relevance of commercial

Table 3: Relevance of commercial diplomacy regression models.

Dependent variable	Service relevance		
	B	**SE**	**t-Value**
Constant	7.204	0.465	15.495[*]
Cognitive dimension	−0.288	0.097	−2.974[*]
N	110		
R^2	0.222		
F	8.843[*]		

[*]Coefficient is significant at the 0.01 level (1-tailed).

diplomacy decreases when the cognitive institutions (knowledge and skills possessed by the people in a country) improve. This does not apply to developing countries.

Before proceeding to the perspectives shared by the interviewees, some other interesting results appeared. Previously, the statistical analysis did not indicate that business promoters demonstrate a higher quality of commercial diplomacy than the civil servants and generalists. However, the results indicated that business promoters do demonstrate more empathy than civil servants and generalists. Moreover, locally hired commercial diplomats do demonstrate a higher quality of commercial diplomacy than expatriate commercial diplomats.

The Perspectives of the Interviewees

The interviewees stressed the importance of the client firm in commercial diplomacy: A 'good question from the company is very important'. They also noted that the client firm's request is very often unrealistic or unspecific. Another interviewee nuanced the importance of a business network by giving the following response: 'I think this differs across countries. I can imagine that a business network is much more important in China [...] culture plays a major role'.

Statistics indicated that locally hired commercial diplomats were more successful than expatriate commercial diplomats. Although this might be the case, some responses gave some interesting insights. For instance, locally hired commercial diplomats are often more useful in trade missions, since they know the markets, culture and language. They can also guide the expatriate commercial diplomats, who often rotate between foreign posts. Expatriates, on the other hand, are most useful to open doors and put pressure on government bodies within the host country. Furthermore, a few of the interviewees stressed that commercial diplomacy is somewhat overrated. They mentioned that commercial diplomacy should not focus on assisting firms specifically, but that it should focus on general issues that arise (e.g. when a country closes its borders).

Summary of the Findings

This research aimed to identify and test which factors determine commercial diplomacy effectiveness. The central research question was: To what extent do characteristics within the field of commercial diplomacy determine the effectiveness of commercial diplomacy? A research model was constructed which included the characteristics of the commercial diplomat, the foreign post, the client firm and the host country as determinants of commercial diplomacy effectiveness. Commercial diplomacy effectiveness was further conceptualized as value added and composed of the quality and the relevance of commercial diplomacy.

The findings support the hypothesis that the amount of experience that a commercial diplomat has acquired while serving at foreign posts, such as embassies, is positively related to the quality of commercial diplomacy. Interestingly, the experience acquired while working in private firms or in the host country seems to be less relevant for a commercial diplomat. The particular field of study and level of education, and the style of a commercial diplomat, do not determine the quality of commercial diplomacy. Furthermore, the business network of a foreign post positively influences the quality of commercial diplomacy, as well as client firm preparedness to start doing business with a host country. Client firm preparedness can even be marked as one of the key determinants pertaining to the quality of commercial diplomacy. Thus, the better a client firm is prepared in terms of knowledge and abilities, the higher the quality of commercial diplomacy is. The findings only confirm the negative relationship between the host country's cognitive environment and the relevance of commercial diplomacy for developed countries. This implies that a less favourable cognitive institutional environment, for instance information availability, will lead to an increase in the relevance of commercial diplomacy. There is no significant evidence in support of the relationship between the regulatory institutional environment and the normative institutional environment and the relevance of commercial diplomacy. Finally, commercial diplomats who possess a business promoter style do tend to demonstrate more empathy than civil servants or generalists. Commercial diplomats who are locally hired also demonstrate a higher quality of commercial diplomacy.

Discussion of the Findings

The conclusions reinforce, embellish and contradict the existing literature. First Naray (2008), Kostecki and Naray (2007) and Hogan et al. (1991) conclude that business knowledge and business experience are critical characteristics of a successful and effective commercial diplomat. This research did not find any evidence in support of a relationship between business experience and business education and the quality of commercial diplomacy. Indeed, researchers have suggested that it is important for a commercial diplomat to have business affinity, but if the quantitative results are examined, this may not directly lead to achieving a greater quality of commercial diplomacy. Client firms might be more pleased with a commercial diplomat who displays empathy towards them, but this does not necessarily generate a greater quality of commercial diplomacy, nor does it increase international trade or stimulate economic growth. An explanation for this finding may be that essentially a commercial diplomat who has an affinity for business has similar capabilities as the client firm, since they both act business. In contrast, a commercial diplomat who has no affinity for business, but for instance, who has a political affinity, may use his or her capabilities in favour of the client firm, since these capabilities differ from those of the client firm. Therefore, a commercial diplomat who has less of an affinity for business can still be of added value to the client firm.

Commercial diplomats who interpret their role as business promoters display more empathy than those who consider themselves to be civil servants and generalists. This partly conforms to the existing body of literature. The most successful commercial diplomats are those who act as business promoters (Kostecki & Naray, 2007; Naray, 2008; Visser, 2011). Visser (2011) notes that business promoters are proactive and rely on practical business skills. They are often less involved in politics than civil servants and generalists and therefore they can focus more on the client firm. This reasoning seems to fit together with the finding that business promoters display more empathy than civil servants and generalists do. The first discussion of this section reasoned that commercial diplomats who have an affinity for business do not necessarily increase the quality of commercial diplomacy directly. The same holds true for the debate between business promoters versus civil servants and generalists. Civil servants and generalists may have their own strengths which can be used in favour of the client firm. Since the empirical findings are not conclusive, it appears that it would be difficult to argue which type of commercial diplomat is most successful and to what extent they contribute to the objectives of commercial diplomacy. However, the findings indicate that it may be more nuanced than Naray (2008) and Kostecki and Naray (2007) argue. Business promoters are not necessarily the most successful commercial diplomats since they do not directly demonstrate a greater quality, and consequently show effectiveness of commercial diplomacy.

The positive relationship between a foreign post's business network and the quality of commercial diplomacy is in alignment with the current body of literature. Up until now, little research has been done on the determinants of commercial diplomacy effectiveness, yet all of them suggest that resources, especially a business network, are indeed key success factors of commercial diplomacy (Hogan et al., 1991; Keesing & Singer, 1991; Kostecki & Naray, 2007; Lee & Hudson, 2004; Naray, 2008; Potter, 2004). Kotabe and Czinkota (1992) and Wilkinson and Brouthers (2006) imply that foreign post's resources indeed increase the client firm's informational and experiential knowledge. This is in line with the application of the resource-based view. Resources do not produce a sustainable competitive advantage, but they do enhance commercial diplomacy effectiveness by enabling firms to make use of a foreign post's resources temporarily in order to enhance their competitiveness and successfully operate abroad. The results indicate that a business network is the most important resource. The importance of the other resources diminished after allowing for all other resources. This is indicative that the variables mutually relate. This does not imply that these resources are less important. It could be that these resources are a precondition for resources such as a business network. A business network cannot be sufficient without the presence of human resources, financial resources and communication facilities. This indicates the presence of an 'inus condition': 'An insufficient but non-redundant part of an unnecessary but sufficient condition' (Shadish, Cook, & Campbell, 2002). Thus, all resources are important, but not all resources may directly influence the quality of commercial diplomacy.

Many recognize the importance of clients in the service process (Bettencourt, 1997; Mills, Chase, & Marguiles, 1983; Mills & Morris, 1986). Hogan et al. (1991) specifically stress the importance of client firms in commercial diplomacy. The empirical findings in this chapter are in keeping with this line of thought. Client firms have an important role to fulfil in commercial diplomacy. The input of the client firm reflects the quality of the output of commercial diplomacy. Service output which has been based on inaccurate or insufficient information and unrealistic or unspecific requests can lead to less quality and effectiveness of commercial diplomacy. Finally, a host country's cognitive environment negatively influences the relevance of commercial diplomacy. The less favourable a host country's cognitive environment for foreign firms is, the more relevant commercial diplomacy will be in that particular setting. This is in line with institutional theory and in accordance to empirical findings in other domains (Busenitz et al., 2000; Kostecki & Naray, 2007; Kostova & Rott, 2002). The host country's institutional environment provides insight into the relevance of commercial diplomacy, particularly its cognitive environment. However, it would seem that the relevance of commercial diplomacy does not fully rely on a host country's institutional environment since the regulatory and normative environment cannot explain the relevance of commercial diplomacy.

Practical Implications

The conclusions present a few practical implications for commercial diplomats, for foreign posts and for commercial diplomacy policymakers. The current body of literature has stressed the importance of commercial diplomacy. It increases international trade and economic growth (Rose, 2007; Yakop & van Bergeijk, 2009). However, there may be also another side. Interviewees have suggested that commercial diplomacy is overestimated. It should focus on managing agreements instead of supporting firms specifically, especially since it is becoming increasingly more and more convenient to trade internationally, for instance within the European Union. They argue that government bodies should resolve problems when for instance borders are closed or import taxes are raised. Because economic diplomacy focuses on managing policies and agreements, the interviewees basically suggest that economic diplomacy should be prioritized over commercial diplomacy. This argument is subject to definitional issues. It is difficult to separate commercial diplomacy from economic diplomacy. Nevertheless, one should be careful when overestimating the power and importance of commercial diplomacy, especially in times when governments cannot spend money recklessly on such programmes.

Since commercial diplomacy forms an important part of governmental pro-grammes, several noteworthy remarks should be made. Firstly, government bodies should consider prioritizing business networks of foreign posts. Business networks yield increased commercial diplomacy effectiveness. The literature points to the importance of identifying potential partners and the facilitation of doing business with them is one of the key ingredients in successful commercial diplomacy. Business networks can only work successfully when a foreign post is present in the host country. Managing business networks cannot easily be done from within the home country.

Secondly, firms which make use of commercial diplomacy should also play an active role in the process. Many of the client firms' requests are often unspecific or unrealistic. Some instruments could help to improve the input of client firms. Fees or selection methods are good examples of this. The introduction of fees may, in effect, decrease the number of firms that make use of commercial diplomacy, but stimulate those firms that do contact commercial diplomats to prepare themselves better for doing business in a host country. Often these firms contact an embassy but are not ready to trade internationally. Setting a minimum fee for the services of commercial diplomacy would make firms think twice before engaging in these services. This seems quite feasible as currently a number of countries are already successfully working with fees (e.g. Finland). Selection methods are comparable to the introduction of minimum fees. Instead of charging a minimum fee, a foreign post could screen client firms and their requests by using a set of criteria. Firms that prove to be unprepared, not serious, specific, realistic, etc. should be filtered out and they would be considered as not being entitled to receiving assistance from a commercial diplomat.

Thirdly, the current body of literature makes it clear that having an affinity for business is very important for a commercial diplomat (Hogan et al., 1991; Kostecki & Naray, 2007; Naray, 2008). While the findings of this chapter are not conclusive, it does not necessarily mean that such a commercial diplomat might enhance commercial diplomacy effectiveness considerably more so than other commercial diplomats. Therefore, government bodies should not solely focus on hiring commercial diplomats who possess business experience or who have had a business education. Commercial diplomats who possess other backgrounds can also contribute to commercial diplomacy very much, for instance when a commercial diplomat knows the country's language or culture, or when a commercial diplomat can use his or her political influence.

Limitations

Firstly, the sample of this study was taken from a single country, the Netherlands. This has implications on the generalizability of the conclusions. Results should hold for at least Western European countries that have similar arrangements in regard to commercial diplomacy. Nevertheless, a replication of this research study should elucidate on this. Secondly, a response rate of almost 41% is above expectation.

Questionnaires sent through e-mail and Internet-mediated questionnaires normally achieve response rates of 11%. However, the response rate seems ambiguous since convenience and snowball sampling techniques were used. Due to this, the total number of respondents who were precisely invited is unclear since respondents may have forwarded the invitation to others who they thought might be eligible to fill out the questionnaire. Thirdly, missing values could pose a minor issue, since a few respondents did not fully complete the questionnaire. These issues may exist and they may raise some concerns. Therefore, non-response bias may be present. Fourthly, the unit of analysis is commercial diplomacy. The unit of observation was commercial diplomats who work for Dutch foreign posts across the globe. We asked the commercial diplomats to fill out a questionnaire. The questionnaire included self-assessment questions and respondents' perceptions. The respondents assessed how they thought about commercial diplomacy. This self-assessment is somewhat limited since it is subjective. The responses may be biased. Finally, the sample size varied across the variables. The sample size had a minimum of $N = 110$ respondents. A relatively low sample size could have led to low statistical power. Lowered statistical power could have led to erroneously failing to reject the null hypotheses, and it could have led to Type II Error (). In particular, the coefficients of country experience (Saunders, Lewis, & Thornhill, 2009), employees, budget and communication facilities were insignificant in the regression model whereas the initial results were indicative of significant relationships regarding service quality. Therefore, it is hoped that researchers might replicate (parts of) this study in order to clarify this issue.

Future Research

This research should be seen as a starting point for a holistic framework of commercial diplomacy effectiveness. That is why other researchers are invited to extend and retest the framework. Determinants which could be included in future research are as follows: home country factors, the commercial diplomat's social competences in particular networking competences, client firm characteristics and host country factors such as complexity and changeability of the regulatory environment, or economic factors such as GDP. Naray (2008) classified different home country arrangements that can influence commercial diplomacy. He proposed several criteria such as independence of trade promotion agencies (e.g. foreign posts), decentralization, positioning and the responsible ministry that affects the role of commercial diplomacy. Decentralization is also described by Mercier (2007). Gil, Llorca, and Serrano (2007) distinguished central, regional and local arrangements. These criteria and/or typologies can be included when examining the effect of home country arrangements on commercial diplomacy effectiveness. The commercial diplomat's social skills (competences) can also be examined. Up until now, there has not been any literature available that incorporates, or even suggests the importance of social competences for successful commercial diplomats. Only characteristics such as experience, education or role have been suggested. In addition, client firm characteristics might also influence the way commercial diplomacy is arranged. The size of a client firm does matter (Hogan et al., 1991), whereas the industry might also be an important attribute of the client firm that could be included in the framework. Client firms with different sizes and industries have different needs and thus, the relevance of commercial diplomacy varies across firms with different sizes and in different industries. Furthermore, instead of examining the presence or quality of a host country's regulatory environment, researchers would be well advised to focus on the complexity and changeability of such an environment. It appears that many have focused their attention on the role of the commercial diplomat (Kostecki & Naray, 2007; Naray, 2008; Visser, 2011). Researchers have mainly focused on characterizing and describing the three roles. These studies have also stressed that business promoters are the most successful commercial diplomats. There seems to be some uncertainty about what a successful commercial diplomat is and what the outcomes are. This research study's findings suggest that business promoters do not necessarily contribute more to effective commercial diplomacy than civil servants and generalists do. Future studies could elaborate on the outcomes instead of characterizing and describing the three different roles. Sequentially, researchers could examine whether business promoters are truly more successful than civil servants and generalists. Instead of using the term successful, researchers should then be clearer concerning the specific outcomes of business promoters, civil servants and generalists and their true contribution to commercial diplomacy.

Rose (2007) and Yakop and van Bergeijk (2009) have all studied the effectiveness of commercial diplomacy on a macro-economic level. It also has been measured in terms of export success for firms specifically (Wilkinson & Brouthers, 2006). This research study observed the effectiveness on a micro (individual commercial diplomat level) level and conceptualized commercial diplomacy effectiveness into quality and relevance which both are value added for client firms and serve as a basis for effective commercial diplomacy. While this may be satisfactory, future researchers should shift their focus to measure commercial diplomacy effectiveness on a lower operational level. Future research should indicate that these elements form a prerequisite for effective commercial diplomacy.

The previous section stressed the relative (un)importance of commercial diplomacy as an instrument that can be used to achieve economic growth. Researchers should further investigate the importance of commercial diplomacy compared to other instruments such as economic diplomacy. The results might provide an answer to a public interest, since governments cannot spend money on these programmes without considering the effect it will have on the economy. Sequentially from time to time, many governments rethink their economic and commercial diplomacy. Many have introduced fees to make use of commercial diplomacy. While experts believe that this boosts commercial diplomacy effectiveness, future researchers could investigate the effect that paying for commercial diplomacy has on the effectiveness. Client firms may have increased the expectations of commercial diplomacy, and they may be more serious, better prepared, provide more feedback and participate more in the commercial diplomacy service process. Researchers could investigate the effect that making payments or requesting fees has on commercial diplomats. It would be interesting to see whether they can cope with higher expectancy levels.

Conclusion

Commercial diplomacy is important in that governments of developed countries are then in a better position to support their economies as the global economic power is shifting more and more towards the East. Foreign posts are at the very heart of commercial diplomacy and are crucial in providing effective support for home country businesses doing business in a host country. Up until now, it has been unclear which factors of commercial diplomacy provided by foreign posts determine its effectiveness. In this chapter, the results of a survey conducted among Dutch foreign post commercial diplomats were presented. It appeared that the experience that a commercial diplomat acquired at the foreign post, a foreign post's established business network and the client firm's preparedness to do business with a host country, all had a positive impact on the service quality of commercial diplomacy. Furthermore, the results indicate that a less favourable cognitive institutional environment increases the relevance of commercial diplomatic services. These findings are largely in line with the hypotheses drawn from the literature, but in certain instances they are contradictory. All in all, this study is the first of its kind to lay the foundation for a holistic framework for achieving commercial diplomacy effectiveness. That is why future research is needed to confirm and expand this framework.

Acknowledgement

The authors would like to thank Harry van der Kaap for his support and help in the statistical analyses presented in this chapter.

References

Barney, J. (1991). Firm resources and sustained competitive advantage. *Journal of Management, 17*(1), 99–120.

Berridge, G., & James, A. (2001). *A dictionary of diplomacy*. Basingstoke: Palgrave.

Bettencourt, L. (1997). Customer voluntary performance: Customers as partners in service delivery. *Journal of Retailing, 73*(3), 383–406.

Bitner, M. J., Faranda, W., Hubbert, A., & Zeithaml, V. (1997). Customer contributions and roles in service delivery. *International Journal of Service Industry Management, 8*(3/4), 193–205.

Bryson, J., Ackermann, F., & Eden, C. (2007). Putting the resource-based view of strategy and distinctive competencies to work in public organizations. *Public Administration Review, 67*(4), 702–717.

Busenitz, L., Gómez, C., & Spencer, J. (2000). Country institutional profiles: Unlocking entrepreneurial phenomena. *The Academy of Management Journal, 43*(5), 994–1003.

Carron De La Carriere, G. G. M. (1998). *La Diplomatie Économique: La diplomate et le marché*. Paris: Economica.

Caves, R. E. (1980). In R. Priem & J. Butler (2001). Is the resource-based view a useful perspective for strategic management research? *The Academy of Management Review, 26*(1), 22–40.

Cronin, J., Jr., & Taylor, S. (1994). SERVPERF versus SERVQUAL: Reconciling performance-based and perceptions-minus-expectations measurement of service quality. *Journal of Marketing, 58*(1), 125–131.

Gençtürk, E. F., & Kotabe, M. (2001). The effect of export assistance program usage on export performance: A contingency explanation. *Journal of International Marketing, 8*(2), 51–72.

Gil, S., Llorca, R., & Serrano, J. (2007). Measuring the impact of regional trade promotion: The Spanish case. *Papers in Regional Science, 87*(1), 139–147.

Hodgson, G. (2006). What are institutions? *Journal of Economic Issues, 40*(1), 1–25.

Hogan, P., Keesing, D., & Singer, A. (1991). *The role of support services in expanding manufactured exports in developing countries.* Washington, DC: Economic Development Institute, World Bank.

Keesing, D., & Singer, A. (1991). Development assistance gone wrong: Failures in services to promote and support manufactured exports. In P. Hogan, D. Keesing, & A. Singer (1991). *The role of support services in expanding manufactured exports in developing countries.* Washington, DC: Economic Development Institute, World Bank.

Kostecki, M., & Naray, O. (2007). *Commercial diplomacy and international business.* Discussion Papers in Diplomacy, No. 107. Netherlands Institute of International Relations 'Clingendael', The Hague.

Kostova, T. (1991). Transnational transfer of strategic organizational practices: A contextual perspective. *Academy of Management Review, 24*(1), 308–324.

Kostova, T., & Rott, K. (2002). Adoption of an organizational practice by subsidiaries of multinational corporations: Institutional and relational effects. *Academy of Management Journal, 45*(1), 215–233.

Kotabe, M., & Czinkota, M. (1992). State government promotion of manufacturing exports: A gap analysis. *Journal of International Business Studies, 23*(4), 21.

Landrum, H., Prybutok, V., & Zhang, X. (2007). A comparison of Magal's service quality instrument with SERVPERF. *Information & Management, 44*(1), 104–113.

Lederman, D., Olarreaga, M., & Payton, L. (2007). *Export promotion agencies: What works and what doesn't.* Policy, Research Working Paper 4044, Vol. 1. The World Bank, The World Region.

Lee, D. (2004). The growing influence of business in U.K. diplomacy. *International Studies Perspective, 5*(1), 50–54.

Lee, D., & Hudson, D. (2004). The old and new significance of political economy in diplomacy. *Review of International Studies, 30*(1), 343–360.

Mercier, A. (2007). *Commercial diplomacy in advanced industrial states.* Discussion Papers in Diplomacy, No. 108. Netherlands Institute of International Relations 'Clingendael', The Hague.

Mills, P., Chase, R., & Marguiles, N. (1983). Motivating the client-employee system as a service production strategy. *Academy of Management Review, 8*(2), 301–310.

Mills, P., & Morris, J. (1986). Clients as partial employees of service organizations: Role development in client participation. *Academy of Management Review, 11*(4), 726–735.

Naray, O. (2008). Commercial diplomacy: A conceptual overview. Paper presented at the 7th World conference of TPOs, The Hague, The Netherlands.

North, D. (1990). *Institutions, institutional change, and economic performance.* Cambridge: Cambridge University Press.

Okano-Heijmans, M. (2010). Hantering van het begrip economische diplomatie. *Internationale Spectator, 64*(5), 73–74.

Okano-Heijmans, M., & Ruël, H. J. M. (2011). Commerciële diplomatie en internationaal ondernemen. *Internationale Spectator, 65*(9).

Parasuraman, P., Zeithaml, V., & Berry, L. (1988). SERVQUAL: A multiple-item scale for measuring consumer perceptions of service quality. *Journal of Retailing, 64*(Spring), 12–40.

Potter, E. (2004). Branding Canada: The renaissance of Canada's commercial diplomacy. *International Studies Perspective, 5*(1), 55–60.

Priem, R., & Butler, J. (2001). Is the resource-based view a useful perspective for strategic management research? *The Academy of Management Review, 26*(1), 22–40.

Rose, A. (2007). The foreign service and the foreign trade: Embassies as export promotion. *The World Economy, 30*(2), 22–38.

Saunders, M., Lewis, P., & Thornhill, A. (2009). *Research methods for business students*. Essex, UK: Pearson Education Limited.

Scott, R. (2008). *Institutions and organizations: Ideas and interests*. Sage.

Shadish, W., Cook, T., & Campbell, D. (2002). *Experimental and quasi-experimental designs for generalized causal inference*. Boston, MA: Houghton Mifflin Company.

Simpson, J., Weiner, E., & Press, O. (1989). *The oxford English dictionary* (2nd ed.). Oxford: Clarendon Press.

The Economist. (2011, March 10). Rookies abroad: The government's foreign missteps are multiplying. *The Economist*. Retrieved from http://www.economist.com/node/18338830. Accessed on March 10, 2011.

Van Aken, J. E., Berends, H., & van der Bij, H. (2009). *Problem-solving in organizations: A methodological handbook for business students* (3rd ed.). Cambridge: Cambridge University Press.

Visser, R. (2011). How commercial diplomats work. Master thesis, University of Twente, Enschede.

Wilkinson, T., & Brouthers, L. E. (2006). Trade promotion and SME export performance. *International Business Review, 15*(1), 233–252.

Yakop, M., & van Bergeijk, P. A. G. (2009). *The weight of economic and commercial diplomacy*. Working Paper No. 478. International Institute of Social Studies, The Hague.

Yiu, L., & Saner, R. (2003). *International economic diplomacy: Mutations in post-modern times*. Discussion Papers in Diplomacy, No. 84. Netherlands Institute of International Relations 'Clingendael', The Hague.

Appendix 1

Table A.1: Operationalization of the constructs and variables included in this research.

Construct and/or variable	Dimension	Item/indicator	As in the questionnaire	Type, attributes and level
Institutional profile: The humanly devised constraints that shape interaction (North, 1990).	Regulatory institutions: Existing laws and rules in a particular national environment, which promote certain types of behaviour and restrict others (Kostova, 1991).	This country's government assists foreign firms in doing business in this country. This country's government sets and communicates clear rules regarding the entry of foreign firms in the country. This country's government pays much attention to respecting the rules in regard to doing business with foreign firms. This country's government sanctions foreign firms for not respecting the rules in the country. Contracts with foreign firms are secure and respected in this country.	Think of the country you currently work in. The following statements apply to this host country. Please indicate the extent to which you agree with each of the following statements: [statements in the left column].	1–7 Likert scale (1 = strongly disagree, 2 = disagree, 3 = disagree somewhat, 4 = neutral, 5 = agree somewhat, 6 = agree, 7 = strongly agree, and 0 = unknown). Ordinal measurement level.

Table A.1: (*Continued*)

Construct and/or variable	Dimension	Item/indicator	As in the questionnaire	Type, attributes and level
		Intellectual property of foreign firms is secure and respected in this country.		1–7 Likert scale (1 = strongly disagree, 2 = disagree, 3 = disagree somewhat, 4 = neutral, 5 = agree somewhat, 6 = agree, 7 = strongly agree, and 0 = unknown). Ordinal measurement level.
		A (commercial) court makes independent and unbiased decisions with regard to claims arising out of transactions of trade and commerce with foreign firms in this country.		
		Stability and freedom for foreign firms is created in this country due to its friendly legal environment.	Think of the country you currently work in. The following statements apply to this host country. Please indicate the extent to which you agree with each of the following statements: [statements in the left column].	
	Cognitive institutions: Knowledge and skills possessed by the people in a country (Busenitz et al., 2000).	For foreign firms, it is easy to find reliable information about this country.		
		Procedures for entering this country are clear and easy to find.		
		In this country potential partners can be easily located by foreign firms.		
		Information about procedures on the development of new businesses in the		

Construct (definition)	Items	Question	Scale
Normative institutions: Social norms, values, and beliefs and assumptions that are socially shared and are carried by individuals (Kostova, 1991).	country is available for foreign firms. Information about firms and quality of goods is widely available for foreign firms throughout this country. Foreign firms and goods are greatly admired in this country. The presence of government officials is greatly appreciated at business occasions in this country. The government has a high informal influence over local business. In this country many companies are state-owned. Corruption is widely accepted in this country.	Think of the country you currently work in. The following statements apply to this host country. Please indicate the extent to which you agree with each of the following statements: [statements in the left column].	1–7 Likert scale (1 = strongly disagree, 2 = disagree, 3 = disagree somewhat, 4 = neutral, 5 = agree somewhat, 6 = agree, 7 = strongly agree, and 0 = unknown). Ordinal measurement level.
Preparedness of client firm: A state of readiness (Simpson et al., 1989).	As in left column. The client firm's request can easily be executed. The client firm's request is clearly defined. The client firm is prepared to go abroad. The client firm conducted prior research before requesting support.	Please indicate the extent to which you agree with each of the following statements: [statements in the left column].	1–7 Likert scale (1 = strongly disagree, 2 = disagree, 3 = disagree somewhat, 4 = neutral, 5 = agree somewhat, 6 = agree, 7 = strongly agree, and 0 = unknown). Ordinal measurement level.

Table A.1: (*Continued*)

Construct and/or variable	Dimension	Item/indicator	As in the questionnaire	Type, attributes and level
Resources: A stock or supply of money, materials, staff and other assets that can be drawn on by a person or an organization in order to function effectively (Simpson et al., 1989).	Employees: Persons employed for wages or salary, especially at non-executive level (Simpson et al., 1989).	There are enough employees to meet the demand of business support.	Please indicate the extent to which you agree with each of the following statements: [statements in the left column].	1–7 Likert scale (1 = very insufficient, 2 = insufficient, 3 = somewhat insufficient, 4 = neutral, 5 = somewhat sufficient, 6 = sufficient, 7 = very sufficient, and 0 = unknown). Ordinal measurement level.
	Budget: Amount of money needed or available for a purpose (Simpson et al., 1989).	Size of the budget is sufficient to meet the demand of business support.		
	Network: Group of people who exchange information and contacts for professional or social purposes (Simpson et al., 1989).	Business network is sufficient to meet the demand of business support.		
	Communication facilities: Piece of equipment provided for sending or receiving information.	Communication facilities are sufficient to meet the demand of business support.		
Experience of employee: Knowledge or skill acquired by a period of practical experience of something, especially that gained in a particular profession (Simpson et al., 1989).	Business experience.	Number of years that the employee has worked in a private firm.	How many years have you worked in a private firm?	Natural logarithm. Ratio measurement level.
	Host country experience.	Number of years that the employee has worked in the host country.	How many years have you lived in this country?	Natural logarithm. Ratio measurement level.
	Commercial diplomatic experience.	Number of years that the employee has worked at a foreign post.	How many years have you worked at a foreign post (e.g. embassy)?	Natural logarithm. Ratio measurement level.
Education of employee: Process of receiving systematic instruction, especially at a school or	Level of education.	Highest completed level of education of employee.	What is your highest completed level of education?	Multiple choice (1 = secondary school, high school, or Associate degree,

Concept / Definition	Variable / Definition	Question	Measurement
university (Simpson et al., 1989).			2 = Bachelor degree, 3 = Master degree, 4 = Doctoral or Professional degree, and 0 = other). Ordinal measurement level.
	Type of education.	What field of study was your completed education?	Open. Nominal measurement level.
Training of employee: The action of teaching a person a particular skill or type of behaviour (Simpson et al., 1989).	Amount of training.	How many hours of business training do you receive per year?	Natural logarithm. Ratio measurement level.
Commercial diplomatic style of employee:	Approach: Deal with (a situation or problem) in a certain way).	How do you approach the tasks belonging to your job?	Multiple choice (1 = focus on business issues, 2 = focus on international relations, and 3 = focus on diplomatic and political perspective). Nominal measurement level.
	Goal: An aim or desired result (Simpson et al., 1989).	What is your goal of the tasks belonging to your job?	Multiple choice (1 = client firm satisfaction, 2 = Ministry of Trade satisfaction, 3 = Ministry of Foreign Affairs satisfaction). Nominal measurement level.
Quality: How well the service level delivered matches customer expectations.	Reliability of the service: Ability to perform the promised service dependably and accurately (Landrum,	This foreign post provides service as promised. Staff at this foreign post can handle client firm's problems.	Please indicate the extent to which you agree with each of the following statements: [statements in the left column]. 1–7 Likert scale (1 = strongly disagree, 2 = disagree, 3 = disagree somewhat, 4 = neutral, 5 = agree somewhat, 6 = agree,

Table A.1: (*Continued*)

Construct and/or variable	Dimension	Item/indicator	As in the questionnaire	Type, attributes and level
	Prybutok, & Zhang, 2007).	Staff at this foreign post performs the right service the first time. Staff at this foreign post provides service at the promised time. Client firms are informed when services will be performed.		7 = strongly agree, and 0 = unknown). Ordinal measurement level.
	Assurance of the employees: Knowledge and courtesy of employees and their ability to inspire trust and confidence (Landrum et al., 2007).	Staff at this foreign post is courteous. Staff at this foreign post instils confidence in client firms. Client firms feel secure in their transactions. Staff at this foreign post has the knowledge to answer client firm's questions.	Please indicate the extent to which you agree with each of the following statements: [statements in the left column].	1–7 Likert scale (1 = strongly disagree, 2 = disagree, 3 = disagree somewhat, 4 = neutral, 5 = agree somewhat, 6 = agree, 7 = strongly agree, and 0 = unknown). Ordinal measurement level.
	Tangibles of the service: Physical representation of the service (Landrum et al., 2007).	This foreign post has modern equipment and facilities. This foreign post looks appealing. Staff at this foreign post looks and behaves neat and professional. Online and offline documentation of this foreign post is appealing.	Please indicate the extent to which you agree with each of the following statements: [statements in the left column].	1–7 Likert scale (1 = strongly disagree, 2 = disagree, 3 = disagree somewhat, 4 = neutral, 5 = agree somewhat, 6 = agree, 7 = strongly agree, and 0 = unknown). Ordinal measurement level.

Construct/Definition	Item	Instruction	Measurement
Empathy of employee: Caring individualized attention provided to clients (Landrum et al., 2007).	This foreign post provides convenient hours of operation. Staff at this foreign post provides individual attention to client firms. Staff at this foreign post has the client firm's best interests at heart. Staff at this foreign post deals with client firms in a caring fashion. Staff at this foreign post understands the needs of client firms.	Please indicate the extent to which you agree with each of the following statements: [statements in the left column].	1–7 Likert scale (1 = strongly disagree, 2 = disagree, 3 = disagree somewhat, 4 = neutral, 5 = agree somewhat, 6 = agree, 7 = strongly agree, and 0 = unknown). Ordinal measurement level.
Responsiveness of employees: Willingness to help client firms and to provide prompt services (Landrum et al., 2007).	Staff at this foreign post provides prompt service to client firms. Staff at this foreign post is willing to help client firms. Staff at this foreign post is ready to respond to requests.	Please indicate the extent to which you agree with each of the following statements: [statements in the left column].	1–7 Likert scale (1 = strongly disagree, 2 = disagree, 3 = disagree somewhat, 4 = neutral, 5 = agree somewhat, 6 = agree, 7 = strongly agree, and 0 = unknown). Ordinal measurement level.
Overall assessment of quality.	Overall assessment of the services offered to support firms.	Please indicate your overall assessment of the services offered to support firms.	1–7 Likert scale (1 = extremely poor, 2 = poor, 3 = insufficient, 4 = neutral, 5 = sufficient, 6 = good, and 7 = extremely good). Ordinal measurement level.
Relevance of the service: Importance and applicability of the Relevance: Important and applicable in a given context.	Offered services are relevant for firms that want to do business in this country.	Please indicate the extent to which you agree with each of the following	1–7 Likert scale (1 = strongly disagree, 2 = disagree, 3 = disagree somewhat,

Table A.1: (*Continued*)

Construct and/or variable	Dimension	Item/indicator	As in the questionnaire	Type, attributes and level
	service in the host country.	The solution the services provide can be used to resolve problems or compensate for shortcomings in this country. This service is very useful in this country. The solution this service offers is relevant for firms that want to do business in this country.	statements: [statements in the left column].	4 = neutral, 5 = agree somewhat, 6 = agree, 7 = strongly agree, and 0 = unknown). Ordinal measurement level.
	Overall assessment of relevance.	Overall assessment of the relevance of all services in this country.	Please indicate your overall assessment of the relevance of all services in this country.	1–7 Likert scale (1 = extremely irrelevant, 2 = irrelevant, 3 = somewhat irrelevant, 4 = neutral, 5 = somewhat relevant, 6 = relevant, and 7 = extremely relevant). Ordinal measurement level.
	Relevance per type of service.	Services related to intelligence (e.g. market scans) are relevant for firms that want to do business in this country. Services related to assistance with fairs and trade missions are relevant for firms that	Please indicate the extent to which you agree with each of the following statements: [statements in the left column].	1–7 Likert scale (1 = strongly disagree, 2 = disagree, 3 = disagree somewhat, 4 = neutral, 5 = agree somewhat, 6 = agree, 7 = strongly agree, and 0 = unknown). Ordinal measurement level.

Variable	Description	Question	Measurement
	want to do business in this country.		
	Services related to problem solving and trade disputes are relevant for firms that want to do business in this country.		
	Services related to partner search are relevant for firms that want to do business in this country.		
Age.	Age of the respondent.	What is your age?	Natural logarithm. Ratio measurement level.
Gender.	Gender of the respondent.	What is your gender?	Multiple choice (1 = male, 2 = female). Nominal measurement level.
Nationality.	Nationality of the respondent.	What is your nationality?	Open. Nominal measurement level.
Foreign post location.	Location of the foreign post.	In which country is this foreign post located?	Open. Nominal measurement level.
Linguistic skills.	Languages the respondent can speak.	With which languages can you communicate effectively?	Open. Nominal measurement level.

Appendix 2

Table B.1: Correlation matrix for most of the dependent and independent variables.

Variable (N = 113)	1	2	3	4	5	6	7	8	9	10	11	12	13	14	15
1. Reliability	1	0.482**	0.367**	0.516**	0.641**	0.755**	-0.115	0.054	0.253**	0.276**	0.175*	0.349**	0.382**	0.381**	0.313**
2. Assurance		1	0.452**	0.585**	0.523**	0.757**	0.175*	0.077	0.079	0.047	0.103	0.153	0.106	0.134	0.141
3. Tangibles			1	0.408**	0.417**	0.730**	0.028	0.244**	0.218*	0.286**	0.287**	0.239**	0.323**	0.374**	0.256**
4. Empathy				1	0.733**	0.806**	0.013	0.050	0.238**	0.081	0.115	0.230**	0.165*	0.186*	0.180*
5. Responsiveness					1	0.832**	-0.076	0.166*	0.315**	0.297**	0.122	0.353**	0.261**	0.334**	0.358**
6. Quality of CD						1	0.002	0.169*	0.289**	0.278**	0.228**	0.345**	0.326**	0.383**	0.347**
7. Business experience							1	0.172*	0.130	-0.244**	-0.244**	-0.239**	-0.092	-0.276**	-0.044
8. Country experience								1	0.243*	0.121	-0.186*	-0.108	0.038	-0.041	0.077
9. Post experience									1	0.121	-0.070	0.086	0.080	0.072	0.050
10. Employees										1	0.534**	0.496**	0.321**	0.791**	0.425**
11. Budget											1	0.345**	0.276**	0.729**	0.308**
12. Network												1	0.598**	0.786**	0.327**
13. Communication													1	0.712**	0.310**
14. Resources														1	0.448**
15. Client firm															1

*Correlation is significant at the 0.05 level (1-tailed).
**Correlation is significant at the 0.01 level (1-tailed).

Table B.2: Correlation matrix (Kendall's tau-b) for education and quality.

Variable ($N = 113$)	1	2	3	4	5	6	7
1. Reliability	1	0.355[**]	0.315[**]	0.383[**]	0.420[**]	0.544[**]	−0.005
2. Assurance		1	0.358[**]	0.424[**]	0.413[**]	0.568[**]	−0.029
3. Tangibles			1	0.237[**]	0.353[**]	0.564[**]	−0.020
4. Empathy				1	0.609[**]	0.588[**]	0.063
5. Responsiveness					1	0.685[**]	0.023
6. Quality of CD						1	0.013
7. Education level							1

[**]Correlation is significant at the 0.01 level (1-tailed).

Table B.3: Independent samples t-test for type of education on quality.

Variable ($N = 113$)	N		Mean		SD		Significance (1-tailed)
	Business	Other	Business	Other	Business	Other	
Reliability	27	86	5.79	5.85	0.938	0.649	0.303
Assurance	27	86	6.20	6.09	0.709	0.587	0.205
Tangibles	27	86	5.65	5.50	0.921	0.922	0.227
Empathy	27	85	6.13	6.13	0.761	0.601	0.491
Responsiveness	27	85	6.14	6.17	0.800	0.663	0.401
Quality of CD	27	86	5.98	5.95	0.643	0.531	0.395

Table B.4: Independent samples t-test for role on quality.

Variable ($N = 113$)	N		Mean		SD		Significance (1-tailed)
	Business promoter	Other	Business promoter	Other	Business promoter	Other	
Reliability	70	43	5.86	5.85	0.763	0.666	0.473
Assurance	70	43	6.12	6.11	0.674	0.518	0.470
Tangibles	70	43	5.51	5.58	0.960	0.860	0.333
Empathy	69	43	6.20	6.02	0.660	0.596	0.076[*]
Responsiveness	69	43	6.19	6.13	0.741	0.618	0.345
Quality of CD	70	43	5.97	5.94	0.608	0.447	0.391

[*]Correlation is significant at the 0.10 level (1-tailed).

Table B.5: Correlation matrix for institutional profile and relevance.

Variable ($N = 110$)	1	2	3	4	5
1. Relevance of CD	1	−0.035	−0.156[*]	0.011	−0.079
2. Regulatory		1	0.666[**]	0.540[**]	0.898[**]
3. Cognitive			1	0.384[**]	0.848[**]
4. Normative				1	0.736[**]
5. Institutional profile					1

[**]Correlation is significant at the 0.01 level (1-tailed).
[*]Correlation is significant at the 0.10 level (1-tailed).

Chapter 5

Measuring Export Support Performance

Gorazd Justinek

Abstract

Export support is one of the measures countries prefer to use to boost export activities and, consequently, economic growth. However, because the direct outputs are unclear, export support results are often questioned. The current economic crisis raises these questions again. The effects of export support are very difficult to measure, since numerous factors can distort them. We therefore suggest focussing on the performance of this kind of support; in the following chapter, the methodology (export support performance [ESP]) for its measurement is presented.

Keywords: Export support performance; commercial diplomacy

Introduction

The current economic crisis, which started spreading globally in 2008, took many by surprise. However, economic downturns and recessions are nothing unusual since they occur roughly every 10 years. A quick look at the past reveals the global economy's cyclical downturns. There was a downturn in the mid-1970s, at the beginning of the 1980s, at the beginning of the 1990s, at the beginning of the 2000s and so it was bound to happen again around 2010. We have experienced a crisis almost every 10 years, but people's memories of economic events are often short, which is one reason why financial crises and bubbles tend to recur with such frequency.

The difference with the current crisis was its magnitude and level of synchronisation: this was not just a regional event, like the Asian financial downturn of the late

Commercial Diplomacy and International Business: A Conceptual and Empirical Exploration
Advanced Series in Management, 141–150
Copyright © 2012 Emerald Group Publishing Limited
ISSN: 1877-6361/doi:10.1108/S1877-6361(2012)0000009009

1990s, but rather a global crisis — at least in its onset. The numbers were striking. According to the IMF, the global economy contracted by 2.3% in 2009 — an unprecedented fall in the post-war era. In the OECD area, the economy contracted by 4.7% between the first quarter of 2008 and the second quarter of 2009. A plunge in global trade was another sign of the seriousness of the crisis. Worldwide, the volume of trade in goods and services fell by 12% in 2009, according to the WTO (Keeley & Love, 2010).

A solution to some crises in the past (especially in smaller and more open economies) was to redirect the economic focus of interest to other regions or countries. Let us look at a hypothetical situation where country 'A' is mainly trading with region 'B', which is going into recession (according to forecasts) or has very low economic growth forecasts. The government of country 'A' could start intensifying its focus on region 'C', where economic conditions are more favourable. The government of country 'A' could implement different trade and investment liberalisation mechanisms with region 'C' through economic diplomacy. Through commercial diplomacy, it could at the same time provide assistance to domestic exporters and other business subjects willing to internationalise to region 'C'. Consequently, the drop in trade between country 'A' and region 'B' could be compensated for through the rise in trade with region 'C', and economic growth in country 'A' should recover. Unfortunately, this manoeuvre was not possible in the present situation since almost all economies (except some emerging ones) were in some kind of trouble.

Searching for economic growth through export support is in fact nothing exceptional. The first export promotion agency (which still exists) was established in Finland in 1919, and in the mid-1960s, export support became a very popular instrument to boost exports, under the auspices of the International Trade Centre (Keesing & Singer, 1991). Export support activities are usually concentrated within the framework of specialised agencies (usually referred to as trade promotion agencies), as is the case in Finland, Sweden and Slovenia. In some countries, national chambers or other associations are responsible for providing this kind of support (Austria and Germany), or the ministries of foreign affairs take on this role (Denmark). Export support is usually carried out by state representatives with diplomatic status — commercial diplomats (Naray, 2008). We agree with Ruel and Zuidema (2012), however, that this is not always the case. We have to be careful to bear in mind that commercial diplomacy is not the same as export support. Export support represents only one of the many activities of commercial diplomacy. The others include investment support, promoting the country's brand, country image building and facilitation in trade disputes. In this chapter, we focus on export support carried out within the framework of commercial diplomacy.

The economic justification for government involvement in export promotion is based on the theory of asymmetric information and other market failures. Private firms alone will not provide foreign market information, as companies are reluctant to incur research and marketing costs that would also benefit competitors. The same applies to pioneer exporters, which make a considerable investment in attempts to open foreign markets, cultivate contacts and establish distribution chains and other costly activities that can be used by their rivals (Hausmann & Rodrik, 2003).

But is governmental involvement in exports justified? Can governmental support open new markets, re-boost exports and mitigate the effects of a crisis? Some ask, for instance, why the French government should support a French company willing to expand into Germany, while this same government does not help the company back home in Paris (Carrière de la, 1998). Others put forward the view that firms might even become dependent on this type of government assistance (Naray, 2008). From my personal experience, working in a national export promotion agency, I remember instances when managers complained about the government helping companies 'going abroad' since they would later employ people and pay taxes in another country. Another issue often raised was that if this same company wanted to expand to some other region in the home country, it would not be eligible for any governmental support.

Many questions are asked in this regard. The only undisputed, known, quantitative fact is the cost of this support, since maintaining a network of offices and qualified personnel abroad requires a great deal of financial resources. Especially nowadays, as governments around the world are cutting costs and a variety of information is relatively easily accessible online, the question of whether this support is justified is back on the agenda. We are therefore aware of the inputs — but what about the outputs?

In the following section, we look at the work already carried out by different authors in the field of measuring export support outputs, and then present a new measure — export support performance (ESP) methodology. This is a method for monitoring export support activities 'on the spot' and focuses on its performance, since we believe that there is a logical linkage of positive results and outputs if the performance of the activity is high.

Measuring Export Support

Several attempts have been made in the past to measure the results of export support at the business level. Kedia and Chhokar (1986), for example, found that export support programmes in the United States had little impact. Seringhaus and Botschen (1991) surveyed the opinions of nearly 600 firms in Canada and Austria, and found that the use of export support services was low, and that the programmes were not well oriented to the specific needs of exporters. Gencturk and Kotabe (2001) tested the link between programme usage and export performance in a sample of 162 US firms and found that the use of export programmes increased profitability but not sales. Keesing and Singer (1991) argued that export support activities have failed to achieve their goals and, in many cases, have even had a negative impact, except in those countries that already had favourable policies vis-à-vis exports, namely Singapore, Hong Kong, South Korea and Taiwan (Keesing, 1993). In a survey of 137

Canadian companies, Yannopopulos (2010) found that some export services were more useful (foreign market information, training, finding agents/distributors) than others (language training, export business planning, advice on logistics). Wilkinson and Brouthers (2006) found a positive relationship between trade shows and satisfaction with export performance. Additionally, a survey was carried out on 88 footwear and textile manufactures from Eritrea, a small country in Africa. The results revealed that, on average, the quality of export services was rated only as satisfactory and small enterprises had less access to them than large firms (Tesfom & Lutz, 2008).

At the national level, Coughlin and Cartwright (1987) estimated that a US$ 100 increase in export promotion expenditure generated US$ 432,000 in increased exports. Using a gravity model, Rose (2005) estimated how the presence of an embassy or a consulate may impact on bilateral trade. He argued that as communication costs fall, foreign embassies and consulates lose much of their role in decision-making and information-gathering processes and are therefore increasingly marketing themselves as export support agents. In a sample of 22 exporting countries and around 200 potential trading partners, he found that for each additional consulate abroad, exports increased by 6–10%.

The Rose study was enhanced with a larger sample of exporting countries and with data for more recent years (Bergeijk, 2009; Yakop & Bergeijk, 2009). They confirmed the thesis that embassies and consulates do facilitate trade. Positive significant estimates have consistently been obtained for the number of embassies and consulates in various specifications, ranging from 6% to 16% for export facilitation. For trade by and with developing countries, even larger elasticities were estimated. The same was confirmed by Bergeijk, de Groot, and Yakop (2011).

An interesting new perspective was recently presented in the paper by Ruel and Zuidema (2012), involving a holistic framework for monitoring commercial diplomacy effectiveness on the basis of a survey of commercial diplomats. The results showed that the experience acquired by a commercial diplomat at a foreign post, a foreign post's established business network and the client firm's preparedness to do business with the host country, all had a positive impact on the service quality of commercial diplomacy. The paper provides interesting findings and correlations but has its limitations, since commercial diplomats were evaluating their own work, which could have led to distorted results due to subjectivity.

Export Support Performance — ESP

Measuring export support activities on the basis of subjective answers provided through questionnaires (even in large numbers) or through data collected from trade flow statistics can be risky. Questionnaires are subjective, while on the other hand experience shows that large or medium and even small companies often direct revenue (and also expense) flows through subsidiaries or affiliated companies in different countries — usually those with lower taxes (not necessarily tax havens). These legitimate business actions distort official trade flow records, and the official statistics therefore do not necessarily provide an accurate picture of trade flows between countries. For these reasons, we suggest focussing on the performance of these activities instead. If the ESP is good, positive outputs in the form of export growth can also be expected. In order to measure export support performance, we created the export support performance methodology — ESP.[1]

With the ESP methodology, we first define the export support activity most required for the country observed, since this varies significantly between countries. The various surveys conducted in the past are therefore very difficult to compare since we do not know why the companies were satisfied with the support (or not). The reasons could vary from one country to another. Therefore, the support activity most required needs to be defined at the outset for each country observed.

The second issue arises with regard to the companies participating in the survey and being questioned about their satisfaction with export support. This is another factor which differs significantly. In most countries, if small and medium-sized enterprises (SMEs) were asked about their satisfaction with export support, we would probably receive negative or neutral feedback — in contrast to large companies, where positive feedback is more usual. The explanation lies in the fact that commercial diplomats like to prioritise large companies. This is understandable since many small companies are just trying their luck, most of them do not even have the capacity or resources required to internationalise. We should also point out that in most of the evaluations carried out in the past, the groups surveyed were not comparable. The ESP methodology precisely defines the characteristics of a 'typical' test company, which ensures the possibility of later comparisons.

Nevertheless, we believe that an accurate evaluation of export support activities cannot be based solely on surveys and questionnaires. In the ESP model, we therefore combine different methodologies. On the basis of the survey (carried out in the first phase) and the predefined 'typical company' (second phase), we determine ESP using the methodology of first-hand observation with participation. This is a structured type of research strategy and is widely used in many disciplines, particularly cultural anthropology, but also sociology, communication studies and social psychology. Its aim is to gain a close familiarity with a given group of individuals and their practices after having been exposed to a stimulus. This method originated in the fieldwork carried out by social anthropologists and in the urban research of the Chicago School of Sociology (Douglas, 1976). In accordance with this method, commercial diplomats are exposed to a stimulus (the request sent from the test company) and are observed at the same time, although they are not aware of it.

By requesting the support activity most required (by the majority of surveyed companies) in comparable circumstances and observing the reactions of commercial

---

[1]The methodology was primarily designed to measure export support performance in Slovenia, which is also where the pilot case study was carried out. More in Justinek (2012).

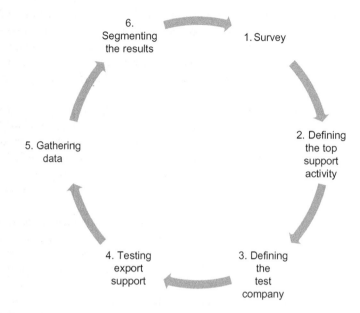

Figure 1: Steps in calculating export support performance (ESP).

diplomats surreptitiously, we believe the actual performance of export support is captured 'on the spot'. The ESP methodology is presented in Figure 1, where the six steps of calculating it are explained in detail.

Step 1. Survey concerning the export support needed.[2] We are aware of the fact that export-oriented companies often have different needs and characteristics owing to different levels of internationalisation, historical issues, general economic development, linguistic specifics, etc. The survey in Step 1 should point out these needs for every country individually. The questionnaire has to be carried out anonymously in order to ensure that truthful answers are provided, and the number of companies questioned has to be adequate in order to assure the legitimacy of the statements (representativeness among export-oriented companies).

Step 2. Defining the support activity most required on the basis of answers provided by the companies. The data received in the survey (Step 1) has to be analysed and a scale defined, ranging from the 'the support most needed' to 'the support least needed'. The activity exposed as the one most needed by the majority of the companies surveyed will be applied in Step 4.

Step 3. Defining a 'test company' that meets the characteristics of a typical company in terms of number of employees, size, revenues, export revenues, etc. This is another factor that differs significantly from country to country. Since SMEs

---

[2]For example, information on foreign markets, potential business contacts, help in finding suitable legal and marketing assistance, help at trade fairs, trade missions, conflict resolution, etc.

usually need the most support for internationalisation, the test company should meet the following criteria:

- The test company selected should, in terms of size,[3] be represented in the segment of SMEs (not large and not micro). This means it should have
  - a headcount of between 10 and 250;
  - a yearly turnover of between EUR 2 and 50 million; and
  - a balance sheet total of between EUR 2 and 43 million.
- In order to ensure the seriousness of the company's request, the test company must already be actively exporting, with at least 10% of its total revenue obtained from foreign markets.
- The test company must have the best or the second best credit rating (A or B).
- The company should have been in operation for at least 2 years. We believe that even 'born globals' need to have been in operation for at least for 2 years in order to demonstrate some past achievements (annual balance).

We have to make an agreement with the company that meets all the above-mentioned criteria and gain access to their official e-mail, from which the requests for support can be sent (Step 4).

Step 4. Testing export support. This step requires particular attention, since it is in fact very similar to the procedures in natural science. First, we need to prepare a request for support (the support activity most required as defined in Step 2) and send it directly to commercial diplomats from the official company's address (e-mail) defined in Step 3. In the formal request, we have to briefly present the company, define the reasons for the support required and request it. This must be done for every commercial diplomat separately. Throughout the testing process, we also have to be aware of the fact that commercial diplomats are in contact with each other. Therefore, the request cannot be sent to all commercial diplomats at once as we could receive distorted feedback if the company is not taken seriously. For this reason, the requests should be sent in multiple stages, but comparable circumstances have to be assured (e.g. the request is always sent on Monday mornings).

Step 5. Gathering data. The time needed for every answer has to be tracked separately. The same should be done regarding the quality of the information sent. On the basis of the data received, the cumulative results of the parameters (the responsiveness of commercial diplomats and the quality of the information sent) can be segmented.

Step 6. Segmenting the results. We focus on two crucial parameters which we believe are essential in international business: the time and quality (usability) of information. It is often said in business circles that 'time is money', and this is also true for export support. If the information requested is not sent within a reasonable amount of time, it is practically useless. Therefore, the time limit set in the model is 7

---

[3]In accordance with the definition of the European Commission. More on http://ec.europa.eu/enterprise/policies/sme/facts-figures-analysis/sme-definition/index_en.htm

days; within this deadline we believe it is still reasonable to expect some useful, quality information. With regard to the responsiveness of commercial diplomats, the following framework was set:

- Answer within 3 days — excellent responsiveness (positive)
- Answer within 4–7 days — good responsiveness (positive)
- Answer within 8–10 days — slow responsiveness (negative)
- Answer within 11–20 days — poor responsiveness (negative)
- More than 21 days — no reply (negative)

The quality of the information sent is the second parameter we focus on. If the information received is sent on time but has no added value, the support can again be considered useless. However, in the case of qualitative information segmentation, we encountered some difficulties, since we are tracking qualitative data. Therefore, we need to group answers with similar characteristics, such as

- no reply (negative);
- reply that he/she cannot provide support, but presents no objective explanation as to why (negative);
- courteous reply that he/she will provide support, but does not (negative);
- provides information from different databases, which can also be accessed from home, but are often fee-based or in a foreign language (positive);
- a custom-made answer containing valuable and useful information (positive);
- others.

With regard to information quality, positive results are understood as being custom-made answers, as well as even answers containing data from different databases, where commercial diplomats provide some assistance on the basis of their foreign market know-how. All other cases are negative, and further detailed explications are required in order to elaborate on the negative deviation.

Concluding Remarks

Export support has been used for decades as a governmental measure to boost exports and, consequently, economic growth. Most research carried out in the past at the macro level confirms the positive results derived from export support activities. In contrast, most of the research carried out at the micro level (on the basis of company surveys) reveals that this form of support is not used very often, and companies do not rate it as being very efficient. However, surveys always include some subjectivity, while official trade statistics do not necessarily reflect accurate business flows between countries. We therefore focused on measuring the performance of export support activities and, in this framework, presented the ESP methodology.

The ESP methodology represents a platform for the evaluation of export support using different methodologies, where tangible data on the usability and responsiveness of the export support activities are defined 'on the spot'.

However, the ESP methodology is not without its limitations, which represent work for further research. The support activity most required — defined in Step 2 of the model — also varies over time, and so it would be helpful to carry out the survey every few years. In addition, the support activity most required may differ by country. Let us look at a hypothetical situation, where most companies from country 'A' would need support 'b' while expanding to country 'C'. It is most likely that the same companies from country 'A' could need support 'c' while expanding to country 'D'. However, in our test we focus on the export support activity most required, not taking any of the differences between foreign countries into account.

We also agree that there is much more to export support than just measuring the time taken to respond to a specific request from a 'typical company' and the quality of the information sent. However, by focusing on the two most relevant parameters regarding the support activity most required, we believe that ESP is captured 'on the spot' and, by doing so, we receive a clear picture of the average ESP. In this sense, we emphasise the word 'average', since we found out through the ESP methodology that even when the ESP results are negative, this does not necessarily mean that some commercial diplomats had not performed their job excellently.

Another limitation to the ESP methodology lies in the fact that it has thus far been tested in only one country (Slovenia), and at the present time we therefore do not have data for other countries to enable an international comparison of results. We intend to carry out the test once again in Slovenia in 2012, and then in Croatia and Serbia in 2013.

It is probably due to the global crisis that some governments have started prioritising export support measures and some have started questioning its output. The ESP methodology represents a contribution to this debate and to the literature published in the field of measuring export support activities and its justification.

We conclude by stating that governments should be able to count on the positive effects of export support (boosting exports, trade and, consequently, economic growth). However, the support measures have to work in practice. The ESP methodology can, in this sense, serve as an orientation for policymakers, since it clearly presents how the support measures are perceived in real life by a typical company requesting the support most required. In this framework, it can serve to help governments implement the changes and policy recommendations needed, and as a result expect better outputs for the support provided.

References

Bergeijk, P. A. G. (2009). *Economic diplomacy and the geography of international trade.* Cheltenham: Edward Elgar.

Bergeijk, P. A. G., de Groot, H. L. F., & Yakop, M. (2011). The economic effectiveness of diplomatic representation: An economic analysis of its contribution to bilateral trade. *The Hague Journal of Diplomacy, 6,* 101–120.

Carrière de la, G. C. (1998). *La diplomatie économique: Le diplomate et le marché.* Paris: Economica.

Coughlin, C. C., & Cartwright, P. A. (1987). An examination of state foreign export promotion and manufacturing exports. *Journal of Regional Science, 27*(3), 439–449.

Douglas, J. D. (1976). *Investigative social research.* Beverly Hills, CA: Sage.

Gencturk, E., & Kotabe, M. (2001). The effect of export assistance program usage on export performance: A contingency explanation. *Journal of International Marketing, 9*(2), 51–72.

Hausmann, R., & Rodrik, D. (2003). Economic development as self discovery. *Journal of Development Economics, 72*(2), 603–633.

Justinek, G. (2012, in print). Measuring export support performance — Case of Slovenia. *International Journal of Diplomacy and Economy, 1*(1).

Kedia, B., & Chhokar, J. (1986). An empirical investigation of export promotion programs. *Columbia Journal of World Business, 21*(4), 13–20.

Keeley, B., & Love, P. (2010). *From crisis to recovery: The causes, course and consequences of the great recession.* Paris: OECD Publishing.

Keesing, D., & Singer, A. (1991). *Assisting manufactured export through services: New methods and improved polices.* WB: Economic Development Institute.

Keesing, D. B. (1993). *The four successful exceptions: Official export promotion and support for export marketing in Korea, Hong Kong, Singapore and Taiwan.* Occasional Paper 2. UNDP/World Bank Trade Expansion Program, Washington, DC.

Naray, O. (2008). Commercial diplomacy: A conceptual overview. Conference paper. *7th world conference of TPOs,* The Hague, The Netherlands.

Rose, A. (2005). *The foreign service and foreign trade. Embassies as export promotion.* NBER Working Paper 11111, National Bureau of Economic Research, Cambridge.

Ruel, H., & Zuidema, L. (2012). *The effectiveness of commercial diplomacy. A survey among Dutch embassies and consulates.* Discussion Papers in Diplomacy, No. 123. Netherlands Institute of International Relations 'Clingendael', The Hague.

Seringhaus, F. R., & Botschen, G. (1991). Cross national comparison of export promotion services. The views of Canadian and Austrian Companies. *Journal of international Business studies, 22*(1), 115–133.

Tesfom, G., & Lutz, C. (2008). Evaluating the effectiveness of export support services in developing countries — A customer (user) perspective. *International Journal of Emerging Markets, 3*(4), 364–377.

Wilkinson, T. J., & Brouthers, L. E. (2006). Trade promotion and SME export performance. *International Business Review, 15*(3), 233–252.

Yannopopulos, P. (2010). Export assistance programs: Insight from Canadian SMEs. *International Review of Business Research Papers, 6*(5), 36–51.

Yakop, M., & Bergeijk, P. A. G. (2009). *The weight of economic and commercial diplomacy.* The Hague: Institute of Social Sciences.

Chapter 6

The Commercial Diplomat in Interaction with International Business: Results of an Empirical Study

Olivier Naray

Abstract

Government, business support organisations (BSOs), support services and client business firms constitute the key actors involved in the business–government interaction within commercial diplomacy. While businesses are interested in support in their international operations, commercial diplomats (CDs) work towards both objectives: supporting individual firms and promoting the home country's national economy in general. BSOs, public or private or mixed such as bilateral chambers of commerce, sector associations, investment promotion agencies and other self-help business organisations, complete the CD's offer, and are often referred to, and participate directly and indirectly in the home country's trade promotion effort.

The nature of the CD's service to beneficiaries is highly people based, and contains both a consistent amount of government instruction and CD's own personal judgment and initiative in promoting various sectors/sub-sectors and spotting business opportunities. The 'intermediary' function of the CD between the beneficiary business and its potential future business partner is important. The interaction may start on either side: the business firm may approach the CD or vice versa. To a large extent, export issues remain the most important enquiries from business to CD vs. other issues such as foreign direct investment, joint venture and debt issues.

From a business perspective the main advantages to use the CD's service are threefold. The CD appears to business firms as the central platform, the starting point to promote bilateral business. Second, CDs enjoy trust as an institution: they are

Commercial Diplomacy and International Business: A Conceptual and Empirical Exploration
Advanced Series in Management, 151–181
Copyright © 2012 Emerald Group Publishing Limited
ISSN: 1877-6361/doi:10.1108/S1877-6361(2012)0000009010

considered credible and neutral (credibility and neutrality). Last but not the least, CDs are found useful in helping out firms in their first steps in foreign markets (not necessarily first exporters but for the firms to which the host country market only is new). The transaction between CD and beneficiary business firm has a material price: some services such as market research are for fee and are often subcontracted. Others being part of a 'basic service' of diplomats are free of charge.

Keywords: Commercial diplomat; commercial diplomacy; trade promotion; business promotion; business–government relations; trade representation; trade representative; FDI promotion; business internationalisation

> My home government's instruction may be to write a report about the consequences of the financial crisis for the next year — how on earth do I know? The commercial diplomat is pressured by both government and business because he/she is measured by both: government checks on costs, and business clients evaluate the service via client surveys. (A commercial diplomat representing Canada)

Introduction

Commercial diplomats (CDs) are state representatives with diplomatic status conducting trade and business promotion activities between a home and a host country. Their work aims at encouraging business development through a series of roles CDs perform in various activity areas such as trade promotion, foreign direct investment (FDI), country image and intellectual property rights. The spectrum of actors ranges from (i) the high-policy level (head of state, prime minister, minister or a member of parliament) to (ii) ambassador and the lower level of specialised diplomatic envoy. It is the latter group of specialised professional CDs that remain our main concern.

The central question this chapter addresses: who are the main stakeholders in commercial diplomacy with focus on the CD and also how these interact in the context of international business.

The existing literature justifies CDs' activities by their usefulness in dealing with both business and governmental concerns. Government's aim in business promotion (including trade, investment and tourism) – although differing country by country – is ultimately to create jobs, increase tax revenue and economic growth (Kotabe & Czinkota, 1992). Government ultimately seeks country competitiveness by engaging in various business promotion programmes. On the other hand, business beneficiaries ultimately seek profitability; for them engaging in international operations constitutes a risk. Businesses are generally satisfied with commercial diplomacy service if they can thereby reduce the risk of entering a foreign market and obtain a service at a competitive price or for 'free', i.e. financed by tax revenue. This chapter will tackle the business perspective vis-à-vis CDs.

The *multi-stakeholder* element emerged as key in our research and demonstrates that commercial diplomacy cannot be reduced to a simple interaction/transaction with direct beneficiaries or as an advisory type of transaction only. Some of the relationships are better understood seeing them as networks:

> In network modes of resource allocation, transactions occur neither through discrete exchanges nor by administrative fiat, but through networks of individuals or organisations engaged in reciprocal, preferential, mutually supportive actions. The basic assumption of network relationship is that one party is dependent upon resources controlled by another and that there are gains to be had by the pooling of resources.

Traditional diplomats and generally government officials are sometimes not perceived as really effective or business-friendly enough by business managers needing support in international operations. The criticism that applies to CDs in particular goes from accusing them to service their private friends to the lack of effectiveness and efficiency and business understanding (Kostecki & Naray, 2007). While these criticisms may all be legitimate in single cases, we have observed in the last decade a constant evolution into the direction of business orientation to meet business needs in commercial diplomacy in our and others' empirical research (Kostecki & Naray, 2007; Ruël, De Boer, & Ten Haaf, 2011; Ruël & Zuidema, 2012).

Indeed, some companies working in specific areas so that the respondent (diplomat) is not able to provide useful information, lack of knowledge and understanding of the industry. That is why some companies are working primarily with their own networks and with local and bilateral chambers of commerce. We note differences in judgments by various concerned business people. This is also confirmed by Ruël et al.'s (2012) recent empirical study of Dutch commercial diplomacy in Malaysia. It is argued throughout the findings of Ruël and Zuidema (2012) that there is a relationship between 'the extent to which a client firm is prepared to do business internationally and the quality of commercial diplomacy'. Ruël and Zuidema (2012) show, furthermore, that a 'less favourable cognitive environment in a host country, for instance information availability, leads to an increase in the relevance of commercial diplomacy'. Lee (2004) and Lee and Hudson (2004) acknowledge that Anglo-Saxon CDs assist both small and middle enterprises (SMEs) and large multinational enterprises (LMNEs). For example, since the Foreign Service Organisation in the United Kingdom was reformed, the government–business partnerships have become a key organising principle in contemporary UK diplomacy to such an extent that public interest is increasingly conceptualised as a collective of private business interests (Lee, 2004).

Moreover, Sherman and Eliasson (2006) state that commercial diplomacy is undergoing a gradual process of privatisation. These institutional developments are generating a move towards private sector influence (Sherman & Eliasson, 2006) in the government's foreign policy. To impede this influence, CDs serving business beneficiaries (clients) should be ensured that their activities are carried out according to pre-determined guidelines and codes of integrity to reduce conflicts of interest.

In this chapter, we will complete existing research by adding the following:

- Key stakeholders in business–government interaction and what are their interests
- The nature of the service provided by the CD and the sequence
- Business firms' frequent demands on CDs

- Advantages and shortcomings of using CDs for the business firm
- Transaction between CD and business and its implications.

Methods

This chapter is based on in-depth interviews held with concerned business firms: 39 progressively semi-structured in-depth interviews were held with concerned business executives (export managers) and 5 semi-structured in-depth interviews with independent experts on commercial diplomacy. Data are also presented from a quantitative study via a survey questionnaire on 146 CDs from Switzerland, Denmark, Austria, Finland, Spain and Taiwan (Republic of China).

Semi-structured interviews were conducted (various versions of interview guides, increasingly focused) with concerned business firms, i.e. CEOs and export/investment managers. Export managers' experience with the CD's service with a broader perspective on the interaction between business and the CD's activities/roles and their value added quality of service was addressed. Moreover, a survey questionnaire (19 questions) on CDs in function at the time of the survey was conducted and some elements used for this research (but rather a reduced amount). The number of observations returned and processed was 146, i.e. filled-in survey questionnaires returned. The questionnaires were sent to 234 CDs (39 host locations multiplied by 6 home countries) and finally 146 answered questionnaires (about 62%) were returned, which provided the base of the further investigation as sample.

In the theory development approach from qualitative research that we used, patterns are expected to emerge from the empirical research (Eisenhardt, 1989; Eisenhardt, 2007). Data coding and codification were carried out according to the following categories:

- The nature of the activity performed by CDs
- The value added of commercial diplomacy in various national foreign services from the client's business perspective
- The CD's relationship with their clients and other members of the network.

Not all research interviews were led personally by the author. Research teams were constituted by students participating in the Masters (MSc) programme on international business development (in 2006 and 2009) as well as in the bachelor's (BSc) course on management (in 2007) at the University of Neuchatel (Switzerland). These three research teams were trained in the subject of commercial diplomacy and in interview techniques by the author and were supervised during the data collecting and drafting phase. The BSc and MSc papers being all empirical research brought insights and some relevant interview quotes in some cases.

Research methods and procedures followed recommended guidelines for theory/ concept development in exploratory qualitative research (Eisenhardt, 1989; Eisenhardt, 2007). Overall, we led 39 interviews with business executives, and 5 with independent experts, progressively structured (semi-structured) in-depth interviews following Kvale's (1996) recommendations in interviewing techniques.

Economic Environment

Global or national business firms in an internationally competitive environment seek survival, performance and reputation in global markets. Governments representing their national economies, particularly from developed nations, evolve in a context of endless economic competition including a general pressure on prices and national reputation (country image).

Business firms operating internationally are submitted to constraints coming from national and international market place, such as rules and regulations, pressure of global competition and trends. Commercial diplomacy responds basically in two ways: (1) promoting generally the business and economic interests of the *home country* (promotion of FDI, tourism, country image/made-in) and (2) delivering a particular service to a particular beneficiary *individual business firms*.

A series of concerns arise as typical to the bilateral trade promotion context in which businesses evolve as beneficiaries of CDs' support.

From the government's point of view, commercial diplomacy is part of a broader 'programme' in the implementation of various trade promotion policies in order to reach the governments' trade promotion objectives. Yet, the service dimension is clear for the government too: beneficiaries behave as clients and pressure increasingly for concrete results and solutions in exchange of taxes and fees. The home country's economy as well as the home government, public institutions participating in bilateral partnerships, benefit in terms of country image and reputation.

Box 1 sums up elements in (a) trade relationship as framework for trade between the countries and firms, (b) what could be at stake from the home country's economic characteristics and (c) the main demands of businesses on CDs.

The effect of positive image works both ways: internationally successful companies give the home country and its government 'credit' in reputation and image. In turn, a generally attractive country as a destination for FDIs, tourism, research and development for instance help home companies in their image building efforts and potential partnerships too. A CD representing Brazil points out:

> Now for example, we are working on the matter of Biodiesel, an energy matrix in technology and knowledge we have and can offer to other countries. Look at China, which has a huge market to explore for small airplanes or the chicken market for the Persian Gulf. Here in Switzerland, the focus is on leather or precious stones. In short, projects depend on the various situations and on the diversity of the various markets.

In developed countries the tendency that was confirmed by our qualitative research is that efficiency and effectiveness matter increasingly. 'The bang for the buck' approach dominates in most governments, which leads to increased professionalisation and professionalism; for instance, governments increasingly offer trainings to their CDs in order to better understand and be up to date with business issues of

---

Box 1.   Concerns in the bilateral trade promotion context

(a) Trade relationships
- Neighbouring, close and natural markets vs. market distance (cultural difference)
- Bilateral agreements on free trade, scientific cooperation, research and development etc., e.g. CH-EU
- Customs union, e.g. EU
- Regional trade agreements
- WTO rules and other relevant international agreements

(b) Home country's economic characteristics
- Abundance in raw materials
- Strategic goods and industries
- Natural resources (limited supply)
- Comparative advantages

(c) Main demand on CDs according to the weight and size of enterprises
- Small enterprise, sole trader, and medium enterprise: first steps in new markets, market information and networks for partnering
- Large multinational enterprise: intelligence and strategic information, lobbying in foreign countries (to influence foreign governments)

Source: Own empirical research.

---

supported sub-sectors (such as IT and life science). Box 2 illustrates the pressure on performance by government.

Stakeholders in Commercial Diplomacy

From the business firm (beneficiary) point of view, commercial diplomacy is a service; in other words, CDs provide a service for the company in exchange of both regularly paid taxes and service fees on occasion. These firms may be SMEs or large. The purpose might vary according to size:

- *SMEs, sole traders* use commercial diplomacy in their first steps of internationalisation with the given target market (host country for the CD): market information, list of potential buyers, distributors, importers or simply contacts for more specific information. The service offered to SMEs is more technical and diversified and less relationship based than with LMNEs (Ruël et al., 2012). The problem-solving function is very important too: should businesses encounter legal issues, non-payments in the foreign markets, then CDs may help to find a friendly solution.
- *Larger firms* use the diplomatic channel at a higher level starting with ambassadors up to the government's ministerial level, mostly to gain advocacy support in

---

Box 2. Illustration of pressure on performance by government

A retired CD from Ireland pointed out: 'Measurement of performance can be carried out by industry's feedback, number of clients, repetition of clients, revenue (if you charge)'.

An MFA official of Switzerland in charge of trade promotion and the foreign trade representation (CD) network says, 'For example, businesses often lack resources when they could be participating in trade fairs, which can cost up to CHF 10000. It would be the CHF2000 final helping hand that could make the difference and allow the company to participate. For example, a neighbouring country of us gives three times more money and four times more staff for promotion, with poor results in exports! Their campaign on the wine is simply not worth it: spending CHF25,000 for promoting sales of 500,000 is too much. Obviously, this means also "selling" the country, so we could put a Swiss label on each Swiss cheese'.

Our interviewees confirm a trend towards more result-based management, thus pro-activeness and initiative encouraged in many developed countries, as a Swiss MFA official expresses:

> The 'agreement on objectives' of each CD (embassies and hubs) measures effectiveness. Whether CDs achieve the agreed objectives or not, this would affect the wages, for example, if poor performance is no compensation for inflation or even reduced. It also applies KPIs (key performance indicators). The objectives are quantifiable and measurable. The ambassador, however, must sign these adaptations.

---

international tenders, access strategic resources, influence relevant policy-making and regulations in the host country (Kostecki, 2005; Kostecki & Naray, 2007). In the case of the LMNEs, the emphasis is also on public relations involving the host country government and private sector personalities. Support for LMNEs involved in negotiations with authorities or corporations from the host country are also an important form of support offered by commercial diplomacy services.

Figure 1 sums up the main stakeholders having demands on the commercial diplomat. These stakeholders correspond to the commercial diplomat's public.

Commercial diplomats work for their governments to fulfil economic and business objectives and constitute at the same time a government, public, commercial and diplomatic service. Government, business support organisations (BSOs), support services (banks, consultants, importer groups, etc.) and client business firms constitute the key actors involved with commercial diplomacy. While businesses are interested in support in their international operations, CDs work towards both supporting individual firms in their needs and promoting the home country's national economy in general. BSOs, public or private or mixed such as bilateral chambers of commerce, sector associations, investment promotion agencies and other self-help business organisations, complete the CD's offer, and are often referred to, and participate directly and indirectly in the home country's trade promotion effort.

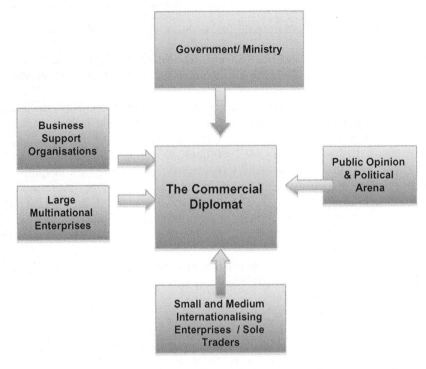

Figure 1: The publics of the commercial diplomat. *Source*: Own empirical research.

Commercial diplomats work for their governments to help realise economic and business objectives and constitutes at the same time a government, public, commercial and diplomatic service. A CD representing Canada shows the ambiguous pressure:

> Home government instruction may be [to] write a report about the financial crisis consequences of the next year -how on earth do I know? The commercial diplomat is pressured by both government and business because he/she is measured somehow by both: government checks on costs, and business clients evaluate the service via client surveys.

Further, a CD representing Canada notes:

> Other examples of enquiries include custom duties, regulatory issues, EU/non-EU differences, free trade agreements, access to research, immigration/emigration free movement of labour, permits, tax issues. [...] Government demands on commercial diplomats has reached some limits as our interviews confirm: 'The commercial diplomat has to be the master of everything. Our hiring skills are very bad. Requirements are too large and various, the pressure is huge from both government and business beneficiaries. Clients are in my terminology anyone who has a demand: businesses, governments, and other institutions'.

Instead of talking about 'clients' as anyone who has a demand or something at stake, we use the term 'stakeholder'. It becomes thus clear that tension might arise since various stakeholders have various and even contradictory demands.

It is thus clear that developed countries, in particular in countries of the European Union, commercial diplomacy remains under a certain pressure. Another CD representing Hungary recognised the trend towards professionalisation with business-like methods but does not agree with it. The kind of argument is perhaps representative of many CDs that were socialised in traditional diplomacy or as civil servants:

> One should separate CDs from the business promotion function. The latter is not compatible with the traditions of diplomacy. If business promotion is to be a public service, the concerned sectors should develop their networks. I wouldn't imagine government people doing that. Either the local chamber of commerce or sectoral business and professional associations. Moreover, the work process thinking such as at KPMG is not for me. They don't allow individual creative thinking; they prepare schemes of thinking i.e. uniform processes to be followed by everyone. That's OK for industrial production but not for intellectual work [...]. Nowadays CDs get instruction from the home government; if enquiries come from outside, he/she has to justify why he/she responded, and be careful with time management (time sheet pressure). Just like at Price Waterhouse ....

This does not make the work of the CD easier, obviously. We shall now see more in detail the nature of the service to beneficiaries. The following stakeholders are distinguished, their relationship with the CD; we explain their key interests in Table 1, which are

– *Government*: the executive and legislative, thus political, concerned with regulation and power

Table 1: Stakeholder characteristics and interests.

Stakeholder	CD's relationship with the stakeholder	Environment	Interest of the stakeholder
The government ministries: Ministry of Foreign Affairs/ Ministry of Trade, Economy or equivalent	Home country: internal, superior in hierarchy Vis-à-vis the host government authorities: official bilateral diplomatic relationship	Trade promotion policy-making — government	Growth, prosperity, national economy and government's political motives: the CD is an implementing agent
Actual business beneficiaries	External, client	International business — for profit	Entering new markets at possibly low price and low risk Business interests advocated and good business–government relationship

Table 1: (*Continued.*)

Stakeholder	CD's relationship with the stakeholder	Environment	Interest of the stakeholder
Potential business beneficiaries	External, potential client, network	International business — for profit	Developing mid-/long-term relationship with the CD Enter new markets at possibly low price and low risk Any support in internationalisation at better quality/price ratio than on the market Commercial diplomats are one option among others
Parallel business support organisations, chambers of commerce, sector associations trade promotion organisations and investment promotion agencies	Internal or external; affiliated organisation or part of network	Business support — non-profit	If government funded: justify their existence if funded by public money and implement their mandate If privately funded: satisfy their members' demands BSOs' activities complete commercial diplomats' activities; some overlap is possible

Source: Conclusions of semi-structured interviews with CDs and trade promotion experts.

- *Not-for-profit organisations*: BSOs and TPOs concerned with the implementation of trade promotion policies
- *For-profit organisations*: private business — business competition in global markets with national starting point.

Nature of the Service Offered by the Commercial Diplomat

In our empirical research, numerous exporting firms' managers, mainly export managers and CEOs, were interviewed and helped us understand the nature of the service that CDs provide. We provide characteristics on both the supply (CD) and demand (business firm) sides. Some tables and boxes were established to sum up the key characteristics found. By the same token, we illustrate the findings with interview

---

Box 3. Nature of the support for various beneficiaries

Beneficiary (recipient, client):	SMEs, LMNEs.
Nature of support for SME:	Non-equal partners: SME needs CD more than the opposite.
Content of service:	First steps in foreign markets, intelligence, sector, sub-sector information, contacts, networks. Business firms and public institutions involved in the bilateral relationship between home and host countries.
Nature of support for LMNE:	Mutual need for one another, equal partners.
	Strategic intelligence for large deals, procurement, business advocacy, equal partners.
Content of the service:	It is directed at intangible assets: knowledge, contacts, network and relationship building etc.

Source: Conclusions of semi-structured interviews with export managers and trade promotion experts.

---

quotes. As already mentioned, both small and large firms may need the CD. A trade promotion organisation (TPO) director dealing with CDs explains:

> The commercial attaché is not specialist but generalist. Our role is not to do everything, but to be a service platform and to give the right names and addresses of good lawyers, associations, representatives and specialists. On the private sector level this would be neither fundable nor profitable.

The nature of the support service for business provided by the CD is summed up in Box 3.

The Supply Side

We found that the nature of the supply side, i.e. the CD's service to beneficiaries, is highly people based and contains both a consistent amount of government instruction and CD's own personal judgment and initiative in promoting various sectors/sub-sectors and spotting business opportunities.

Nature of the offer. We see from our semi-structured interviews with export managers and trade promotion experts that the CD offers a platform, meaning that beneficiaries are often recommended to other agencies/companies for further help and support. The transaction goes two ways: the beneficiary goes to CD and CD goes to

Box 4.   Characteristics of the CD as provider

Public service:	Open to anyone funded by tax revenue, fees may be required for special and more labour and knowledge intensive services.
Delivery:	Might be both continuous and discrete transaction. Volatility in CD's delivery, performance and quality as perceived by IB. Importance of the individual, human factor.
Type of service:	Typical foreign market knowledge and facilitation. Some customisation possible, e.g. country reports, general economic information, 'how to do business in XYZ' country briefs.
Peculiarity of service:	CD's judgment is important in the interaction with the beneficiary since it expresses an official opinion. Tailor made service is the trend.

Source: Conclusions of semi-structured interviews with export managers and trade promotion experts.

beneficiary. It is an 'intermediary' type of service: beneficiary might benefit of CDs relative objectivity when receiving referral. The leading concern is that CDs have to draw the line in how far they answer the business enquiry or delegate to other agencies/private consultants.

The 'intermediary' function of the CD between the beneficiary business and its potential future business partner is important too. The interaction may start on either side: the business firm may approach the CD or vice versa. Box 4 sums up the characteristics of the CD as a provider.

The Demand Side

On the demand side, a key finding is the volatility of expectations, meaning that businesses expect either too little or too much from the CD. This might in turn stem from by the experienced volatility in service provided by the CD. The latter will be dealt with more in detail when addressing the question of fees. A company working in the telecommunications sector in Switzerland and another company working in the computer software sector illustrate:

'There is a large discrepancy in the ability to help businesses. CDs should be closer to SMEs and help develop the home country's economy'.

'The services that I paid private consultants for I could also pay CDs working closer with the target market; that dialogue is more simple. So we said why not!'

Table 2: Users' characteristics.

Kinds of users	Experience of foreign market	Own network in target market
1. *Regular*	Yes	Not necessarily
2. *Random*	Yes	Not necessarily
3. *Typical first-time user*	Should not be first-time exporter	No
4. *Potential*	Should not be first-time exporter	Yes or No

Source: Conclusions of semi-structured interviews with export managers and trade promotion experts.

Nature of the business firms' demand. We see from our semi-structured interviews with export managers and trade promotion experts that demands are regular and permanent. They are specific to the economic sector, sub-sector in which the firm operates, and the market as well as trade regulations. The service provided by the CD is highly people based, usually constituted by a senior CD and his/her staff team composed of consultants and trade assistants. Facilities have less importance than people. A *leading concern* is the high volatility in the CD's attitude, quality and engagement for the business firm.

Furthermore, based on our qualitative research with concerned businesses' export managers, we found out that users can be categorised. Table 2 shows a possible categorisation. Various cases need to be distinguished, whether a firm becomes a user or not or whether it has its own network in the *specific target market* and whether it has enough experience in international business — especially for inexperienced SMEs; one mistake abroad could be fatal as an interviewee ex Swiss diplomat pointed out. The interviewed trade promotion experts insisted that the very first time exporter should not use the CD, and if filtering policy were consistent these would not be handled anyway. The reason being that the very first exporter with no export experience should first address the competent BSOs in the home country and make sure it becomes export ready.

Sequence of the Interaction

In the organisation of commercial diplomacy, the service marketing function in the classical sense (Lovelock, 1991, Chapter 12) such as evaluating and selecting markets, service product characteristics, location, and communication to customers works in a relatively loose way. Since government objectives and priorities are set, i.e. the service beneficiaries are per definition national firms, and the national economy, the market is not as much studied and considered as in the case of a typical international service firm in private business sector.

The basic sequence of service delivery (see Lovelock, 1991) may be described in the three phases as follows:

1. *The business firms are to be made aware: "'Service organisation goes to the customer' or 'word of mouth'* (Lovelock, 1991)

Firms discover the services, networks and information they may access through a CD through the national TPO, a business association or chamber of commerce. To illustrate, an international firm in the telecommunications business says: 'We will use the service offered by TPO (at home) to gain a first impression. Thereafter and for a specific area, we will appeal to embassies and chambers of commerce involved'.

It is to be noted that the TPO headquarters, normally located in the business capital of the home country, is meant to support exporters in general, especially first time exporters. CDs come in at a second stage when the firm has chosen the host country as target market.

2. *Business firm from home or host country contacts the CD: 'Customers goes to service organisation' (Lovelock, 1991)*

Nowadays electronic communication facilitates the process of first contact. CDs posted abroad report directly to the responsible ministry and national TPO — if the CD is located outside the embassy he/she sometimes has a more or less close relationship with it. To illustrate, a company in the watch industry says:

> If faced with exporting and encountering payment problems, we may address diplomatic service. For exporting, the service is rather "technical". Obviously, if the company opts for a direct investment then policy aspects are involved including the understanding of the tax rates'.

3. *Interaction: 'One-stop Shop' or delegation to other BSO*

Collaboration takes place either through a transaction between the CD and the business firm alone or in coordination and even cooperation with other BSOs such as the binational (home–host) chamber of commerce; special services are often subcontracted to specialists such as specific market research, legal aspects, or even for public relations campaigns.

Advantages and Shortcomings of Using CDs from a Business Perspective

Advantages

International business firms (IB) address CDs on a regular basis and most various levels of IB such as sole traders, SMEs, and LMNEs. The main reasons for this imply both practical and symbolic ones. The specific reasons imply that business people trust the institution of commercial diplomacy and thus consider it as:

1. A central platform for international business to government relations
2. Neutrality and credibility

3. Support in the first steps to be made in foreign markets (good price/quality ratio).

1. *Central platform*

Commercial diplomats offer a centralised platform with location in the host country (from a CD perspective) or 'target market' (from a business perspective). The difference with other business support institutions (BSOs) is this actual and physical presence in the host country and thus the general and specific knowledge about and connectedness with it.

Centralisation carries the advantage to work with many companies at the same time — these being independent from another but might send similar enquiries to the CD. The CD may thus work with various 'portfolios' and carry out his/her mission for a group of companies at the same time. A TPO director in charge of the trade representation network argues in favour of a government-owned trade representation network in the world:

> A private service firm could not afford to supply market studies of the whole world! [...] Also in the long run we can gather the companies in clusters with linked products and mandate the CD to find new markets e.g. for micro-technical products, plastic.

The same Swiss TPO director follows:

> Some private firms are offering similar services, but to set up such a structure in the world (as the TPO) it is virtually impossible. A company cannot afford a market study of the world. So the role of the state, in the first phase is to dig, but then it must find a specialist.

International business firms that interact with CDs also tend to recognise that CDs constitutes a central platform from a bilateral standpoint. As a company points out:

> In fact, in almost all firms know CDs they know the basic organisation in Spain that is in charge i.e. ICEX is owned by the Ministry of Economy, it is an institute. So everyone knows them but I would still recommend them.

Specific knowledge may be available indirectly: CDs should possess an extensive address book with the relevant lawyers, experts, local authorities, politicians, etc. Being government's central diplomatic hub in the host country gives the advantage of centralisation and the resulting economies of scale, possibility of linking business with politics and dealing with government's strategic concerns in the area of business such as access to supplies of energy, strategic trade policy or technological leadership.

- *Access to decision-makers.* High-ranking diplomats tend to have better access to executive of large corporations, policy-makers, bureaucracies and elites in the host country. Increasingly frequent business missions and visits of politicians may improve access of CDs to decision-makers or provide greater value to 'door opening' aspects of their activities. Their diplomatic functions may be particularly important since access to business elite may be facilitated through political or cultural activities of diplomatic mission.

- *Diplomatic immunity* may also encourage CDs to take risks in collecting intelligence data since *legati iure gentium sancti sunt* (diplomats are untouchable under international law). As one of our respondents noted, the *ambassador may step in to increase access and credibility*. A former ambassador that embraced a business career argues firmly and clearly that in commercial diplomacy as well as in the private sector *contacts are everything*.

An Australian businessman says that 'certain investments would have never taken place without a close contact between our ambassador and a CEO of a major foreign company. A former ambassador argues that hierarchy may be very important. The trade representative (i.e. the commercial diplomat) is not always received, when alone, by managers of large corporations and the ambassador has to go along as well to gain access to top management'.

- *Access to markets.* CDs facilitate access to markets by providing relevant information and contacts in a relevant market for business and also by helping business becoming familiar with culturally distant markets. For instance, a Swedish business manager expresses that established companies need services by CDs particularly in new markets. Experience with the Swiss Business Hub (SBH) suggests that business support is perhaps less urgently needed in neighbouring countries than in major distant markets. Several European and US managers refer to cultural problems in China, Japan or other Asian countries and recognise that CD may facilitate interaction. "The US Commercial Service [...] aligns the [...] resources to developing markets that are of growing importance to future US business opportunities". It is meant to move CDs and their teams from developed markets such as France and Canada to developing (emerging) markets such as India and China. (US 'Transformational Commercial Diplomacy Initiative')

2. *Neutrality and credibility*

By neutrality we mean that firms are not discriminated or treated better or worse versus their competitors. A developed Western European trading nation's government ministry (confidential source) formulates the following in its guidelines for trade representations (diplomatic network) about competing companies both being from the home country:

> Two competing [...] companies may enlist the guidance of the missions at the same time for the same matter. In principle, it is not up to the missions to work selectively. The companies must be treated equally, given the same information and be introduced in the same manner. This does not however mean that an undesirable situation cannot arise in which the two companies are played off against each other.

Public or semi-public channels provide information and support too, such as bilateral chambers of commerce. Nevertheless, the role of certain bilateral chambers is not free of ambiguity. As noted by another CD representing a European country:

The chamber is usually a place where businesses meet in the foreign country to network with each other and to make deals and it is not clear why they should offer support to newcomers who are likely to become their competitors.

The issue of neutrality is important in intelligence, as the CD sponsored business information may be more reliable. Another CD from Portugal adds, 'We cannot know everything but we make an effort to provide credible information'. A CD from Brazil concludes, 'We also have a more secret side; we go beyond the information found in newspapers and statistics; we have relevant political and macro-economic information.

By credibility it is meant that diplomats generally enjoy good reputation, and are considered to be well informed about the home and host country's political and economic affairs. Both serving a government administration and carrying the diplomatic status provide additional weight when it comes to the provision of information, referral or any recommendation, and generally trust between home and host country business and government actors. The idea of credibility comes out also in various comments and judgments made with the interaction. A company producing cameras for the industry in Switzerland that paid for the service remembers:

[…] Commercial diplomats are really able to imagine and also to quickly understand our needs and perform well.

Interesting enough, firms recommend in general CDs to other firms independently from the quality of their own experience (trust in the institution), as the following business firm illustrates:

Very helpful, the foreign trade representation in Japan […] I recommend them rather in conversations with acquaintances or with people in the business who have the same interests.

3. Supporting the first steps in foreign markets

Commercial diplomat as government representative and diplomat is an important advantage, particularly for smaller or less internationally known firms, operating in new markets or in countries with strong government involvement in business sector. Examples include support in organising trade fairs and information needed to settle down in a new market. Moreover, diplomats also enjoy more credibility when making promises and commitments to foreign investors than private actors. They also have greater weight when dealing with public administration, state-owned enterprises and government procurement agencies. The *market-entry function* of CD is particularly critical for SMEs that are newcomers to a particular region.

A developed Western European trading nation's government ministry (confidential source) formulates the following in its guidelines for trade representations (diplomatic network) saying that CDs:

[…] may provide assistance when a company plans on setting up activities in a specific market. They may, for instance, introduce the company to authorities in the host country and other businesses. They may also give tips and advice about potential business partners (e.g. concerning their reputation). Missions will want to brainstorm with the company on how to best develop its activities.

A CD from an Eastern European country located in Switzerland says that Swiss businesses also need to be reassured that their information, in particular financial figures, is handled and labelled 'confidential', otherwise they do not give relevant information. The advantages of various experiences of CD in IB are illustrated with further interview quotes in Table 3.

Figure 2 sums up the elements that the business firm considers before addressing the target market abroad. As explained, the CD is one counterpart feeding the decision-making process in international operations of the firm along with chambers of commerce, other BSOs, the firm's own subsidiaries if any and other networks. The double arrow shows that the firm gathers the information and contacts within its own

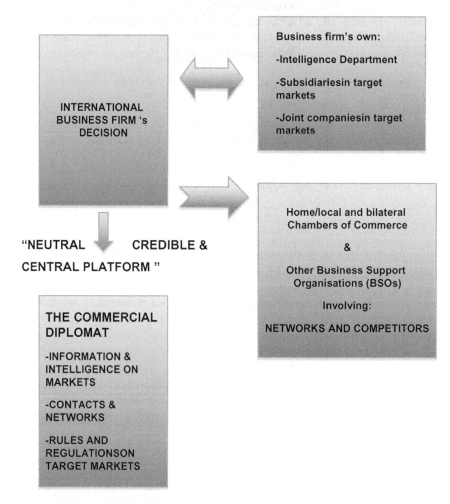

Figure 2: The advantages of using CDs: A business perspective.

Table 3: Leading quotes on advantages to use the CD from a business perspective.

Advantages from a business perspective	Leading quotes by export managers
Central platform for bilateral business	'Well, I think that SMEs would not settle down in a country that is unfamiliar, etc. ...The SME would do if it already has an address of someone who knows the country'. Company in the food sector, chocolate — country of origin: Belgium — Service for Free. 'It is certain that the experience of these people on the ground (CDs) is non-negligible and it saves a lot of time. [...] At first I did not think the proposed service could be so important. [...] At first I started business negotiations without help, but soon my staff advised to contact CDs for help. Since I can't do without'.
Neutrality and credibility	'For us, it's good to have contact with commercial diplomats in Switzerland because they know the issues'. Company in the Retail Trade and Food Country of origin: Switzerland, 'We made positive experiences with their know-how, consultations, collaboration, best. [...] In any case, we are very satisfied, everything is great'.
Supporting first steps in foreign markets	'The (collaboration) was very helpful. We can recommend it for everyone who enters a new foreign market'. 'I would recommend without a doubt. As a source of information about a country is the first thing we have. It's pretty basic, but enough to make the first steps ...'. 'So I have told some people that we addressed some countries and with this service, we have advanced more quickly than if we had done it alone'.

Source: Empirical in-depth interview research with concerned business firms.

system, whereas the simple arrows mean that the firm addresses external organisations such as various BSOs and the CD.

Shortcomings

Many criticisms are made especially for diplomats and their lack of practice and a 'too general' point of view. Some firms do little or no use of CDs and work with their personal networks; others use 'the service' mainly when exploring new markets, or for

Table 4: Shortcomings related to the quality of information: quotes by export managers.

Leading concern related to quality of information	Leading interview quote by export managers
Not very quick	1. 'I would say that CDs are very friendly, ready to help you, who have many contacts, but they lack pragmatism in relation to SMEs. [...] They are not really concrete, while we as SMEs need something very concrete, very quickly'.
Double checking is needed	2. Company in surgical appliances; country of origin: Switzerland: 'Commercial attachés are not specialised; we asked for lists of companies and we had to check them, then we realized that some do not even working in our sector. Double-checking everything gave us even more work'.
Does not meet the criteria requested	3. Company in the automotive sector; country of origin: Spain; service: free: The information we receive from CDs might be useful, still, the quality of contacts, CDs have given us, have not met our critieria.
Lack of updating	4. 'In some cases, lack of updating. [...] It's normal, I would recommend them. Everyone recommends them'.
Lack of commitment for business success	5. 'It helped me [...]. Subsequently, nobody helped us [...].' Yes, I would recommend, because there's still support. 'The attachés have not bothered to see whether we had business opportunities thereafter'.
Business firm has own department/ network for international intelligence	6. Businessman working for a company (consortium) in Moldova: 'Generally speaking, our company prefers to have a department that deals with international issues to use services of commercial diplomats. Our employees are more competent and professional in business techniques. Even with double taxation

Table 4: (*Continued.*)

Leading concern related to quality of information	Leading interview quote by export managers
	information we can find it easily at the finance ministry and [there] is no need to contact commercial diplomats'.
	7. Business firm in the metal industry: 'If our firm establishes in a new country, we do not use the diplomatic service, but rather by knowledge networks (other known companies based in the same country) to learn more about the political-economic conditions'.
	8. Swiss watch-making company: 'We did a lot of things internally. Precisely, we have the chance to build on our 28 subsidiaries within people who are employed by us. In other countries, there are people who have knowledge, significant expertise in their country, their market and also give us the valuable business information: our agents and our subsidiaries are a major source of information and that we see regularly'.
IB uses private consultant to follow up the changes in the business conditions or does not do it	9. Company; country of origin: Belgium: 'For me there is no follow up. If they do this work and then on the other hand nobody does anything to see later, it is no use they do this work like before. [...]'

exports. Table 4 presents the observed shortcomings relating to the quality of information received from CDs and alternative action.

Interviewed firms have told us about the following problem: as a company, they do not know what CDs can bring, what the company can expect from them and how to contact 'them'. This is not a lack of willingness to cooperate, but rather a misunderstanding of the services offered by commercial diplomacy and TPOs (Box 5).

Table 5 sums up the observed shortcomings from a business standpoint and presents alternative action. Ambiguous is that the general trust in some credibility and neutrality even pushes many international business managers to recommend CDs and

Box 5. Shortcomings related to communication (publicity and advertising): quotes by concerned managers

- 10: Swiss surgical equipment company: "We don't know much about them (CDs) and we do not know if we can call them for certain activities. [...] It was actually not me who called on him it was he who came to me, I had never worked with them before.
- 11: "At the beginning when we started we wanted to know what the CDs have done before with other companies and ask for recommendations. And then we asked them if they are satisfied with the CDs. We move faster than if we had done it alone."
- 12: Swiss surgical equipment company: "I have not worked with the commercial attachés out of ignorance I suppose. I work with the Chamber of Commerce."
- 13: "I rather think that commercial attachés should be marketing themselves (instead of being recommended)."

praise them even if their own experience was not good — in particular meant the service free of charge.

Price of the Transaction between the Commercial Diplomat and the Beneficiary

The transaction between IB and the CD varies in nature. Simple interactions where only a discussion, a referral or basic economic information about the host country is at stake, no fees are asked generally. More specific and knowledge-based services, however, have a price; sometimes the given research or market study is even subcontracted by the CD to TPOs or other relatively low-price consultants. Borer-Fielding (2003) argues that services should be for free since companies already pay corporate tax and people pay taxes on an individual level too and that otherwise some potential businesses not being able to afford the fees would be *de facto* discriminated.

The main arguments put forward to a large extent by IB in favour of fees are that by paying one can expect and ask for higher quality and precision. The services free of charge carry the advantage of being accessible to all and constitute a good basis to start with when dealing with a foreign market.

Even though no one really questions that both types of services are needed because they are often different in nature, the embassy/trade representation charges for *consultancy services* that requires specific knowledge required such as market research for a particular product, while the *facilitation of contacts* and recommendations take place for free. Our research led with concerned export managers from various

Table 5: Shortcomings and alternatives from the business firm standpoint.

Aspects experienced as shortcomings from Business perspective
A. Shortcomings related to the quality of information

- Lack of pragmatism
- Not concrete
- Not very quick (See quote 1 in Table 4)
- Not specialized
- Double-checking is needed (see quote 2 in Table 4)
- Does not meet the criteria requested (see quote 3 in Table 4)
- Lack of updating (see quote 4 in Table 4)
- Lack of commitment for business success (see quote 5 in Table 4)

Alternatives for the firm
- Business firm has own department/network for international intelligence (see quotes 6, 7 and 8 in Table 4)
- IB uses private consultant to follow up the changes in the business conditions or does not do it (see quote 9 in Table 4)

B. Shortcomings related to communication (publicity and advertising) on the support offered by CD

- Lack of knowledge on the support offered by CD as a possibility at all (see quote 10)
- Lack of knowledge on the types of support (see quote 11)

Alternatives for the business firm
- IB learns about commercial diplomacy (see quote 12)
- IB calls for more effective information on this activity from official bodies (see quote 13)

Source: Own empirical research.

Table 6: Descriptive statistics.

	N	Mean	Standard deviation
Filtering by firm's willingness to pay	146	.27	.44
N valid (listwise)	146		

European countries and CDs on an international level show that the fee issue is by far not unanimously interpreted among stakeholders.

As mentioned under various filtering criteria in the quantitative evidence, in our survey *willingness to pay* is relatively rarely applied as a filtering criterion by CDs — about 26% of cases out of the 146 surveyed CDs. The data reflect the extent to which CDs filter business firms per suggested criteria (ordinal variables, originally yes/no answers converted into '1' for yes and '0' for no). Table 6 below shows the population size, mean and standard deviation.

Services Free of Charge

Our research interviews with concerned companies show that there are those who think that fees should not be charged because 'it would be beneficial for SMEs with small budgets' or those who tell us that government service should not be paying because 'it is already financed by taxes'. And finally there are the interviewees who are of the opinion that the services not only benefit the company but the entire country in general and therefore the costs should not be borne solely by companies. When the service is for free, companies are quite satisfied, rather they regard the service as 'better than nothing'. They consider it a good tool to make first steps into foreign markets. Companies often said, 'We are happy with what they give us'. Still, in most cases *service for fees* and *for free* co-exist. Box 6 contains cases where services are provided free of charge.

Services with Fee

The rationale behind asking for and paying fees lies in the question of expectations in value and quality of the service received by IB users. For particular services such as

---

Box 6.   Services free of charge

A CD representing Brazil points out: 'It is up to us to promote efficient trade relations between countries, respecting their different interests. As for prices, there isn't a list, we do not sell services; we represent government action whose responsibility is to promote Brazilian interests'.

A CD representing Moldova illustrates: 'All the services are free because we are civil servants. Sometimes investors ask us what Moldovan wine is better "Milestii Mici" or "Cricova" or "Purcari" and we answer that our opinion is subjective because we are not connoisseurs of wines'.

Box 7.   Services with fee

Half of our sample of companies in our in-depth research interviews (qualitative) believes that to pay is not a bad idea because they can then expect a service, which is 'more reliable', 'more efficient' and 'better monitored'. Companies can then 'require more of them'. Even in countries where for the moment the service is free, we are told that 'it does not matter paying more if we could expect more of the service provided by commercial attachés'.

market research and in-depth consultancy and advisory, many concerned export managers/CEOs declare that they are ready to pay and CDs through their governments do not hesitate to charge. Box 7 contains explanations by companies on services with fee.

Average fees vary according to countries' trade promotion policies and lie between 100 and 150 euro per hour and move up to 450 euro per half a day. Also, many services are sub-contacted if an embassy does not have the resources to carry them

Table 7: Summary of favourable and unfavourable aspects of service fees.

	Favourable aspects	**Unfavourable aspects**
Service for fees	1. • More reliable service • Better follow up • Can expect more	2. • Price might be prohibitive for some SMEs • Commercial diplomacy is already financed by taxes — public money
Service free of charge	3. • Good basic service • Any firm can access • Part of country image	4. • May be low quality • Cannot expect high quality

Source: In-depth interviews with 25 export managers and commercial diplomats.

Box 8. Quotes illustrating arguments for and against fees relating to Table 7

1. Company in the food sector; country: Spain; service: free
   'If they want to pay, they do. [...] Yes, but then they must produce results. [...] By paying, I think they will be more reliable, more efficient',
2. CD representing Canada: 'Funding and service fees. The UK for instance has an absolute cost-recovering system, where every single step has to be justified. It is a big mistake. Moreover, they charge companies. As a diplomat one should not charge for services, except if I need to hire someone — which I do very rarely — for a task, e.g. market research'.
3. Company; country of origin: Belgium; service: free
   'If I had to pay there would be a better track. But if it is for free, it allows companies who can't afford this type of service otherwise'.
4. Company in the food sector; country of origin: Switzerland; service: with fee.
   'I also understand that one must pay for the service because what is for free is worth nothing at all. There are many risks, for example, that the services available are not useful' anyway.

out, and the market determines the fee level. Most interviewed businesses seemed satisfied with services for fees and would continue paying and even recommend the service.

We met with very opposite opinions about fees of commercial attachés, but eventually the vast majority of companies believe that by paying to qualify for this service you will obtain better performance. In some countries, the image of a free service stands for work of poor quality and unreliability. In fact billing the service makes many businesses more demanding.

Table 7 sums up the favourable and unfavourable aspects of a service for and without fees.

Box 8 contains some interview quotes illustrating the arguments for and against including both business and CD perspectives.

Business Firms' Frequent Issues

Content of Business Enquiries

Our survey allowed us to present some quantitative data, namely what type of enquiries CDs receive from business firms. Of course, prudence is needed when interpreting the data, since the questions were not detailed about firms' issues. Table 8

Table 8: The content and frequency of business enquiries (issues).

Firm's issue	N	Mean	Standard deviation
Exports	145	5.81	1.6
Regulatory	139	3.6	1.76
Tax	145	3.37	1.71
Subsidiary	145	3.36	1.51
Human resources	144	3.17	1.53
Production	143	3.14	1.52
Outward investment	145	3.01	1.49
Authorities	1	3.0	
Debt	1	3.0	
Joint venture	141	2.63	1.34
Research and development	143	2.52	1.31
Other	10	4.5	2.59

Source: Quantitative research based on survey questionnaire.
Remark: On the scale 1 means weak interest or low frequency; 7 means vivid interest or high frequency .It can be observed that according to the mean values (MV) three groups can be separated: (a) MV > 4.5; (b) 3 < MV < 3.6; (c) MV < 3.
Exports issues and regulatory issues dominate the list. 'Other issues' have a high mean but $N = 10$, so it is a very small sample compared to the others. Further research might find out about the 'other' element, which seems important on the scale and could not be captured precisely.

presents the answers by CDs to the question asked on the content and frequency of enquiries on a scale from 1 to 7 (whole numbers). Table 8 presents the content and frequency of business enquiries CDs receive.

So 'export issues' are by far the most frequent enquiries that CDs receive and tackle.

At this stage, we provide an analysis with descriptive statistics according to the CD's home and host countries (where he/she is located).

We sum up the following trends:

- 'Exports' dominate by far for CDs from all home countries that have median above 5.
- The other business enquiries such as subsidiary issues, joint venture, production, R&D, and even regulatory issues (surprising!) do not reach very convincing results on the scale.
- Host location where CDs are located does not seem to influence the content of business enquiries.

It is to be examined in further research whether the outward investment issue is more frequent in emerging/developing host countries such as Poland, Hungary, Belgium and Vietnam, while the research and development issues are stronger in developed host countries such as France, Canada, Hungary and Sweden.

Filtering and Priorities

The data reflect the extent to which CDs filter business firms per suggested criteria (ordinal variables, originally yes/no answers converted into '1' for yes and '0' for no).

'Filtering by nationality' is clearly the dominant criterion. Not even the half of 'yes' answers is reached by 'filtering by commitment to home country's economy' as second

Table 9: Prioritisation of business firms' enquiries per criteria.

Priorities when using filtering by	N	Mean	Standard deviation
Nationality	146	.73	.45
Commitment to home country's economy	146	.39	.49
Degree of internationalisation	146	.29	.45
Firm's willingness to pay	146	.27	.44
Firm's size	145	.26	.44
Technology orientation	146	.19	.40
Economic sector	146	.08	.28
Time factor	145	.08	.27
Other criteria	146	.08	.26
Membership	145	.0	.14
N valid (listwise)	144		

Source: Questionnaire survey on commercial diplomats (quantitative analysis).

Box 9. General and particular comments on findings on application of filtering

- Filtering by nationality seems to be an important criterion compared to all others.
- Many other criteria such as technology orientation, commitment to home country's economy, firm's size, degree of internationalisation, economic sector and willingness to pay are not applied by a majority of CDs, quite clearly.
- The location of host country/markets does not influence much the prioritisation of enquiries per criteria, meaning there is no striking difference with the analysis according to the home country.
- The service appears to be accessible to any business in that CDs do not filter by 'firms' willingness to pay' except in China where a majority of CDs does, and half/half in India, Japan, Sweden and the United States: 'large market' effect might be further tested perhaps.
- No majority filters by economic sector.

---

in the list. This shows that CDs work in relatively 'mercantile' mind-set. Criteria such as technology orientation, commitment to home country's economy, firm's size, degree of internationalisation, economic sector, and willingness to pay are not applied by a majority of CDs (Table 9).

There are only some exceptions, which may be worthwhile studying further: a slight majority of Denmark's CDs do filter degree of internationalisation and willingness to pay. Further, CDs from Switzerland and Taiwan show only about half/half in terms of filtering per commitment to home *country's economy*. Box 9 presents general and particular comments on what was found regarding application of filtering.

It is worthwhile noting that some of this is in contradiction with some in-depth interviewees that were insisting on the importance of government instruction and sector policy priorities: it does not seem to be implemented by the large majority of CDs of all surveyed home countries. We did not find a considerable number of CDs that filter by economic sector (nor any important variance according to host country), which might contradict what we heard in our in-depth research interviews many times that the government's trade promotion priorities and instructions had a great influence on the filtering.

Discussion and Conclusion

Wrap up

We have seen that the nature of the CD's service to beneficiaries is highly people based, and contains both a consistent amount of government instruction and CD's own personal judgment and initiative in promoting various sectors/sub-sectors and spotting business opportunities. The 'intermediary' function of the CD between the beneficiary business and its potential future business partner is important. The interaction may start on either side: the business firm may approach the CD or vice versa. To a large extent, export issues remain the most important enquiries from business to CD vs. other issues such as FDI, joint venture and debt issues. From a business perspective the main advantages to use the CD's service are threefold. The CD appears to business firms as the central platform, the starting point to promote bilateral business. Second, CDs enjoy trust as an institution: they are considered credible and neutral (credibility and neutrality). Last but not the least, CDs are found useful in helping out firms in their first steps in foreign markets (not necessarily first exporters but for the firms to which the host country market only is new). The transaction between CD and beneficiary business firm has a material price: some services such as market research are for fee and are often subcontracted. Others being part of a 'basic service' relating to general information and 'how to do business in (whatever country)' briefs in the host country remain 'free of charge', meaning they are funded from national tax revenue. Business beneficiaries seem to appreciate both, yet they expect higher quality as in the private sector once they pay for the service and seem more demanding.

Discussion: Define and Clarify the Target Beneficiary

First, regarding filtering: the target group should be clearly defined, which our commercial diplomacy intends to serve. Does this include non-home-country-based firms and to what extent is our commercial diplomacy to support them? We found a 'mercantile' tendency in that the 'nationality of the firm' was the filtering criterion most applied. Overall the survey showed that criteria such as technology orientation, commitment to home country's economy, firm's size, degree of internationalisation, economic sector and willingness to pay are not applied by a majority surveyed CDs. As already noted, we found a contradiction with our in-depth CD interviewees (as opposed to the survey): they were insisting on the importance of filtering by sector, and other priorities; however, most of the surveyed CDs do not seem to implement the alleged filtering. There are only some exceptions, which may be worthwhile studying further: a slight majority of Denmark's CDs do filter by degree of internationalisation and by willingness to pay. This seems in line with hands-on attitude and high CD initiative of Danish CDs. The second point is whether filtering at HQ level (in the home country capital) is enough (assumed it is done properly) or should the CD further filter.

Discussion: Service Content and Price/Quality

Our research has found that export promotion and export development remain the main concern of businesses when addressing the CD. Other issues such as regulation, tax, production and HR received an average score clearly below 'export issues', thereby clearly indicating the dominant issue in business enquiries. Though the question was not further detailed, these clear responses give an indication where to specialise or at least expect demands.

The question of charging fees is a fundamental issue in relation to the concept of 'public service', diplomacy and their fundamental role in business support. A 'purist' approach would be to strictly refer to the Vienna convention and not mix diplomacy with services that cost directly to the beneficiary and generally stay away from the business transaction. This option, in reality however, is only a formality: other government-sponsored BSOs (chambers of commerce for instance) offer the needed service without the 'diplomatic sponsor' for fees that concerned businesses can afford, meaning that they are below regular consultancy market prices. If fees are charged in most cases it is for various reasons: first, the trade representation office abroad is often also managed as a decentralised organisational unit that works to remain efficient and financially sustainable in order to stay in business; second, extra costs are involved when firms ask for detailed advice involving for instance market research or a feasibility study, therefore CDs charge a fee. Consequently, the managerial decision on service is not about whether or not to charge but rather concerns a clear delineation and limitation of the service to be provided by the CD and on the division of labour among BSOs.

Concerning the shortcomings on service quality mentioned by concerned businesses such as 'lack of pragmatism', 'inaccurate information' or not enough up-to-date information or even a too general (probably too macro-economic) perspective should give us to think. In light of our aggregate findings, the following suggestions can be made: general improvements in terms of accuracy of information, commitment to help businesses, updated information and timeliness of responses are to be undertaken in any case and should be integrated, if not yet, into a basic quality control system. Regarding the content, neither all shortcomings can be nor should be addressed. It was said more than once that the CD cannot become a specialist in various sub-sectors — but indeed trained to follow up on evolutions and trends — and should be used to refer to a database or even to a specialist that would be able to tackle the issue. The CD is not meant to substitute of any specialised consultancy to serve business firms that do not seem to obtain or afford advice and answers elsewhere for whatever reason. The idea of 'central platform for bilateral business' is indeed about referring to specialists when and if needed. This is where good communication and publicity on scope and limits of commercial diplomacy comes in.

The question of advertising or at least making the CD well known to target beneficiaries came up as well as part of the interaction between government and business. Once government invests considerable amount of funds in opening and maintaining trade representation offices abroad it would make sense to inform potential key targets, once defined who these are, as suggested above. This does not prevent any business firm to use the service as an ordinary taxpayer also. Information campaigning may take place through the home country's BSOs where exporters and other internationalised firms gather.

Conclusion

Our research demonstrated that too often almost 'everything' is expected from the CD (by both government and business) at the same time without specifying the intensity. In concrete terms this means continuously maintaining an overview of business needs, becoming quickly familiar with a given complex sector (such as IT or biotech), providing the right networks and connections, and also knowing well enough local regulations, institutions, evolution of the economy and reporting about them, looking for potentially new business areas, attracting investments and promoting positive corporate and country image, etc. One could fairly raise the question whether all these functions have to be included in one person's portfolio that often has limited resources. An important question is to what extent CDs should focus on a reduced number of roles, activity areas and sectors and to what extent remain broad in areas covered.

References

Borer-Fielding, T. (2003). *Public Affairs: Bekenntnisse eines Diplomaten*. München: Econ 20.

Eisenhardt, K. (1989). Building theories from case study research. *Academy of Management Review, 14*, 532–550.

Eisenhardt, K. (2007). Theory building from cases: Opportunities and challenges. *Academy of Management Journal, 50*(1), 25–32.

Knights, D., & Willmot, H. (2007). Organization, structure and design. In D. Knights & H. Willmot (Eds.), *Introducing organisational behaviour and management* (pp. 194–255). Bath, UK: Thomson Learning.

Kostecki, M. (2005). *Business advocacy in the global trading system: How business organizations may shape trade policy* (pp. xiv–180). Geneva: ITC.

Kostecki, M., & Naray, O. (2007). *Commercial diplomacy and international business*. Clingendael Discussion Paper in Diplomacy. Clingendael Institute, The Hague. Retrieved from http://www.clingendael.nl/publications/2007/20070400_cdsp_diplomacy_kostecki_naray.pdf

Kotabe, M., & Czinkota, M. R. (1992). State government promotion of manufacturing exports: A gap analysis. *Journal of International Business Studies, 23*, 637–658.

Kvale, S. (1996). *Interviews: An introduction to qualitative research interviewing*. London: Sage.

Lee, D. (2004). The growing influence of business in U.K. diplomacy. *International Studies Perspective, 5*, 50–54.

Lee, D., & Hudson, D. (2004). The old and new significance of political economy in diplomacy. *Review of International Studies, 30*, 323–360.

Lovelock, C. H. (1991). *Services marketing text, cases and reading*. London: Prentice-Hall.

Sherman, R., & Eliasson, J. (2006). Trade disputes and non-state actors: New institutional arrangements and the privatization of commercial diplomacy. *The World Economy, 29*(4), 473–489.

Ruël, H. J. M., De Boer, S., & Ten Haaf, W. (2011). Commercial diplomacy in practice: Experiences of international business executives and representatives. *Proceedings 1st REDETE Conference on economic Development and Entrepreneurship in Transition Economies* (pp. 537–546), Banja Luka Bosnia-Herzegovina, October 27–29, 2011.

Ruël, H. J. M., & Zuidema, L. (2012). *The effectiveness of commercial diplomacy: A survey conducted among embassies*. Clingendael Discussion Paper Series. The Netherlands Institute of International Relations Clingendael, The Hague, the Netherlands.

Chapter 7

Competitors or Collaborators: A Comparison of Commercial Diplomacy Policies and Practices of EU Member States

Annette Stadman and Huub Ruël

Abstract

Commercial diplomacy within the EU is currently a matter for the individual EU member states (MS). This results in different policies and practices. But to what extent do they really differ? This chapter presents the results of a comparative study on EU MS commercial diplomacy policies and practices. The policy goals and practices of all 27 MS were assessed via document analysis and interviews with commercial diplomats. The findings show considerable differences in terms of the responsible ministry, the policy focus, the network of foreign posts and the work performed at the foreign post. However, countries that entered the EU first seem to have similar commercial diplomacy *policy* and *practices* characteristics, as do the countries that entered the EU after 2003. Furthermore, the results of statistical tests show that countries that entered first are similar in size, wealth, share of EU trade, number of embassies inside the EU, number of employees at the foreign post and the activism of the foreign post. These similarities apply as well for the countries that entered the EU after 2003. Overall, this study concludes that home country characteristics (size, culture, government), host country characteristics (institutions, culture, regime) and the relationship between a home country and a host country affect the commercial diplomacy policies and practices.

Keywords: Commercial diplomacy; diplomacy; EU; foreign post; comparative study

Commercial Diplomacy and International Business: A Conceptual and Empirical Exploration
Advanced Series in Management, 183–225
ISSN: 1877-6361/doi:10.1108/S1877-6361(2012)0000009011

Introduction

Commercial diplomacy is about how governments and diplomats promote and support international economic activities of and for home country companies (Naray, 2011; Ruel & Visser, 2012; Ruel & Zuidema, 2012). Commercial diplomacy is different for each country in the world because it depends on the political structure of a country, its regulations and government policies. This creates many different styles and approaches to commercial diplomacy around the world (Kostecki & Naray, 2007). In Europe, the EU makes rules and regulations about economic affairs that its MS have to implement (Chalmers, Hadjiemmanuil, Monti, & Tomkins, 2006; Nugent, 2006). The policy decisions of the EU affect the MS' government policies on commercial diplomacy. One of the most important policy decisions is the creation of a single European market with no trade barriers and free movement of goods and services to stimulate trade and economic affairs within the EU (Chalmers et al., 2006; Moravcsik, 1991; Nugent, 2006). The policy decisions of the EU and the internal market change the commercial diplomacy policies and practices of each MS. There are mutual relations among the MS, and some bilateral diplomacy has been taken over by the EU (Keukeleire, 2003). The fact that there are no trade barriers and that economic affairs have been mostly aligned has made some of the export tasks of embassies within the EU unnecessary (Kostecki & Naray, 2007; Naray, 2008). This means that MS should re-order their embassies within the EU to align them with the Council and Commission decisions concerning economic affairs (Bátora & Hocking, 2008). EU MS exercise different commercial diplomacy policies and practices when operating within the EU and outside the EU.

It is unclear whether the commercial diplomacy policies and practices of the MS will harmonise within the EU. The EU MS have to align their policies and practices to the rules and regulations of the internal market, but this does not directly affect commercial diplomacy. Kostecki and Naray (2007), Naray (2008), and Bátora and Hocking (2008) acknowledge that within the EU there are still differences between the commercial diplomacy policies and practices of the EU MS. Bratberg (2007) gives an example of four EU MS and shows that they have different commercial diplomacy policies and practices. This comparison is not that extensive, however. There is currently no research and knowledge about how exactly all the EU MS differ from each other or what they have in common in terms of their commercial diplomacy policies and practices within the EU. This research aims to identify and compare the differences and similarities between the commercial diplomacy policies and practices of the EU MS and to uncover how these differences and similarities can be explained.

This chapter continues with a literature review about commercial diplomacy. Its definitions and the factors that influence commercial diplomacy are highlighted. Then the research methodology is explained. In the findings the commercial diplomacy factors of the MS are compared. We conclude with a discussion about the results, the limitations of the research and the possible options for further research.

Diplomacy

Diplomacy, in the broad sense, is an instrument for foreign policy to manage external relations. It involves communication, information-sharing and negotiations between states. It contains rules, regulations and procedures about the interaction and activities of diplomats of different countries who work in foreign posts or other organisations (Bátora & Hocking, 2008; Baylis & Smith, 2005; Kostecki & Naray, 2007; Lee & Hudson, 2004). There are different types of diplomacy. In this research the focus is on commercial diplomacy.

Commercial Diplomacy

The literature has different definitions of commercial diplomacy, and there is no agreement about its extent. In general, commercial diplomacy focuses on the business community (Kostecki & Naray, 2007). It is about the 'promotion of inward and outward investment and exports in trade' (Berridge & James, 2003, p. 42; Lee, 2004, p. 51; Saner & Yu, 2003, p. 13). A detailed definition of commercial diplomacy was given by Naray (2008) and extended by Ruel and Visser (2012): 'commercial diplomacy is an activity conducted by state representatives which is aimed at generating commercial gain in the form of trade and inward and outward investment for the home country by means of business and entrepreneurship promotion and facilitation activities in the host country based on supplying information about export and investment opportunities, keeping contact with key actors and maintaining networks in relevant areas' (Ruel & Visser, 2012, p. 2). This definition indicates that commercial diplomacy embraces the work of diplomats in embassies or foreign posts who support home country business in host countries and develop international business ventures (Berridge, 2010; Kostecki & Naray, 2007; Ruel & Visser, 2012; Ruel & Zuidema, 2012). Commercial diplomacy is performed by government employees, diplomats and other employees of foreign posts. Commercial diplomats are normally state representatives, but they can also be private actors with a diplomatic status who work on business promotion between the home and host country (Naray, 2011).

In this study, commercial diplomacy will be defined as the services of foreign posts that support export promotion and business development. It is about the diplomatic activities that help home country companies to sell their products abroad, and to find new business partners and investment opportunities. The services of the foreign posts are the commercial diplomacy practices of a country and display their implementation. The commercial diplomacy policies of a country depend on its government policies. Hocking and Spence (2005) and Kostecki and Naray (2007) indicate that within the EU, commercial diplomacy has changed because of policy integration. They mention that commercial diplomacy within the EU might move to become one commercial diplomacy system (Hocking & Spence, 2005; Kostecki & Naray, 2007). In the next section, a closer look is taken at commercial diplomacy in the EU and between the MS.

Diplomacy in the EU

Diplomacy within the EU dates back to the beginning with the creation of ESCS. The first delegation of the EU was opened in London in 1955. It had no actual diplomatic function and only served as a communication and information office (Bátora, 2003; Bruter, 1999). In 2011, the EU had 130 delegations and offices all over the world, with 14 of them at international agencies: African Union, UN, WTO, ASEAN, UNCESO, OECS, FAO, WFO, IFAD, Council of Europe, IAEA, ONEDC, UNIDO and OSCE (Europa, 2011b).

Diplomacy in the EU has its own styles, rules and procedures that are created by the treaties (Bátora, 2003). The first basis for external relations, mostly in the field of economics, was established by the EEC treaty in 1957. The biggest change to external relations was made in the treaty that established the EU (TEU) in 1992 in Maastricht. This treaty divided the EU into three pillars: the first is the European Commission (EC) pillar, the second is the CFSP pillar, and the third pillar is about JHA (Nugent, 2006). Thus, commercial diplomacy falls under the EC pillar (Kostecki & Naray, 2007). To say something about the commercial diplomacy of each member state, a closer look should be taken at the EC pillar and its influence on the EU MS.

Commercial Diplomacy in the EU

The EC pillar contains the European market and the free movement of production (Chalmers et al., 2006; Nugent, 2006). The primary goal of the EEC was to create an area in which there was 'free movement of goods, persons, services and capital'. In order to achieve this, the EEC created a customs union in which trade barriers, quotas and tariffs were abolished (Lindberg, 1963). The next big step was taken in 1985 with the creation of the SEM within the SEA. The SEM liberalised procedures and ensured the completion of the internal market without internal frontiers by 1992 (Moravcsik, 1991; Nugent, 2006). The SEM contains its own four pillars: 'the free movement of goods, persons, services and capital between the MS; the approximation of such laws, regulations or administrative provisions of the MS as directly affect the establishment or functioning of the common market; fair competition; and equal trade with common trade barriers for the whole EU and no barriers inside the EU' (Nugent, 2006, pp. 356–360).

As predicted in the SEM, the internal market was completed in 1992 in Maastricht with the creation of the TEU (Pollack, 1997). From then on, the internal market contained the 'free movement of goods, persons, services and capital'. The internal market is about fair competition where there are no internal frontiers, borders, controls or checkpoints (Chalmers et al., 2006; Kleiner, 2008; Moravcsik, 1991; Pollack, 1997). The EU makes decisions about the internal market and about product standards, product testing, certifications, labels, protectionism and monopolies of companies (Nugent, 2006). MS gave the EU the competence and right to create policies about trade and economic development through the treaties (Bruter, 1999; Hill & Wallace, 1979; Kenis & Schneider, 1987). Already since 1957, the EC pillar has had a legal person status, and today all the regulations, directives and decisions that are and have been made within this pillar are binding for all the MS (Chalmers et al., 2006; Hocking & Spence, 2005).

MS' Commercial Diplomacy

The competences of the EC to create policies that are binding for all the MS have changed their commercial diplomacy policies. The internal market has created an intense EU integration and 'Europeanisation' with no borders that brings the MS closer together (Bratberg, 2007; Hocking & Spence, 2005; Kostecki & Naray, 2007). This European integration created a so-called intra-EU order where domestic politics and MS' commercial diplomacy overlap (Bátora & Hocking, 2007, 2008). This overlap means that MS have to take the EU framework and Commission policies into account when making national politics. The responsible ministry for commercial diplomacy and the foreign posts have to align their policies to the EU ones, since parts of bilateral diplomacy have been taken over by the EC/EU (Bátora & Hocking, 2008; Keukeleire, 2003). For commercial diplomacy this means that diplomats have to modify their duties because the internal market without trade barriers changes the tasks of export promotion of embassies within the EU considerably (Kostecki & Naray, 2007), but it is not clear how the tasks of the embassies will change.

According to the literature, it would seem that the intra-EU order within the European integration creates a convergence between the commercial diplomacy policies and practices of EU MS whereby commercial diplomacy within the EU looks more like one concept (Bátora & Hocking, 2008; Hocking & Spence, 2005; Kostecki & Naray, 2007). MS can create alliances with other MS in multiple ways and strengthen bilateral relations where there are mutual interests in multiple forums (Bátora & Hocking, 2007, 2008). In this situation the MS will be collaborators. However, there are some articles that indicate that this integration does not mean that commercial diplomacy in each MS will be created in exactly the same way since there is, for instance, a variation in the range of capabilities (Bátora, 2003; Rijks & Whitman, 2007). There is space within the free trade zone to operate in the way each MS wants, and there is no common policy concerning commercial diplomacy (Bátora & Hocking, 2008; Hill & Wallace, 1979). This means that MS can diverge: some might stick to their traditional structure, while others shift commercial diplomacy in a new direction (Bátora & Hocking, 2008). Especially in this European integration, embassies and foreign posts remain important communication and promotion services for the MS (Bátora & Hocking, 2008) and are shaped in the way each MS thinks best, and then the MS will be competitors.

The discussion above makes it clear that commercial diplomacy in the EU is changing because of the binding policies in the EC pillar, but it also makes it clear that the commercial diplomacy policies and practices of all the EU MS will not automatically be the same. The MS have the option to be collaborators or competitors. In the next sections, all the factors that might explain the differences or similarities between the MS are discussed.

Factors Influencing Diplomacy

The literature on diplomacy is very extensive. There are many factors involved. It is assumed that these factors also influence commercial diplomacy, because they are interconnected and overlap in several areas.

The factors that have been mentioned in the literature are the country's characteristics: identity, character, law, norms, values, rules, traditions, structure, culture, size of the country, time of entry into the EU, degree of EU scepticism, the 'international' strength/power of a country and the strength of the responsible ministry (Bátora & Hocking, 2007; Bratberg, 2007; Duke, 2002; Galtung & Ruge, 1965; Hill & Wallace, 1979; Hocking & Spence, 2005; Hoffman, 2003; Kleiner, 2008; Rijks & Whitman, 2007); a country's capabilities and resources: the size and number of embassies, the budget and number of employees at foreign posts, training, competencies, academic background, working requirements, communication, tasks, staff category, function, access and presence (Bátora & Hocking, 2007, 2008; Bratberg, 2007; Duke, 2002; Hill & Wallace, 1979; Kleiner, 2008; Szondi, 2008); the policy focus of a country and the policy goals (Bruter, 1999; Kleiner, 2008; Szondi, 2008).

Factors influencing commercial diplomacy. In the literature on commercial diplomacy, there are several factors that overlap with diplomacy, especially when looking at the country characteristics. The main factors mentioned are the government's structure, its political issues, the country's homogeneity, size (Mercier, 2007), and organisational and institutional arrangements (Naray, 2008). The literature also describes factors that specifically influence commercial diplomacy. They can be categorised into ones concerning the government of a country and its foreign posts. The two levels are discussed below.

On the government level, the commercial diplomacy policies are influenced by the responsible ministry, the centralisation/decentralisation from the ministry, the independence of trade promotion organisations (TPO), and the structure of the ministry (Naray, 2008). An example of different systems based on the responsible ministry is given by Naray (2008) and by Kostecki and Naray (2007). Naray (2008) shows that the responsible ministry can be the Ministry of Trade, which is the case in Poland, France and Russia, or the Ministry of Foreign Affairs, as in Sweden, Norway, Denmark, Finland, and Iceland. There can also be joint oversight between both ministries, which is the case in the United Kingdom. This joint oversight may also be controlled by the Ministry of Trade, which cooperates in some cases with the Ministry of Foreign Affairs, as in Italy and Germany (Kostecki & Naray, 2007; Naray, 2008).

On the foreign post level, the commercial diplomacy practices are influenced by the structural form of the agencies responsible for commercial diplomacy and by the level of government (central, regional and local) where the services of these agencies are provided (Mercier, 2007). The local government level contains the bodies that implement the services, also known as the foreign posts. The structural forms of agencies or foreign posts can be divided into private, public or a mix of both. Most

European countries seem to adopt a private–public mixture (Mercier, 2007). The foreign posts use different programmes and practices for the promotion of export and inward investment. The export promotion programmes can be divided into market development programmes and export service programmes. The export promotion practices are trade shows and trade missions (Mercier, 2007). Market development programmes are concerned with the dissemination of sales leads, the participation in trade shows, the preparation of analyses and the sending of newsletters. Export service programmes involve holding seminars for exporters, counselling those exporters, providing 'how-to-export' handbooks and helping with the financing of export (Mercier, 2007). Trade shows are used to promote home country firms and their products abroad. They form a big part of market development programmes. Trade missions are used more for commercial diplomacy than trade shows. Trade missions provide aid to firms for future business and FDI in a simple and cost-effective manner. Diplomats in trade missions provide knowledge of a host country's culture and market to home country firms by contacting government representatives and local business persons (Mercier, 2007).

The influential factors on the foreign post level are affected by the number and the characteristics of the diplomats and employees working there. The education of the employees, their background, skills, motivation, experience and mindset influence the commercial diplomacy practices (Kostecki & Naray, 2007; Saner & Yu, 2003). Commercial diplomats in foreign posts can be civil servants, trained diplomats or representatives of a country's chamber of commerce (Saner & Yu, 2003). A common way in commercial diplomacy to verify and improve a diplomat's skills is cross-fertilisation. Cross-fertilisation schemes place diplomats in different settings for short periods of time. For instance, diplomats may be placed in business settings, while the business representatives temporarily occupy a post at the mission (Lee, 2004; Mercier, 2007). When diplomats leave the embassy, cross-fertilisation can again come into play. Ambassadors may be appointed to the international relations departments of global companies, or work in investment firms, consulting companies, law firms or policy advisory agencies (Saner & Yu, 2003).

Finally, along with all these factors that influence the commercial diplomacy policies and practices, there are also different types of diplomats. Within the literature on diplomacy, three types of diplomats have already been mentioned by Galtung and Ruge (1965): the 'elite-oriented', the 'treaty-oriented' and the 'structure-oriented' diplomats. Although these are rather extreme types, they are still valid (or mixtures of them) and can also apply in commercial diplomacy. An elite-oriented diplomat mostly comes from the upper class. His/her job consists of meetings, parties, social gatherings and conferences. This diplomat has a lot of connections and knows people who can help him/her to achieve a goal. The treaty-oriented diplomat should have a law degree and be an expert in legal matters. He/she should be able to negotiate and draft treaties in order to reach an agreement that is acceptable to his/her own country's laws and preferences. Finally, the structure-oriented diplomat should be an academic who has specialised in social sciences. His/her job is to read as many books and articles about the political, economic and social structure of the host country. All of his/her observations and reports should provide enough insight into the host country for the home country to take further action (Galtung & Ruge, 1965).

Alternatively, Kostecki and Naray (2007), Naray (2008) and Ruel and Visser (2012) describe three basic types of commercial diplomats: business promoter, civil servant and generalist commercial diplomat (Kostecki & Naray, 2007; Naray, 2008). A business promoter is a diplomat who is very business-oriented. He/she seeks proactively to support companies by performing consultancy services for them. A civil servant mostly works for the Ministry of Foreign Affairs and has a reactive role. He/she keeps a distance from business and only does the work that is requested by the ministry. A generalist is a diplomat who works for businesses on an *ad hoc* basis. He/she does the work for the foreign post, and when he/she feels like it, the diplomat supports business (Kostecki & Naray, 2007; Naray, 2008).

Commercial Diplomacy Policy and Practice

The previous section showed that the first factors that influence commercial diplomacy policies and practices are the country characteristics. They reflect similarities and differences between EU MS on the national government level and on the foreign post level. The national government level involves the commercial diplomacy policies, and the foreign post level concerns the commercial diplomacy practices of a country. Figure 1 shows that the country characteristics directly affect the government's focus and the policy goals of a country, and indirectly influence the commercial diplomacy policies and practices. The country characteristics lay down the basis for a government and its decision-making process, but it is the government

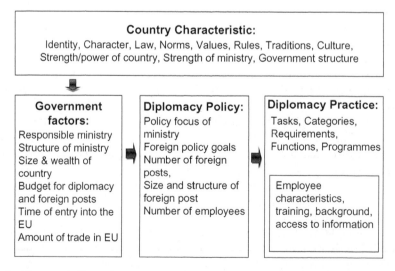

Figure 1: Factors influencing commercial diplomacy.

that creates the focus and the commercial diplomacy policies of a country. A government policy specifies a government's goals. It defines what should be accomplished and which behaviour of the underlying staff is needed for that (Wies, 1994). The government policy focus of a country directly influences its commercial diplomacy policies and indirectly its commercial diplomacy practices. The commercial diplomacy policies that are laid down by the responsible ministry directly influence the commercial diplomacy practices. The commercial diplomacy practices contain elements of human resource management such as training, job description, staff selection and involvement in decision-making (Ahmad & Schroeder, 2003; Delery & Doty, 1996; Way, Lepak, Fay, & Thacker, 2010) and can be separated into the content and the employee characteristics that influence the diplomatic job. The former are the tasks, staff categories, functions of employees, the requirements for employees and the programmes that can be used by commercial diplomats to implement the policy. The latter are an employee's personality, training, academic background, and access to information.

In this study, the EU MS will be compared on the basis of their government and its commercial diplomacy policies and practices. The comparison is performed on both the national government level and foreign post level to show the differences and similarities between their commercial diplomacy policies and practices. The government factors and commercial diplomacy policies and practices will be compared on the basis of clear, separate concepts or numbers as discussed in the methodology.

Method

The comparison of the commercial diplomacy policies and practices of EU MS is based on the principles of policy analysis and qualitative research. Policy analysis is used to understand the MS' policy setting to learn what the different policies are and to better compare all the policies based on clear concepts. Policy analysis is also used to see how the policies are implemented and uncover the methods used by the MS for dealing with commercial diplomacy. Qualitative interviews are used to gather information about the work on commercial diplomacy of employees of foreign posts.

Commercial Diplomacy Policy Factors

The first part is an examination of primary and secondary data to uncover the policies of the MS. In this part, the level of analysis is the organisational unit of the MS (also referred to as the government). The policy goals and documents examined come from the government of a country and its current cabinet. This study does not look at how the policies changed over time but at what they are in the current government. We can state that the policies of a country did not change drastically during the study and can be considered constant. This means that the data is reliable, and the policy goals are similar over a short time period. The policies will be compared on the basis of the following factors: the responsible ministry, the structure of the ministry, the size of the country, the wealth of a country, the budget for diplomacy and foreign posts, the time of entry into the EU, the amount of import and export within the EU market, the policy focus of the ministry, the foreign policy goals, the number of embassies, the number of trade offices and the number of employees dedicated to commercial diplomacy. These factors were chosen because they are relatively straightforward to find and they can be compared based on clear categories. The operationalisation of these factors is shown in Table 1.

Commercial Diplomacy Practice Factors

The second part of the study consists of qualitative, semi-structured interviews and unstructured field observations to uncover the commercial diplomacy practices of the MS. The interviews were conducted among diplomats and employees of foreign posts. The interviews with the employees were conducted to gather empirical data about the commercial diplomacy practices of the EU MS, how employees perform their work, which of the practices are used and how the policies are implemented. The practice factors that are compared in this study are the size of the foreign post, the structure of the foreign post, the economic function of the foreign post, the number of employees at the foreign post, the tasks and staff categories of the employees at the foreign post, the programmes used by the employees, the activism of the foreign post, the training of employees, the requirements of the foreign post, the academic background of the employees and the access to information. The operationalisation of the practice factors can be found in Table 1.

The interviews were conducted face to face with diplomats and employees of foreign posts (Eisenhardt & Graebner, 2007). The units of analysis in this part are the commercial diplomats and the other employees of the foreign posts. The interviews were semi-structured and consisted of open-ended and closed-ended questions. Closed-ended questions are used to obtain similar answers that are more easily comparable based on the concepts given for the practice factors. Open-ended questions are used to provide space for new aspects of commercial diplomacy that are addressed by the respondents but not used in the literature and that can bring new light to the situation. The language that is used is English; in combination with the closed-ended questions, this is meant to avoid differences in definitions and to make sure the answers can be compared (Atkinson & Brandolini, 2001). It has to be kept in mind that interviews can be biased because of the personality and position of a respondent (Eisenhardt & Graebner, 2007) and their desire to present themselves in a better light (Newman et al., 2002). In order to avoid this bias, several respondents of one country were asked for an interview to make sure that this country is evaluated by different persons, hopefully at a similar level. The answers to the questions will always differ, but because of the way the questions are formulated, the possibility to categorise the answers into clear factors, and the direct contact with the respondents, this part of the study is considered valid, and the answers are good enough to make a clear comparison of the practices of the EU MS (Sorensen, Sabroe, & Olsen, 1996).

Table 1: Operationalisation of the comparable factors of commercial diplomacy.

Policy factors	Definition	Indicators	Labels	Code
Responsible ministry	The ministry that creates the policies about commercial diplomacy and trade	Policy goals of the responsible ministry	Ministry of Trade Ministry of Foreign Affairs Both	1 2 3
Structure of responsible ministry	The hierarchy and freedom to operate the ministry	If the ministry has to follow the government policies step by step or has some freedom to decide on its own	Decentralised Independent Centralised Dependent	1 2 3 4
Size of country	The size of a country based on square kilometre area and number of inhabitants	Square kilometre, and population	Small Medium Large	1 2 3
Budget for commercial diplomacy and foreign posts	The amount and percentage of the total budget that is spent on commercial diplomacy and foreign posts	X total budget X for commercial diplomacy and foreign posts	X% of total budget	Numerical numbers
Wealth	The wealth of a country is the amount of income (GDP) the country and its inhabitants have	GDP per capita in PPS and euro per inhabitant	Rich Average Poor	1 2 3
Intra-EU trade	The amount of import and export of a MS within the EU	Share of the amount of imports and exports in percent per MS	High Average Low	1 2 3
Entry time in the EU	The date and time period when a country entered the EU	1957: EU six Between 1958 and 2003 is the middle From 2004 till 2011 is the last	First Middle Last	1 2 3
Policy focus of ministry	The general focus on trade and business of the government of an MS	Foreign policy goals of the ministry	Business oriented Mixed oriented Trade oriented	1 2 3

Table 1: (*Continued*)

Policy factors	Definition	Indicators	Labels	Code
Number of embassies	The number of embassies a country has within the EU and outside the EU	Number of embassies within the EU and outside the EU	X embassies outside the EU X embassies inside the EU Total number of embassies	Numerical numbers
Number of embassies in EU	Category of the number of embassies a country has within the other MS	20 or less 21–25 In all other MS 26	Few Average High	1 2 3
Number of trade promotion organisations (TPOs)	The number of offices abroad that are not embassies or consulates, but do focus on trade and commercial diplomacy	Number of offices of trade agencies	Total trade promotion offices	Numerical numbers
Number of employees	The number of employees who work on commercial diplomacy under the ministry and/or trade agency	Number of employees abroad (and the number of employees within the home country)	Number of employees abroad	Numerical numbers

Practice factors	Definition	Indicators	Values	Code
Structure of foreign post	The way the foreign post is organised and how it is funded	Government budget or private member fees	Private Public	1 2
Economic function	The kind of function that the employees have within the foreign post	The tasks and activities of the employees of the foreign post	Business promoter Civil servant /business promoter Generalist	1 2 3
Staff categories	The categories of the staff (employees) of the foreign post based on their activities and work	The work and activities of the employees of the foreign post	Structure Elite Treaty	1 2 3

			Number of employees	Numerical numbers
Size of foreign post	The size of the foreign post expressed in the number of employees working on commercial diplomacy	The number of employees working on commercial diplomacy	Number of employees	
Programmes	The activities and events that the employees of a foreign post perform and organise for commercial diplomacy	The activities and events the employees work on	Trade shows (fairs); Reporting; Seminars; Counselling; Trade missions; Workshops	Yes or No; 1 = Yes; 2 = No
Activism of foreign post	The number of programmes and tasks the employees of a foreign post perform and work on	Number of tasks and programmes, 3 or less is reactive, more than 3 is proactive	Proactive; Reactive	1; 2
Requirements	The requirements that have to be met in order to work at the foreign post	Requirement for a degree, learning languages and other requirements	Degree; Language; Other	Yes or No; 1 = Yes; 2 = No
Training	The amount of training and the kind of training while working at the foreign post	If the employees have training or not while working at the foreign post	Yes; No	1 = Yes; 2 = No
Academic background	The educational background of the employee of the foreign post	The employee's educational background	Economic/business; Political; Economics and political; Economics and law; Politics and law	1; 2; 3; 4; 5
Access to information	The way and possibility of employees (and companies) to find information	The employees indicate whether the way of gathering information is good or bad	Good; Bad	1; 2

Data Collection

This research covered all 27 current MS of the EU: Austria, Belgium, Bulgaria, Cyprus, Czech Republic, Denmark, Estonia, Finland, France, Germany, Greece, Hungary, Ireland, Italy, Latvia, Lithuania, Luxembourg, Malta, the Netherlands, Poland, Portugal, Romania, Slovakia, Slovenia, Spain, Sweden and the United Kingdom (Europa, 2011a). For this study, the goal was to get in touch with each MS to achieve a full comparison of commercial diplomacy within the EU. The first part looks at the commercial diplomacy policies, especially the policy focus and policy goals of each country. The commercial diplomacy policies of all 27 MS were compared by looking at primary and secondary sources, such as books, journals, government publications and newspapers. The country characteristics and general information were found on the EU website (Europa, 2011a, 2011c) and data was taken from Eurostat (Eurostat, 2011). To find out what the policies of a government are, their websites were thoroughly searched for their policy documents and all policy goals. Still, it was not always easy to find the correct information on the government website. A lot of information is spread over many pages, and often important information can only be found in the local language. This affects the validity of the data, because not all of it can be accessed (Sorensen et al., 1996). For some governments the policy documents could not be found or correctly translated. Nevertheless, enough data was obtained for each government to show what the policy goals of the country are, and the data is considered valid.

The commercial diplomacy practices of the EU MS were collected via interviews with diplomats and employees of foreign posts. We strove to get a response from large and small countries, the new members and the ones that had been in the EU the longest to check the effect of size and time of entry into the EU. The extent of this research is dependent on the respondents' willingness to participate and the time limits of the participants and of the researcher. For practical reasons and to improve comparability, only one foreign post of a country was visited, and all the foreign posts were located in one MS, in this case Sweden (Stockholm). The practices of the MS vary across countries and can create bias with practices in other countries. To avoid any bias, the data collected can be seen as a sample or a case study looking at the practices of one foreign post of a MS in one other MS (Eisenhardt & Graebner, 2007). The research is reliable when looking at the commercial diplomatic practices in the case of Sweden, but it cannot be generalised to all commercial diplomatic practices of a member state within and outside the whole EU (Sorensen et al., 1996).

All the employees were contacted via post, e-mail or telephone and asked whether they wanted to participate in this research. Each interview with the employee was conducted at the foreign post. In the findings, the foreign post is classified as an embassy or a different kind of foreign post. During the interview, notes are made, and where possible the interview was recorded. After each interview, the notes and information were written down as soon as possible. The interview information contains the location, date, time, setting and impression of the interview. Each session was saved as a separate Word file. The notes and recordings of the interviews were translated into an interview transcript. This transcript was sent to the interviewee for comments and cross-checking. After receiving the respondent's comments, the final version of the interview transcript was created, and this was used later in the data analyses.

Data Analyses

The commercial diplomacy policy and practice factors of the EU MS were gathered via policy analyses and interviews. To be able to compare them, they were transformed into categorical data. The chunks of data were classified in the categories shown in Table 1. These categories will be shown next to each other in the tables of differences and similarities between the policy factors and the practice factors of the EU MS. From these tables the comparison between the factors was drawn. To be able to see a relationship between the policy and practice factors and if an explanation can be found for these differences and similarities, the policy and practice factors were statistically tested. To do so, they have to be changed into quantities. The factors are arranged into categorical variables or quantitative variables and are put in a statistical data set as nominal data or numerical data. The tests used for the categorical data are the Pearson chi-square test, the Phi test and Cramer's V test. For the categorical data there is no test that can show a linear relationship, but the chi-square test and Phi test show if the values are independent of each other or not. If the values are dependent, then there is a relationship between them. The Cramer's V test shows any association between two variables. The association between two categories does not show the strength of the direction of the relationship, but only indicates that there is one. For the numerical data, the chi-square test, the Phi test and the Cramer's V test are also used, but one additional test is done to see if there is a correlation between two numerical factors. The association for the numerical data shows if there is a linear relationship, and the correlation shows its direction and strength (De Veaux, Velleman, & Bock, 2008). The operationalisation of the factors and the corresponding statistical values (codes) can be found in Table 1. Table 2 shows the number of times the labels of the factors were found. The total of the policy factors is 27 MS. The total of the practice factors is 14 MS. The results of the policy analysis and interviews are explained and discussed in the next section.

Findings

As mentioned before, this research compares the commercial diplomacy policies and practices of EU MS in two ways: a policy analysis and a practice analysis. In this section the two analyses are performed, and the MS factor comparison is discussed. The first part contains the policy analysis of the 27 EU MS. The second part contains the practice analysis of a selection of 14 MS: Austria, Belgium, Denmark, Estonia, Finland, France, Germany, Greece, Hungary, Latvia, Lithuania, the Netherlands, Romania, and Slovakia.

Table 2: Descriptive statistics.

Policy factors	Labels	Frequency	Percentage
Responsible ministry	Ministry of Trade	4	14.8%
	Ministry of Foreign Affairs	5	18.5%
	Both	18	66.7%
Size of country	Small	8	29.6%
	Medium	13	48.1%
	Large	6	22.2%
Wealth	Rich	11	40.7%
	Average	3	11.1%
	Poor	13	48.1%
Share of intra-EU trade	High	6	22.2%
	Average	6	22.2%
	Low	15	55.6%
Entry time in the EU	First	6	22.2%
	Middle	9	33.3%
	Last	12	44.4%
Policy focus	Business oriented	12	44.4%
	Mixed oriented	14	51.9%
	Trade oriented	1	3.7%
Number of embassies inside the EU	Few	4	14.8%
	Average	15	55.6%
	High	8	29.6%

Practice factors	Labels	Frequency	Percentage
Structure of foreign post	Private	1	7.1%
	Public	13	92.9%
Economic function	Business promoter	11	78.6%
	Civil servant/business promoter	3	21.4%
	Generalist	0	0%
Staff category	Structure	2	14.3%
	Elite	4	28.6%
	Treaty	1	7.1%
	Mixed	7	50%
Programmes	Trade shows (fairs)	9	64.3%
	Reporting	14	100%
	Seminars	9	64.3%
	Counselling	3	21.4%
	Trade missions	14	100%
	Workshops	2	14.3%
Activism	Proactive	9	64.3%
	Reactive	5	35.7%

Table 2: (*Continued*)

Practice factors	Labels	Frequency	Percentage
Requirements	Degree	14	100%
	Language	10	71.4%
Background	Economic/business	5	35.7%
	Political	2	14.3%
	Economics and political	4	28.6%
	Economics and law	2	14.3%
	Politics and law	1	7.1%
Access to information	Good	14	100%

Member State Policy Comparison

Each country has its own network of responsible ministries and other parties that are involved in commercial diplomacy. Most MS have a network with a shared responsibility between the Ministry of Foreign Affairs and the Ministry of Economic Affairs. This network is used in 17 MS: Austria, Bulgaria, Cyprus, Czech Republic, Denmark, Estonia, Finland, Germany, Hungary, Italy, Latvia, Lithuania, Luxembourg, Malta, the Netherlands, Romania and Slovakia. The other possible scenarios are that only the Ministry of Foreign Affairs is responsible as is the case in Belgium, Greece, Ireland, Sweden and the United Kingdom, or that the Ministry of Economic Affairs is responsible, mostly with some support from the Ministry of Foreign Affairs and its embassies, as is the case in France, Poland, Portugal, Slovenia and Spain. The responsible ministry is the main actor working on commercial diplomacy together with the foreign posts that implement its policies. In the network, the chambers of commerce are also taken into account, because they play a large role in commercial diplomacy. Other organisations and institutions can also play a role in commercial diplomacy, but because they vary widely from country to country, this makes the network too complex, and they are not discussed here.

The policy focus of most MS is classified as business-oriented. It is derived from their policy goals. Many countries indicate in their policy goals that they want to improve trade and abolish barriers, increase export and attract investment. These policy goals are very trade-oriented. In addition, the MS have written down in their policy programmes and website how they want the policies to be implemented by the trade agencies and trade offices. It is there that one sees a focus on supporting businesses and helping them with their export and investment and finding new business opportunities. Determining the policy focus was not easy, because a lot of the information was dispersed. The policy focus in this study shows what the predominant policy goals of a country are. It is possible that data is missing and that countries might have a different policy focus, but from the data gathered, the countries are categorised as having a certain policy focus. Thirteen countries were classified as being predominantly business-oriented: Austria, Denmark, Estonia, France, Greece, Italy, Luxembourg, the Netherlands, Romania, Poland, Portugal, Sweden and the United Kingdom. Based on the data that was found, one country was classified as being predominantly trade-oriented: Bulgaria. Some countries could not be classified as being predominantly trade- or business-oriented and are classified as mixed. These countries are Belgium, Cyprus, Czech Republic, Finland, Germany, Hungary, Ireland, Latvia, Lithuania, Malta, Spain, Slovenia and Slovakia.

In this study, the number of foreign posts has been divided into the number of embassies within the EU, the number of embassies outside the EU and the number of trade offices. The embassies within the EU have been categorised into three groups. There are eight countries with an embassy in each MS: Belgium, France, Germany, Greece, Ireland, Italy, Portugal and Spain. Most MS have between 21 and 25 embassies in the EU, and have a consulate or high commission in the MS where they do not have an embassy. There are a few small countries that have 20 or fewer embassies within the EU: Estonia, Malta, Latvia and Luxembourg. The MS also have trade offices that work on commercial diplomacy. They almost always fall under the responsibility of the Ministry of Economic Affairs and/or a trade agency. Only Bulgaria, Hungary, Slovakia and Slovenia do not have trade offices abroad. In these countries all the work of commercial diplomacy abroad is done at the embassies and consulates, and often the embassy has an economic section or commercial counsellors working on commercial diplomacy. In Austria and Germany, the chambers of commerce act as trade offices, and the Austrian chambers of commerce are often named as the economic department of the embassy. The policy factors of the EU MS are summarised and shown next to each other in Table 3.

Member State Practices Comparison

As mentioned before, the MS all have a network of embassies and/or trade offices that work on commercial diplomacy (Table 2). Almost all MS have embassies and trade offices abroad; only Bulgaria, Hungary, Slovenia and Slovakia do not. Austria and Germany have chambers of commerce abroad (AWO and AHK) that operate as a trade office. The German embassies work on a part of the commercial diplomacy, and the rest is done at the AHK. No commercial diplomacy is performed by the Austrian embassies, as everything is done by the AWO. The AWO is often considered the economic department of the embassy, and some employees of the AWO have a diplomatic status. Denmark, Estonia, Finland, France, Greece, Latvia, Lithuania, the Netherlands, and Romania all have embassies and trade offices that work on commercial diplomacy. Often the trade office is part of the embassy (as its economic department), but in Estonia, Finland and the Netherlands, they have separate trade (business) offices outside the embassy. The employees of the trade offices or of the economic departments of the embassies can all be classified as business promoters. The employees who work on commercial diplomacy within an embassy who are not part of an economic department and/or also have to perform other activities are classified as civil servants. In the embassy of Estonia and

Table 3: Policy factors.

Policy factors	Austria	Belgium	Bulgaria	Cyprus	Czech Republic
Responsible ministry	Combination of Ministries of Economy, Family and Youth and Ministry of European and International Affairs	Ministries of Foreign Affairs, Foreign Trade and Development Cooperation	Ministry of Foreign Affairs and Ministry of Economy	Ministry of Foreign Affairs with the Ministry of Commerce, Industry and Tourism	Ministry of Foreign Affairs with the Ministry of Industry and Trade
Structure of ministry	Decentralised and autonomous (independent)	Autonomous (independent), decentralised	Decentralised		Individually (independent)
Size of country	Area: 83,870 km², population: 8.3 million; medium	Total area: 30,582 km², population: 10.7 million; medium	Area: 111,910 km², population: 7.6 million; medium	Area: 9250 km², population: 0.8 million; small	Total area: 78,866 km², total population: 10.5 million inhabitants; medium
Wealth of country	Rich	Rich	Poor	Average	Poor
Budget for diplomacy	6.4% of total budget	15.7% of total budget	13.2% of total budget	7.63% of total budget	Export strategy: 3330 million CZK
Entry time in the EU	1995: middle	First, 1957	Last, 2007	Last, 2004	Last, 2004
Share of intra-EU trade	Average	High	Low	Low	Low
Policy focus	Business oriented	Mixed oriented	Trade oriented	Mixed oriented	Mixed oriented
Policy goals	More efficiency; bilateral economic agreements and economic policy support, provide businesses and organisations with incentives for cooperation. Hub and lobby centres for EU decision-making	Create inward and outward investment Abolish tariffs and trade obstacles Develop trade promotion Provide business support	Improve participation in economic cooperation and international trade Promote economy abroad	Promote development Increase economy Promote export of goods and services Increase inward investment	Promote export Promote economic interests abroad Improve services for companies abroad

Table 3: (Continued)

Policy factors	Austria	Belgium	Bulgaria	Cyprus	Czech Republic
Number of embassies	23 embassies in the EU, 45 embassies outside the EU; average	26 inside the EU, 60 outside the EU; high	24 inside the EU, 60 outside the EU; average	21 inside the EU, 27 outside the EU; average	58 outside the EU, 25 inside the EU; average
Number of foreign trade offices	AWO: 75 offices abroad	Flanders: 70 offices, Wallonia: 20, Brussels: 20		11 trade centres	33 offices in 30 countries
Number of employees	2167 abroad	Foreign trade advisers: 403, living abroad: 221			Total: 375, head office: 235, abroad: 140

Policy factors	Denmark	Estonia	Finland	France	Germany
Responsible ministry	Ministry of Foreign Affairs with Ministry of Business and Growth	Ministry of Foreign Affairs with Ministry of Economy and Communications	Ministry of Foreign Affairs and Ministry of Employment and Economy	Ministry of Economy, Finance and Industry	Ministry of Trade with Ministry of Foreign Affairs
Structure of ministry					
Size of country	Total area: 43,094 km², total population: 5.5 million inhabitants; medium	Total area: 45,000 km², total population: 1.3 million inhabitants; Small	Total area: 338,000 km², total population: 5.3 million inhabitants; medium	Total area: 550,000 km², total population: 64.3 million inhabitants; large	Total area: 356,854 km², total population: 82 million inhabitants; large
Wealth of country	Rich	Poor	Rich	Rich	Rich
Budget for diplomacy		0.3% of total budget	66% of foreign service budget, 0.3% of total expenditure	Total expenditure is 176.3 billion euro	2% of total budget
Entry time in the EU	Middle, 1973	Last, 2004	Middle, 1995	First, 1957	First, 1957
Share of intra-EU trade	Low	Low	Low	High	High

Policy focus / Policy goals	Mixed oriented / Free trade / Increase value, knowledge and growth	Business oriented / Support businesses abroad / Improve export for new companies / Enter more markets	Mixed oriented / Remove trade barriers (free and fair trade) / Improve services of missions for companies / Promote and improve internationalisation of Finnish companies, especially SMEs	Business oriented / Support French companies with their export and entry into foreign/international markets	Mixed oriented / Abolish trade barriers / Work on international agreements for global free trade and fair competition / Promote export and investment
Number of embassies	60 outside the EU, 25 inside the EU; average	13 outside the EU, 20 inside the EU; low	52 outside the EU, 25 inside the EU; average	139 outside the EU, 26 inside the EU; high	124 outside the EU, 26 inside the EU; high
Number of foreign trade offices	Located in 60 countries	10 offices in 9 countries	66 locations in 45 countries	48 agencies: 33 outside the EU and 15 inside the EU	AHK: 120 offices in 80 countries
Number of employees	100 in Denmark, 300 abroad	Estonia Enterprise: 285 employees	1800 employees at missions abroad		

Policy factors	Greece	Hungary	Ireland	Italy	Latvia
Responsible ministry	Ministry of Foreign Affairs	Ministry of Foreign Affairs with Ministry of Industry, Trade and Tourism	Ministry of Foreign Affairs and Ministry of Trade	Ministry of Trade with Ministry of Foreign Affairs	Ministry of Economics with assistance of Ministry of Foreign Affairs
Structure of ministry		Autonomous	Decentralised		
Size of country	Total area: 131,957 km^2, total population 11.2 million inhabitants; medium	Total area: 93,000 km^2, total population: 10 million inhabitants; medium	Total area: 70,000 km^2, total population: 4.5 million inhabitants; medium	Total area: 301,263 km^2, total population: 60 million inhabitants; large	Total area: 65,000 km^2, total population: 2.3 million inhabitants; small

Table 3: (Continued)

Policy factors	Greece	Hungary	Ireland	Italy	Latvia
Wealth of country / Budget for diplomacy	Poor / 0.03% of total	Poor	Rich / 1.5% of total	Average	Poor / 16% of total
Entry time in the EU	Middle, 1981	Last, 2004	Middle, 1973	First, 1957	Last, 2004
Share of intra-EU trade	Low	Low/Average	Low/Average	High	Low
Policy focus / Policy goals	Business oriented / Promote Greek business abroad / Provide information to Greek businesses abroad	Mixed oriented / Free competition and increase Hungarian competitiveness, and enter new markets / EU integration / Trade development	Mixed oriented / Promote trade and investment / Increase access to new markets	Business oriented / Increase trade / Internationalise business / Support access to new markets	Mixed oriented / Competitiveness / Free trade
Number of embassies	58 outside the EU, 26 inside the EU; high	53 outside the EU, 24 inside the EU; average	34 outside the EU, 26 inside the EU; high	100 outside the EU, 26 inside the EU; high	14 outside the EU, 20 inside the EU; low
Number of foreign trade offices	60 bureaus abroad in 49 countries	Network with diplomatic services via the embassies in over 50 countries	30 international offices	117 offices in 87 countries	13 representation offices abroad
Number of employees			Total: 1260, in Ireland: 900, abroad: 360		LIAA: 200 employees

Policy factors	Lithuania	Luxembourg	Malta	The Netherlands	Poland
Responsible ministry	Ministry of Foreign Affairs with Ministry of Economy	Ministry of Foreign Affairs with Ministry of Economy and Ministry Foreign Trade	Ministry of Foreign Affairs with Ministries of Finance, Economy and Investment	Ministries of Economic Affairs, Agriculture and Innovation together with the Ministry of Foreign Affairs	Ministry of Economy
Structure of ministry				Decentralised	

Size of country	Total area: 65,000 km², total population: 3.3 million inhabitants; small	Total area: 3586 km², total population: 0.5 million inhabitants; small	Total area: 316 km², total population: 0.4 million inhabitants; small	Total area: 41,526 km², total population: 16.4 million inhabitants; medium	Total area: 312,679 km², total population: 38.1 million inhabitants; large
Wealth of country	Poor	Rich	Poor	Rich	Poor
Budget for diplomacy		0.4% of total expenditure	0.04% of total budget	4.6% of total budget	
Entry time in the EU	Last, 2004	First, 1957	Last, 2004	First, 1957	Last, 2004
Share of intra-EU trade	Low	Low	Low	High	Average
Policy focus	Mixed oriented	Business oriented	Mixed oriented	Business oriented (innovation)	Business oriented
Policy goals	Work closely on EU trade policy; Add value to business and create innovation	Export to new, international markets; Support economic activities abroad	Bring investment to Malta; Improve export; Support international commerce; Maximise economic benefits	Strengthen international competitiveness; Ensure more innovation through cooperation; Enlarge and secure global economic position	Improve trade, export and inward investment; Help Polish companies to do business abroad, especially SMEs
Number of embassies	20 outside the EU, 22 inside the EU; average	23 outside the EU, 19 inside the EU; low	12 outside the EU, 14 inside the EU; low	85 outside the EU, 25 inside the EU; average	64 outside the EU, 25 inside the EU; average
Number of foreign trade offices	9 commercial attachés, Enterprise Lithuania: 18 representation offices	Trade and investment offices in 9 countries	5 overseas offices	Business supports offices in 9 countries	48 offices in 44 countries
Number of employees					

Table 3: (Continued)

Policy factors	Portugal	Romania	Slovakia	Slovenia	Spain
Responsible ministry	Ministry of Economy and Employment	Ministry of Economy with Ministry of Foreign Affairs	Ministry of Economy with Ministry of Foreign Affairs	Ministry of Economy	Ministry of Economy
Structure of ministry					
Size of country	Total area: 92,071 km², total population: 10.6 million inhabitants; medium	Total area: 237 500 km², total population: 21.5 million inhabitants; medium	Total area: 48,845 km², total population: 5.4 million inhabitants; small	Total area: 20,273 km², total population: 2 million inhabitants; small	Total area: 504,782 km², total population: 45.8 million inhabitants; large
Wealth of country	Poor	Poor	Poor	Poor	Average
Budget for diplomacy		11.9% of total budget			0.45% of total budget
Entry time in the EU	Middle, 1986	Last, 2007	Last, 2004	Last, 2004	Middle, 1986
Share of intra-EU trade	Low	Low	Low	Low	Average
Policy focus	Business oriented	Business oriented	Mixed oriented	Mixed oriented	Mixed oriented
Policy goals	Internationalization of economy More inward investment and export	Promote export: organise events and meetings, support with regulations and laws, support network Attract inward investment	Liberalise market Remove trade barriers Change legislation to make business easier	Make enterprise more competitive Internationalise market (more export) Attract inward investment	Make enterprise more competitive Internationalise market (more export) Attract inward investment

Number of embassies	50 outside the EU, 26 inside the EU; h gh	24 outside the EU, 23 inside the EU; average	41 outside the EU, 22 inside the EU; average	37 outside the EU, 24 inside the EU; average	91 outside the EU, 26 inside the EU; high
Number of foreign trade offices	50 offices in 44 countries	80 offices	21 economic sections outside the EU and 22 economic sections inside the EU		13 business centres
Number of employees					1000 specialists

Policy factors	Sweden	UK
Responsible ministry	Ministry of Foreign Affairs	Ministry of Foreign Affairs (FCO)
Structure of ministry		Decentralised
Size of country	Total area: 449,964 km², total population: 9.2 million inhabitants; medium	Total area: 244,820 km², total population: 61.7 million inhabitants; large
Wealth of country	Rich	Rich
Budget for diplomacy	4.99% of total budget	
Entry time in the EU	Middle, 1995	Middle, 1973
Share of intra-EU trade	Average	High
Policy focus	Business oriented	Business oriented
Policy goals	Free trade More export Support for companies, especially of SMEs	Increase growth and international competitiveness Make it easier for SMEs and entrepreneurs to enter a market and to grow
Number of embassies	56 outside the EU, 21 inside the EU; average	78 outside the EU, 24 inside the EU; average
Number of foreign trade offices	50 offices in 52 countries	Offices in 96 countries
Number of employees		2400 employees

Finland, the employees working on commercial diplomacy cannot be classified as being predominantly business promoters, because they also perform tasks that do not fall within the scope of commercial diplomacy and because both countries have trade offices (Estonia Enterprise and Finpro) outside the embassy that work on commercial diplomacy. The embassy of Germany has an economic department, but its employees work more on economic policy affairs than on commercial diplomacy and cannot be classified as business promoters, but more as civil servants. Germany has an AHK that acts as the trade office, and the employees of the AHK are exclusively business-oriented.

The work of the employees of the foreign posts can be divided into several tasks. The first one is to write reports. Each employee updates the government or the HQ of a trade office on the current status of the post, the work that has been accomplished, the events that have been organised, what the economic situation of the host country is, and what the position of the host country government is on economic affairs. The second task is to arrange missions. Each foreign post, often in cooperation with the home government and other institutions, arranges missions of trade and/or political delegations that come to the host country. Another important task is to respond to questions received from companies, institutions and individuals asking for information about economic sectors of the host country and/or possible business opportunities and partners. Some of the employees indicated that they would help companies to set up meetings with possible business partners and provide some advice concerning business opportunities. They made it clear that they provide information and set up meetings, but do not take part in the business meetings. The foreign post is not a consultancy firm and is not involved in the firm's strategy. The employees give options to the firm, and the firm decides which strategy to follow.

The employees of the foreign post also arrange particular events. Most foreign posts organise shows to bring companies together or to display what their country has to offer in terms of export and investment opportunities. Fairs and trade shows are two big events where countries show their home products. Often the embassy or trade office arranges a national booth where companies can display their products. The embassies of Estonia, Finland, Germany, Hungary and the Netherlands indicated that they did not arrange fairs, but Estonia Enterprise, Finpro, the AHK or the agency at home (EVD) arranges national booths at international fairs or trade shows. A second option to promote and highlight the business opportunities of the home country is by organising workshops and seminars. The employees at the foreign posts of Lithuania, Romania, France, Greece, Latvia, Finland, Estonia, Denmark and Austria said that they organise seminars. The employees of Lithuania and Greece stated that they also organise workshops. The task row in Table 4 shows which kind of events countries organise to promote their companies and country. Based on these results, the countries are labelled as proactive or reactive. Reactive means it only organises missions and fairs, while proactive implies it also organises seminars, workshops and other events that actively promotes the country. The foreign posts of Austria, Denmark, Estonia, Finland, France, Greece, Latvia, Lithuania and Romania are labelled as proactive. The foreign posts of Belgium, Germany, Hungary, the Netherlands and Slovakia are labelled as reactive.

The events that are organised by the employees depend on the structure and the resources of the foreign post. Embassies have fewer resources, such as money and employees, for commercial diplomacy than the trade offices. Trade offices have more employees working on commercial diplomacy. In an embassy there are often only one or two commercial attachés working on economic affairs. The number of employees working at the foreign post and the activities they perform are decided by the ministry, but this is also influenced by the working requirements, the training, and the background of the employees at the foreign post. All the employees of an embassy have had diplomatic training. They have an academic background in economics and politics. The employees at trade offices have not all had diplomatic training, and they have an academic background in economics and law. The requirements for a person who wants to work at the foreign post differs per country. The foreign posts of Austria, Finland, France, Greece, Latvia, Lithuania and Romania indicated that speaking several languages is a requirement. The foreign posts of Belgium, Denmark, Estonia, Germany, Hungary, the Netherlands and Slovakia indicated that speaking the local language is not a requirement, but it is a benefit if an applicant does speak the local language and/or other languages. The foreign post of each MS has a university bachelor degree as a requirement. The working requirements and number of employees can explain the differences and similarities between the practice factors of the 14 MS. The practice factors together with the country characteristics and the policy factors were statistically tested for a relation between the factors and any possible explanations for the differences and similarities between the MS (Table 4).

Results of Statistical Analysis

The comparison of the commercial diplomacy policy and practice factors showed that there are clear differences and similarities between the EU MS. The commercial diplomacy policies and practices of the MS depend on the country characteristics. The country characteristic factors show differences and similarities between the MS, but they also provide a possible explanation for the differences and similarities between the commercial diplomacy policy and practice factors of the MS. The country characteristics together with all the policy and practice factors have been statistically analysed for possible relations between them and for possible explanations for the differences and similarities between the MS. The statistical analysis for possible relations is based on the chi-square test, the Phi test, the Cramer's V test and the correlation test (De Veaux et al., 2008). From a theoretical point of view, we would expect to find relationships between several factors. Six interesting relationships are discussed in this section.

Responsible ministry and policy focus. On the policy side, a relationship is generally assumed between the responsible ministry and the policy focus of the MS. Within a country, we would expect that the policy focus and policy goals of a government depend on the responsible ministry creating the policies. It would make sense that the Ministry of Foreign Affairs is less business-oriented than the Ministry of Trade, but

Table 4: Practice factors of EU MS.

Practice factors	France	Germany	Greece	Hungary	Latvia
Structure of foreign post	Chamber of commerce, private.	Trade agency, public	Embassy, public	Embassy, public	Embassy, public
Economic function	Business promoter	Business promoter	Business promoter	Civil servant/business promoter	Business promoter/civil servant
Tasks	Problem solver; answer questions; provide information; organise events, fairs, trade shows, missions, delegations, ministry visits, business to business meetings; partner search; briefings; reports	Reporting, answering questions, trade missions, trade fairs, market study, country profile	Promoting investment and export; market analysis; partner search; exporting strategies; events, trade shows and seminars; meetings; reports; briefings; company visits; missions	Assisting business with their export and going abroad, answer questions, promote Estonia, cooperate on EU affairs, attend briefings, organise events	Reporting, answering questions, events, meetings, briefings, visits
Staff category	Elite oriented	Structure oriented	Structure oriented	Mixed oriented	Elite oriented
Number of employees	7 in the office	2 on economic affairs	8 on economic affairs	1 on economic affairs	1 on economic affairs
Programmes	Seminars, fairs, missions, reports	Fairs, trade missions, reporting	Seminars, fairs, missions, reports	Reporting, seminars, missions	Trade missions, reporting, seminar
Activism of foreign post	Proactive	Reactive	Proactive	Proactive	Proactive

	France	Germany	Greece	Hungary	Latvia
Requirements	German and English, economic and law degree	University degree, diplomatic test, affinity with country and economic degree recommended	Experience within economic sector, business degree; local language is a plus	Diplomatic requirements	University degree, 4 languages: Finish, Swedish, English and language of own choice
Training	On-the-job training, with seminars and personal training	Assessment and test, after that no training	Team-building, competence development courses	Diplomatic training	Diplomatic training
Background	Economics and law	Politics and economics	International business	Politics	International politics, law and communication
Access to information	Good	Good	Good	Good	Good
Practice factors	**France**	**Germany**	**Greece**	**Hungary**	**Latvia**
Structure of foreign post	Trade agency, public	Embassy, public	Embassy, public	Embassy, public	Embassy, public
Economic function	Business promoter	Civil servant/ business promoter	Business promoter	Business promoter	Business promoter
Tasks	Give advice, provide information, show benefits, provide contacts, find partners and opportunities, provide tools for public and	Contact for companies, answer questions, report to ministry and other agencies, support EU affairs, go to	Increase export; promote investment; organise conferences, symposia and workshops; develop	Organise events, reports, arrange delegation visits, find investors, work on export, travel to find	Attract investment; promote Latvia; organise seminars, fairs,/ exhibitions;

Table 4: (*Continued*)

Practice factors	France	Germany	Greece	Hungary	Latvia
	press relations and advertising, coordinate young graduate programme, organise fairs and events, make studies	briefings, do market studies, organise missions and visits, advice companies	business relations; organise trade and business delegations; provide information; arrange options for exhibitions	and help companies	matchmaking; trade missions; individual visits; market research; provide information
Staff category Number of employees	Mixed oriented 12 people in the office	Mixed oriented 12 in the economic department (50 in the chamber of commerce)	Elite oriented 2 employees in the economic section	Treaty oriented 1 employee on economic affairs	Elite oriented 1 employee on economic affairs
Programmes	Reporting, fairs, seminars, counselling, missions	Reporting, missions, counselling	Fairs, trade missions, workshops, seminars, reports	Reporting, missions	Seminars, fairs, missions, reports
Activism of foreign post	Proactive	Reactive	Proactive	Reactive	Proactive
Requirements	English, trade/business education, learn local language	Diplomatic requirements	University degree, fluent English and French	Diplomatic requirements	Business and trade, 3–4 languages, higher education

Practice factors	Lithuania	The Netherlands	Romania		Slovakia
Training	Exam, experience is training	Diplomatic training	Exam, no further training	Exam for each country you go to, special job training	Presentation exam, experience
Background	Business	Politics, some economics	Business and economics and mass communication	Politics	Economics, journalism
Access to information	Good	Good	Good	Good	Good
Practice factors	**Lithuania**	**The Netherlands**	**Romania**		**Slovakia**
Structure of foreign post	Embassy, public	Embassy, public	Embassy, public		Embassy, public
Economic function	Business promoter	Business promoter	Business promoter		Business promoter
Tasks	Promote export, investment and tourism; provide information; provide consultancy; organise events	Reporting, answering questions, trade missions, market scan, promoting brand Holland	Export promotion and investment attraction; organise missions, fairs, exhibitions, study and work visits, meetings, presentations; go to conferences; answer questions; provide information; partner search; provide contact information; write reports; go to briefings		Identify trends, strengthen competition, attract investment, look for innovation and knowledge, answer questions, briefings, reports, fairs, missions, presentations

Table 4: (*Continued*)

Practice factors	Lithuania	The Netherlands	Romania	Slovakia
Staff category	Mixed oriented	Structure oriented	Mixed oriented	Mixed oriented
Number of employees	1 on economic affairs	2 on economic affairs	1 on economic affairs	1 on economic affairs
Programmes	Fairs, seminars, report, workshops, counselling, missions	Missions, reporting	Seminars, fairs, missions, reports	Fairs, trade missions, reporting
Activism of foreign post	Proactive	Reactive	Proactive	Reactive
Requirements	5 years business experience, English+one other language, degree in economics, international trade and law	Affinity with and knowledge of country, economic degree and language recommended	Romanian citizenship, bachelor degree (economic or law), 2 foreign languages (local is a plus)	University degree, diplomatic test, business degree recommended
Training	Test with verbal discussion	Training and test at beginning, after that no training	Training programme with written test and interview before going abroad (applying for job abroad)	Assessment and test, after that no training
Background	Degree in economics, international trade and law	Politics, economics and social	Economics/business	Politics and economics
Access to information		Good	Good	Good

the statistical analysis did not prove this relationship. The Ministry of Trade as well as the Ministry of Foreign Affairs that are solely responsible for commercial diplomacy were both labelled as business-oriented. If the responsibility lay with both ministries, then they were labelled as business-oriented, mixed-oriented, but also as trade-oriented.

Economic function and background of the employees. On the practice factor side, we would expect to find a relationship between the economic function of the foreign post and the background of the employees. If the foreign post is business-oriented, then we would assume that the employees have a background in economics. This relationship has not been proven by the statistical analysis. The foreign post that is labelled as business-oriented can have employees with a background in economics, politics or law. The employees do not need an economic background to work for a foreign post that is business-oriented.

Staff category and background of the employees. Also on the practice side, we would assume that there is a relationship between the staff category and the academic background of the employees. According to the literature, a treaty-oriented diplomat has a background in law, and the structure-oriented diplomat has a background in the social sciences (Galtung & Ruge, 1965), but this has not been confirmed by the statistical analysis. The background of an employee cannot be classified into one staff category. An employee with an economic background can be labelled as elite-oriented, but also as structure-oriented or treaty-oriented.

Policy focus and economic function. Concerning the implementation of the policies of an MS, practice factors have been tested with the policy factors to see if there is a link between them. We would assume that there is a relationship between the policy focus of a country and the economic function of a foreign post. We would expect that the economic function and activities of the foreign post are directly derived from the policy goals of the government. The statistical analysis did not prove this relationship. This means that the employees have some freedom in deciding the function and activities of the foreign post.

Wealth and the number of embassies inside the EU and the number of employees. Finally, we would assume that there is a relationship between the wealth of a country, the number of embassies a country has inside the EU, and the number of employees at the foreign post. A country labelled as rich should have more money and resources to set up an embassy in each MS and to employ more persons at a foreign post than a country that is labelled as poor. This has not been proven by the statistical analysis. Countries labelled as rich do not have significantly more embassies and employees than countries labelled as poor. A country that is labelled as rich might have the resources to set up more embassies and to employ more persons, but that does not mean that the country will do so and will employ more persons than countries labelled as poor. Both can have the same number of embassies within the EU and

have one person working on commercial diplomacy at a foreign post. The results of
the six interesting relationships are shown in Table 5.

Besides these six relationships, the statistical tests found relationships between
other factors. The relationships and the values of the factors that have a relationship
can be found in Table 6. In addition, the statistical tests found a weak positive
correlation between the number of trade offices and the number of embassies within
and outside the EU (and the total number of embassies). This means that when the
number of trade offices increases, the number of embassies also increases or vice
versa. For instance, if the number of trade offices of a country is higher, then the
number of embassies of that country also will be higher.

After having tested all the factors in order to see if there is a relationship between
pairs of them, it became clear that the MS can be arranged into two groups that have
the same categories for several factors. There are only a few countries that fall outside
the category, and some factors do not apply to all the countries, but the categories
make a clear distinction between the MS. The categories contain the country
characteristics, policy factors and practice factors. The data shows that countries
labelled as small mostly entered the EU last; they are labelled as poor and have a
lower percentage of intra-EU trade. The responsibility for commercial diplomacy lies
with both the Ministry of Foreign Affairs and the Ministry of Trade. They also have
fewer embassies and fewer employees at the foreign post. These countries are almost
all proactive in promoting trade and investment and have a staff category at the
foreign post that is labelled as mixed-oriented. The countries that are labelled as large
almost all entered the EU first; they are labelled as rich and have a high percentage of
intra-EU trade. The responsibility for commercial diplomacy lies with both the
Ministry of Foreign Affairs and the Ministry of Trade or only with the Ministry of

Table 5: Interesting relationships.

Relationship	Test value[a]
Responsible ministry and the policy focus of a country	0.893
Economic function, foreign post and the background of the employee(s)	0.160
Staff category of the employees of the foreign post and the background of the employee(s)	0.208
Policy focus of a country and the economic function of its foreign post	0.707
Wealth of a country and the number of embassies inside the EU	0.394
Wealth of a country and the number of employees at a foreign post	0.095

[a]The test values are similar for the chi-square test, the Phi test and Cramer's V test. A relationship
is significant when the value is smaller than 0.05.

Table 6: Statistical relationships.

Relationship	Test value[a]
Entry time in the EU and the size of a country	0.018
Wealth of a country and the entry time in the EU	0.001
Entry time in the EU and the share of intra-EU trade	0.001
Entry time in the EU and the number of embassies inside the EU	0.020
Entry time in the EU and the activism of the foreign post	0.047
Entry time in the EU and the number of employees at the foreign post	0.019
Size of a country and the wealth of a country	0.039
Size of the country and the number of embassies inside the EU	0.003
Size of the country and the number of employees at the foreign post	0.015
Size of the country and the share of intra-EU trade	0.004
Share of intra-EU trade and the number of employees at the foreign post	0.002
The academic background of the employees and the activism of the employees of the foreign post	0.019
The total number of embassies and the number of trade offices	0.02

[a]The test values are similar for the chi-square test, the Phi test and Cramer's V test. A relationship is significant when the value is smaller than 0.05.

Foreign Affairs. They have more embassies and more employees at the foreign post, but are mainly reactive in promoting their country and have different kinds of staff categories.

Conclusion

The results of the research show the differences and similarities between the commercial diplomacy policies and practices of the EU MS. To begin with, it is obvious that the MS are different in terms of their country characteristics. It is more interesting to compare the commercial diplomacy policy and practice factors. The first difference between the MS is that they all have their own commercial diplomacy network of ministries, foreign posts, chambers of commerce and other institutions that are involved in commercial diplomacy. The most common network is a shared responsibility between the Ministry of Foreign Affairs and the Ministry of Economy. Almost all countries have embassies and trade offices abroad that are working on commercial diplomacy. Often, the trade office is part of the embassy (as an economic department), but in some countries they have separate trade (business) offices outside the embassy. MS have different policy goals and policy focus. They also vary in the number of embassies, the number of trade offices and the number of employees at the foreign post. Furthermore, the MS have different staff categories, working requirements, types of training and employees at the foreign posts. Finally, the MS vary in terms of the tasks of the employees at the foreign post and the events they organise. Some MS can be classified as being proactive and some as being reactive. There are also similarities between the MS. They can be categorised into two groups: countries that entered the EU first and countries that entered the EU last. Figure 2 shows the two categories that are opposite of each other in almost all aspects.

The categories in Figure 2 look general, and not all of them count for each country, but it shows in what way the MS are similar to each other. The countries that entered the EU between 1958 and 2003 do not form a third group, rather they can be placed in one of the two categories. Examples of countries that fall in the 'first' category are France, Germany, Italy, Belgium, the Netherlands, the United Kingdom and Spain. Countries that fall in the last category are, for instance, the Czech Republic, Estonia, Latvia, Lithuania, Romania, Slovakia, and Slovenia. There is a big difference between countries that have been in the EU for a long time: they have set up a good trade network. Countries that are new to the EU still have to set up a trade network and promote the business and investment opportunities of their country, because they are not well known in the EU. These categories make the effect of the policies created within the EU clear, and it shows the EU how countries shape their commercial diplomacy policies and practices within the single European market, and whether these regulations have been implemented or if they should be changed. Finally, these categories reveal the relevance of this research because it shows what the commercial diplomacy policies and practices are of the other MS. It is relevant for governments to know what the other MS are doing, because it affects their political and especially their economic relation. It raises the questions of whether they should collaborate or if they should be competitors. Especially the countries labelled as small would do well to collaborate within the EU to increase trade and investment.

Figure 2: Member state categories.

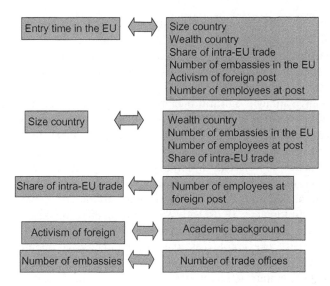

Figure 3: Relationship between commercial diplomacy factors.

The commercial diplomacy policy and practice factors were also statistically tested for a relationship between them and for a possible explanation for the differences and similarities between the MS. Figure 3 shows the relationships between the commercial diplomacy policy and practice factors.

The statistical tests show that there is a positive relationship or correlation between pairs of factors, but it does not show which factor can explain the differences or similarities between the MS. We would assume that the size of a country explains the number of employees at a foreign post. However, the statistical tests do not support a causal relationship; in other words, which factor is the dependent factor and which is the independent factor (de Veaux et al., 2008). Also, some of the relationships do not reflect the influence of one factor over the other. There is theoretically no explanation for the relationship between the time of entry into the EU and the size of a country. This means that there is no absolute clarity about which factors explain the differences and similarities between the MS and which factors affect commercial diplomacy. The next section contains a discussion about the factors that influence commercial diplomacy according to the employees interviewed, and to what extent these factors have been mentioned in the literature.

Discussion

The literature review showed that the commercial diplomacy policies and practices of a country are influenced by different factors. During the interviews, some of these factors were discussed with the participants. Almost all of the respondents mentioned that the practices of the foreign posts are performed differently in each country around the world. Four important points influencing the commercial diplomacy practices that some of them mentioned are the host country characteristics, the economic relationship between the countries, the kind of foreign posts in the host country and whether the host country is located inside or outside the EU.

The first point has been mentioned in broad terms before. According to the literature, the environment, cultural background, regime and institutions of the host country affect commercial diplomacy (Kostecki & Naray, 2007; Ruel & Zuidema, 2012; Yakop & van Bergeijk, 2009). The literature acknowledges that the host country affects commercial diplomacy, but most articles do not mention which characteristics specifically influence commercial diplomacy. The only authors who talk about the host country factors are Kostecki and Naray (2007). They say that 'the host country's market size and market potential is the most significant determinant of the investment in commercial diplomacy' (Kostecki & Naray, 2007, p. 13). They stress the importance of the host country characteristics in the performance of commercial diplomacy practices. The employees who were interviewed mentioned more host country characteristics that influence commercial diplomacy than those given in the literature. The host country characteristics should contain the general characteristics of the country, such as identity, character, law, norms, values, rules, traditions, culture, strength/power of the country and government structure, but they should also include its market characteristics like the type of market (upcoming or developed), size of the market, specific market sectors, specialisations, the added value of top sectors and the way of doing business (local business culture).

The second factor that is important is the economic relationship between the home and the host country. Several studies show the link between export and demographic factors. Rose (2006) finds in his study that export is negatively linked to the economic distance between two countries. This means that if a host country is further away, then the amount of export from the home country to that host country is lower than if the host country is located nearby. He also finds a positive link between export and countries with trade agreements, a common language or land border. Finally, he shows that the relationship between the two countries matters and proves this in the point that colonies trade much more with their coloniser than with other countries (Rose, 2006). Yakop and van Bergeijk (2009) extend the study of Rose. They confirm that distance influences the amount of trade between two countries and introduce new factors that are linked to export. They find that export is positively linked to the economic size and the important markets in the host country, and that it is negatively related to transaction costs, transportation time, land border, currency union, product area and common language (Yakop & van Bergeijk, 2009). The employees who were interviewed raised similar points. They indicated that distance and the economic interaction between the two countries influence the commercial diplomacy practices. The economic interaction between the two countries depends, according to the employees, on the economic priority of the countries, their current trade relation, possible trade barriers, their cultural differences, the amount of trade, perceptions of the country and what a country can gain from the other country (added value).

The third point that influences the commercial diplomacy practices are the types of foreign posts a country has in the host country. In the literature review it was already mentioned that the structural form of the foreign posts affects commercial diplomacy and that they can be divided into private, public or mixed (Mercier, 2007). The results of this research made it clear that practices are performed differently within an embassy or a trade office. The employees of the foreign posts indicated that the practices depend on the number and the types of foreign posts in the host country. The literature found that an additional consulate or embassy in the host country increases the amount of export (Rose, 2006; Yakop & van Bergeijk, 2009). These studies only looked at consulates and embassies related to export, but did not include trade offices or chambers of commerce related to commercial diplomacy. The employees at the foreign posts mentioned that the practices of an embassy in the host country are different if there is also a trade office and a chamber of commerce. Then the embassy performs different and fewer practices, because the rest are performed by the trade agency or by the chamber of commerce. If the embassy is the only foreign post in the host country, then obviously it has to perform all the practices that are normally performed at the trade office or the chamber of commerce.

The final factor that was mentioned by the employees is the location of the foreign posts within other EU countries and in countries outside the EU, especially in third world countries. The literature review mentioned that the internal market of the EU changes the commercial diplomacy of the MS and that diplomats should modify their duties (Bratberg, 2007; Hocking & Spence, 2005; Kostecki & Naray, 2007). The literature, however, does not show in which way it will change and what duties the diplomats perform. The employees of the embassies said that within the

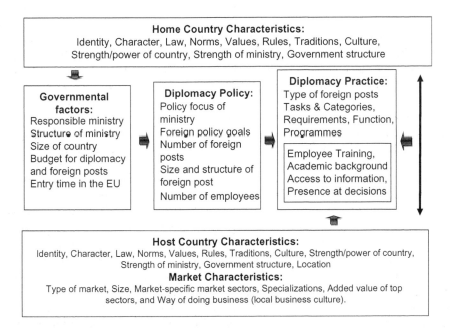

Figure 4: Factors influencing commercial diplomacy.

EU they work more on economic affairs and the political decisions within the EU framework. They look for cooperation options with countries for all EU affairs and inform the government about a MS position on a certain policy issue. The employees in the EU do not need to work on issues about trade regulations and barriers because of the free trade area. According to the employees, the embassies outside the EU have to work on removing trade barriers and controlling the rules and regulations of the host country. In third-world countries, embassies may only get involved when a company has trouble with the rules, regulations and other trade barriers of the host country. In those countries, the political relations and active roles of diplomats are needed to help a company to venture abroad and find business opportunities.

This discussion makes it clear that there are more factors that influence the commercial diplomacy practices than those mentioned in the literature review. This means that the figure showing the factors that influence commercial diplomacy has to be extended. Figure 4 contains the home country characteristics, the host country characteristics, its market characteristics, the economic relationship between the two countries, and the commercial diplomacy policy and practice factors.

Limitations and Further Research

This study looked at the commercial diplomacy policies and practices of the EU MS. Their policies were examined based on a policy analysis. The information was found on the government websites and in policy documents. This information is limited because not everything is published online, and a lot of information is only written down in the local language. Still, for this study enough information was found to analyse the policies of a government and to compare the MS. The practices were researched through interviews. The participation rate is a limitation for this study, because not all of the MS practices could be compared. The fact that all the foreign posts were located in Stockholm (Sweden) makes it hard to generalise the data, but it is good for comparing the factors, because all the posts are located in the same economic market and country.

These limitations and the discussion about the factors that influence commercial diplomacy indicate that there is still plenty that is unclear about what influences commercial diplomacy policies and practices and what effect EU membership has. Future research should focus on the differences in commercial diplomacy policies and practices within and outside the EU. Researchers and decision-makers have to realise that the internal market changes the way commercial diplomacy is performed. Furthermore, studies should be done to prove which factors that have been mentioned in this study really influence commercial diplomacy. More statistical tests have to be performed to confirm the direction of the relationship between factors and which factors deter commercial diplomacy. Also, the practice factors of the MS have to be tested in different countries to see if this data can be generalised to account for practice factors of all the foreign posts of an MS within the EU. These practice factors should also be tested outside the EU, paying special attention to the significance of the host country characteristics, the relationship and the distance between the home and host country.

Acknowledgement

The authors would like to thank Nico Groenendijk for his comments to an earlier version of the chapter.

References

Ahmad, S., & Schroeder, R. G. (2003). The impact of human resource management practices on operational performance: Recognizing country and industry differences. *Journal of Operations Management, 21*, 19–43.

Atkinson, A. B., & Brandolini, A. (2001). Promise and pitfalls in the use of secondary data-sets: Income inequality in OECD countries as a case study. *Journal of Economic Literature, 39*(3), 771–799.

Bátora, J. (2003). *Does the EU transform the institution of diplomacy?* Discussion Papers in Diplomacy. The Netherlands Institute of International Relations 'Clingendael', The Hague, the Netherlands.

Bátora, J., & Hocking, B. (2007). *Bilateral diplomacy in the EU: Towards post-modern patterns?* Vienna: Institute for European Integration Research, Austrian Academy of Sciences.

Bátora, J., & Hocking, B. (2008). *Bilateral diplomacy in the EU: Towards 'post-modern' patterns?* Discussion Papers in Diplomacy. The Netherlands Institute of International Relations 'Clingendael', The Hague, the Netherlands.

Baylis, J., & Smith, S. (2005). *The globalization of world politics: An introduction to international relations* (3rd ed.). Oxford: Oxford University Press.

Berridge, G. R. (2010). *Diplomacy, theory and practice* (4th ed.). New York, NY: Palgrave Macmillan.

Berridge, G. R., & James, A. (2003). *A dictionary of diplomacy* (2nd ed.). Basingstoke, Hants, UK: Palgrave Macmillan.

Bratberg, O. (2007). Bilateral Diplomacy in an integrated Europe: the co-existence of institutional orders? Working Paper no. 10. ARENA – Centre for European Studies, University of Oslo, Oslo, Norway.

Bruter, M. (1999). Diplomacy without a state: The external delegations of the European Commission. *Journal of European Public Policy, 6*(2), 183–205.

Chalmers, D., Hadjiemmanuil, C., Monti, G., & Tomkins, A. (2006). *EU law* (1st ed.). Cambridge, UK: Cambridge University Press.

De Veaux, R. D., Velleman, P. F., & Bock, D. E. (2008). *Stats data and models* (2nd ed.). Amsterdam, The Netherlands: Pearson Education.

Delery, J. E., & Doty, D. H. (1996). Modes of theorizing in strategic human resource management: Tests of universalistic, contingency and configurational performance predictions. *The Academy of Management Journal, 39*(4), 802–835.

Duke, S. W. (2002). Preparing for European diplomacy. *Journal of Common Market Studies, 40*(5), 849–870.

Eisenhardt, K. M., & Graebner, M. E. (2007). Theory building from cases: Opportunities and challenges. *Academy of Management Journal, 50*(1), 25–32.

Europa. (2011a). *Countries.* Retrieved from http://europa.eu/about-eu/countries/index_en.htm

Europa. (2011b). *EU delegations.* Retrieved from http://www.eeas.europa.eu/delegations/index_en.htm

Europa. (2011c). *Panorama of the EU.* Retrieved from http://ec.europa.eu/publications/booklets/eu_glance/79/en.pdf

Eurostat. (2011). *Statistic database comparing themes between the MS.* Retrieved from http://epp.eurostat.ec.europa.eu/portal/page/portal/statistics/search_database

Galtung, J., & Ruge, M. H. (1965). Patterns of diplomacy. *Journal of Peace Research, 2*(2), 101–135.

Hill, C., & Wallace, W. (1979). Diplomatic trends in the European community. *International Affairs, 55*(1), 47–66.

Hocking, B., & Spence, D. (2005). *Foreign ministries in the EU: Integrating diplomats* (rev. ed.). Basingstoke, Hants, UK: Palgrave Macmillan.

Hoffman, J. (2003). Reconstructing diplomacy. *British Journal of Politics and International Relations, 5*(4), 525–542.

Kenis, P., & Schneider, V. (1987). The EC as an international corporate actor: Two case studies in economic diplomacy. *European Journal of Political Research, 15*, 437–457.

Keukeleire, S. (2003). The EU as a diplomatic actor: Internal, traditional and structural diplomacy. *Diplomacy & Statecraft, 14*(3), 31–56.

Kleiner, J. (2008). The inertia of diplomacy. *Diplomacy and Statecraft, 19*, 321–349.

Kostecki, M., & Naray, O. (2007). *Commercial diplomacy and international business.* Discussion Papers in Diplomacy. The Netherlands Institute of International Relations 'Clingendael', The Hague, the Netherlands.

Lee, D. (2004). The growing influence of business in UK diplomacy. *International Studies Perspectives, 5*, 50–54.

Lee, D., & Hudson, D. (2004). The old and new significance of political economy in diplomacy. *Review of International Studies, 30*, 343–360.

Lindberg, L. N. (1963). *The political dynamics of European economic integration* (online ed.). Stanford, US: Stanford University Press.

Mercier, A. (2007). *Commercial diplomacy in advanced industrial states: Canada, the UK and the US.* Discussion Papers in Diplomacy. The Netherlands Institute of International Relations 'Clingendael', The Hague, the Netherlands.

Moravcsik, A. (1991). Negotiating the single European act: National interest and conventional statecraft in the European community. *International Organization, 45*(1), 19–56.

Naray, O. (2008). *Commercial diplomacy: A conceptual overview.* Paper presented at the 7th World Conference of TPOs, The Hague, the Netherlands.

Naray, O. (2011). Commercial diplomacy in the context of international business. *The Hague Journal of Diplomacy, 6*, 121–148.

Newman, J. C., Des Jarlais, D. C., Turner, C. F., Gribble, J., Cooley, P., & Paone, D. (2002). The differential effects of face-to-face interviews and computer interview modes. *American Journal of Public Health, 92*(2), 294–297.

Nugent, N. (2006). *The government and politics of the EU* (6th ed.). Basingstoke, Hants, UK: Palgrave Macmillan.

Pollack, M. A. (1997). Representing diffuse interests in EC policy-making. *Journal of European Public Policy, 4*(4), 572–590.

Rijks, D., & Whitman, R. (2007). European diplomatic representation in third countries: Trend and options. In: *The EU Foreign Service: How to Build a More Effective Common Policy* (November edition, pp. 35–47). Brussels: European Policy Centre.

Rose, A. K. (2006). The foreign service and foreign trade: Embassies and export promotion. *The World Economy, 30*(2), 22–38.

Ruel, H. J. M., & Visser, R. (2012). Commercial diplomacy as corporate entrepreneurs: Explaining role behaviour from an institutional perspective. *International Journal of Diplomacy and Economy, 1*(1), 1–34.

Ruel, H. J. M., & Zuidema, L. (2012). *The effectiveness of commercial diplomacy: A survey conducted among embassies.* The Clingendael Discussion Papers Series. The Netherlands Institute of International Relations 'Clingendael', The Hague, the Netherlands.

Saner, R., & Yu, L. (2003). *International economic diplomacy: Mutations in post-modern times.* Discussion Papers in Diplomacy. The Netherlands Institute of International Relations 'Clingendael', The Hague, the Netherlands.

Sorensen, H. T., Sabroe, S., & Olsen, J. (1996). A framework for evaluation of secondary data resources for epidemiological research. *International Journal of Epidemiology, 25*(2), 423–442.

Szondi, G. (2008). *Public diplomacy and nation branding: Conceptual similarities and differences.* Discussion Papers in Diplomacy. The Netherlands Institute of International Relations 'Clingendael', The Hague, the Netherlands.

Way, S. A., Lepak, D. P., Fay, C. H., & Thacker, J. W. (2010). Contingent workers' impact on standard employee withdrawal behaviours: Does what you use them for matter? *Human Resource Management, 49*(1), 109–138.

Wies, R. (1994). Policies in network and systems management – Formal definition and architecture. *Journal of Network and Systems Management, 2*(1), 63–83.

Yakop, M., & van Bergeijk, P. A. G. (2009). *The weight of economic and commercial diplomacy.* Working Paper no. 478. International Institute of Social Studies, Erasmus University Rotterdam, The Hague, the Netherlands.

Chapter 8

Entering the United States Federal Procurement Market: Success Factors and Barriers for Foreign Firms

Tim Vehof, Huub Ruël and Jan Telgen

Abstract

The US federal procurement market is the largest procurement market in the world. Therefore, it is an attractive market for foreign companies to enter. Existing literature indicates the success factors and barriers for public procurement market entry in general, however not for the US procurement market. To get an in-depth understanding of the US federal procurement market entry process for foreign companies, an expert study was conducted, involving successful foreign companies, procurement market entry consultants, and US government officials. The findings indicate that company-specific factors and product-specific factors can be labeled as "qualifiers," while relational factors can be labeled "winners."

Keywords: Market entry; federal procurement

Introduction

On the road to economic recovery in the United States after "The Great Recession," the deepest recession since "The Great Depression" in the 1930s, government expenditure in the United States is playing a major role. Examples are the economic stimulus packages of the Obama administration, totaling nearly $1.2 trillion since the nation descended into recession in late 2007. The economic recovery of the United States so far has relied for a great deal on these stimulus packages of the government and is expected to stay reliant on them for years to come.

Commercial Diplomacy and International Business: A Conceptual and Empirical Exploration
Advanced Series in Management, 227–250
ISSN: 1877-6361/doi:10.1108/S1877-6361(2012)0000009012

Where American government expenditure will be the main source for economic recovery, it appears that there could be opportunities for foreign companies. Federal procurement in the United States is very extensive, and growing. Since 2005, the amount of federal procurement has increased by almost $150 billion, to over $540 billion in fiscal year (FY) 2008. Additionally, the $787 billion American Recovery and Reinvestment Act (ARRA) of 2009 includes a big package of public investment regarding infrastructure, sustainable energy, and water management. Although the overall procurement under the regular budget decreased slightly in 2009 ($535 billion), the procured goods from the stimulus packages have to be added in the 2009 procurement overview. When including those figures, the total amount of federal procurement increased significantly in 2009, totaling $636 billion (Federal Procurement Database). This makes the federal public procurement market in the United States the biggest in the world and potentially very relevant for exporting countries.

This chapter aims to gain insight into the critical success factors and barriers for foreign companies to acquire federal procurement contracts. Although public procurement and its procedures and the factors playing a role in getting contracts as such is not an underresearched topic, it is not clear though how foreign companies can become successful on the US public procurement market. The US federal procurement market is the largest in the world and specific in nature. We conducted an expert study involving foreign companies that have been successful in the US federal procurement market, consultants offering services to support foreign companies, and US federal government officials. All the experts were US based and the study was carried out in the United States.

Managerial Relevance

With the new shift in government spending regarding the economic recovery, there are opportunities for foreign companies to expand their business toward the US federal procurement market. However, winning public procurement contracts is not an easy matter. Supposed to be transparent though, the procedures are complex and time-consuming. The US federal procurement market is still the largest in the world. Especially an expert study based research provides an in-depth understanding of what factors play a crucial role for successfully entering the federal procurement market and on how they play a role.

Theoretical Framework

Public Procurement: Definitions and Aims

Public procurement is big business; in most countries, it accounts for a sizeable share of economic activity, depending on the scope of the government's responsibilities and involvement in the economy (Berrios, 2006; Maskin & Tirole, 2007; Reich, 2009;

Walker & Brammer, 2007; Weiss & Thurbon, 2006). Government is often the single biggest customer within a country, and governments can potentially use this purchasing power to influence the behavior of private sector organizations.

Public procurement is an arrangement between a public entity and a private entity in which the private entity promises, in exchange for money, to deliver certain products or services to the public entity for public consumption, which is guided by principles of transparency, accountability, and achieving *value for money* for citizens and taxpayers (Kelman, 2002; Walker & Brammer, 2007; Weiss, 1993). It is through public procurement that the State, or its territorial or functional subdivisions, undertakes public works, builds roads, and cares for health, education, and public order (Erridge & McIlroy, 2002).

Even though there are many similarities, it is commonly accepted that public procurement is quite different from procurement in the private sector (Erridge, 1996; Telgen, 2006; Thai, 2001; Thai et al., 2004). It is widely acknowledged that the decision by a private entity to outsource a transaction often involves efficiency issues. Nevertheless, when it comes to public services activities organized by governments, contracting out is often viewed through the lens of ideology, leading to clear-cut positions (positive or negative) that contrast with the more balanced way that contracting strategies between private firms are analyzed (Saussier, Staropoli, & Yvrande-Billon, 2009). When comparing public and private sector procurement, the demands on public procurement seem to be more extensive than those on private procurement; in public procurement, there are additional demands that must be satisfied (Telgen, 2006), and it seems justified to the state that public sector procurement is more complex than private sector procurement. In his study, Spiller (2008) found that a fundamental difference between public and private contracting is the potential scrutiny of public contracts by "third party opportunism," which he explains as third parties[1] providing information only when it is in their interest; this limits the potential for relational public contracting. Thus, public contracting will not only be more complex, involving multiple rules and procedures, but will also be more subject to litigation.

Contract and Contractor Selection

According to the procurement regulations in the United States, government contracts are supposed to be awarded to the bidder providing "best value" to the government. The "best value" determination is based on cost and noncost factors such as excellence, management capabilities, and professional experience. Not much empirical research exists on practices of this process of awarding contracts.

According to Maskin and Tirole (2007), the standard presumption in academic and policy work on public procurement is that the government acts to maximize social

---

[1]Interested third parties who may benefit politically from exposing a hint of corruption in a public agent's actions.

welfare. They state that this assumption oversimplifies reality because, amongst other reasons, "government officials may have preferences that differ from those of a social welfare maximizer" (Maskin & Tirole, 2007). In addition, Levin and Tadelis (2010) show that politicians' project choices are influenced significantly by the desire to please constituencies and by budgetary constraints.

A study that underlines these statements is that of Berrios (2006). In his paper, he explores which contractors are most likely to win government contracts. He states that many of the for-profit government contractors rely on selling to the government for nearly all of their business. "Most are well-established firms with a staff of proposal writers, accountants, auditors, engineers and lawyers. Some of these firms can afford to spend large sums putting together a proposal. Quite often the selection weighs heavily on the technical content of the proposal and less so on the actual cost. The procedure tends to favor the larger and more established contractors. They have a distinct advantage over small firms even if those groups have the technical expertise in the field" (Berrios, 2006).

Where most literature on public procurement focuses on the government perspective, this study focused on the foreign business perspective of public procurement. In the field of international business, it is well accepted that foreign firms face disadvantages while doing business abroad (Eden & Miller, 2001; Elango, 2009; Hymer, 1976; Kindleberger, 1969). This concept has been referred to as Liability of Foreignness (LOF) and has been defined as "all additional costs a firm operating in a market overseas incurs that a local firm would not incur" (Zaheer, 1995). We found that LOF holds for the US federal procurement market as well, and we try to find what factors contribute to LOF: the barriers for foreign companies for doing business with the US federal government. Also, we try to find what success factors exist for coping with LOF and thus contribute to the successful acquisition of government contracts in the United States. We decided to use categories of factors because "in the case of complex procurement, the mechanism design approach is indeed often irrelevant in practice: the suitability of each awarding procedure depends on many economic and institutional factors that can hardly be taken into account in most formal models" (Milgrom, 2004). This study focused on the process after the decision of the US federal government to contract out and after making a decision on contracting practices: the process of contractor selection. We found three categories of endogenous variables and four categories of exogenous variables.

Endogenous Variables

Three categories of endogenous variables (success factors) are identified: company-specific factors, product-specific factors, and relational factors. These are categories of factors that should contribute to the acquisition of government procurement contracts by foreign vendors.

Company-specific factors.   We define company-specific factors as the factors that apply to a company and distinguish it from other companies. Several scholars have mentioned the importance of company-specific factors in public procurement processes. Saussier et al. (2009) state that "the reliability of private partners should be assessed on the basis of their past performances, their reputation, or their attitude to team-working and innovation" (Saussier et al., 2009). Berrios (2006) already noted that procurement procedures tend to favor the more established contractors because of these reasons: "The procedure tends to favor the larger and more established contractors. They have a distinct advantage over small firms even if those groups have the technical expertise in the field" (Berrios, 2006).

Nielsen and Nielsen (2010) found that international experience of a top management team of a company influences a company's choice for a foreign entry mode, which could influence their success in a foreign environment. In addition, Burpitt and Rondinelli (2004) state that entry mode choices are also determined by the firm's experience with particular types of marketing channels in their home countries. Zhou (2007) found that for early internationalizing firms, entrepreneurial proclivity impacts on the pace of born global development through foreign market knowledge. Also, he found that firm size and international experience were significantly related to foreign market knowledge. Consistent with most of the evidence in the literature, relatively larger firms seem to have more resources and capabilities to learn about foreign market knowledge, and such knowledge tends to be richer as international experience increases (Zhou, 2007). While not directly related to public procurement, these findings underline the importance of company-specific factors for companies competing in foreign markets.

Product-specific factors. According to Saussier et al. (2009), a "public–private project can be awarded according to either the 'lowest price only' or the 'most economically advantageous tender.' The choice of a particular criterion essentially depends on the project's complexity and on the level of uncertainty." The importance of economic advantages is underlined by several scholars. Ya Ni and Bretschneider (2007) state that "the core argument for the economic rationale is that public sector organizations can deliver services at a lower cost by contracting with private or nonprofit sector organizations than it can through the direct production of services." Private contractors operating in competitive markets are under constant pressure to keep costs low and quality high often through innovative service delivery (Donahue, 1989; Kettl, 1993; Pack, 1987; Savas, 1987). We define product-specific factors, such as price, quality, or uniqueness of a product, as the factors that create added value to the product/service being sold compared to similar, competitive products.

Elango (2009) stresses the importance of product variety for companies trying to sell abroad: "First, by having a greater number of product choices, the foreign firm increases its odds of offering the customer a product which is desirable compared to a local firm. Second, increased product variety will allow the foreign firm to gain exposure in underserved segments of the local markets, allowing for growth with relatively less competition." Levin and Tadelis (2010) found that contracting difficulties such as problems in monitoring performance, the need for flexibility, or sensitivity to service quality might lead to less private contracting by local governments in the United States. These findings indicate an influence of product-specific factors on public procurement processes.

Relational factors.   According to Guttman and Willner (1976), the public contracting processes "are dominated by the network of relationships that exist between contractor and agency, and these relationships are crucial in the awarding and administration of contracts." Therefore, "from a business standpoint, former contracting officers and other key officials with [procurement] expertise are essential to have on board. They are attracted to the private sector because their expertise and inside knowledge, they retain inside contacts, and are specially adept at securing contracts because they know their way in and out of government" (Berrios, 2006). The nexus between former government officials and their new role as clients to the government has been criticized as representing a conflict of interest, but former government officials are seen as prized commodities for their intimate knowledge of government policies affecting their business. In this study, relational factors are defined as the factors that contribute to maintaining good relationships between parties involved in procurement processes.

Erridge and McIlroy (2002) outline different (roles of) relationships in procurement processes and their influence on eventual partnerships between governments and private parties. They state that if an organization's strategy involves a closer relationship, then partnership models are likely to be explored. The general principle underlying these relationships involves trust, mutual commitment, and sharing (Ellram, 1991). Macbeth and Ferguson (1994) argue that a cooperative approach such as partnerships reduces transaction costs through a clearer understanding of requirements and reduces monitoring requirements such as quality control which will have a positive benefit on cost reduction. Furthermore, this approach tries to share risks and rewards although this will tend to be to varying degrees (Ellram, 1991a; Macbeth & Ferguson, 1994). However, Spiller (2008) argues that "third party opportunism" limits the potential for relational public contracting: "Public agencies will have difficulty entering into a close relation with a supplier, in which contract adaptation takes place without formal renegotiations, and/or litigation." These regulatory factors are indeed identified as one of the categories of exogenous variables, on which we will elaborate in the following section.

Exogenous Variables

Four categories of exogenous variables (barriers) are identified: regulatory factors, nonregulatory factors, industry-specific factors, and political factors. These are categories of assumed barriers to acquiring government procurement contracts by foreign vendors.

Regulatory factors.   Public procurement is bound to be executed within strict limits imposed by legal rules and organizational procedures at various levels (Murray,

1999). Sometimes the rules and regulations are cumulative (international, national, local) or mutually contradictory or elusive. In the case of the US federal government, the rules and regulations are quite extensive; the Federal Acquisition Regulation[2] contains about 2000 pages.

For foreign companies, this could mean a disadvantage vis-à-vis domestic companies. Zaheer (1995) states that one of the factors that create the before-mentioned LOF is costs, due to lack of familiarity in the local environment. This lack of familiarity requires foreign firms to collect information that is already known to local firms (Hennart, Roehl, & Zeng, 2002). On the other side of the coin, there is a lack of awareness by customers and regulators leading to discrimination hazards (Zaheer, 1995) and time compression diseconomies during market entry (Elango, 2009; Markides & Williamson, 1994).

In the case of federal procurement in the United States, protectionist regulations appear to play an additional disadvantage for foreign companies. More specifically, the "Buy American" provision as part of the ARRA (2009) has enhanced the protectionist precautions of the Buy American Act of 1933, which requires the United States government to prefer US-made products in its purchases. Other federal legislation extends similar requirements to federal purchases. Miyagiwa (1991) explains this disadvantage in terms of political goals: "governments typically wield their purchases as a policy tool, favoring domestic over foreign suppliers. By doing so, they aim to return tax money to domestic residents, create more jobs at home, and reduce imports." Thus, an overlap appears to exist between regulatory factors and political factors, on which we will elaborate further below.

Nonregulatory factors. Transparency is an important issue in public procurement for obvious reasons. It refers to the ability of all interested participants to know and understand the actual means and processes by which contracts are awarded and managed. It implies the existence of a "level playing field" (equal opportunities for all participants). In addition, integrity of all participants of public procurement processes is expected, to do what they promise to do, and to avoid improper, wasteful or corrupt and fraud practices (Telgen, 2006). We refer to these practices as nonregulatory factors: factors that limit fair competition apart from regulations.

In public procurement, the evaluation of proposals mostly requires special expertise that the buying agency may not possess. Often, the procured goods and services involve new technologies and/or nonstandard designs, which are difficult to objectively measure or evaluate. According to Burguet and Che (2004), this need for relying on a third-party assessment of contract proposals creates a potential for bribery and corruption. In their article, they show how bribery affects the nature of procurement competition and the welfare of the involved parties and how the scoring rule should be designed to mitigate the harmful effect of corruption. Burguet and Che (2004) found that bribery competition and contract bidding play

---

[2]https://www.acquisition.gov/Far/

fundamentally different roles, and that when bribery and contract bidding occur together, the former undermines the effectiveness of the latter in selecting the most efficient contractor.

Industry-specific factors. We define industry-specific factors as the factors that characterize an industry (other than the differences in product groups). In this case: the industry/market the US federal government wants to buy from is not based on products but other factors. Examples of these factors would be the competitive forces such as economics of industries, new entrants, the bargaining power of customers (US government agencies) and suppliers, and the threat of substitute services or products (Porter, 1979).

Both theoretical and empirical works highlight that public–private agreements' failures are connected to the environment in which they are embedded (Saussier et al., 2009). Levin and Tadelis (2010) argue that a lack of a competitive market could lead to less use of private sector services by public entities in the United States. Another example of the influence of industry-specific factors on public procurement processes is given by Telgen (2006), who discusses the similarities of the well-known concept of reciprocity: buying from a supplier that is buying from you. He states that in public purchasing, it is well realized this complicated relationship structure poses additional demands on the buyer–supplier interaction at both the policy level and the operational level. Indeed, these demands may differ per industry.

Political factors. As Spiller (2008) points out, "a fundamental difference between private and public contracts is that public contracts are in the public sphere, and thus, although politics is normally not necessary to understand private contracting, it becomes fundamental to understanding public contracting." Additionally, framing contracting decisions strictly in economic terms would make sense if government organizations were insulated from politics. "Public agencies, however, unlike their private counterparts, are heavily influenced by politics. Public decision makers have to balance efficiency with political considerations" (Ya Ni & Bretschneider, 2007). Empirical evidence on the influence of political factors on public contracting practices is given by Levin and Tadelis (2010), who found that large cities in the United States do more private contracting. Similar results for recently incorporated cities were found, and they observed more private contracting by cities governed by an appointed city manager rather than an elected mayor. We assume that political factors have an influence on the US federal procurement processes as well.

Evidence that supports this assumption is provided by Ya Ni and Bretschneider (2007), who conclude that "arguments associated with market and economic rationality are clearly politically motivated, at least in part. The benefits from contracting out must, by their nature, have political benefits and cannot be completely understood as a managerial activity aimed solely at enhancing the efficient provision of public goods."

Methods

This study aims to gain insight into the critical success factors and barriers for foreign companies to acquire federal procurement contracts. Existing research in the field of business and management does not provide insights in how foreign companies can become successful in the US public procurement market. The foreign business perspective regarding this topic has been fully disregarded so far. For that reason we decided to opt for a qualitative study, more specifically an expert study design. This design is especially appropriate for gaining insights in unexplored and theoretically undeveloped topics. The results of our study will be an initial model identifying the factors that facilitate and inhibit foreign companies to be successful in the US federal procurement market. This model then can be taken as a point of departure for a confirmative quantitative study.

Setting up the expert study was done based on a protocol, to increase the reliability (Yin, 2009), consisting of five stages. *Stage 1* concerned gaining insight into the federal procurement market and its characteristics. The *Federal Procurement Data System* was used to provide information on all federal contracts. In collaboration with the International Trade Administration, part of the Department of Commerce, we mapped the size of the federal procurement market and the share of non-US companies in it. This provided us with additional initial insights in possible factors that could play a role in being successful in the US procurement market, which was needed for preparing for the interviews. *Other Internet-based sources*, including many US government websites concerning federal procurement, were also used in this first stage. These were rich sources for information for vendors on procurement procedures. It helped us to get a better understanding of the federal procurement market from a vendor's perspective, which was very useful in developing the interview protocols and for conducting the interviews. *Key informants* were used to get more insights in foreign private sector business and in the US business climate. Seven officials of the Economic Department of The Royal Netherlands Embassy in Washington, DC, served as key informants. *Observations in meetings, events, and conversations* played an important role in providing contextual information. Examples of meeting and events were some particularly focusing on public procurement in the United States, round-table meetings with business at the World Bank, and meeting in Washington, DC, on the US economic situation, the business environment, and political issues.

Stage 2 concerned the selection of the experts. We considered three groups of people to be experts: (1) business owners or business representatives that had been successful in winning US federal procurement contracts, (2) consultants who support foreign companies in doing business with the US federal government, and (3) officials from the US federal government who are involved in procurement. The first group and the second group were considered as the main groups of experts; the expertise of the third group was considered to be meaningful in order to place the outcome from the interviews with business and consultancy in perspective. We used purposive sampling and selected 12 non-US company representatives that had been successful in the US federal procurement market, based on the *Federal Procurement Data System* and with the help of the International Trade Administration. The companies selected were all from the Netherlands. The Netherlands is the third largest investor in the United States (after Japan and the United Kingdom), and the Netherlands ranks first when it comes to US direct investment abroad.[3] This made Dutch companies a very interesting and relevant subject for a study on federal procurement in the United States.

We selected seven consultants who offer support services to foreign companies, based on information provided by the Economic Department of the Royal Netherlands Embassy, and six US government officials. In total 25 experts were invited and were willing to participate.

Stage 3 focused on developing the interview questions. The questions needed to reflect the essence of our study and serve as the major tools to collect data to answer our research question. However, as the predominant technique we used semi-structured interviews and we aimed for guided conversations with the interviewees rather than structured, closed questions-based queries. Or in line with Yin (2009), interviews pursued a consistent line of inquiry, but the actual stream of questions is likely to be fluid rather than rigid. Four major questions were chosen to lead the interviews, though each question consisted of subquestions, topics, and issues that had to be covered in the interviews. The four main questions were: (1) Could you describe the process from inducement to signing a contract? (2) What are the main barriers for foreign companies wanting to do business with the US federal government, and why? (3) What factors are determinative for foreign companies for acquiring US federal government procurement contracts, and why? (4) What boundary conditions exist for foreign companies acquiring US federal contracts, and why? These sets of main questions were used for all the three groups of experts. *Stage 4* consisted of conducting the actual interviews with the experts. The interviews were held face-to-face and individually at the experts' offices. The interviews were not recorded, as we believed that it could have a negative effect on the answers given. As an alternative, detailed notes were taken and interviewees were asked to confirm those afterward. The interviewees preferred to stay anonymous. The final stage, *stage 5*, of the expert study protocol, dealt with the analysis of the interviews, though triangulated with the data collected during stage 1. The data collected from the interviewees, as well as secondary data and the notes made during meetings, events, and conversations were analyzed in a structured way. First, we analyzed the results for the exogenous variables (barriers), then the results for the endogenous variables (success factors) that are perceived to address those barriers. Ultimately, this way of analyzing the data contributed to development of the model, allowing clear conclusions to be drawn.

Findings

We found that for foreign companies, company-specific factors and product-specific factors play an important role in the early stages of procurement processes. Factors

---

[3]http://www.bea.gov/international/

like quality and uniqueness of a product are important because they should meet the technical requirements of RFPs, which determine what products will compete for a contract, or "qualify for the shortlist." In other words, when a company's product cannot meet the requirements of the RFP of a contract they decided to compete for, they are not "qualified" and can thus never win the contract. Price does not always seem to be as important in these initial stages, depending on the contract. The larger the contract is in monetary terms, the less important the role of price seems to be. For commodity products, price is obviously very important. With larger contracts, company-specific factors like an extensive track record and a good reputation seem to be more important than price in the process of being selected to compete for a government contract. However, as indicated by two international trade specialists of a federal department:

> **G3a+G3b.** *"Price should be determining in all cases, but everybody knows this is not always the case."*

The importance of company-specific factors in the early stages of a procurement process can be attributed to the concept of trust to a great extent. Government agencies prefer to make "safe choices" for obvious reasons: the agencies do not want to waste any money, and government contractors want to keep their job. Where trust is important, an overlap between company-specific factors and relational factors seems to exist. A metaphor was sketched by the executive vice president of a company involved in aero structures:

> **P11.** *"It's like buying a second-hand car, which everybody prefers to buy from a good friend instead of a stranger."*

Regulatory factors have a direct, obvious influence on the relationships company-specific factors and product-specific factors have with the possibility to compete for a certain contract, since companies should comply with procurement regulations, and products should meet the RFPs' specifications. In addition, industry-specific factors have a direct influence on the process of "shortlisting" qualified companies for a certain contract.

> **P9.** *"There are many ways for an agency to purchase products and services, but they are regulated, so an understanding of what is allowed and what isn't is important for being successful in this market. However, it's a regulation and not necessarily a law. Some agencies abide by the regulations and some don't, so having a clear understanding of the procurement process and what guidelines that particular office uses is key to saving time and maximizing effort."*

Another category of exogenous variables that seems to have an influence in the initial stages of government procurement is political factors. For foreign companies, it seems wise to take these political factors into account when trying to do business with the US federal government. An overlap between regulatory factors and political factors exists, e.g., protectionist regulations ("Buy American").

P11. *"The US procurement market is a global, imperfect world and most definitely not an open market. Protectionist regulations of the US are the main barrier for foreign companies in doing business with the federal government. Americans are very, very risk-averse."*

C5. *"Foreign companies have to work much harder and should cope with the discrimination of foreign suppliers."*

We found that in the stage of vendor selection after "shortlisting" qualified candidates for a contract, relational factors are of critical importance for actually winning government contracts. The results of this study show that in different ways, social relations can play a major role in procurement processes. Also, our empirical findings reveal that relational factors are critical for obtaining information on opportunities to do business with the US federal government, e.g., information on upcoming RFPs.

C5. *"Building and maintaining relationships is determining for winning contracts. That is, in addition to price and quality, but every company can compete on price and quality, you have to do more. When you have real good relationships, you can make sure RFPs are written in a way that the choice for your company is justified."*

In the processes after selecting qualified candidates for a contract, product-specific factors and company-specific factors play a complementary role when it comes to winning that contract. By selecting a company as a qualified vendor, the procuring government agency has already considered those factors. However, the results indicate that a "mix of factors" is important, and therefore none of the endogenous variables is redundant for winning government contracts.

P2. *"Content (a good product), form (a good reputation) and timing (talk to the right people at the right time) are all important for winning federal contracts; it is the mix that makes the determinative big picture."*

The results of this study further indicate that in this stage of the model, nonregulatory factors and political factors can influence the relationship between the endogenous variables and the dependent variable. Companies should take these possible barriers into account when competing for a government contract.

C5. *"Success factors for winning contracts are always about advantages for the contractor. Therefore, when doing business with the federal government, companies should focus on advantages for congressmen. American politicians only think about two things: reelection and money. Therefore, the bigger the advantage for the contractor, the bigger the chances for winning the contract. Thus, a presence in the US is very important: creating jobs, taxes in the US and other sorts of economical advantages make a contractor look good."*

Referring to Hill (1993), the concepts of "qualifiers" and "winners" seem to apply to the US federal procurement market. The results of this study indicate that for foreign companies trying to do business with the US federal government, product-specific factors and company-specific factors are the "qualifiers," the factors that are necessary for competing for government contracts. Relational factors can be considered the "winners," the factors that will be determinative for actually winning contracts (Tables 1 and 2).

P3. "*Product-specific factors, company-specific factors and relational factors are all important. However, the first two will get you to the door; the last one will get you through it.*"

Table 1: Endogenous variables.

Endogenous variables	Summary of perceptions
Product-specific factors	*Overall, 17 of the 25 interviewees thought that product-specific factors play a role in federal procurement processes. Of those, only 4 (3 of them US government officials) agreed that product-specific factors are determinative for winning contracts. The 13 other interviewees believed that product-specific factors are complementary to company-specific factors and relational factors.*
Company-specific factors	*Company-specific factors are considered important by 20 of 25 interviewees. However, only 6 interviewees (2 of 12 interviewees of the Dutch private sector group and 4 of 6 interviewees of the government officials group) see them as determinative.*
Relational factors	*All interviewees from the Dutch private sector group (12) and the consultant group (7) thought that relational factors are important for success in the federal procurement market. Of the government officials, 4 of the 6 interviewees felt relational factors play a positive role. That makes 23 of 25 interviewees who believed relational factors can contribute to winning government contracts in several ways. Of those 23, 13 interviewees (9 from the Dutch private sector group, 4 from the consultants group) thought relational factors are determinative.*

Table 2: Exogenous variables.

Exogenous variables	Summary of perceptions
Regulatory factors	*Nine of 12 interviewees from the Dutch private sector group perceive "regulatory factors" as the main reason this market is as difficult as it is. The consultant group agreed that political factors such as protectionist regulations can play a role in procurement processes. All interviewees from the government officials group perceive regulatory factors as the most important barrier for companies trying to do business with the federal government.*
Nonregulatory factors	*Six of the 25 interviewees think that nonregulatory factors like corruption and errors in procedures play an important, negative role in the process of selling to the federal government. None of the interviewed government officials thought that nonregulatory factors play a role in procurement processes; they are of the opinion that the perceived influence of nonregulatory factors is mostly created by the media and companies who did not win contracts they competed for.*
Industry-specific factors	*Industry-specific factors like nonlevel playing fields are considered an important barrier by 11 of 25 interviewees. Most of these interviewees refer to protectionist precautions taken by the US government as a cause for nonlevel playing fields (see above), which could indicate an overlap with regulatory factors.*
Political factors	*All interviewees agree that political factors are important to address when trying to sell to the federal government. Political factors are perceived to play different roles in procurement processes. An overlap appears to exist between political factors and the other exogenous variables presented in the research model.*

Toward a Model

In stage 5, during the analysis of the interviews, we referred to the four phases of public procurement processes that companies pass, which we identified in stage 1. First, we analyzed the perceptions on the negative influence of the exogenous variables (barriers) toward each phase. Second, we analyzed the perceptions on

Table 3: Influence of exogenous variables.

Exogenous variables	Phase in procurement process			
	Toward awareness of opportunities	Toward "long list" of qualified companies	Toward "shortlist" of qualified companies	Toward acquisition of contract
Regulatory factors	-	***	-	-
Nonregulatory factors	-	-	-	**
Industry-specific factors	-	-	***	-
Political factors	-	**	**	**

(-) No influence; (**) indirect, negative influence; (***) direct, negative influence.

Table 4: Influence of endogenous variables.

Endogenous variables	Phase in procurement process			
	Toward awareness of opportunities	Toward "long list" of qualified companies	Toward "shortlist" of qualified companies	Toward acquisition of contract
Company-specific factors	-	***	**	-
Product-specific factors	-	-	**	-
Relational factors	***	-	-	***

(-) No influence; (**) complementary, positive influence; (***) determinative, positive influence.

the positive influence of the endogenous variables (success factors) on each phase. This way of analyzing contributed to the development of our model, presented in this section. The model is based on the results of our analysis, of which we made a summarizing table for both the exogenous and the endogenous variables.

For the exogenous variables, we made the distinction between direct and indirect negative influence. For instance, regulatory factors — for obvious reasons — have a direct, negative influence on the phase of qualifying for the "long list," where political factors have an indirect, negative influence. The results of our analysis are depicted in Table 3.

A similar table for depicting the results of our analysis is developed for the endogenous variables (Table 4). The endogenous variables should exert a positive influence on winning federal procurement contracts. We made the distinction between complementary and determinative positive influence. The influence of a category of endogenous variables is determinative when this category can be fully accountable for passing a phase. A complementary influence requires another category of endogenous variables for successfully passing a phase.

Combining the summarizing tables, the following model is developed, visualizing the findings of our qualitative expert study (Figure 1). The vertical areas represent the ending of each phase of the procurement process as identified in stage 1 of the study. When successfully passing each phase (following the big grey arrow), a company acquires the contract they compete for. The vertical grey arrows represent the negative influence exerted on the process by the exogenous variables. The horizontal arrows represent the positive influence exerted by the endogenous variables. The validity of our results and model are discussed in the next section.

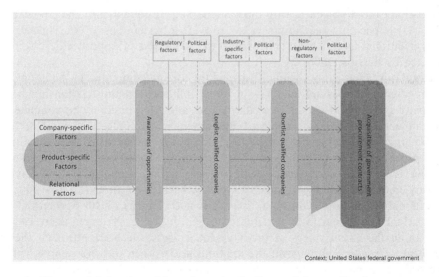

Figure 1: The model developed based on the findings of the qualitative expert study.

Discussion

We found that in the initial stages of government procurement processes, company-specific factors and product-specific factors play a major role. That is, in the stage where government agencies are writing RFPs for a contract and where they choose qualified companies based on their proposals for that contract, company-specific factors and product-specific factors are important selection criteria.

For new entrants as well as incumbents, proactive participation is very important to gain experience and a good understanding of the complexities in public procurement markets, as has already been emphasized by several scholars (Erridge, 1996; Telgen, 2006; Thai, 2001; Thai et al., 2004). Our results show that this is applicable to the US federal procurement market as well. An active participation in the market also helps with developing a good reputation and good references, which are key to winning trust and thus to being perceived as a qualified candidate for a contract.

In addition to this emphasis on company-specific factors, product-specific factors are found to be of major importance in the initial stages of procurement processes as well. Our results indicate that the statement of Saussier et al. (2009) that contracting out public services "might allow public authorities to take advantages of scale and scope economies and to benefit from their private partners" applies to the US federal procurement market. Especially in the phase of selecting qualified vendors, this reasoning seems critical.

Our model depicts a complementary role for relational factors in the initial stages of procurement processes. That is, relational factors can play a role in the selection of qualified vendors in addition to company-specific factors and product-specific factors. Our results show that relational factors can contribute to gaining information on whom to talk to about characteristics of the market and its procedures, and on opportunities to do business with the US federal government, e.g., the publication of RFPs. Also, personal acquaintances can provide introductions to "the right people." Thus, relational factors can contribute to the awareness of opportunities, as already depicted by Berrios (2006).

Regulatory factors are the main barriers for foreign companies in the initial stages of procurement processes and have a direct influence on the relationship between company-specific and product-specific factors and the possibility to compete for a government contract. This confirms the statement of Spiller (2008) that "public contracting seems to be characterized by formalized, standardized, bureaucratic and rigid procedures." Our results show that this applies to the US federal procurement market as well. Also, an overlap with political factors exists. Several scholars have already emphasized that governments typically wield their purchases as a policy tool to win public support (Guttman, 2004; Levin & Tadelis, 2010; Miyagiwa, 1991). Political factors appear to be taken into account by US government agencies and its officials in the initial stages of procurement processes as well, although the exact influence of political factors on the relationship between the endogenous variables and being selected as a qualified vendor is not clear. The results confirm that foreign companies should take into account the additional demands of public procurement vis-à-vis private procurement as mentioned by Telgen (2006) and that "politics are fundamental to understanding public contracting" (Spiller, 2008).

Other barriers that play a role in the early stages of procurement processes are industry-specific factors. They may yield the existence of nonlevel playing fields, thereby directly influencing the companies' chances of winning government contracts. Berrios (2006) already stated that "the procedure tends to favor the larger and more established contractors. They have a distinct advantage over small firms even if those groups have the technical expertise in the field" (Berrios, 2006). Our empirical results imply that this statement holds for the US federal procurement market.

We found that in the process of vendor selection after the shortlisting of qualified candidates for a contract, relational factors are of critical importance. Therefore, our results indicate that relational factors can be considered "winners," the factors that will determine who actually wins a contract. Our results confirm the statement of Berrios (2006) that "one of the broad categories of reasons for behavior that contradicts the very tenets that the government claims to be embracing in turning to contractors to do government work is the close relationship between many contractors and government officials who deal with them, including the revolving door that often sends contractors into government positions and former government officials into contracting firms." We found that relational factors become more important in situations that are characterized by a high level of difficulty and a need for expertise, which was already depicted by Chong, Huet, Saussier, & Steiner (2006).

The effect of social relations on the development of exchanges was already recognized by Granovetter (1985), who states that networks of social relationships strongly influence the development of exchanges, and he argues that where relationships are embedded, behaviors "are so constrained by on-going social relations that to construe them as independent is a grievous misunderstanding." In addition, Burt (2000) defines social capital as "the player's relationship with other players *of a competitive arena+*", and he views social capital as "the final arbiter of competitive success." The results of this study show that these views apply to the US federal procurement market.

In the stages after the shortlisting of qualified candidates for a contract, product-specific factors and company-specific factors play a complementary role as the procuring government agency selected the vendors based mainly on those factors. To some extent this applies to the influence of regulatory factors as well; they do not play a role in the stages after selecting qualified candidates, because those vendors already meet the required regulations. Most government officials interviewed did not agree on the critical importance of relational factors for winning government contracts and thus have a different perception than the interviewees from the other two groups. However, government officials are expected to think that procurement processes are executed "by the book," that product-specific factors like price and quality and company-specific factors like reputation and past performance are critical for winning government contracts.

In these stages too, political factors appear to have an influence on the relationship between company-specific factors, product-specific factors, relational factors, and winning a government contract. Our results indicate that the following statement of

Ya Ni and Bretschneider (2007) holds for the US federal procurement market: "public decision makers have to balance efficiency with political considerations. Therefore, policy or management practices that are adopted are typically based on a mixture of both political and economic rationales."

An overlap appears to exist between political factors and the other exogenous variable that appears to have an influence in this stage of procurement processes, nonregulatory factors. For instance, political rationales may be an incentive for government officials to exercise some form of corruption (e.g., assign a contract to a company in exchange for election money) (Berrios, 2006; Burguet & Che, 2004; Saussier et al., 2009). The results of this study do not clarify when, how, and to what extent the influence of the perceived barriers is present, making it an interesting subject for future research. We will present our recommendations for further research in the following sections. First, we will discuss the limitations of this study.

Managerial Implications

Our results show that for foreign companies, the US federal procurement market is a complex market to compete in that should not be entered without sound preparation. Before entering the US federal procurement market, foreign companies should do extensive research on what industry they want to compete in. Based on this industry scan and an analysis of their own products, they should choose a strategy for entering and competing in this market, while taking into account the results of this study.

One major reason for the market being so difficult is that the US federal government requires vendors to meet many regulations, with accompanying complex procedures. For foreign companies, it is wise not to try to deal with this alone. Instead, a collaboration with an intermediary could be initiated before actually competing in this market.

It can take up to five years before new entrants start winning profitable contracts. Therefore, first of all, it is important that companies are able to survive these long acquisition processes. Second, companies need patience and a willingness to invest a lot of money, time, and effort before establishing profitable returns. In their first years in the US federal procurement market, foreign companies should build networks to obtain information on the characteristics of the market, regulations, procedures, unwritten rules, and upcoming opportunities. Also, participating in the market by means of "small" contracts seems wise for building experience, reputation, and a track record, which have shown to be very important for competing for and winning bigger contracts. By building and maintaining an extensive network with relevant people from the public and private sectors, a company can increase its chances of getting information on opportunities before RFPs are made public. A presence in the United States can be of major importance for foreign companies; this study has shown that it can contribute to winning government contracts in different ways. It can address certain barriers (e.g., protectionist regulations, political considerations) and contribute to building and maintaining an extensive network of relationships.

References

Berrios, R. (2006). Government contracts and contractor behavior. *Journal of Business Ethics*, *63*, 119–130.

Burguet, R., & Che, Y.-K. (2004). Competitive procurement with corruption. *RAND Journal of Economics*, *35*(1), 50–68.

Burpitt, W. J., & Rondinelli, D. A. (2004). Foreign-owned companies' entry and location strategies in a U.S. market: A study of manufacturing firms in North Carolina. *Journal of World Business*, *39*, 136–150.

Burt, R. S. (2000). The network entrepreneur. In R. Swedburg (Ed.), *Entrepreneurship: The social science view*. Oxford: Oxford University Press.

Chong, E., Huet, F., Saussier, F., & Steiner, F. (2006). Public private partnerships and prices: Evidence from water distribution in France. *Review of Industrial Organization*, *29*(1–2), 149–169.

Donahue, J. D. (1989). *The privatization decision: Public ends, private means*. New York, NY: Basic Books.

Eden, L., & Miller, S. (2001). Opening the black box: Multinationals and the costs of doing business abroad. In *Proceedings of the Academy of Management*, C1–C6.

Elango, B. (2009). Minimizing effects of "liability of foreignness": Response strategies of foreign firms in the United States. *Journal of World Business*, *44*, 51–62.

Ellram, L. (1991). Supply chain management: The industrial organization perspective. *International Journal of Physical Distribution and Logistics Management*, *21*(1), 13–22.

Erridge, A. (1996). *Innovations* in public sector and regulated procurement. In A. Cox (Ed.), *Innovations in procurement management*. UK: Earlsgate Press.

Erridge, A., & McIlroy, J. (2002). Public procurement and supply management strategies. *Public Policy and Administration*, *17*, 52–71.

Granovetter, M. (1985). Economic action and social structure: The problem of embeddedness. *American Journal of Sociology*, 481–510.

Guttman, D. (2004). Governance by contract: Constitutional visions; time for reflection and choice. *Public Contract Law Journal*, *33*(2), 321–360.

Guttman, D., & Willner, B. (1976). *The shadow of government: The government's multimillion dollar giveaway of its decision-making to private management consultants, "experts" and their thinks tanks*. New York, NY: Pantheon Books.

Hennart, J., Roehl, T., & Zeng, M. (2002). Do exits proxy a liability of foreignness? The case of Japanese exits from the U.S.. *Journal of International Management*, *8*(3), 241–264.

Hill, T. (1993). *Manufacturing strategy: Text and cases* (2nd ed.). London: Macmillan.

Hymer, S. (1976). *The international operations of national firms: A study of direct investment*. Cambridge, MA: MIT Press.

Kelman, S. J. (2002). Contracting. In L. M. Salamon (Ed.), *The tools of government: A guide to the new governance* (pp. 282–318). New York, NY: Oxford University Press.

Kettl, D. F. (1993). *Sharing power: Public governance and private markets*. Washington, DC: Brookings Institution.

Kindleberger, C. (1969). *American business abroad*. New Haven, CT: University Press.

Levin, J., & Tadelis, S. (2010). Contracting for government services: Theory and evidence from US cities. *Journal of Industrial Economics*, *58*(3), 507–541.

Macbeth, D., & Ferguson, N. (1994). *Partnership sourcing*. London: Pitman.

Markides, C. C., & Williamson, P. J. (1994). Related diversification, core competencies and corporate performance. *Strategic Management Journal*, *15*, 149–165.

Maskin, E., & Tirole, J. (2007). Public-private partnerships and government spending limits. *International Journal of Industrial Organization, 26,* 412–420.

Milgrom, P. (2004). *Putting auction theory to work.* Cambridge: Cambridge University Press.

Miyagiwa, K. (1991). Oligopoly and discriminatory government procurement policy. *American Economic Review, 81,* 1320–1328.

Murray, J. G. (1999). Local government demands more from purchasing. *European Journal of Purchasing and Supply Management, 5*(1), 33–42.

Nielsen, B. B., & Nielsen, S. (2010). The role of top management team international orientation in international strategic decision-making: The choice of foreign entry mode. *Journal of World Business, 46*(2), 185–193.

Pack, J. R. (1987). Privatization of public-sector services in theory and practice. *Journal of Policy Analysis and Management, 6*(4), 523–540.

Porter, M. E. (1979). How competitive forces shape strategy. *Harvard Business Review, 57*(2), 137–145.

Reich, A. (2009). The new text of the agreement on government procurement: An analysis and assessment. *Journal of International Economic Law, 12*(4), 989–1022.

Saussier, S., Staropoli, C., & Yvrande-Billon, A. (2009). *Public*-private agreements, institutions and competition: When economic theory meets facts. *Review of Industrial Organization, 35,* 1–18.

Savas, E. S. (1987). *Privatization: The key to better government.* Chatham, NJ: Chatham House.

Spiller, P. (2008). *An institutional theory of public contracts: Regulatory implications.* NBER Working Paper No. 14152. National Bureau of Economic Research, Cambridge, United Kingdom.

Telgen, J. (2006). Public procurement in perspective. In L. A. Knight, C. M. Harland, J. Telgen, G. Callender, K. V. Thai & K. E. McKen (Eds.), *International public procurement: Cases and commentary.* Routledge.

Thai, K. V. (2001). Public procurement re-examined. *Journal of Public Procurement, 1*(1), 9–50.

Thai, K. V., Araujo, A., Carter, R. Y., Callender, G., Drabkin, D., Grimm, R., ... Telgen, J. (2004). Challenges in public procurement. Boca Raton, FL: Academics Press.

Walker, H., & Brammer, S. (2007). *Sustainable procurement in the United Kingdom public sector.* Working Paper Series 15. School of Management, University of Bath, Bath, United Kingdom.

Weiss, F. (1993). *Public procurement in European community law.* London: The Athlone Press.

Weiss, L., & Thurbon, E. (2006). The business of buying American: Public procurement as trade strategy in the USA. *Review of International Political Economy, 13*(5), 701–724.

Ya Ni, A., & Bretschneider, S. (2007). The decision to contract out: A study of contracting for e-government services in state governments. *Public Administration Review, 67,* 531–544.

Yin, R. K. (2009). *Case study research: Design and methods.* Sage.

Zaheer, S. (1995). Overcoming the liability of foreignness. *Academy of Management Journal, 38*(2), 341–363.

Zhou, L. (2007). The effects of entrepreneurial proclivity and foreign market knowledge on early internationalization. *Journal of World Business, 42,* 281–293.

Appendix 1: List of Interviewees

Group	Indicator of interviewee	Function of interviewee
Dutch private sector	P1	*Managing Director of a company involved in sustainable building management*
	P2	*Founding partner of a company involved in sustainable energy*
	P3	*Federal contracts manager at a company involved in infrastructure*
	P4	*Account manager (federal government as main client) at a company involved in natural resources*
	P5	*Salesman (to the federal government) of a company involved in water management*
	P6	*Salesman (to the federal government) of a company involved in security and safety*
	P7	*Senior Area Vice President at a human resources company*
	P8a	*Vice President Federal Programs at a company involved in natural resource management*
	P8b	*Vice President Marketing at a company involved in natural resource management*
	P9	*Vice President Government Sales at a company involved in knowledge-driven solutions*
	P10	*Commercial Director Industrial Services at a company involved in defense and security*
	P11	*Executive Vice President at a company involved in Aero structures*
Consultants	C1a	*Official at the Defense Department of the Royal Netherlands Embassy*
	C1b	*Official at the Defense Department of the Royal Netherland Embassy*
	C2	*Founding partner of a consulting firm specialized in the US federal government marketplace*
	C3	*Managing director at a consulting firm specialized in foreign investment in the United States*
	C4a	*Senior Vice President Business Development at a consulting firm specialized in doing business with the Department of Defense*
	C4b	*Associate at a consulting firm specialized in doing business with the Department of Defense*
	C5	*Founding partner of a consulting firm specialized in government contracting*

Appendix 1: (*Continued*).

Group	Indicator of interviewee	Function of interviewee
US federal government	G1	*Director of Research and Technical resources at an institute for public procurement practitioners*
	G2	*Senior Director Procurement Policy at a lobbying group representing businesses and associations across the United States*
	G3a	*International trade specialist at a federal department*
	G3b	*International trade specialist at a federal department*
	G4a	*Director, Acquisition Operations at a federal agency*
	G4b	*Acquisition Management Official at a federal agency*

Chapter 9

Lobbying of Commercial Diplomats: Institutional Setting as a Determining Factor

Elena Bondarouk and Huub Ruël

Abstract

The aim of this research is to contribute to the understanding of how commercial diplomats lobby for public procurement contracts. The institutional environment has ramifications for the manner of lobbying and for the practice of commercial diplomacy. This research brings together these streams of literature, and a conceptual model is developed. By means of an in-depth, single-case study, investigating the lobbying activities of EU diplomats in Indonesia, the study aimed to illustrate the model and draw the list of lobbying activities applicable for commercial diplomats. The findings reveal that in a weak institutional development environment, the diplomats focus on informational lobbying and rely heavily on their networks. If the decision-making powers are decentralized, the diplomats target more decision-makers. If diplomats do not have an access to decision-makers then 'voice' lobbying is applied. If the decision-makers are not elected, the diplomats do not engage in constituency-building lobbying. The findings illustrate the plausibility of the introduced conceptual model. They also suggest that domestic factors, such as interest in the host country, priority status of the host country and historical bilateral ties can positively influence the lobbying activities of the diplomats as well.

Introduction

The role of commercial diplomats is slowly changing. The Internet epoch makes it possible for companies to conduct their own investigations of the market characteristics and opportunities in a country of interest; such gathering of intelligence was historically one of the tasks of a commercial diplomacy unit. Nowadays, the

Commercial Diplomacy and International Business: A Conceptual and Empirical Exploration
Advanced Series in Management, 251–291
Copyright © 2012 Emerald Group Publishing Limited
All rights of reproduction in any form reserved
ISSN: 1877-6361/doi:10.1108/S1877-6361(2012)0000009013

added value of commercial diplomats revolves more and more around their expertise and contacts in the host country. Especially in emerging countries where the political, economic, legal and social environment tends to change unpredictably, companies find themselves relying increasingly on the commercial diplomats to explain the rules of the game to them and what channels should be used for the business start-up and promotion.

At the same time, despite the difficulties companies might face in emerging countries, these countries also offer a lot of opportunities for them to grow and expand their market. The population is young and demanding the same standards the developed countries enjoy whether it comes to, for example, mobile phones, computers or hospitals (Egan & Ovanessoff, 2011). One of the sectors where companies from developed countries can seize great opportunities is infrastructure, as in most of the emerging countries airports, harbours, and roads, which could meet the developed countries' standards, are yet to be built (Wooldridge, 2010).

Because of these opportunities in these countries, public procurement becomes an interesting subject for a closer examination. It is through public procurement that a company can contract itself to, for example, building roads, railways, dams, or other projects. In foreign countries, it can be challenging to get a public procurement contract because companies might not be aware of the local rules and procedures. Moreover, foreign companies will be disadvantaged compared to domestic companies because they will not have proper connections which could ease the process. This is where the commercial diplomats' familiarity with the host market and its regulations can play a crucial role. As one of the responsibilities of commercial diplomats is the establishment of good relations with the authorities in the host country, they manifest themselves as essential players that can assist a firm in acquiring a public procurement contract and can channel the company through their networks to a successful result.

Despite its obvious practical importance, little is known about how commercial diplomats assist companies in successfully acquiring such contracts. One of the ways to influence the authorities responsible for public procurement is by lobbying them. But *how* do commercial diplomats lobby? How do they build their network? What lobbying techniques are used? Article 3 of the Treaty on the Functioning of the European Union lays down EU competence in external economic policy. Having a framework in which the countries are obliged to work together, do European diplomats lobby in a similar way? What determines the lobbying techniques of the commercial diplomats? The current literature on lobbying or commercial diplomacy does not provide for answers to these questions.

Most of the research on lobbying is done on interest groups and other non-state actors (e.g. Ihlen & Berntzen, 2007; Miller & Harkins, 2010). Little is known about how states themselves engage in lobbying activities (Panke, 2012). There is no knowledge on how commercial diplomats lobby. The existing literature on lobbying points out that the institutional setting of a country has ramifications for the manner of how groups lobby (e.g. Eising, 2007; Hamada, 2007; Holyoke, 2009; Lowery, 2002; Lowery, Poppelaars, & Berkhout, 2008). Kostecki and Naray (2007) also determined that the commercial diplomats' activities depend on the host country characteristics of the institutional setting. Hence, the following research question emerges:

To what extent does the institutional setting of a host country determine the lobbying activities of European commercial diplomats in the case of public procurement contracts in emerging countries?

Such theoretical question calls for a large-scale empirical research. However, the current state of knowledge on the lobbying activities of commercial diplomats is incomplete, making it difficult for such research to be conducted. Consequently, it is necessary to explore these activities first. A single case-study design is chosen to accommodate this need. At the same time it provides for an opportunity to see whether there is any plausible link between institutional setting and lobbying activities at all. Hence, the aim of this research is twofold: (1) drawing a list of lobbying activities applicable for commercial diplomats and (2) illustrating the plausibility of a link between the concept of institutional setting and lobbying activities of commercial diplomats.

The study is presented in the following sections. The literature review section identifies the streams of literature and ties them into a conceptual model. The section on methodology explains how the data on lobbying activities was gathered, and how the model is examined. The findings are presented in the results section, followed by conclusions and a reflection on the research.

Literature Review

This section identifies the streams of literature that are relevant to the central research question. The objective is to construct a research model which will frame the concepts and guide the research in its empirical stage. Academic databases were used to track the literature on the basis of keywords. Backward and forward referencing was applied to locate other sources of information. This amounted to a vast pile of literature resources, which enabled assessment of the *status quo* on the subject and revealed theoretical gaps.

In order to answer the research question, there is a need to establish (2.1.) what is implied by commercial diplomacy. As the activities of a commercial diplomat are uncovered, it will bring the subjects of (2.2.) public procurement contracts and (2.3.) lobbying to the surface. (2.4.) The institutional setting will then emerge as a possible shaping factor of the lobbying activities. (2.5.) The conceptual model will be introduced to guide the empirical part of this research. (2.6.) At last, the propositions about the model will be derived in conclusion.

Commercial Diplomacy

Commercial diplomacy has been receiving more attention in the academic world in the past few years (e.g. Busschers, 2011; Naray, 2008; Okano-Heijmans & Ruël, 2011;

Reuvers, 2012; Ruël & Zuidema, 2012; Visser, 2011). It has been identified as one of the ingredients of economic diplomacy (Buschers, 2011; Okano-Heijmans & Ruël, 2011; Potter, 2004; Reuvers, 2012; Ruël & Zuidema, 2012). While economic diplomacy is a broad term covering different economic means available to diplomats when seeking foreign policy goals (Haan, 2010; Muller, 2002; Okano-Heijmans, 2008), commercial diplomacy is a more specific term reflecting the support that diplomats can offer to the business sector by facilitating specific commercial gains through export promotion, attracting inward investment and preserving outward investment opportunities (Kostecki & Naray, 2007; Mercier, 2007; Naray, 2008; Potter, 2004). It is important to note that this research will use a broader conceptualization of diplomats in order to answer the main question. It will depart from the usual assumption that diplomats are government representatives with a diplomatic status, and will include the local staff working in the economic department of the embassy without diplomatic status into the definition.

Buschers (2011) presents an overview of the activities performed by the commercial diplomats that have been outlined in the literature. The common ingredients identified by different authors seem to be (1) the provision of intelligence, which implies gathering and disseminating market information to the firms, (2) establishing relationships with the authorities which can help companies in their search for projects and partners, (3) promoting home country products and services via different channels of communication and trade fairs and (4) assisting companies in disputes.

Governments have different reasons to invest in commercial diplomacy (Naray, 2008). Although the Internet has made a lot of intelligence publicly accessible, there are still *missing markets* where reliable and neutral business information can only be accessed by the diplomats due to their special relations with the country. Sukiassyan and Nugent (2011) argue that especially in transition economies, it is difficult for companies to operate due to unstable and unclear market conditions. Hence, the knowledge and experience of commercial diplomats in these countries prove to be indispensable. Commercial diplomats contribute to strengthening the commercial ties with the host country by establishing and maintaining *a country image*, which plays a role when a domestic company is recommended to the host country business and government. *Networking opportunities and partner search* which the commercial diplomats can offer to the companies form yet another reason why commercial diplomats are indispensable. Their 'local knowledge is particularly useful in helping business people to participate in trade fairs, trade displays, store promotions, social receptions for local leaders, trade and technical symposia' (Naray, 2008, p. 5). Large companies rely on the important contacts that commercial diplomats can offer when it comes to complicated markets where useful networks are essential. Commercial diplomats are familiar with the judicial system of a host country and can assist in *conflict resolution*. The preparation of *business and government delegation* is usually something that commercial diplomats are responsible for. By helping the businesses, the commercial diplomats contribute to the competitiveness of domestic economies and export growth (Naray, 2008; Ruël & Zuidema, 2012). This rationale for commercial diplomacy becomes especially relevant when considering the support provided by the diplomats to the companies that engage in large contracts, where the national image counts (Naray, 2008).

Public Procurement Contracts

One area in which commercial diplomacy can have special relevance is public procurement contracting. Public procurement can be defined as the process of 'public purchase of goods and services from the private sector' (Weiss & Thurbon, 2006, p. 703). The outcome of such process is a 'business arrangement between a government agency and a private entity in which the private entity promises, in exchange for money, to deliver certain products and services to the government agency or to others on the government's behalf' (Ya Ni & Bretschneider, 2007, p. 533). Public procurement represents 'one of the sources of demand for companies in sectors such as construction, health care and transport' (Edler & Georghiou, 2007, p.950).

The public procurement market is immense. At the end of 20th century, it amounted to 82.3% of international trade in goods and services (Kommerskollegium, 2011). The Organisation for Economic Co-operation and Development (OECD) has estimated that its members' spending on public procurement amounts on average to 12–25% of their GDP (2011). In developing countries it amounts to 14% of their GDP (Kommerskollegium, 2011). The OECD expects that the percentages will only grow: due 'to the economic downturn, many countries have launched fiscal stimulus programmes that include a large procurement component, often related to infrastructure projects' (OECD, 2011, p. 148). Therefore, public procurement presents lots of opportunities for companies.

Public procurement is known to be a complex arrangement because there are many demands the company must fulfil in order to get the contract (Ruël, Vehof, & Telgen, 2012). A company should take into account the different political goals and many stakeholders' different objectives when answering the public procurement call (Telgen, 2007). Companies should be aware of the cultural setting of the country, different rules and organizational procedures at the various levels that apply in public procurement contract appointment (Telgen, 2007). Moreover, different long-term relationships of the government with the country's business sector should be considered (Telgen, 2007).

The need for information about these demands, different rules, and culturally and politically sensitive intelligence which plays a role in whether a company gets the public procurement contract or not brings the subject back to the rationale of the existence of commercial diplomacy. One of the responsibilities of commercial diplomats is the establishment of good relations with the authorities in the host country. Therefore, they manifest themselves as essential players that can assist a firm in acquiring a public procurement contract and can channel the company through their networks to a successful result. And for that reason, the knowledge, experience and network of commercial diplomats constitute valuable assets for the companies striving to get the public procurement contracts.

Despite its practical importance, little is known about how commercial diplomats assist companies in their successful acquiring of such contracts. One of the ways to influence the authorities responsible for public procurement is by lobbying them. The current literature on commercial diplomacy has been oblivious to the lobbying literature. The next section attempts to set this straight.

Lobbying

A wealth of research has been done on lobbying. Most of it focuses on interest groups and other non-state actors (e.g. Ihlen & Berntzen, 2007; Miller & Harkins, 2010). Little is known about how states themselves engage in lobbying activities (Panke, 2012). And this is fundamentally different from business groups. For example, the diplomats do not have a budget which they can use to make a donation in order to persuade the decision-makers to assign the public procurement contract to a particular company. A study on public procurement in the United States has shown that companies that made political donations were more likely to receive the public procurement contract (Hogan, Long, & Stretesky, 2010). Neither can commercial diplomats capture the fields of sciences, civil society and the media completely due to budget constraints (Miller & Harkins, 2010). Moreover, the usual stage where lobbying is examined is the US congress or the EU institutions (e.g. Coen, 2007; Mack, 2005; Mahoney & Baumgartner, 2008). Another important aspect of this stream of literature is that lobbying is usually performed to influence a policy outcome, regulation or other legislation (e.g. Gray, 1989; Lowery, 2002). And as public procurement competition is not about changing a policy but about who is getting the contract, the lobbying activities will differ. Yet another stream of literature on lobbying focuses on the personal characteristics of a lobbyist which can make lobbying successful (McGrath, 2006; Nownes & DeAlejandro, 2009; Spencer & van Schendelen, 2002; Van Schendelen, 2002). This section attempts to distil the lobbying aspects which are relevant for this kind of lobbying, concentrating on state actors who do not target policy change, rules or other legislation.

Lobbying is defined as a strategic activity of providing information to legislators (Hojnacki & Kimball, 1998; McGrath, 2007), 'contacting government officials or elected politicians to influence their decisions on matters of interest' (Mack, 2005, p. 340). Ihlen and Berntzen (2007) define it as 'influencing political decision-making in the interest of a group by communicating with publics relevant to the political process of a certain issue' (p. 236). And Vining, Shapiro, and Borges (2005) define it as 'all attempts to communicate information to political actors' (p. 151). Panke (2012) defines it in a similar way: 'lobbying is an informal pathway to influence policies in arenas or bodies in which lobbyists themselves have no formal decision-taking competencies' (p. 130). The combination of these definitions results in the following synthesis, where the concept of lobbying for this research captures *all attempts by the commercial diplomats to communicate information to host government officials in order to influence their decision about whom to assign a public procurement contract to.*

Although lobbying effectiveness is very difficult to measure due to its concealed nature in the process of decision-making (Lowery, 2002; Svendsen, 2011) and the great variety of ways the lobbying takes place (Lowery et al., 2008; Van Schendelen, 2012), it has empirically been shown that it does have an effect on the outcome of a lobbied concept (e.g. Baron & Hirsch, 2012; Gawande, Krishna, & Robbins, 2006; Gawande, Maloney, & Montes-Rojas, 2009; Husted, 1991; Kee, Olarreaga, & Silva, 2007; Panke, 2012; Vining et al., 2005). Lobbying plays an important role as it can shape the decisions that are taken, make sure that a *status quo* prevails and influence the attitudes of decision-makers by moulding the political agenda (Baron & Hirsch, 2012; Gawande et al., 2009; Hojnacki & Kimball, 1998; Svendsen, 2011). The pursuit of economic benefits is usually the reason for lobbying (Crosby & Orsini, 1996; Mack, 2005). And although this could be considered a negative motivation (Van Hulten, 2011), it does not necessarily have to be denoted that way as it is another way of interest representation and assurance that the government officials take decisions that are not mismatched to society's needs (Eising, 2007; Ihlen & Berntzen, 2007; Mack, 2005; McGrath, 2005). For example, in the case of lobbying for a free-trade agreement between countries, tariff-barrier-lifting measures or access to the foreign market agreements, lobbying even benefits the consumers by lowering the prices through facilitating intensified competition and thus improving welfare (Gawande et al., 2006; Husted, 1991; Kee et al., 2007; Solis & Katada, 2007). Hence, even though the commercial diplomats will be driven by the interest of their home countries' firms, the outcome of their lobbying does not necessarily harm the host country.

Lobbying involves a lot of preparation which is indispensible for success (Van Schendelen, 2012). Different relevant documents are studied for stakeholders, their position on the matter, and when and how they are likely to intervene, and the time frame which is prescribed by procedures and agendas (Gray, 1989; Van Schendelen, 2012). The literature identifies several methods and techniques lobbyists can use to best achieve their goal (Furlong & Kerwin, 2005; Nownes & DeAlejandro, 2009; Schlozman & Tierney, 1986). However, the lists of such techniques and methods are not directly applicable to the lobbying of commercial diplomats and especially not in the case of lobbying for public procurement contracts. This brings the matter to the first aim of this research: the identification of lobbying techniques that are applied by the commercial diplomats. Even though the literature does not provide such list of techniques, it helps to identify different elements of lobbying which the commercial diplomats have to be aware of. It will also serve as a guide in the search for lobbying activities that commercial diplomats use. Hence, the remaining part of this section will outline different aspects of successful lobbying which are relevant for the commercial diplomats.

Lobbyists need to make a selection of priority projects they want to focus on, as they have limited financial and human resources (Crosby & Orsini, 1996; Panke, 2012; Vining et al., 2005). Domestic interests can play a role, but also the host country's needs are to be considered. When a lobbying group chooses a project which reflects popular and salient matters, for example lobbying for the need to build a new public transport system which will lessen congestion and contribute to a healthier environment, it will have a better chance of getting through (Klüver, 2010a, 2010b; Lowery, 2002).

The notion of salience draws attention to the timing of lobbying, one of its most vital aspects (Crosby & Orsini, 1996; Gray, 1989; Mack, 2005). A delay could result in somebody else getting the public procurement contract, at the same time 'lobbying an issue before it has become salient to the decision-maker will cause it to fall on deaf ears' (Crosby & Orsini, 1996, p. 2). Therefore, if lobbyists want to address an issue the public is not familiar with yet, they need to make it salient and attract attention to it. They have to plan their actions to be timely and anticipate the trends.

Once the issue is chosen, there is a decision to be made on how to structure and present the message (McGrath, 2007). Vining et al. (2005) identify three major categories of lobbying argumentation. *Fact and science* arguments are crucial in the fields where technical knowledge is indispensible like health and environment issues. *Economic efficiency* arguments focus on the notion of maximizing social surplus, and *equity* arguments have strong persuasion powers when they can be described in terms of big losses to large groups of society. Thus, the lobbying commercial diplomats can use their technical intelligence and present the arguments differently depending on the matter and the goals.

The decision-makers need this technical intelligence in order to design policies and justify the decisions that are taken (Bouwen, 2002; Crosby & Orsini, 1996). Lobbying groups employ informational lobbying to shape the decision-makers' opinion on the subject (Gawande et al., 2009; Heitshusen, 2000). The lobbyists can disseminate to the relevant decision-makers' informational materials containing different technical data and arguments (Gawande et al., 2009; Sukiassyan & Nugent, 2011). They can provide information about the positive and negative consequences of the decision or measure to be taken, or even draft legislation or amendments (Heitshusen, 2000; Hojnacki & Kimball, 1998). In this way the lobbyists can mould the point of views of decision-makers in their favour.

Along with technical intelligence, there is a need for political intelligence in order to accomplish successful lobbying. A lobbying group should monitor what is going on in the relevant government ministries. It is important to meet regularly, formally and informally with the decision-makers (Haug & Koppang, 1997; Hojnacki & Kimball, 1998; Mack, 2005). The ability to have frequent meetings with the decision-makers is essential for successful lobbying (Hamada, 2007, Nownes & DeAlejandro, 2009). Nownes and DeAlejandro (2009) explain why organizing personal meetings and receptions with decision-makers are so effective. It provides an opportunity to listen as well as to speak. In this way the lobbying party can find out about the upcoming calls for public procurement and other projects, for example. Frequent meetings allow lobbyists to build close relationships with decision-makers. And finally, it works because 'government officials and their staffers like them' (Nownes & DeAlejandro, 2009, p. 449). The level of familiarity with the decision-makers and their agenda has a positive effect on the lobbying success (Eising, 2007; Holyoke, 2009). So if there are ties that were historically formed due to a long bilateral relationship between the domestic and host country, it will benefit the lobbying because the lobbying group will know how the government works, and in turn the government will also be familiar with it (Panke, 2012). Such networking and acquiring of an influential mass of befriended stakeholders determine the effectiveness and efficiency of lobbying, as lobbyists can rely on their influential network when required (Mack, 2005; Van Schendelen, 2012).

Lobbyists have to identify with whom they will cooperate, as different authors have indicated that the ability to form a coalition is one of the most important determinants of successful lobbying (Furlong & Kerwin, 2005; Klüver, 2010a, 2010b; Nownes & DeAlejandro, 2009). And although lobbying for public procurement signifies a singular national interest, there are possibilities to form coalitions with domestic groups, such as businesses and associations. This is also referred to as constituency-building lobbying, where lobbying can persuade decision-makers by offering them the proof that the lobbyists' demands are supported by a large group in society or key players in the domestic industry (Haug & Koppang, 1997; Hojnacki, 1997; Hojnacki & Kimball, 1998; Holyoke, 2009; Vining et al., 2005). Hence, the earlier mentioned equity arguments would be effective. Collective lobbying can also lead to economies of scale, and hence efficiency, as different groups will merge resources to obtain the desired outcome. At the same time the lobbying group should be aware which other countries will be lobbying and keep an eye on their activities (Holyoke, 2003).

There are different lobbying strategies such as 'access' driven or 'voice' driven, where the former relates to direct lobbying of a decision-maker through appointments and meetings, and the latter relates to indirect lobbying through, for example, media attention, campaigns and grassroots lobbying[1] (Bergan, 2009; Bouwen & McCown, 2007; Vining et al., 2005). If possible the lobbyists will always try to have appointments with the decision-makers, i.e. 'access' lobbying. The literature shows that influential committee members or decision-makers who are responsible for the decision-taking will always be targeted (Eising, 2007; Heitshusen, 2000; Hojnacki & Kimball, 1998; Holyoke, 2009; Mack, 2005). The lobbyists will also lobby their allies or decision-makers who will be likely to favour them (Austen-Smith & Wright, 1996; Hojnacki & Kimball, 1998). When the group wants the matter to be put on political agenda, then again they will lobby their allies, providing them with more information tools to convince other decision-makers (Eising, 2007; Hojnacki & Kimball, 1998).

When a lobbying group cannot get access to decision-makers, it will engage in indirect lobbying — 'voice' lobbying. However, lobbyists can also apply indirect lobbying when there is a need to strengthen their direct lobbying efforts. Media lobbying is one of such indirect ways to lobby, where the lobbyists try to shape the decision-makers' opinion through newspaper articles or journals. When using media for lobbying, the lobbying group should avoid too much confrontation with the decision-makers by pointing out the flaws or suggesting that other ways different from what the decision-makers have chosen are better. The ability to keep the 'license to operate' is most important when it comes to lobbying, hence the lobbyists should frame their information well (Ihlen & Berntzen, 2007; Van Schendelen, 2012).

---

[1]Grassroots lobbying refers to the mobilization of the members of the lobby group, or the members of the political party, to contact a policy-maker to influence the desired outcome (Bergan, 2009).

When projecting the lobbying literature on the field of commercial diplomacy, it emerges that commercial diplomats need to make a selection of priority projects to lobby for and ensure that the projects trigger the host country's public interest. Commercial diplomats can structure their technical intelligence into different types of arguments for their *informational lobbying*. They must acquire political intelligence, be closely familiar with the rules, and *establish networks* with the influential members of the public procurement committee and officials who are likely to back their candidates. At the same time they should be aware of other countries lobbying the same committees and people. *Constituency building* can be a powerful way to persuade decision-makers. That is why the diplomats could choose to ally with domestic actors as much as possible. Overall, the diplomats can engage in both *'access'-driven* (direct) and *'voice'-driven* (indirect) lobbying, depending on the access they can get to the decision-makers.

Institutional Setting

Many of the lobbying aspects depend on the political structure and institutional setting of the country. The literature identifies that the institutional environment has ramifications for the manner of lobbying (Eising, 2007; Hamada, 2007; Holyoke, 2009; Lowery, 2002; Lowery et al., 2008; Messer, Berkhout, & Lowery, 2010; Nownes & DeAlejandro, 2009; Sukiassyan & Nugent, 2011; Vining et al., 2005). Kostecki and Naray (2007) also determined that the commercial diplomats' activities depend on the host country characteristics of its institutional setting. Buschers (2011) showed that in a less developed institutional setting, the SMEs consult commercial diplomats more often than in more developed ones. Telgen (2007) draws attention to the importance of the institutional setting of the host country for the public procurement contracts. Chan, Isobe and Makino (2008) have also recognized that businesses will behave differently in different countries depending on the institutional structure. As a lot of authors devote attention to the institutional setting in these streams of literature, the following section will classify different aspects of the institutional setting that can have ramifications for the lobbying of commercial diplomats for the public procurement contracts.

'Institutions are the rules of the game in a society or, more formally, are the humanly devised constraints that shape human interaction' (North, 1990, p. 3). The role of the institutions is to reduce uncertainty by providing a stable framework of how humans operate in a particular society (Hall & Taylor, 1996). Hence, acquiring knowledge of the structure of an alien part of the world ensures a reduction in information costs and provides an opportunity to engage in international trade (North, 1991). As Hodgson (2006) points out, it is important to be aware of the formal and informal institutional aspects, as the former relates to 'political and (judicial) rules, economic rules, and contracts' (North, 1990, p. 47) and the latter concerns 'codes of conduct, norms of behaviour, and conventions' (North, 1990, p. 36) — i.e. the social institutions (Chan et al., 2008).

When the formal institutions do not evolve, economies tend to be less productive and not live up to their potential (Campos, 2000; North, 1991; Scully, 1988). At the same time, countries with better institutions tend to trade more (Dollar & Kraay, 2003). And with the trade comes economic growth and development (e.g. Rodriguez & Rodrik, 2001). Better institutions, or strongly developed institutions, indicate that the rules are respected, in a sense that the government and public obey these rules, which also means that in case of violation of rules there are certain measures to be taken. Hence, strong institutional development ensures certainty that the rules are conformed to, which leads the companies to conclude that it is safe to do business in a country.

There are different kinds of this (un)certainty. Political uncertainty, or political instability, which refers to the likelihood that the government will be destabilized or overthrown by unconstitutional or violent means (Kaufmann, Kraay, & Mastruzzi, 2010) has less of an effect on the decision of a company to trade in certain countries (Knack & Keefer, 1995). Knack and Keefer (1995) argue that property rights protection and other forms of legal certainty play a more crucial role when it comes to the size of foreign trade and investment in a host country. Campos (2000) also showed that the rule of law is one of the conditions for the economic development and growth of a country. For example, if a company is sure that it has legal protection when it comes to ownership and property rights in a specific country and thus the risk of being deceived and losing money is low, then this company feels safer to trade in this country. Hence, such institutional environment can be denoted as friendly for the foreign companies. Corruption, which refers to capture of the state by elites and private interests (Kaufmann et al., 2010), can stand in the way of this legal certainty, because it makes it possible for some companies to disobey the rules as long as they can capture the state. When it is accepted that the rules are disobeyed by some companies, it becomes difficult for other companies to anticipate how the market operates and they refrain from doing business in this country or even entering this market (Tsui-Auch & Möllering, 2010). When the rules are disregarded, it indicates that institutional development is weak.

Accordingly, commercial diplomats seeking to promote businesses in a country with a weak institutional development — where information is difficult to obtain due to pliable rules, corruption and a lack of transparency — are likely to engage in 'market-preparation' measures first. These measures would be directed at helping the country to strengthen its institutions, before lobbying for specific business interests. The efforts will also be directed at creating a level playing field, where all companies have to play by the same set of rules. For example, the diplomats would try to contribute to improvement of rules by suggesting different policy designs, or other check-and-balance tools that could ensure that the rules are obeyed in a country. As a result, the institutional development will improve and it will become more attractive for companies to trade with the host country. On the other hand, if the institutional development is weak, a lot depends on personal networks (North, 1991). Hence, diplomats would have to rely on their personal networks when assisting companies. In countries where institutional development is strong, the commercial diplomats would not have to engage in such 'market-preparation' measures and can assist companies in their specific needs more.

One of the important decisions in lobbying is the decision of whom to lobby. The answer can be found when looking at the institutional structure of government. This variable can be conceptualized two dimensionally, as it can involve a lot of different layers of government and different interest group consultation mechanisms. The decentralized structure of the government signifies that there are many interacting decision-making levels of government among which the authority and responsibility is distributed. Thus, it implies that not only central government bares the responsibility for decision-making, but different committees or other public authorities and regional or municipal levels of government are also involved in the decision-making process. Hence, the more decentralized the government is, the more levels of the government the diplomats would have to address in their lobbying strategy as more people are involved in the decision-making process (Eising, 2007; Heitshusen, 2000; Mahoney & Baumgartner, 2008). If the decision-making process moves slowly, lobbyists will take advantage of it to lobby more decision-makers (Hojnacki & Kimball, 1998). Also, when the lobbying group needs a majority of decision-makers to approve the candidacy, the lobbyists are likely to target more people (Hojnacki & Kimball, 1998; Mack, 2005; Vining et al., 2005). Accordingly, when the government structure reflects centralized government, the diplomats would engage in less extensive lobbying as the number of decision-makers will be smaller.

When looking at whom to lobby, it is also interesting to see whether there is any interest group consultation mechanism in a country. If the system reflects corporatist structures, which means that there is room for negotiations between organized interests of civil society and decision-makers (Schmitter, 1974), the lobbying group will be able to work closely with the decision-makers, as the system allows for an opportunity to target the decision-makers directly (Lowery, 2002; Mahoney & Baumgartner, 2008). On the other hand, if the system reflects totalitarian structures, where there is no room for interest group consultation mechanism as there is only one body taking decisions, the lobbying diplomats will have to 'devise creative ways to get the attention of decision-makers and have their message stand out from the cacophony of lobbying communications' (Mahoney & Baumgartner, 2008, p. 1266). When it comes to whether a lobbying group is used to the system of interest representation — due to the resemblance of the host and domestic institutional structures — Eising (2007), against his expectations, found that it does not have an influence on the success of lobbying. Hence, the lobbying diplomats will not be disadvantaged if they come from a different institutional structure when compared to the host country. At the same time, Hamada (2007) also found that the flexibility of the lobbying diplomats to adapt to different environments is a better determinant of success.

Another aspect of institutional setting that has an effect on the manner of lobbying is whether decision-makers are elected or not. Decision-makers who are elected are more responsive to the wishes of their constituency, as they recognize their electoral vulnerability (Mahoney & Baumgartner, 2008). If the decision-makers can be hold accountable for their actions through (re)elections, then lobbyists will engage in coalition building and acquiring of as much support from the decision-makers' constituency as possible in order to persuade decision-makers of their outcome preference (Mahoney, 2007). On the other hand, as the positions of the appointed decision-makers are not dependent on the results of election and thus are not sensitive to constituency pleasing, they will be 'more attuned to information about policy feasibility and direct communications about policy details' (Mahoney & Baumgartner, 2008, p. 1264).

Summing up, when the institutional development is weak, the companies will not feel as safe to invest and trade and thus may stay away from the market. In such cases the commercial diplomats will likely try to engage in 'market-preparation' measures first. These measures would be directed at helping the country to strengthen its institutions, before lobbying for specific business interests. A weak institutional development is also characterized by a dependence on the networks. Thus, diplomats would have to rely on their personal networks when assisting companies. In countries where institutional development is strong, the commercial diplomats would not have to engage in such 'market-preparation' measures and can assist companies in their specific needs more. A system which is characterized by corporatist structure will offer more opportunities to lobby the public procurement decision-makers directly ('access' lobbying). If there is no such mechanism (in case of a totalitarian structure), the diplomats would be forced to lobby in other — creative and probably indirect — ways ('voice' lobbying). If decision-making powers in a public procurement process are decentralized, diplomats would have to lobby more people to be effective. Accordingly, when the government structure reflects centralized government, the diplomats would engage in less extensive lobbying as the number of decision-makers will be smaller. And finally, whether the officials are appointed or elected will determine whether diplomats will engage in coalition building and acquiring of as much support as possible for the diplomats' outcome preference.

Conceptual Model and Conclusion

Based on the literature, there is support that the institutional setting influences the lobbying style of commercial diplomats (Fig. 1).

By linking these streams of literature, different perceptions about the relationship between the concepts emerge.

When the weak institutional development of the host country creates an environment where international companies do not feel safe, the commercial diplomats will direct their efforts at informational lobbying of the decision-makers in order to persuade them to invest in institutional development. In such an environment, the commercial diplomats are likely to rely on their network and their influential mass of befriended stakeholders and invest in good relationships with them. Due to the weak institutional development leading to a lack of information and transparency of the system, the commercial diplomats are also likely to have difficulties with getting the timing of their lobbying actions right. On the other hand, if the institutional development is strong, the commercial diplomats can focus more on lobbying for specific commercial interests.

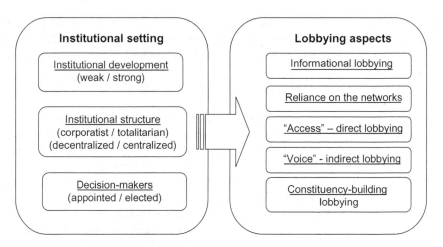

Figure 1: Conceptual model.

If the institutional setting reflects corporatist structures, the commercial diplomats are likely to have more direct and frequent contact with the decision-makers responsible for public procurement. Their lobbying activities are likely to correspond to an 'access'-driven strategy, where they focus their lobbying directly on the authorities. If the decision-making powers are dispersed and there are many levels of decision-making, the commercial diplomats are likely to target them all. Moreover, they are likely to target even more people if the decision-making process takes a lot of time. Accordingly, when the government structure reflects centralized government, the diplomats would have to lobby fewer decision-makers. If it is difficult to gain access to the authorities due to totalitarian structure, the commercial diplomats are likely to focus more on a 'voice'-driven strategy, where they would have to find other ways to get noticed and indirectly influence the decision of the decision-makers.

When the decision-makers in the public procurement committee are elected, the commercial diplomats are likely to pursue constituency-building lobbying. When the authorities are appointed, the commercial diplomats are likely to focus on informational lobbying.

The following sets of propositions are derived from the conceptual model.

P1. If commercial diplomats find themselves in a weak institutional development environment, they are likely to focus on informational lobbying and rely heavily on their networks. If institutional development is strong, commercial diplomats are likely to focus on lobbying for specific commercial interests.

P2. If the institutional setting reflects corporatist structures, the commercial diplomats are likely to focus on 'access'-driven strategy. If it reflects totalitarian structures, the commercial diplomats are likely to focus more on 'voice'-driven strategy.

P3. If the institutional structure of the decision-making body is decentralized, the commercial diplomats are likely to engage all levels of it in their campaign. If it is centralized, the commercial diplomats are likely to concentrate on lobbying of only few decision-makers.

P4. If the decision-makers are democratically chosen, the commercial diplomats are likely to pursue constituency-building lobbying. If the decision-makers are appointed, the commercial diplomats are likely to focus on informational lobbying.

Methodology

The reviewed literature indicated how the institutional setting can influence lobbying. Important scientific contributions of this research involve applying this literature to commercial diplomacy and examining the plausibility of a link between the lobbying activities of the commercial diplomats and the institutional setting, as described in the conceptual model of the previous section. However, the literature on itself does not provide all the necessary tools to examine the model. So far, it has only been possible to distil certain determining aspects of lobbying and not uncover specific lobbying techniques that are relevant for the commercial diplomats. Therefore, this study aims at another scientific contribution: identifying the practice of commercial diplomats' lobbying that could be translated into measurable indicators of lobbying activities. With such contribution, this research intends to build a foundation for larger scale research on the topic.

Research Design

A single-case study approach was selected as a means of uncovering the so far unknown lobbying activities of the diplomats. Siggelkow (2007) argued that 'research involving case data can usually get much closer to theoretical constructs' (p. 22). Therefore, it allows for a certain depth to explore the still unmeasured lobbying activities of the commercial diplomats. At the same time it provides for an opportunity to see whether there is any plausible link between institutional setting and lobbying activities at all. A single case cannot prove causality; it can only exhibit a link (Siggelkow, 2007). Hence, such design allows for a 'pilot' illustration of the introduced conceptual model and understanding of its mechanism (Eisenhardt, 1989; Gerring, 2004; Gschwend & Schimmelfennig, 2007; Siggelkow, 2007; Swanborn, 2010).

It is important to pay attention to the criticism of a single-case study approach, where it is argued that it does not provide for the possibility to generalize upon the results (Bennett, 2004; Gerring, 2001; Grix, 2004, Yin, 2003), its internal validity can be weak (Bennett, 2004; Siggelkow, 2007; Yin, 2003), and construct validity and reliability are threatened (Gerring, 2001; Yin, 2003).

Swanborn (2010) notices that '*all* research boils down to comparison' (p. 15), which facilitates the ability to generalize from the findings, thus also a single-case study is no exception. Gerring (2001) and Bennett and Elman (2006) explain that external validity does not have to be jeopardized if the case is selected well: if it represents a typical case[2] then representativeness can be high as there is an indirect comparison with other cases (which have a peripheral position in the research design). At the same time, a single case relies on the within-case comparison (Gerring, 2001; Swanborn, 2010). Hence, this study chose a typical case of an emerging country: Indonesia (OECD, 2009). It employed within-case comparison of the units of analysis — i.e. the commercial diplomats. Internal validity is increased by employing pattern-matching logic, where the expectations from a theoretical model are reflected on the findings (Bennett, 2004; De Vaus, 2001; Yin, 2003). The data was analyzed for possible alternative explanations (Siggelkow, 2007; Yin, 2003), like the interest of the home country in the host country. By choosing the case not on the dependent variable, the internal validity is increased as well (Geddes, 2003). Construct validity is warranted by using different sources for data collection. The reliability of the research is safeguarded by the case-study protocols (Gerring, 2001; Yin, 2003).

Data Collection

Semi-structured interviews were chosen to research the lobbying activities of the commercial diplomats, as they provide an opportunity to explore the subject of the still unknown lobbying activities. Interviewing suits the purpose of the study well, as it allows a certain degree of flexibility and leaves room to consider unexpected lines of enquiry (Fontana & Frey, 2000; Grix, 2004). The aspects of lobbying that were identified in the literature guided the questions. Despite the advantages of such interviewing, the replicability of such research may be low; to counteract this challenge, this study provides a detailed protocol.

In Jakarta, there are 19 embassies of the members of the EU. The interviews were conducted with the commercial diplomats of 12 embassies. No response was received from four embassies. One embassy no longer has a commercial/economic department in Jakarta, and no appointment could be scheduled with two embassies due to the diplomats' busy agendas. Additionally, three interviews were conducted with commercial diplomats from two chambers of commerce and one commercial diplomat from the EU delegation. This was done in order to increase the scope of understanding of the commercial diplomats' lobbying activities from a third party. In total, this amounted to 15 interviews.

The data for the institutional setting is collected from different sources: Worldwide Governance Indicators (WGI) research project index and recent reports on the public procurement system in Indonesia. The former identifies governance as institutions by

---

[2]This approach seeks to find the most usual case in a particular population.

which authority in a country is exercised, thus political institutions.[3] Chan et al. (2008) developed an institutional development index for the years 1996–2001 for different countries and found that political institutions have the highest correlation with the development index, when compared to economic and social institutions. Hence, this index suits this study when it comes to making conclusions about institutional development.

WGI reflects the statistical compilation of 31 sources such as surveys on the quality of governance given by many enterprises, citizens, experts, think tanks, NGOs, and other international organizations (Kaufmann et al., 2010). It covers more than 200 countries. It identifies six dimensions of governance: voice and accountability (VA), political stability and absence of violence (PV), government effectiveness (GE), regulatory quality (RQ), rule of law (RL) and control of corruption (CC) (Kaufmann et al., 2010). The range of possible scores differs from −2.5 (weak) to +2.5 (strong) governance performance. The index also uses a percentile ranking of the countries.

To learn more about the public procurement system in Indonesia, its institutional structure, the most recent reports were studied: TI-USA, and CIPE, and TII (2011) and Attström and Ismail (2010). They were chosen because of the independence of their authors. The document presented by Attström and Ismail (2010) evaluates an Australian aid project given to the government of Indonesia in order to help it to strengthen its public procurement institutions. At the same time, it also evaluates the progress the Indonesian government has booked so far. TI-USA et al. (2011) assessed the extent to which the APEC[4] procurement transparency standards in Indonesia reduced corruption. Thus, these reports also shed light on its institutional structure and on the decision-makers.

Data Analysis

In order to analyze transcribed interviews, the constant comparative method (Boeije, 2002) was applied. Open coding is a first stage where in a single interview 'interactions are compared with others for similarities and differences. They are also given conceptual labels. In this way, conceptually similar interactions are grouped together to form categories and subcategories' (Corbin & Strauss, 1990). This presented the core of the interview content. The next stage was to compare the categories between the interviews to come up with a typology, the so-called axial coding (Boeije, 2002). The typologies of activities were then categorized along the lines of the theoretical model: informational lobbying, reliance on the networks, 'access' lobbying, 'voice' lobbying, and constituency-building lobbying.

---

[3]Kaufmann et al. (2010) specify further that governance concerns 'the process by which governments are selected, monitored and replaced; the capacity of the government to effectively formulate and implement sound policies; and the respect of citizens and the state for the institutions that govern economic and social interactions among them' (p. 3).
[4]Asia-Pacific Economic Cooperation.

The WGI was analyzed for the scores that Indonesia has on the six dimensions and the relative ranking of the scores among all countries. In order to draw conclusions about its institutional development, the scores and the ranks were compared with other emerging countries — Brazil, Russia, India, China and South Africa — to see how the institutional development of Indonesia scored in its own group. The average scores and average rankings of the six dimensions were computed per country to make the comparisons possible. Moreover, the information of Indonesia was compared to the scores and ranks of 12 members of the EU whose commercial diplomats were interviewed, to see how the host countries' institutional development differs from the domestic one. Again, the comparisons relied on the individual scores and also on the means per country and per group. This put the scores and ranking of Indonesia in perspective of the participating commercial diplomats, and thus it provided more insights into how commercial diplomats themselves could perceive the institutional development.

The reports on the public procurement system in Indonesia were studied for the institutional structure of the system: whether it is decentralized or centralized, and whether the system allows for interest group representation (corporatist or total-itarian structures). Moreover, the documents were studied for how the decision-makers gain their post and to whom they report.

The final step of data analysis was bringing the information acquired through interviews, indices, and reports together in order to see whether the model illustrated the findings. The propositions were examined, and the findings were also discussed in terms of how influential the interest of the home country in the host country is on the lobbying activities the diplomats undertake.

Results

This section first presents the lobbying activities, then the findings on the institutional setting are laid out, and finally, it concludes with applying the conceptual framework to the findings.

Lobbying Aspects

The interviews provided rich insights into how commercial diplomats lobby in Indonesia. The conceptual categories of the lobbying aspects gained a more practical meaning. This is summarized in Table 1.

Informational lobbying. Lobbying activities were categorized as informational lobbying, if they captured activities that are aimed at informing the government officials of the consequences of their measures, pointing out the need to change some regulations as they are disadvantaging certain groups, and cooperating with the government officials on certain policies. Typically, this was exhibited in printed communication.

Table 1: Lobbying activities of EU diplomats in Indonesia.

Lobbying aspects	Activities[a]	Frequency score[b]
Informational lobbying	• A joint committee on some field of cooperation $[H_{p1}]$ • Distribute advanced leaflets to top sectors of government or potential partner companies $[C_{p5}, J_{p2}, O_{p1}]$ • Responsiveness to the disadvantageous measures $[A_{p2+p4}, B_{p6}, D_{p4}]$ • Close cooperation on trade and investment policies in the EU framework $[A_{p4}, B_{p6}, C_{p12}, E_{p5}, F_{p1}, G_{p5}, H_{p3}, I_{p1+p3}, J_{p4}, N_{p6}]$	12
Reliance on the networks	• Introduce the companies to the contacts of the acquired network $[A_{p8+p9+p13}+B_{p3}+C_{p3}]$ • Answer the invitations of associations, government events $[A_{p1}, C_{p1}, F_{p1}, I_{p2}]$ • Organize informal lunches and receptions $[B_{p8}, C_{p1+p2}]$ • Invite government officials to the home country (otherwise advise home companies to invite them) $[C_{p2}, F_{p1}, M_{p1+p4+p6}, N_{p3}]$ • Organize visits of home countries' high-level people (royal, ministers, president) $[C_{p5}, D_{p13}, J_{p2}]$ • Business trips, trade missions $[B_{p4}, E_{p1+p3+p4}, M_{p1+p2}, N_{p3}]$	10
'Access' lobbying	• Different levels of government are contacted on a frequent basis $[A_{p1}, H_{p2}, M_{p1+p4+p6}, N_{p2+p3+p5}]$ • Explanation meeting after publication of the public procurement tender $[G_{p1}]$ • Organize business lunches with government officials $[C_{p2}]$	6
'Voice' lobbying	• Organize theme seminars on a frequent basis $[A_{p3+p7}, B_{p4}, C_{p5}, D_{p11}, E_{p1+p3+p4}, F_{p1}^{+}, I_{p1+p3}, J_{p1+p2}, M_{p1+p2}, N_{p2+p3+p5}^{+}, O_{p1}]$	11

Table 1: (*Continued*)

Lobbying aspects	Activities[a]	Frequency score[b]
	• Invite country's national champions to attract other players $[E_{p3}]$ • Invite journalists to events organized by the embassy $[C_{p5}]$ • Frequent section/columns in newspaper $[A_{p7}, B_{p8}, I_{p1+p3}]$ • Matchmaking events $[A_{p19}, B_{p2+p3}, C_{p10}, I_{p1+p3}]$ • Business to business events $[J_{p1+p2}]$	
Constituency building	Involve host country's civil society organizations or associations in the campaign $[D_{p10}, H_{p3}]$	2

[a]Capital letters refer to different commercial diplomats; p numbers refer to the number of the paragraph of the transcribed interview where the reference can be found; a plus refers to special importance given by the diplomat to the activity.
[b]Frequency score tells how many diplomats have practiced the activities of a particular category.

Almost all diplomats (12) indicated they were involved in close cooperation on trade and investment policies in the EU framework. Every month the commercial diplomats are invited to the EU delegation to discuss pressing matters and the progress the EU has made in its talks with the Indonesian government. The diplomats are welcome to raise issues of concern, so that the EU is aware of any problems and could channel the information to the Indonesian government in the appropriate manner. The EU delegation collects these complaints in order to make a credible case towards the Indonesian government.

G. 'With EU embassies we have once a month (even more usually) economic council meeting, and sometimes there are subgroups for food, pharmacy, logistics — it depends on the issues. Then there is a political council meeting, the development council meeting [...] and the EU delegation is very active. We for sure meet and cooperate, give input to each other, inform on the state visits, so what are they organizing'.

Sometimes it is more effective to present a complaint from a big investor company than have diplomats deploring about it for a long time:

D. 'It is much more impressive if a CEO of such a company says such a thing, when compared to civil servant or even EU ambassador saying the same thing'.

However, there were also diplomats who were having bilateral talks with the Indonesian government. This is done in order to stress how important the matter is.

A. 'Usually there will be letters sent, in some cases it is done under the EU authority. In addition to that, we also talk to the relevant actors. The decision to point something out on behalf of the EU depends on how important the issue is'.

Fewer countries had joint committees in a certain field of cooperation. Another important aspect is that the diplomats have to be very careful not to criticize the Indonesian government in public. If they do disagree with the Indonesian government, it is important to present solutions and present the home country as a partner without being too aggressive.

A. 'You always have to think what is the best strategy to approach the matter, and in this country you have to be very careful. If you would seek confrontation too obviously it would bounce back and work against you. Loosing face or damaging somebody's image is here very sensitive. So it is not done to demand something in the papers or something like that. You would lose immediately then'.

An interesting observation by the EU delegate was that some other countries, like China, Japan or Australia, engage in financing of advisory committees to the decision-making body. In this way they can influence the policy formation at an early stage, for example what Indonesia would regard as standards for green ecological cars. Japan has different standards than the EU, so it can be disadvantageous for the EU companies if Japan advises on these standards. Hence, EU countries should also use these opportunities to influence the rules and standards in their favour. According to one diplomat:

D. 'The embassies and people that work here all deliver great job. What they could do is lobby to get more money for the offensive interests, so that we could indeed finance a parliamentarian committee here for. It is just a simple example, but there are lots of things where you could think of different cooperation. Last year, we did something interesting with the postal industry; we invited European regulators for a workshop to explain to Indonesians the postal reform (liberalization) in Europe and how can you make it work. This kind of contact is very important. While the EU does not have the budget to invite people to do this, we are dependent on the member states' willingness to send somebody'.

Reliance on the networks. Lobbying activities were categorized as reliance on the networks, if they captured different attempts where diplomats make use of their network in order to get the results (e.g. introduce the company to a decision-maker), and different ways in which the diplomats attempt to strengthen the ties by attending different events, or inviting different people, which would strengthen the relationship between the countries. It was usually exhibited in a lot of face-to-face communication.

Almost all diplomats (10) indicated that they work on their networks, building relationships with relevant decision-makers and using these contacts whenever it is helpful for the companies (e.g. introducing them to relevant decision-makers or influential parties).

A. 'For a part it [list of contacts] indeed comes from the network that we have built up through the years, and then we often know that if we bring the company in contact with that person then most likely that person will be able to guide them further and introduce them to other people. [...] So usually we go to a person who knows people and how things work, and of course he should be willing and prepared to help us. Next to it, it comes down to calling around. You start with a few people that you do know and then go further. We call them and tell about the matter, ask whether he knows anybody whom they should talk to, etc. And then you call those people and go on and go on. So it is very labour intensive, but this is the way how it works, especially in this country where you do not have good databases, directories or sort alike'.

The diplomats made sure they showed up at the different events they were invited to by different Indonesian authorities, in this way showing them respect by paying attention to their cause:

A. 'That is why all the meetings and sessions to which we are invited are not always directly interesting for us, but from this perspective they are very important to attend to. So your presence is usually noticed and appreciated. So if you do such a gesture then people are more prepared if you asked them for something to help you and do their gesture in return'.

The diplomats also organized different informal events to which important stakeholders were invited. Some diplomats effectively managed to invite Indonesian officials from different levels and committees of the government to their home country to show different examples of progress in their industries. Some have suggested to the companies they assist to invite certain people to their country and to show them in practice what the companies are talking about. It is much easier to persuade decision-makers if they can be shown the achievements. What many diplomats acknowledged, although not everybody was able to practise it, is the importance of having top people from their own government pay a visit to Indonesia. They explained that this strengthens the relationships between the countries, which usually lead to more interest in the things the diplomat's country has to offer. An example of a diplomat who answered whether political interest from high-level officials of his country would have been helpful for the businesses:

G. Absolutely, yes, definitely! In this type of country the government is very important. Because, first you send a MOU [memorandum of understanding] on whatever: a technical cooperation, scientific cooperation, commercial cooperation. Then they start trusting you because they know that the government is behind the private — the business initiative. So first you have to open with a memorandum. And then the business can easily come and do business. [...] If you have big companies they can go absolutely by themselves, they do not need us even to reach a minister — no problem. But because my country is more composed of SMEs they do not have the strength, the means to go alone by themselves. So this is for whom such political actions would help a lot'.

Business trips and trade missions have the same effect on the relationship with the country, indicated diplomats. The existence of historical bonds certainly helped the diplomats in their work because the Indonesian authorities were familiar with them or knew what the diplomat's country had done for Indonesia in terms of investment. Hence, the interest was easier to trigger.

'Access' lobbying.   Lobbying activities were categorized as 'access' lobbying, if they captured the direct attempts of the diplomats to contact government officials with the aim to discuss different measures and propose different ideas. This was typically exhibited in a lot of formal meetings and exclusive appointments.

These historical bonds might also be the reason why only a few diplomats were able to have direct appointments with the Indonesian decision-makers on a frequent basis.

A. 'My country has then the advantage that we have a very good access to the government and ministerial level, as we still have a very special relation. Especially when you compare it with other European countries. [...] And of course we try to take the full advantage of it'.

Diplomats acknowledged that the direct lobbying intensifies if the host country is a priority for the home country. And not all EU countries see Indonesia as a priority in the international economic relations. At the same time, there were diplomats indicating that Indonesia has an extremely difficult institutional environment, which makes it difficult for diplomats to have direct meetings with the officials. One diplomat referred to having appointments with the Indonesian authorities as a challenging task:

G. 'It is really based on personal relationship so if you get to know somebody because of any reason, it is easier. If you just ask for an appointment they usually do not answer. You have to find your own way to get a network or people in every ministry that can help with what you need. Maybe you meet at seminars, exhibitions, conferences. It is good then to invite them if you organize something, or to keep in touch because when you need to get to the right level [...] if you know somebody inside an organization it is helping a lot. Usually face to face contacts work the best'.

At the time the interviews were conducted, there was a government reshuffle, some ministers were appointed to another function and some were replaced. This made the cooperation and appointments with the government officials more difficult. In general, some have also indicated that it was virtually impossible to get through and arrange an appointment.

'Voice' lobbying.   Lobbying activities were categorized as 'voice' lobbying, if they captured the indirect attempts of commercial diplomats to attract the attention of the decision-makers, by organizing different events where businesses meet, by inviting decision-makers to join such events and hold speeches, and publishing in newspapers, journals etc. This was displayed in a lot of creative ways to attract attention.

All diplomats with sufficient capacity engaged in organizing different seminars. Only two embassies could not because they do not have enough staff and little commercial competence from their home governments. Two other diplomats even indicated that organizing such seminars was the best way to attract attention. It is important to have such events planned throughout the year and hold them consistently and organize them in a coherent way, paying a lot of attention to whom to invite:

> C. 'We usually try to take to bring a non-business actor from our country, an expert from some academic institution who will present that, for instance, in this city we did this and this and this, and it worked out very well, without mentioning the specific company. But people understand that it is about business but then the politicians might get inspired. It is then not so pushy'.

The diplomats made sure to invite representatives of different levels and committees of the Indonesian government. They also organized different business and match-making events. What was noticed by most of the diplomats was that competition is fierce in Indonesia. A lot of Chinese companies get contracts. The EU diplomats suspect that Chinese companies are backed by their government, and they present factual information in a better light than it actually is when applying for a project. This gives them a competitive advantage when compared to the European companies, which do not have financial backing from their governments. Therefore, it becomes important when organizing such events to invite different banks and try to erase the advantage of Chinese companies by offering opportunities for the companies to network with the banks about the possible financing of their projects. When it comes to media promotion, some had sections in the newspapers or journals about, for example, industrial innovations and solutions in their countries:

> A. 'Every once or twice a year we publish in the '*Now Jakarta*' a whole section on our country. And there we make sure to highlight some interesting sectors in more detail. Minister of Economic Affairs has agreed to write a passage for the annual report of Oxford Business Group, and then we link it also to this newspaper on the topic of bilateral relationship'.

Although most of the diplomats were pleased with how they organize such events, chambers of commerce expressed that these events were not always organized in a consistent way. For example, sometimes a follow-up was missing after a big event, which is crucial for making some business proposals concrete. The seminars are great in facilitating network opportunities for the companies, but without a follow-up, some companies would be just left with promises from their counterpart without any specific business proposals. Especially smaller companies need that. It was noteworthy that not all diplomats were fully aware of what other European diplomats were doing and organizing.

Constituency building.   Lobbying activities were categorized as constituency building, when they captured the attempts of diplomats to ally with host countries' important business associations or civil societies.

The diplomats did not involve many civil society organizations or business associations in their lobbying. Chambers of commerce found it regrettable that some diplomats did not involve them, especially because they have good networks with the host country's business associations. One diplomat especially did recognize the relevance of involving Indonesian stakeholders:

> **D.** 'It is once again a very intern-oriented country. This also means that the Indonesian ministers will be more inclined to listen to KADIN [Indonesian chamber of commerce], or APINDO [employees association], than when compared to a Dutch company or EU delegation, as an example. So about lobbying, what we have learned here is that, if there is a problem then we should look whether we can find Indonesian champions which have an interest in European pleads. That is always a bit tricky, because if we cannot find the Indonesian counterparts who would lobby with us, then I think there is little sense to lobby at all'.

Miscellaneous findings.   Through interviews it became apparent that diplomats invest a lot of their time in directly assisting companies, as opposed to indirect support through lobbying. Legal assistance was found to be very important: diplomats often engaged in explaining the rules of the country or stood by them in courts. One pointed out that it is very important that their companies understand the business culture in Indonesia, as it differs from what some of them might be used to. For example, the business culture is not that direct and straightforward. There is a legitimate need to invest in building personal relations with the Indonesian companies, and showing respect for the country's traditions.

> **G.** 'Indonesian market is not very easy, because if you want to have success you have to stay here, you have to cultivate your relations on a regular basis, etc.'

The diplomats thus guide the companies in the process of selecting their channels of promotion, encouraging them to come here if they are serious about doing business in Indonesia. They also conduct sector analysis and market scans for the companies, and even search for possible partners for them. Some countries have specific conditional funds for the companies if they engage in development cooperation, or would like to participate in exhibition fairs.

Most of the diplomats stressed the importance of the home companies being interested in Indonesia. Therefore, they invest a lot of time in ensuring that companies back home are aware of the investment and trade opportunities. Some have special websites where they update the information regularly about the public tenders and procurement projects. At home, different events are organized to raise the awareness of the attractiveness of the host country — Indonesia. In this way they hope to trigger the interest of the companies. If there is no interest, the diplomats cannot do that much. Despite all the efforts to provide companies with fresh information, some diplomats pointed out that they are not always successful in bringing useful information to the firms, either because they already know of existing public procurement tenders or the time frame scheduled for the application is too narrow to apply. The diplomats often suspect that the winners have already been selected before the tenders are published because the application deadline is too short, making it impossible for many companies to apply.

Institutional Setting

To find out more on the institutional setting of Indonesia, the data from the WGI and the reports on public procurement system of Indonesia were examined.

The Worldwide Governance Indicators.   The WGI gives insights into institutional development of a country. The WGI data on the countries was examined on six dimensions: voice and accountability, political stability and absence of violence, government effectiveness, regulatory quality, rule of law and control of corruption. Each country has an estimated score of governance performance on each of the dimensions, ranging from −2.5 (weak) to +2.5 (strong), which indicates the level of institutional development. Such score is then put in perspective of the scores of other 200 countries in the percentile rank. Hence, it clarifies what the individual estimated score signifies when compared to other countries' results. For each country an average of the six dimensions per estimated score and per ranking was computed. This gives an indication of overall score and ranking of a country. The scores and ranking of Indonesia were compared to the scores and rankings of other emerging countries, such as Brazil, Russia, India, China, and South Africa, and the scores and rankings of 12 members of the EU whose commercial diplomats were interviewed.

Table 2 summarizes the data from the WGI on emerging countries. The computed average for Indonesia is −0.478. This suggests that institutional development is rather weak, especially if comparing Indonesian score with the other 200 countries: Indonesia ranks in the 35th percentile. Together the group of emerging countries has a score of −0.289, and ranks in the 42nd percentile. This indicates that Indonesia scores fourth within the group of six emerging countries, scoring better than Russia and China. Within its scores, Indonesia scores best for the VA dimension with −0.055, placing Indonesia in the 48th percentile on this dimension. This suggests that Indonesian citizens are able to some extent to elect their government, and to express their freedom of expression and association. However, it is still very limited, as in more than half of the other countries the citizens can do it better. Emerging countries score as a group very low on PV with an average score of −0.639, putting them in the 27th percentile. From all Indonesian scores, RL and CC score very low, −0.630 and −0.727 respectively. This suggests that legal certainty is low in Indonesia.

Table 2: The Worldwide Governance Indicators 2010: emerging countries.

Country		VA	PV	GE	RQ	RL	CC	μ
					WGI			
ID	Estim[a]	−0.055	−0.887	−0.195	−0.375	−0.630	−0.727	−0.478
	Rank[b]	48.34?	18.868	47.847	39.713	31.280	27.272	35.554
BR	Estim[a]	0.499	0.048	0.071	0.189	−0.002	0.056	0.144
	Rank[b]	63.507	48.113	56.938	55.981	55.450	59.808	56.633
RU	Estim[a]	−0.945	−0.887	−0.394	−0.395	−0.784	−1.074	−0.747
	Rank[b]	20.853	18.396	41.627	38.278	26.066	12.919	26.357
IN	Estim[a]	0.424	−1.315	−0.007	−0.393	−0.058	−0.517	−0.311
	Rank[b]	59.242	10.849	55.024	39.234	54.502	35.885	42.456
CN	Estim[a]	−1.650	−0.766	0.123	−0.231	−0.347	−0.603	−0.579
	Rank[b]	5.213	24.057	59.808	44.976	44.550	32.536	35.190
ZA	Estim[a]	0.526	−0.025	0.339	0.391	0.097	0.094	0.237
	Rank[b]	65.403	44.340	65.072	62.679	57.820	60.766	59.347
μ	Estim[a]	−0.200	−0.639	−0.011	−0.136	−0.287	−0.462	−0.289
	Rank[b]	43.760	27.437	54.386	46.810	44.945	38.198	42.589

Source: WGI retrieved from www.govindicatcrs.org
VA, voice and accountability; PV, political stability and absence of violence; GE, government effectiveness; RQ, regulatory quality; RL, rule of law; CC, control of corruption; ID, Indonesia; BR, Brazil; RU, Russia; IN,India; CN, China; ZA, South Africa.
[a]Estimate of governance (ranges from approximately −2.5 (weak) to 2.5 (strong) governance performance).
[b]Percentile rank among all countries (ranges from 0 (lowest) to 100 (highest) rank).

Table 3 presents the data on the European countries and Indonesia. The ranks of Indonesia become even less flattering if they are compared to the average of the 12 European countries, which is a group score +1.145 and are ranked in the 82nd percentile. PV scores of the EU members are also the lowest within their scores on six dimensions. The best score of Indonesia, −0.055 for VA and accordingly its ranking in the 48th percentile, is very low compared to the EU average: +1.197 (84th percentile). Where Indonesia scores −0.630 for RL and −0.727 for CC, EU scores in average +1.242 and +1.155 respectively. Such comparison suggests that Indonesian institutional development could be perceived by diplomats as very low, as most of the scores of the EU are more than double higher when compared to the Indonesian scores. Hence, when classifying the institutional development of Indonesia, these scores suggest that it is very weak.

Reports.   The examined reports, along with revealing how the public procurement system works in Indonesia, strengthened the findings from the index.

Indonesia changed its governance system in 1999, 'enacting two laws that significantly decentralized government power and established regional autonomy' (TI-USA et al., 2011, p. 12). In 2001 a wide range of functions was assigned to districts and municipalities. There are 33 provinces divided into 508 districts and municipal government, each with its own administrative unit responsible for the provision of government service and thus also public procurement. Government services included 'public works, health, education and culture, agriculture, transportation, industry and trade, capital investment, the environment, cooperatives, and manpower' (TI-USA et al., 2011, p. 12).

Indonesian public procurement has a tradition of being regulated through presidential decrees. Unlike the procurement guidelines of the World Bank, which encourage following the principle of economy, efficiency and transparency, the presidential decrees had other objectives strongly influenced by the government policy of that time, 'for example efficient use of the State funds, promotion of domestic product and services, equity and social justice' (Attström & Ismail, 2010, p. 6). The ambiguity of such objectives was disadvantageous when it came to implementation, as they were subject to personal interpretation.

In 2006 the procurement units (ULP) were introduced that would be established at all levels of the government agencies. They would take over the tasks of an *ad hoc* tender committee of BAPPENAS (National Development and Planning Agency) which had few resources and an unclear mandate, and be responsible for the tendering process, 'starting from preparing tender schedules, cost estimate of the tendering package, advertisement, bid evaluation, and proposing bid winner' (Attström & Ismail, 2010, p. 6). In 2007 the Indonesian Public Procurement Agency (LKPP) was established with a mandate to '(i) develop public procurement strategy, policy, and regulation; (ii) conduct monitoring and evaluation; (iii) implement e-procurement; (iv) strengthen the skills of procurement officials; and (v) provide advice, recommendations and complaint resolution' (TI-USA et al., 2011, p. 16). That organization's early years have been marked by recruiting staff and developing its infrastructure. Its ability to improve the regulatory and institutional environment of

Table 3: The Worldwide Governance Indicators 2010: interviewed European countries.

Country				WGI				
		VA	PV	GE	RQ	RL	CC	μ
NL	Estim[a]	1.494	0.934	1.733	1.794	1.809	2.145	1.652
	Rank[b]	96.209	79.717	94.258	98.086	97.156	97.608	93.839
AT	Estim[a]	1.441	1.087	1.888	1.525	1.796	1.643	1.563
	Rank[b]	95.735	88.679	97.608	93.301	96.682	92.345	94.058
SE	Estim[a]	1.583	1.076	2.016	1.720	1.948	2.251	1.766
	Rank[b]	99.052	88.208	98.565	96.651	99.526	99.043	96.841
FR	Estim[a]	1.226	0.699	1.441	1.338	1.524	1.394	1.270
	Rank[b]	89.100	70.755	89.474	87.081	90.521	88.995	85.988
DK	Estim[a]	1.581	1.010	2.167	1.901	1.878	2.374	1.819
	Rank[b]	78.673	84.434	99.043	100	98.578	100	93.455
IT	Estim[a]	0.927	0.473	0.515	0.848	0.382	-0.043	0.517
	Rank[b]	75.829	62.264	67.943	77.033	62.559	57.416	67.174
BG	Estim[a]	0.485	0.377	0.007	0.607	-0.080	-0.183	0.202
	Rank[b]	62.560	57.547	56.459	71.770	53.080	52.153	58.598
PT	Estim[a]	1.123	0.680	1.038	0.818	1.041	1.031	0.955
	Rank[b]	84.834	69.811	81.818	75.598	83.412	81.340	79.469
PL	Estim[a]	1.033	0.999	0.706	0.974	0.687	0.447	0.808
	Rank[b]	81.042	83.491	72.727	79.426	69.194	70.335	76.036
ES	Estim[a]	1.141	-0.177	0.984	1.191	1.195	1.011	0.891
	Rank[b]	85.782	39.151	79.426	84.211	86.730	80.861	76.027
UK	Estim[a]	1.313	0.404	1.561	1.745	1.770	1.482	1.379
	Rank[b]	91.943	58.019	92.344	97.129	94.787	89.952	87.362
CZ	Estim[a]	1.018	0.973	1.008	1.237	0.953	0.307	0.916
	Rank[b]	78.673	82.075	80.861	85.167	80.095	65.550	78.737

Table 3: (*Continued*)

Country		WGI						
		VA	PV	GE	RQ	RL	CC	μ
μ	Estim[a]	1.197	0.711	1.255	1.308	1.242	1.155	1.145
	Rank[b]	84.953	72.013	84.211	87.121	84.360	81.300	82.326
ID	Estim[a]	-0.055	-0.887	-0.195	-0.375	-0.630	-0.727	-0.478
	Rank[b]	48.341	18.868	47.847	39.713	31.280	27.272	35.554

Source: WGI retrieved from www.govindicators.org

VA, voice and accountability; PV, political stability and absence of violence; GE, government effectiveness; RQ, regulatory quality; RL, rule of law; CC, control of corruption; NL, the Netherlands; AT, Austria; SE, Sweden; FR, France; DK, Denmark; IT, Italy; BG, Bulgaria; PT, Portugal; PL, Poland; ES, Spain; UK, United Kingdom; CZ, Czech Republic; ID, Indonesia.

[a]Estimate of governance (ranges from approximately −2.5 (weak) to 2.5 (strong) governance performance).

[b]Percentile rank among all countries (ranges from 0 (lowest) to 100 (highest) rank).

public procurement depends on the 'political support, mandate and the capacity of the organization to define, communicate and realize its role in the procurement system' (Attström & Ismail, 2010, p. 1). Hence, the authors concluded that the development of a good infrastructure for the agency depends highly on political willingness and stability.

On 1 January 2011, the new Presidential Regulation 54/2010 came into effect. The main achievement is that it divides the administration tasks within the procurement system into three separate units. 'The first [unit] is charged with planning and carrying out procurements (the 'Budget Authority'); the second is charged with determining the implementation of individual procurements, such as defining tender specifications, evaluating bids and awarding contracts, and monitoring the implementation of contracts (the 'Procurement Services Unit' or 'PPK'); and the third is the Project Result Receiver Committee in charge of evaluating contracted outcomes' (TI-USA et al., 2011, p. 17).

Several challenges for public procurement in Indonesia were identified by Attström and Ismail (2010) and TI-USA et al. (2011). There is a lot of ambiguity in terms of the legal framework: there are conflicting regulations, missing guidelines, and no national procurement law which could take precedence above other regulations. Moreover, the highly decentralized system resulted into many local officials not being familiar with the new regulation, and they avoid enforcing it (TI-USA et al., 2011). Attström and Ismail (2010) acknowledge that LKPP's success depends on building alliances and a constituency to convince others of its usefulness and benefit, as the organization itself does not have enforcement powers. However, little has been done to include the participants of the system in commenting on the proposed regulations: even the Indonesian Chamber of Commerce and Industry (KADIN) and the Association of Indonesian Employers (APINDO) are sometimes left out (TI-USA et al., 2011). Additionally, while the new regulation 'allows bidders to file a protest, there is no clear protest handling mechanism and no clear sanctions for violation of the procurement procedures' (TI-USA et al., 2011, p. 17).

The organization also requires more professionalization. 'It will require organisational development, skills development of procurement professionals, establishment of incentive systems and career paths etc.' in order for the procurement bodies to function well (Attström & Ismail, 2010, p. 8). Attström and Ismail (2010) found that there is little staff turnover anticipated in LKPP; therefore, the individual knowledge will stay in the organization. At the same time, there is no mechanism to ensure the knowledge transfer within the organization and other deputies.

Another challenge to an effective public procurement system is the high level of corruption and lack of transparency. 'According to a survey conducted by Indonesia's Procurement Watch in 2010, 89% of companies said they need to bribe public officials to get a contract. The government estimates that corruption in Indonesia's public procurement is responsible for US$ 4 billion in losses every year' (TI-USA et al., 2011, p. 14). There is hardly any mechanism which could prevent such corruption. Civil society organizations lack effective access to information which could allow monitoring of the government (TI-USA et al., 2011). When it comes to bidders, the information is available but only for the ones who are familiar with the system. 'Sometimes the rules are changed in the middle of the procurement; other times the deadline is shortened or extended. Winners are publicly announced but it is rare that procurement officials provide technical or economic reasons for the choice' (TI-USA et al., 2011, p. 28).

In conclusion, reports and scores of the WGI index point out that the institutional development of Indonesia is low. The WGI scores suggest that Indonesian institutional development is especially low when it comes to rule of law and control of corruption. Hence, legal certainty is low as well. The reports indicate that the institutional structure is highly decentralized: there are a lot of levels involved, and a lot of actors are determining the course of actions. At the same time the reports reveal that the system reflects to some extent corporatist structures. The WGI score for voice and accountability dimension also suggests that there is some room for interest representation mechanism in Indonesia. However, the interest representation mechanism does not facilitate the participation of the interest groups — i.e. civil society organizations and business associations — as much as the transparency standards of APEC would call for. At the same time it has to be noted that the public procurement body in Indonesia is young. There are still a lot of institutional challenges to be met. Along with a lack of experience, the body also suffers from corruptive malpractices and lack of transparency. This is also supported by the WGI scores. Inefficiency and gaps in the regulation identified in the reports strengthen the idea that institutional development is not high. The reports suggest that the decision-makers in the public procurement system are not elected but appointed. Nevertheless, they need stakeholders' approval to be effective.

Conceptual Model, Propositions and Findings

According to the WGI index, the reports and even some of the interviews, the institutional development of Indonesia is weak and faces a lot of challenges. Under such conditions, the first set of proposition (P1) derived from the conceptual model predicts that diplomats will focus on informational lobbying in order to persuade the decision-makers to invest in institutional development as it would benefit the European companies. At the same time the diplomats will rely heavily on the networks they have acquired.

Indeed, the majority of diplomats engages in informational lobbying and relies and invests in their networks. There are a lot of issues that need improvement in order to make the Indonesian market more attractive for European companies. This is what the diplomats try to achieve with their informational lobbying. A lot comes down to personal relationships and favours. This is also what the diplomats experience as they rely heavily on their network in order to assist the companies. Hence, P1 is illustrated.

With the institutional structure that characterizes the Indonesian public procurement body, where there is no clear interest representation mechanism and decision powers are decentralized, the conceptual model would prescribe 'voice' lobbying targeting different levels (P2, P3).

It is also observed in Indonesia. The diplomats make sure to invite representatives of different levels and committees of the decision-making body. Hence, P3 is illustrated.

As only a few are lucky to have direct appointments with decision-makers, the majority of the diplomats engages in indirect attempts to influence the decision-makers' preference and opinion through seminars, different receptions and other events.

This is the point where findings complement the model. It became apparent that direct 'access' lobbying is a luxury that only the diplomats from countries with historical close ties to the host country can enjoy. It does not mean that for the remainder of the diplomats, it is impossible to make an appointment with the decision-makers, but it does complicate the matter and makes it more difficult. At the same time, the diplomats that could engage in 'access' lobbying also engaged in 'voice' lobbying to strengthen their efforts. Along with historical ties, the priority that the host country has in the home country's external economic policy determines how extensive the lobbying can be. If there is room for extensive lobbying, i.e. 'access' and 'voice' lobbying combined, then the diplomats would engage in both. Some of the diplomats pointed out that they do not have enough means, for example human resources, to extensively lobby Indonesian decision-makers, because their country does not consider Indonesia a priority in their economic relations. This usually implied that the diplomats from these countries did not have enough budget or staff to afford labour- and capital-intensive lobbying. Hence, such diplomats had only restricted room for lobbying, which limited their activities. As Indonesia is not a clear example of corporatist, or totalitarian structure, P2 could not be illustrated, as both 'access' and 'voice' lobbying was also applied.

The issue of priority leads to another aspect of the findings. The diplomats found it very important for their lobbying activities to have companies from their home countries that were interested in Indonesia. Therefore, they spent a lot of time making companies aware of the business opportunities in Indonesia. Often, if Indonesia was not a priority country for the diplomat, then there was usually also little interest from the home country.

The decision-makers in the Indonesian public procurement body are appointed. According to the conceptual model, the diplomats would not invest in constituency building but rather would rely more on informational lobbying and providing factual information (P4).

This is also shown in practice: the diplomats did not invest much energy in constituency-building lobbying. Instead, they focused on informational lobbying. Hence, P4 is illustrated.

Therefore, the findings reflect the model and at the same time complement it.

Conclusion and Discussion

The research question was: to what extent does the institutional setting of a host country determine the lobbying activities of European commercial diplomats in the case of public procurement contracts in emerging countries? In order to answer the research question, two research aims were formulated. The first aim of this research has been to contribute to the understanding of how commercial diplomacy is practised and, more specifically, derive a list of techniques used by the commercial diplomats to lobby for the public procurement contracts for the companies which they assist. The second aim has been to illustrate the plausibility of a link between the concept of institutional setting and lobbying activities of commercial diplomats.

The literature identifies that the institutional environment has ramifications for the manner of lobbying and for the practice of commercial diplomacy. However, the research which would combine these three concepts has not been conducted yet. Therefore, this study brought together these different pieces of the puzzle. The institutional setting was framed by institutional development, institutional structure and whether the decision-makers are elected or not. Lobbying aspects that are relevant for the commercial diplomat were identified as informational lobbying, reliance on the networks, 'access' — direct lobbying, 'voice' — indirect lobbying, and constituency-building lobbying.

The mechanism between the two concepts was expected to reflect the following link. In a weak institutional development environment, the diplomats are likely to focus on informational lobbying in order to persuade the decision-makers to invest in institutional development as it would benefit the home companies which operate in the host country. At the same time, the diplomats are likely to rely heavily on the networks they have acquired. If institutional structure reflects totalitarian structure and decision-making powers are decentralized, the diplomats are likely to engage in 'voice' lobbying, targeting different levels of the decision-making body. If the decision-makers are elected, the diplomats are likely to engage in constituency-building lobbying. If that is not the case, the diplomats are likely to rely more on informational lobbying.

Indonesia has been chosen as a study case to illustrate the conceptual model and come up with a list of lobbying activities used by the commercial diplomats, which could facilitate larger scale research on the topic. Table 4 lists the lobbying activities which could be translated into measurable indicators for a larger scale study.

The findings indeed illustrated the plausibility of the model to some extent. The weak institutional development of the country necessitated informational lobbying and network reliance by the commercial diplomats (P1 is illustrated). As decision-making powers were decentralized, diplomats attempted to target different levels of decision-making body (P3 is illustrated). Indonesia does not have a clear interest representation mechanism. Both 'voice' and 'access' lobbying were applied by the commercial diplomats (therefore P2 is not illustrated). And as decision-makers were not elected, the diplomats almost never engaged in constituency-building lobbying (P4). These findings therefore would lead to the conclusion that the institutional setting of the host country indeed can have ramifications for the lobbying activities of the European commercial diplomats in the case of public procurement contracts in emerging countries.

However, the findings also revealed that the institutional setting of a host country could not be the only determining factor. The domestic factors of the commercial diplomats also play a role in how they lobby. The business interest of the home country in the host country determines whether there is lobbying at all and how extensive it will be. If there is little interest in doing business in the host country, then the commercial diplomats do not lobby intensively. This interest is also related to the priority the host country enjoys in the home country's external economic

Table 4: Lobbying activities.

Lobbying aspects	Indicators
Informational lobbying	• A joint committee on some field of cooperation • Distribution of advanced leaflets on top sectors at government or potential partner companies • Responsiveness to the disadvantageous measures • Close cooperation with host government on trade and investment policies
Reliance on the networks	• Introduce the companies to the contacts of the acquired network • Answer the invitations of associations, government events • Organization of informal lunches and receptions • Invite government officials to home country (otherwise advise companies to invite them) • Organize visits of home countries' high-level people (elite, ministers, president) • Business trips, trade missions
'Access' lobbying	• Different levels of government are contacted on a frequent basis • Explanation meeting after publication of the public procurement tender • Organization of business lunches with government officials
'Voice' lobbying	• Organization of theme seminars on a frequent basis • Invite country's national champions to attract other players • Invite journalists to your events • Frequent section/columns in newspaper • Matchmaking events • Business to business events
Constituency building	Involve host country's civil society organizations or associations in the campaign

policy, as it determines what tools the commercial diplomats have at their disposal. It may concern financial but also human capital means, a lack of which undermines the commercial diplomats' ability to engage in labour- and capital-intensive lobbying, such as organizing expensive events and direct lobbying. Moreover, the historical bilateral ties between the home and the host country can positively affect the lobbying, by making it easier to lobby directly and even attract attention in general.

At the same time, it is fair to state that these domestic factors are likely to play a role in the whole existence of commercial diplomacy. If not for the economic interest of the home country, would there be commercial diplomacy? The assumption emerges that the priority of the host country and historical ties will always intensify the bilateral relationship. Hence, it is only natural that the diplomats from these countries have an advantage over others. This advantage is then transferred to their lobbying power.

Coming back to the second research aim, this study provided the first illustration that the institutional setting can influence the lobbying activities of the European commercial diplomats for public procurement contracts in emerging countries. At the same time, the study suggested a legitimate assumption that domestic factors, such as interest in the host country, priority status of the host country and historical bilateral ties, can positively influence the lobbying activities of the diplomats as well.

Limitations and Further Research

The research was limited in the beginning by the absence of measurable indicators for the lobbying aspects. Therefore, a small-scale, extensive, qualitative study was needed before being able to test the model on a larger scale. This involved a risk of having findings that were not generalisable. Only one study case was chosen to illustrate the model — Indonesia. However, Indonesia represents a typical emerging country (OECD, 2009), and therefore the damage to external validity has been avoided in this sense as much as possible. At the same time, $N = 15$ is rather small, and even though the aim was to illustrate the plausibility of the conceptual model, the findings could be exaggerated because of such a small scale. Thus, future research should test the model, with the introduced indicators, on a larger scale. Moreover, the future research should also include different types of institutional settings, for example countries with weak institutional development and countries with strong institutional development, to make stronger conclusions about the mechanism of the model possible.

In this study the assumption emerged that the priority of the host country and historical ties will always intensify the bilateral relationship. It is only natural that the diplomats from these countries have an advantage over others. This assumption would be interesting to test in further research providing some empirical evidence. Surveys backed by institutional indices and reports on the institutional setting will suit the purpose of expanding this research to a larger scale.

Regarding practical implications, further research is needed on the effectiveness of lobbying in commercial diplomacy. The winners of tenders could be approached and interviewed about the role the commercial diplomats played in their public procurement contract and how they think this role can be improved. Such research, instead of focusing on the process of lobbying, would focus on the outcome and provide suggestions of what makes lobbying successful in commercial diplomacy. A stream of literature on lobbying identifies several personal characteristics of a lobbyist that can make lobbying successful. Such research on the personal characteristics of a commercial diplomat would also contribute to the understanding of successful lobbying in commercial diplomacy. The literature also suggested that effective lobbying involves knowing what other competitors are lobbying for (and how). The findings of this study revealed that diplomats often did not know what the other embassies were organizing. If two embassies organize an event on the same theme during the same period of time, it might decrease the effectiveness of such events. Hence, further research is justified to measure the awareness of commercial diplomats of how other competitors are lobbying.

Acknowledgement

The authors would like to thank Nico Groenendijk for his comments to an earlier version of the chapter.

References

Attström, K., & Ismail, R. (2010). *Indonesia strengthening public procurement program ISP3 INH521: Independent completion report.* Retrieved from OECD. Available at http://www. oecd.org/derec/australia/48473814.pdf

Austen-Smith, D., & Wright, J. R. (1996). Theory and evidence for counteractive lobbying. *American Journal of Political Science, 40*(2), 543–564.

Baron, D. P., & Hirsch, A. V. (2012). Common agency lobbying over coalitions and policy. *Economic Theory, 49*(3), 639–681.

Bennett, A. (2004). Case study methods: Design, use, and comparative advantages. In D. F. Sprinz & Y. Wolinsky-Nahmias (Eds.), *Models, numbers, and cases: Methods for studying international relations.* Ann Arbor, MI: University of Michigan Press.

Bennett, A., & Elman, C. (2006). Qualitative research: Recent developments in case study methods. *Annual Review of Political Science, 9,* 455–476.

Bergan, D. E. (2009). Does grassroots lobbying work? *American Politics Research, 37*(2), 327–352.

Boeije, H. (2002). A purposeful approach to the constant comparative method in the analysis of qualitative interviews. *Quality & Quantity, 36,* 391–409.

Bouwen, P. (2002). Corporate lobbying in the European Union: The logic of access. *Journal of European Public Policy, 9*(3), 365–390.

Bouwen, P., & McCown, M. (2007). Lobbying versus litigation: Political and legal strategies of interest representation in the European Union. *Journal of European Public Policy, 14*(3), 422–443.

Buschers, J. A. (2011). *The value of commercial diplomacy.* Enschede: University of Twente.

Campos, N. F. (2000). Context is everything: Measuring Institutional change in transition economies. World Bank Policy Research Working Paper No. 2269, Washington, DC. Retrieved from http://elibrary.worldbank.org/content/workingpaper/10.1596/1813-9450-2269

Chan, C. M., Isobe, T., & Makino, S. (2008). Which country matters? Institutional development and foreign affiliate performance. *Strategic Management Journal, 29,* 1179–1205.

Coen, D. (2007). Empirical and theoretical studies in EU lobbying. *Journal of European Public Policy, 14*(3), 333–345.

Corbin, J., & Strauss, A. (1990). Grounded theory research: Procedures, canons, and evaluative criteria. *Qualitative Sociology, 13*(1), 3–21.

Crosby, B. L., & Orsini, D. M. (1996). *Developing lobbying capacity for policy reform.* Technical Notes. A publication of USAID's Implementing Policy Change Project No. 7. Retrieved from http://gopher.info.usaid.gov/our_work/democracy_and_governance/publications/ipc/tn-7.pdf

De Vaus, D. A. (2001). *Research design in social research.* London: Sage.

Dollar, D., & Kraay, A. (2003). Institutions, trade, and growth. *Journal of Monetary Economics, 50,* 133–162.

Edler, J., & Georghiou, L. (2007). Public procurement and innovation — Resurrecting the demand side. *Research Policy, 36*(7), 949–963.

Egan, H., & Ovanessoff, A. (2011). Capturing the growth opportunity in emerging markets. *The European Business Review, September–October,* 42–45.

Eisenhardt, K. M. (1989). Building theories from case study research. *The Academy of Management Review, 14*(4), 532–550.

Eising, R. (2007). Institutional context, organizational resources and strategic choices. *European Union Politics, 8*(3), 329–369.

Fontana, A., & Frey, J. H. (2000). The interview: From structured questions to negotiated text. In N. K. Denzen & Y. S. Lincoln (Eds.), *Handbook of qualitative research* (2nd ed.). Thousand Oaks, CA: Sage.

Furlong, S. R., & Kerwin, C. M. (2005). Interest group participation in rule making: A decade of change. *Journal of Public Administration Research and Theory, 15*(3), 353–370.

Gawande, K., Krishna, P., & Robbins, M. J. (2006). Foreign lobbies and U.S. trade policy. *The Review of Economics and Statistics, 88*(3), 563–571.

Gawande, K., Maloney, W., & Montes-Rojas, G. (2009). Foreign informational lobbying can enhance tourism: Evidence from the Caribbean. *Journal of Development Economics, 90*(2), 267–275.

Geddes, A. (2003). *Paradigms and sand castles: Theory building and research design in comparative politics.* Ann Arbor, MI: University of Michigan Press.

Gerring, J. (2001). *Social science methodology: A criterial framework.* Cambridge: Cambridge University Press.

Gerring, J. (2004). What is a case study and what is it good for? *American Political Science Review, 98*(2), 341–354.

Gray, C. (1989). The tobacco industry provides a lesson in effective lobbying. *Canadian Medical Association Journal, 141*(August), 321–322.

Grix, J. (2004). *The foundations of research.* New York, NY: Palgrave Macmillan.

Gschwend, T., & Schimmelfennig, F. (2007). Introduction: Designing research in political science — A dialogue between theory and data. In T. Gschwend & F. Schimmelfennig (Eds.), *Research design in political science: How to practice what they preach.* Basingstoke: Palgrave Macmillan.

Haan, A. (2010). Omvat economische diplomatie ook ontwikkelingswerking? *Internationale Spectator, 64*(2), 70–72.

Hall, P. A., & Taylor, R. C. R. (1996). Political science and the three new institutionalisms. *Political Studies, 44,* 936–957.

Hamada, Y. (2007). The impact of the traditional business-government relationship on the Europeanization of Japanese firms. *Journal of European Public Policy, 14*(3), 404–421.

Haug, M., & Koppang, H. (1997). Lobbying and public relations in a European context. *Public Relations Review, 23*(3), 233–247.

Heitshusen, V. (2000). Interest group lobbying and US house decentralization: Linking informational focus to committee hearing appearances. *Political Research Quarterly, 53*(1), 151–176.

Hodgson, G. M. (2006). What are institutions? *Journal of Economic Issues, 40*(1), 1–25.

Hogan, M. J., Long, M. A., & Stretesky, P. B. (2010). Campaign contributions, lobbying and post-Katrina contracts. *Disasters, 34*(3), 593–607.

Hojnacki, M. (1997). Interest groups' decisions to join alliances or work alone. *American Journal of Political Science, 41*(1), 61–87.

Hojnacki, M., & Kimball, D. C. (1998). Organized interests and the decision of whom to lobby in Congress. *The American Political Science Review, 92*(4), 775–790.

Holyoke, T. T. (2003). Choosing battlegrounds: Interest group lobbying across multiple venues. *Political Research Quarterly, 56*(3), 325–336.

Holyoke, T. T. (2009). Institutional constraints on legislative lobbying: The case of Indian casino advocacy in New York. *Social Science Journal, 46*(4), 756–775.

Husted, S. (1991). Foreign lobbying: A theoretical analysis. *Eastern Economic Journal, 17*(1), 89–99.

Ihlen, Ø., & Berntzen, Ø. (2007). When lobbying backfires: Balancing lobby efforts with insights from stakeholder theory. *Journal of Communication Management, 11*(3), 235–246.

Kaufmann, D., Kraay, A., & Mastruzzi, M. (2010). *The Worldwide Governance Indicators methodology and analytical issues*. Working Paper no. 5430. World Bank Policy Research Department, Washington, DC. Retrieved from http://info.worldbank.org/governance/wgi/index.asp

Kee, H. L., Olarreaga, M., & Silva, P. (2007). Market for sale. *Journal of Development Economics, 82*, 79–94.

Klüver, H. (2010a). *Lobbying and policy-making: How interest groups can shape policy formation in the European Union*. Paper presented at the 5th Pan-European Conference on EU Politics, June, Porto.

Klüver, H. (2010b). *Lobbying and the issue context: A quantitative analysis of interest group influence in the European Union*. Paper presented at the Conference on Quantifying Europe: Pitfalls and Challenges of Data Generation Process, December, Mannheim.

Knack, S., & Keefer, P. (1995). Institutions and economic performance: Cross-country tests using alternative institutional measures. *Economics and Politics, 7*(3), 207–227.

Kommerskollegium. (2011). *Cross-border public procurement — An EU perspective*. Retrieved from http://www.kommers.se/Documents/Dokumentarkiv/Publikationer%20i%20PDF/%C3%96vriga%20publikationer/Report%20-%20Cross-border%20Public%20Procurement.pdf

Kostecki, D., & Naray, O. (2007). *Commerical diplomacy and international business* (pp. 1–41). Den Haag: The Netherlands Institute of International Relations 'Clingendael'.

Lowery, D. (2002). Why do organized interests lobby? A multi-goal, multi-context theory of lobbying. *Polity, 39*(1), 29–54.

Lowery, D., Poppelaars, C., & Berkhout, J. (2008). The European Union interest system in comparative perspective: A bridge too far? *West European Politics, 31*(6), 1231–1252.

Mack, R. (2005). Lobbying effectively in Brussels and Washington — Getting the right result. *Journal of Communication Management, 9*(4), 339–347.

Mahoney, C. (2007). Networking vs. allying: The decision of interest groups to join coalitions in the US and the EU. *Journal of European Public Policy, 14*(3), 366–383.

Mahoney, C., & Baumgartner, F. (2008). Converging perspectives on interest group research in Europe and America. *West European Politics, 31*(6), 1253–1273.

McGrath, C. (2005). Towards a lobbying profession: Developing the industry's reputation, education and representation. *Journal of Public Affairs, 5*, 124–135.

McGrath, C. (2006). The ideal lobbyist: Personal characteristics of effective lobbyists. *Journal of Communication Management, 10*(1), 67–79.

McGrath, C. (2007). Framing lobbying messages: Defining and communicating political issues persuasively. *Journal of Public Affairs, 7*, 269–280.

Mercier, A. (2007). *Commercial diplomacy in advanced industrial states: Canada, the UK and the US*. Clingendael Discussion Paper in Diplomacy. Clingendael Institute. The Hague, the Netherlands.

Messer, A., Berkhout, J., & Lowery, D. (2010). The density of the EU interest system: A test of the ESA model. *British Journal of Political Science, 41*, 161–190.

Miller, D., & Harkins, C. (2010). Corporate strategy, corporate capture: Food and alcohol industry lobbying and public health. *Critical Social Policy, 30*(4), 564–589.

Muller, M. (2002). South Africa's economic diplomacy: Constructing a better world for all? *Diplomacy & Statecraft, 13*(1), 1–30.

Naray, O. (2008). *Commercial diplomacy: A conceptual overview*. Paper presented at the 7th World Conference of TPOs, The Hague, the Netherlands.

North, D. C. (1990). *Institutions, institutional change and economic performance*. New York, NY: Cambridge University Press.

North, D. C. (1991). Institutions. *The Journal of Economic Perspectives, 5*(1), 97–112.

Nownes, A. J., & DeAlejandro, K. W. (2009). Lobbying in the new millennium: Evidence of continuity and change in three states. *State Politics & Policy Quarterly, 9*(4), 429–455.

OECD. (2009). *Globalisation and emerging economies: Brazil, Russia, India, Indonesia, China and South Africa*. OECD Publishing. doi: 10.1787/9789264044814-en

OECD. (2011). Size of public procurement market. In *Government at a Glance 2011* (pp. 148–149). OECD Publishing. doi: 10.1787/gov_glance-2011-en

Okano-Heijmans, M. (2008). Economie en diplomatie in de relatie Japan-China: Voorwaarts ondanks het verleden. *Internationale Spectator, 62*(3), 155–159.

Okano-Heijmans, M., & Ruël, H. J. M. (2011). Commerciële diplomatie en internationaal ondernemen. *Internationale Spectator, 65*(9), 463–467.

Panke, D. (2012). Lobbying institutional key players: How states seek to influence the European Commission, the Council Presidency and the European Parliament. *Journal of Common Market Studies, 50*(1), 129–150.

Potter, E. H. (2004). Branding Canada: The renaissance of Canada's commercial diplomacy. *International Studies Perspective, 5*, 55–60.

Reuvers, S. I. M. (2012). *Research on commercial diplomacy: Review and implications*. Enschede: University of Twente.

Rodriguez, F., & Rodrik, D. (2001). Trade policy and economic growth: A skeptic's guide to the cross-national evidence. In B. S. Bernanke & K. Rogoff (Eds.), *NBER macroeconomics annual 2000* (Vol. 15). MIT Press. ISBN: 0-262-02503-5. Retrieved from http://www.nber.org/chapters/c11058

Ruël, H. J. M., Vehof, T., & Telgen, J. (2012). *Federal procurement market entry in the United States: Success factors and barriers for foreign companies*. Paper presented at the Australian and New Zealand International Business Association (ANZIBA) Conference, 12–14 April 2012, University of South Australia, Adelaide.

Ruël, H. J. M., & Zuidema, L. (2012). *The effectiveness of commercial diplomacy: A survey conducted among embassies and consulates*. Clingendael Discussion Papers Series in Diplomacy. Clingendael Institute, The Hague, the Netherlands.

Schlozman, K. L., & Tierney, J. T. (1986). *Organized interests and American democracy*. New York, NY: Harper & Row.

Schmitter, P. C. (1974). Still the century of corporatism? *The Review of Politics, 36*(1), 85–131.

Scully, G. W. (1988). The institutional framework and economic development. *Journal of Political Economy, 96*(3), 652–662.

Siggelkow, N. (2007). Persuasion with case studies. *Academy of Management Journal, 50*(1), 20–24.

Solis, M., & Katada, S. N. (2007). The Japan-Mexico FTA: A cross-regional step in the path towards Asian regionalism. *Pacific Affairs, 80*(2).

Spencer, T., & van Schendelen, R. (2002). Of fireworks, the Shahman and Machiavelli. *Journal of Public Affairs, 2*(2), 95–98.

Sukiassyan, G., & Nugent, J. B. (2011). Lobbying or information provision: Which functions of associations matter most for member performance? *Eastern European Economics, 49*(2), 30–63.

Svendsen, G. T. (2011). Evaluating and regulating the impacts of lobbying in the EU? The case study of green industries. *Environmental Policy and Governance, 21*, 131–142.

Swanborn, P. G. (2010). *Case study research: What, why and how?* London: Sage.

Telgen, J. (2007). Public procurement in perspective. In L. A. Knight, C. M. Harland, J. Telgen, G. Callender, K. V. Thai & K. E. McKen (Eds.), *Public Procurement: International case and commentary*. London: Routledge.

TI-USA, CIPE, & TII (2011). APEC procurement transparency standards in Indonesia: A work in progress. Retrieved from http://www.transparency-usa.org/documents/Indonesia TIReportFINAL-May2011.pdf

Tsui-Auch, L. S., & Möllering, G. (2010). Wary managers: Unfavorable environments, perceived vulnerability, and the development of trust in foreign enterprises in China. *Journal of International Business Studies, 41*, 1016–1035.

Van Hulten, M. (2011). *Corruptie: Handel in Macht en Invloed*. The Hague: SDU Publishers.

Van Schendelen, R. (2002). The ideal profile of the PA expert at the EU level. *Journal of Public Affairs, 2*(2), 85–89.

Van Schendelen, R. (2012). New trends of public affairs management at the EU level. *Journal of Public Affairs, 12*(1), 39–46.

Vining, A. R., Shapiro, D. M., & Borges, B. (2005). Building the firm's political (lobbying) strategy. *Journal of Public Affairs, 5*, 150–175.

Visser, R. (2011). *How commercial diplomats work: A qualitative study to gain insight into the way commercial diplomats shape their roles*. Enschede: University of Twente.

Weiss, L., & Thurbon, E. (2006). The business of buying American: Public procurement as trade strategy in the USA. *Review of International Political Economy, 13*(5), 701–724.

Wooldridge, A. (2010, November 22). The emerging emerging markets: Businesses will learn to look beyond the BRICs. *The Economist*. Retrieved from: http://www.economist.com/node/17493411

Ya Ni, A., & Bretschneider, S. (2007). The decision to contract out: A study of contracting for e-government services in state governments. *Public Administration Review, 67*, 531–544.

Yin, R. K. (2003). *Case study research: Design and methods* (3rd ed.). Thousand Oaks, CA: Sage.